Positive Neutrality

POSITIVE NEUTRALITY

Letting Religious Freedom Ring

STEPHEN V. MONSMA

Foreword by Michael Novak

CONTRIBUTIONS IN LEGAL STUDIES, NUMBER 69
Paul Murphy, *Series Adviser*

GREENWOOD PRESS
Westport, Connecticut • London

KF
4865
.M66
1993

Library of Congress Cataloging-in-Publication Data

Monsma, Stephen V.
    Positive neutrality : letting religious freedom ring / Stephen
V. Monsma ; foreword by Michael Novak.
        p. cm. — (Contributions in legal studies, ISSN 0147-1074 ;
no. 69)
    Includes bibliographical references and index.
    ISBN 0-313-27963-2 (alk. paper)
    1. Church and state—United States. 2. Freedom of religion—
United States. I. Title. II. Series.
KF4865.M66 1993
342.73'0852—dc20
[347.302852]   92-25738

British Library Cataloguing in Publication Data is available.

Library of Congress Catalog Card Number: 92-25738
ISBN: 0-313-27963-2
ISSN: 0147-1074

First published in 1993

Greenwood Press, 88 Post Road West, Westport, CT 06881
An imprint of Greenwood Publishing Group, Inc.

Printed in the United States of America

The paper used in this book complies with the
Permanent Paper Standard issued by the National
Information Standards Organization (Z39.48–1984).

10   9   8   7   6   5   4   3   2   1

Copyright Acknowledgments

The author and publisher are grateful to the following for allowing use of their material:

Bruce K. Macluary. Foreword to *Politics, Markets, and America's Schools* by John Chubb and
Terry Moe. Washington, DC: Brookings Institution, 1990, p. ix.

Hugh Sidey. Letter to the Editor. *Washington Post*, October 6, 1986. Copyright © The
Washington Post.

To
my wife, Mary Carlisle Monsma,
for her encouragement, patience, and support
over our years together

Contents

Foreword

On a January day some years ago the author of this book stood in a World War II military cemetery for 4,000 slain Americans just outside Florence, Italy. Although this neat, restful, and silence-inducing site is maintained by the U.S. government, these graves are not individually marked by a uniform secular symbol. On the contrary, since most of the U.S. soldiers who died in World War II (like their civilian compatriots) belonged either to the Christian or the Jewish faith, the grave of virtually every soldier is marked by a cross or by a Star of David. In this peaceful cemetery, the public expression of religious differences, for each according to his own communal belonging, seems totally appropriate. In death as in life, the U.S. government does not try to obliterate the religious differences important to its citizens. Without violating its chaste neutrality as between Christians, Jews, and others, it does not use that neutrality to insist either on public denial of religion or on public uniformity. This is neutrality; but it is "positive neutrality." It does not prohibit the expression of religion in the public sphere, and by no means establishes unbelief as the only permissible public expression.

Contrast this situation of only fifty years ago with the contortions the Supreme Court has been going through since, in its efforts to ban or to regulate the public display of communal religious symbols (a creche, a menorah). The Court's recent understanding of religion as a private matter for individuals has plainly become malnourished and impoverished. *This* poverty, Stephen Monsma has decided, needs attention, too.

This remarkable book opens up a new way to understand the relationship between church and state in the United States. It brings together many different strands of scholarship that have hardly been accessible in any one book before. It is marked by a generous and ecumenical spirit. Its theses are set forth in clear relief by prose of workmanlike clarity. To teach from this book will probably also be a joy, because it is a rich compendium of memorable historical opinions about the troubled and tangled relationship of religion and public life.

Monsma describes two disestablishments of religion in the United States: the first at its founding (concrete, nuanced, respectful of religious realities and living traditions); the second in our own time, in the mid-twentieth century (far more thorough-going, abstract, and ideological). On this second occasion mainline Protestantism was too intellectually weak to defend its own traditions; and Catholics and Jews were concerned with putting down solid roots of their own. Emboldened, secularists had the gall to argue that differences of religion were the chief cause of violence in our history — conveniently overlooking violent clashes of region, race, and class, not the least of which was the bloodiest war in history until that time, the Civil War.

Monsma is particularly skilled at bringing together the several strands of "structural pluralism," as he calls it, advanced by several remarkable European Christian thinkers in this century. Among these were the Catholics Jacques Maritain and Yves Simon, the Dutch Calvinist Abraham Kuyper, the Anglican John Figgis, and others who laid the philosophical groundwork for the Christian Democratic parties of Europe. Such thinkers had a much stronger sense than English utilitarians or U.S. pragmatists of the quasi-sovereignty and autonomy of the intermediate communities and associations of civil society, which stand between the individual and the state. They recognized quite clearly — more clearly than many U.S. Supreme Court justices — that much that is most important to individual persons derives from belonging to communities; that these communities play a crucial role in the achievement of the common good; and that, by the principle of subsidiarity, the state ought not to tread on their autonomy. In some ways, the social nature of individual persons is better expressed through such communities and associations than through the state.

Monsma shows in convincing historical detail how the U.S. Supreme Court has worked from an inadequate supply of conceptual materials concerning the social and public dimensions of such religions as Judaism and Christianity. It is a serious error, for example, to hold that religion is a merely private matter. And the practice of treating religion in that way is itself a commitment to a peculiar conception of religion and, in practice, to a "neutrality" that enshrines unbelief as the public expression of the republic's self-understanding. This is both a neutrality that is not neutral and a violation of the "free exercise" clause, whose premise (together with the "no-establishment" clause) is that the religions present at the founding are by nature both public and communal, even when disestablished.

In brief, Monsma's conceptual work calls out for a fresh beginning. With promising results, in fact, he begins applying his new method to a range of perplexities currently before the Court and on the agenda of public policy; or, at least, he sends light cavalry to test the enemy's defenses. Modestly, he insists that in assembling the large array of materials he has brought together, he has only brought his forces to the battlefield; he has not yet developed a strategy for the real fight nor drawn up an order of battle. But like the Confederate troops in the mountains around Antietam, looking out over the long and regular lines of approaching Union troops, and seeing behind them still other columns marching toward the battlefield along several different roads, his opponents will know that a truly splendid assemblage of forces is now being deployed against them.

The true nature of the people of the United States, and the true, rich, and public relationship between their government and their religious communities, deserve something very like the "positive neutrality" that Monsma describes. Until recently, after all, it had been their inheritance.

Michael Novak
American Enterprise Institute for Public Policy Research

Preface

This is not primarily a book about constitutional law, nor about political and social theory, nor about public policy. Rather, it is some of all three. The genesis of this book does not lie in the scholar's disinterested concern with academic questions of constitutional law, political and social theory, or public policy. Instead, it lies in my experiences as a Michigan state legislator for eight years in the late 1970s and early 1980s. There, Thomas Jefferson's wall of separation between church and state, about which I had learned in school, seemed artificial and removed from reality. It was often ignored, as when the legislature opened its sessions with prayer or purchased foster child-care services from religiously based private agencies. However, when the wall of separation was carefully observed, it produced results that seemed to me to be constricted and unnatural, as when a group of senior citizens with whom I was meeting was prohibited from saying grace before a lunch that was state-subsidized.

I was troubled, and no one seemed to have satisfactory answers. The Moral Majority, which was then at the height of its power, seemed insensitive to the religious pluralism of our society, while the American Civil Liberties Union seemed insensitive to the deepest religious beliefs of the majority of our citizens.

Thus, once I had left the legislature and returned to my more accustomed place in academia, I began to read widely and reflect carefully about church and state in the U.S. polity. I approached my topic as a scholar who was acutely aware of a practical, current policy problem and sought to apply the insights of scholarship in such fields as constitutional law, church history, public opinion, and social and political theory.

The result is a book in which I seek, first, to document and analyze the inadequacies both of Supreme Court church-state decisions and of the societal attitudes that underlie them. Next, I seek to describe the historical events and political theories that have contributed to these inadequacies. Then, I seek to develop a new paradigm, rooted in structural, normative pluralism, to guide church-state relations. I term this approach or paradigm *positive neutrality*, and in the last chapter I apply it to the concrete, contentious church-state issues of our day. In all this I seek to be both historically accurate and theoretically sophisticated, while also being practical in terms of throwing light on present-day, concrete, church-state controversies with which the political system and the broader U.S. society are struggling today.

I thank the Earhart Foundation of Ann Arbor, Michigan, for a grant that helped fund my early research on pluralism and church-state relations. Also, I thank a number of scholars who read portions of early drafts of the book: Royce Clark, Richard Hughes, Mark Noll, Paul Marshal, James Skillen, and especially Paul Weber, who read the entire manuscript in draft form. Collectively, they helped enormously by pointing out errors and making suggestions for improvements. However, they should not be held responsible for the ideas or conclusions contained in the book. I alone am responsible for whatever weaknesses or errors of fact or interpretation may still be found on the following pages.

I also thank Mildred Vasan and the other editors at Greenwood Press for their constant encouragement, help, and efficiency during a long process. Finally, I thank my wife, to whom I dedicate this book, for standing by me on this, as well as numerous earlier projects, with her invariable good sense and patience.

Positive Neutrality

1

Church and State in U.S. Society

While on the presidential campaign trail in 1988, George Bush commented on his World War II experience of being shot down as a young navy flier:

> Was I scared floating around in a little yellow raft off the coast of an enemy-held island, setting a world record for paddling? Of course I was. What sustains you in times like that? Well, you go back to fundamental values. I thought about Mother and Dad and the strength I got from them — and God and faith and the separation of Church and State.[1]

As law professor Gerard Bradley commented when citing this incident, one hopes that, while desperately seeking to save his life by eluding enemy patrols, the young flier was thinking of things other than the constitutional principle of the separation of church and state. However, the very fact that the presidential candidate felt the need to follow a reference to God by doffing his hat to the separation of church and state vividly demonstrates the fact that seasoned politicians instinctively sense that they are moving onto dangerous ground when they refer to God in a campaign speech.

There was nothing wrong with George Bush's political instincts. Controversy often accompanies church-state issues, controversy matched by the indecisiveness and uncertainty of the way in which the political system resolves them.[2] This uncertainty and the controversies underlying it sometimes even spill over into the Supreme Court's normally staid opinions. In a 1987 dissenting opinion, Justice Antonin Scalia wrote:

> We have said essentially the following: Government may not act with the purpose of advancing religion, except when forced to do so by the free exercise clause (which is now and then); or when eliminating existing governmental hostility to religion

(which exists sometimes); or even when merely accommodating governmentally uninhibited religious practices except that at some point (it is unclear when) intentional accommodation results in the fostering of religion, which is of course unconstitutional.[3]

A respected legal scholar echoed this sense of frustration when he wrote: "The first amendment's religion clauses have perplexed commentators and Supreme Court Justices for some time. The difficult body of doctrine derived from these clauses seems to consist of contradictory principles, vaguely defined tests, and eccentric distinctions."[4]

The U.S. public is equally ambiguous in its reactions to church-state issues. The authors of a thorough survey of attitudes toward church-state relations concluded: "There is a notable ambivalence in the general public between theory and practice on church-state issues. Rhetorical assent to the separation of church and state is contradicted by nearly constant approval of less rigid separation in practice."[5]

This book explores the controversial and ambiguous — many would say confused — subject of church-state relations. I argue that current church-state uncertainties and confusions result from several inappropriate assumptions long buried in the past, and that until these assumptions are uncovered and fundamental changes have been made in them, church-state problems and tensions will mount, leading to even greater controversy and more indecisiveness than exists today. In this chapter I seek to introduce the subject of church-state relations by looking briefly at the nature of religion in U.S. society and its relationship to government.

THE CHURCH-STATE CONUNDRUM

The separation of church and state is the concept at the heart of Americans' response to church-state questions. U.S. society generally accepts the proposition that both church and state benefit when neither one supports or interferes with the other. The Jeffersonian metaphor of a wall of separation captures the spirit of the traditional U.S. ideal of church-state separation. The survey cited earlier found a 51 percent majority of the general population agreeing with the statement, "There should be a high wall of separation between church and state," while even higher majorities of leadership groups agreed with it (77 percent of government leaders, 92 percent of academics, and 79 percent of media leaders).[6]

A conundrum emerges, however, from the fact that in real life church and state are not, and cannot be, totally separate. The constitutional law scholar Laurence Tribe pointed out that the

Supreme Court's approach to the separation of church and state recognizes "that there are necessary relationships between government and religion; that government cannot be indifferent to religion in American life; and that, far from being hostile or even truly indifferent, it may, and sometimes must, accommodate its institutions and programs to the religious interests of the people."[7] The so-called wall between church and state is breached in countless ways, some of which provoke controversy and debate and some of which are taken for granted and supported by societal consensus. In the latter category are public fire engines rushing to put out a fire in a church building, county health officials certifying a church youth camp as meeting appropriate health standards, property tax exemptions for churches, state certification of parochial school teachers, prayers offered at the start of sessions of Congress, the motto "In God We Trust" on coins, and a member of Congress quietly praying in her office before going on the floor to cast a particularly difficult vote. The list could go on and on. More controversial are a court ordering a hospital to give blood transfusions to a child in contradiction to the parents' religious beliefs, a government agency paying a religiously based child-care agency for children in foster care, a church offering sanctuary to illegal aliens who are fleeing conditions in their home country but whom the State Department does not deem of a nature to indicate political asylum, and a president publicly defending his opposition to abortion on religious grounds. Through actions such as these, whether consensual or controversial, the wall of separation of legal theory proves in real life to be more like latticework. Even so-called strict separationists do not favor total separation of church and state in a literal, absolute sense.

Herein lies the conundrum: if, in actual practice, there neither can be, nor is, a true wall separating church and state, what principles are there to determine what are permissible and what are impermissible forms of church-state cooperation and accommodation? Consensus on such principles eludes us. The wall image itself does not offer guidance. Tribe was surely correct when he pointed out that "the principle evoked by the image of a wall furnishes less guidance than metaphor."[8] The Supreme Court, other political institutions and leaders, political commentators, and academicians have all searched for some firm principles on which to draw that line between the permissible and the impermissible. However, disagreements, conflicts, contradictory positions, and bitter accusations — not consensus or even broad agreement — mark the search.

FROM CONSENSUS TO CONFLICT

The conundrum currently posed by church-state issues is a fairly recent development. Throughout most of U.S. history, church-state issues did not pose any particular problems or provoke many note-worthy controversies. Throughout the nineteenth and early twentieth centuries, the Supreme Court was called on to decide only a handful of religion cases, and, with only a few exceptions, one searches in vain through the newspapers and historical accounts of that era for confrontations over the place of religious organizations and beliefs in the public sphere. Up until the 1940s the religion language of the First Amendment was not even legally binding on the state governments.

In the past forty to fifty years all this has changed. Every year the Supreme Court is confronted by a series of controversial cases dealing with church-state relations, each one seemingly more intractable than the one before, and, like the Hydra of Greek mythology, each one that has been resolved by the Court seems to give rise to additional litigation. The news media are similarly filled with stories and heated debates dealing with church-state issues. One has only to list names or issues such as the Reverend Jerry Falwell, Archbishop John O'Connor, abortion, Christmas displays on public property, and school prayer to illustrate the fact that contentious church-state issues are commonplace on the nation's public policy agenda. There are four trends that are especially important in explaining the explosion of church-state issues that has occurred in the past forty to fifty years. Their continued existence indicates that the contentiousness and prominence of church-state debates on the U.S. agenda are likely to continue for the foreseeable future.

The Comprehensive Administrative State

The continuing rise of big government, leading to the comprehensive administrative state, is one key trend.[9] It is easy to think of examples of activities in which government had little or no involvement at the start of the twentieth century but in which it is now deeply involved, either as a regulator or as the provider of services. These include the provision of welfare services to the poor, regulations forbidding discrimination based on race and gender, the support of a large standing army and massive armaments programs, the promotion of international stability, and the regulation, funding, and (sometimes) running of family-planning, drug treatment, adoption, and spouse abuse programs. Moreover, one has to go back only fifty more years, to the mid-nineteenth century, to find the early signs of government engaging in the universal education of the young. In noting the rise of the administrative state, I do not imply any criticism of this trend — in an urban, highly mobile, highly bureaucratized society, a plethora of government regulations and programs are essential — but this fact of modern societal life has enormous implications for church-state relations.

As the comprehensive administrative state regulates more and more aspects of society, in the natural course of events it will tend also to regulate religiously based organizations and agencies. As political scientist Paul Weber asked, "When governments regulate everything from safety belts on buses to exit signs in public buildings to the sale of bonds, should only church buses, buildings and bonds be exempt?"[10] If one answers "Yes," are not the goals of the regulations being thwarted and is not religion being unfairly advantaged? However, if one answers "No," is not full freedom of religious belief and practices threatened by the long shadow of bureaucratic power? Similarly, when the government funds or runs a wide range of educational and social service programs, it is providing services that at an earlier time were exclusively or primarily provided by religious organizations and that religious organizations often still provide. In such situations, must government avoid any cooperation with the religiously based programs? Many commentators are convinced that for government to do so is to aid religion; many others are equally convinced that for government not to do so is to discriminate against it. The point here is not to try to answer such questions (that will take all the rest of the book); rather, the point is that before the rise of the comprehensive administrative state of the twentieth century, with its far-reaching regulatory and service programs, church-state issues of this nature would not even come up. However, now they do, and neither the administrative state nor the church-state issues to which it has led are going to disappear.

The Strength of Religion

Political scientist Booth Fowler wrote: "The overwhelming fact about religion in the United States today is its enormous pluralist vitality. It is a world of pluralist dimensions which bursts with energy. There is absolutely no sign of a once predicted death."[11] Fowler here emphasizes two characteristics of religion in the United States — its vitality and its pluralism, both of which have given rise to church-state questions and issues. This section looks at the continuing strength and vitality of religion, and the next section examines its pluralism.

Almost every commentator on U.S. society, from Tocqueville to the present-day sociologist Robert Bellah and his colleagues, has commented on the religious nature of Americans.[12] Moreover, survey research supports what these commentators have observed. Gallup poll figures show that 86 percent of the people in the United States report that religion is very or fairly important to them, 65 percent belong to a church or synagogue, and over 40 percent attend religious services weekly.[13] After analyzing polling data gathered over fifty years, George Gallup and Jim Castelli concluded: "Certain basic themes emerge from the mass of survey data collected over more than five decades. . . . The first is the enduring popularity of religion. There have been several periods of heightened interest in religion, but the baseline of religious belief is remarkably high — certainly, the highest of any developed nation in the world."[14]

There are four noteworthy features of religion in U.S. life on which most researchers comment. One is the prevalence, not just of religious beliefs, but of religious beliefs of a traditional, historical Christianity. For example, studies have found that 86 percent of the public believe that the Bible is either the literal or inspired word of God; 84 percent believe that Jesus was God or the Son of God; 84 percent believe that heaven exists, and 67 percent believe that hell exists.[15] It is the theologically conservative, and not the liberal churches, that are growing most rapidly.[16] A second feature of religion in the United States is that religious belief leads to religious practices such as church membership and attendance, both of which are high. This means that churches are strong, vital organizations with a significant effect in their communities and on the lives of their members. As political scientist Kenneth Wald observed, "Institutionally, churches are probably the most vital voluntary organizations in a country that puts a premium on 'joining up.'"[17]

A third feature of religion in the United States worth noting is that the people of the United States, as Gallup and Castelli pointed out, are much more religious than the citizens of any other modern, developed nation in the world. Political scientist Everett Ladd put it even more forcefully: "By just about every measure that survey researchers have conceived and employed, the United States appears markedly more religious than its peers in the family of nations, the other industrial democracies."[18]

A fourth feature of U.S. religion that has impressed researcher after researcher is that, contrary to what many had predicted, as the United States has modernized and as education and affluence have increased, religion has not declined but rather is as vital and dynamic as ever. In the 1920s a team of researchers conducted an in-depth study of Muncie, Indiana, which they termed Middletown. Fifty years later, another team of researchers returned to study the ways in which the city had changed in the intervening years. They found it had indeed changed in many ways: Its population had grown rapidly; education was much more widespread; modern technology, transportation, and communications had arrived; and the administrative hand of government was very much in evidence. The one thing that had *not* changed significantly, however, was the vibrant religious life of the city. In fact, they found that there were "a variety of indications that Middletown citizens were *more* involved in religion today than were their predecessors in the 1920s."[19] The lead analyst concluded: "Meanwhile, the conventional forms of Christian piety — prayer, fasting, meditation, alms-giving — all flourish in contemporary Middletown. What was supposed to be the age of skepticism has turned out to be an age of faith."[20] Church historian Martin Marty, commenting on a comprehensive survey of U.S. religious beliefs and attitudes, noted that it is "astonishing that in a high-tech, highly affluent nation, we have 90 percent [of the populace] who identify" themselves as religious.[21]

The point is clear: Religion, including traditional, institutional religion, is probably the most vital, significant force in U.S. society. It shows no sign of waning or withering into insignificance. If religion were an aging, somewhat tired phenomenon, bound to the traditions of an earlier, less sophisticated generation, it no doubt would be irrelevant to most contemporary issues and trends and would gracefully fade into the distance. In fact, however, religion, with its vital, active nature, and the comprehensive administrative state, with its growing number of regulations and services, are on a collision course. Both are major, active moving forces in end-of-the-twentieth-century, U.S. society; contact, overlap, tension, and conflict are inevitable.

The Increasing Diversity of Religion

A third trend explaining the rise in the number of church-state issues that face the nation is the increasing diversity of religion in the United States. This is the pluralism to which Fowler made reference in an earlier quotation. The twentieth century has seen major changes. Throughout the nineteenth century and well into the twentieth, there was a reigning Protestant consensus that simply assumed the tone and tenor of U.S. society, in its political, educational, and social manifestations, would reflect that consensus. Church historian Mark Noll has noted, "In the years between the presidencies of Thomas Jefferson (1801–1809) and Abraham Lincoln (1861–1865), Christian values and the values of American public life joined in a powerful cultural synthesis."[22] This Christian synthesis held for many years. Marty has noted that, as late as 1927, "French visitor Andre Siegried could still say with plausibility that Protestantism was America's 'only national religion.'"[23]

The carriers of the dominant Christian-Protestant cultural vision were the large, mainline Protestant denominations. It was such groups as the Presbyterians, Methodists, Congregationalists, and Episcopalians that determined the cultural ethos of the United States, defined the religious dimension of public policy issues, and decided what church-state issues were to be on the nation's policy agenda. Their vision of the United States and the United States' vision of itself merged into a single vision of the United States as the carrier of Christian civilization to the masses at home and abroad. The Roman

Catholic Church was largely a church of new immigrants struggling to find their way in a new and strange land. What today would
be called Fundamentalist groups largely existed within the mainline
Protestant churches, not yet having split off and formed their own
institutions and policy positions. African-American churches
struggled with the burdens of grinding poverty and massive discrimination. The Jewish community was very small and generally was in
the same position as the Catholic community — more concerned
with coming to terms and achieving success in a new land than with
influencing that country's public policy debates. Other non-Christian
religions were virtually unknown, and individuals without religious
faith of any kind generally did not advertise this fact. In short, there
existed a societal consensus on church-state relations that was rooted
in the overwhelming dominance of mainline Protestantism. There
were no voices with the desire, courage, and resources to challenge it
successfully.

It takes no great insight into contemporary U.S. religion to
recognize that today all this has changed. The cultural-political
dominance of the old mainline Protestant denominations has so
eroded that they are now often called by their critics the "sideline"
churches.[24] In part, this loss of dominance is a result of numerical
shifts. Pollsters Gallup and Castelli have noted that from 1947 to 1987,
"The nation has become less distinctly Protestant and more
pluralistic in character."[25] Two trends were especially important in
causing them to reach this conclusion: The growth in the population
of the proportions of Catholics and of persons who identify themselves
with a religious position other than Protestant, Catholic, or Jewish.
They found that the percentage of Protestants dropped from 69
percent in 1947 to 57 percent in 1987, while the percentage of
Catholics was increasing from 20 percent to 28 percent.[26] That this
trend is likely to continue is revealed by the fact that among persons
18–24 in age, the gap between Protestant and Catholic is even
narrower, with only 49 percent being Protestant and 31 percent
Catholic. Gallup and Castelli went on to show that from 1947 to 1987,
the proportion of Americans who are not Protestant, Catholic, or
Jewish doubled from 6 percent to 13 percent, and, significantly,
among 18–24-year-olds, it has shot up to 19 percent. Most of those
who are not Protestant, Catholic, or Jewish are nonbelievers (9
percent of the population), while 4 percent are adherents of faiths
other than Judaism or Christianity, up from 1 percent as recently as
1957. Within Protestantism there is also greater diversity, with the
historic mainline denominations losing members to denominations
that are more conservative theologically.

These shifts in religious adherents affect the number and nature
of church-state issues being raised. During the era of Protestant
dominance, a consensus on the appropriate relationship between

church and state existed. Often (as Chapter 3 develops more fully), the reigning Protestant consensus did not grant full religious freedom to those outside this dominant group, but those outside groups were usually too small, too weak, too far outside the mainstream, or too preoccupied with more urgent questions of survival to raise voices of protest. Church-state questions that could have been raised and debated, for the most part went unraised. They never even made it to the nation's public policy agenda. Now, with the mainline Protestant denominations in decline and with Catholics, conservative Protestants, non-Christian believers, and nonbelievers increasing in numbers, a wider diversity of traditions are speaking from greater positions of strength.[27] They are challenging previously accepted church-state accommodations — and are likely to continue doing so.

Expanding Political Involvements

The diversity of the U.S. political scene has also been increased by an upsurge in the number and variety of religious traditions taking a more active interest and role in the social-political world. As a result, the mainline Protestant churches are losing influence not only due to declining membership relative to other Christian traditions, but also due to these other traditions having gained a greater sense of self-confidence and a new social-cultural vitality. This is especially true of conservative Protestants, Roman Catholics, and African-American churches. Conservative Protestants have left an earlier position of cultural isolation and, with increasing numbers and rising self-confidence, are forming social institutions such as schools, colleges, "alternatives to abortion," adoption, and family crisis agencies. In addition, they have developed positions on public policies and entered the political fray with gusto and certainty — and sometimes with thought and care. Catholics, first spurred by the desire to protect their parochial schools and then by the Supreme Court's abortion rights decisions, have also weighed in with carefully researched policy positions that are directly and deeply rooted in the Catholic tradition. In the Reverend Martin Luther King, Jr., and other black clerics of the 1960s civil rights movement, the black Protestant church found its political voice and used it with effectiveness. That tradition continues today in clerical leaders such as the Reverend Jesse Jackson and the recently retired Representative William Gray of Philadelphia.

In addition to these three groupings, one should also note that both the founding of Israel and the lessons driven home by the Holocaust — combined with raising educational and economic achievements — have led the Jewish community to speak directly to the public policies of the nation. Furthermore, the fact that Madilyn Murray O'Hair is a recognizable name to many Americans stands as a symbol of persons of no religious faith who seek to defend their rights and live out their lack of religious faith in the political arena.

What must be emphasized about this development — apart from its magnitude and pervasiveness — is that these groupings do not see their social and political activism as being ancillary to their beliefs, but rather as necessary and required. There is a strain within U.S. thinking that sees religion as simply a private affair. It sees religion as having to do with how persons seek — in the quiet of their hearts and homes — to relate to the Divine. At the most, this strain of thought sees religion as affecting a person's family and other direct, personal relationships. However, this is a cramped, constricted view of religion, and is flatly contradicted by the tenets and practice of most religious faiths. Bellah and his associates have clearly made this point:

> Yet religion, and certainly biblical religion, is concerned with the whole of life — with social, economic, and political matters as well as with private and personal ones. Not only has biblical language continued to be part of American public and political discourse, the churches have continuously exerted influence on public life right up to the present time.[28]

Religion certainly has a private facet, but for many deeply religious persons, it has a most decidedly public facet as well.

Whether the old mainline Protestant churches are indeed mainline or merely "sideline" churches, no one can deny that they are still seeking to influence the broad world of culture and public policy. Their organizational structures produce carefully researched positions on a wide variety of public questions. What is new is that they have been joined by newly energized religious groups, which share in a concern for the social or public dimension of their faith, a dimension that, in their view, is an integral, necessary component. This is true of the three largest, most important of the newly active traditions mentioned earlier: Catholics, African-Americans, and conservative Protestants. The Catholic bishops, for example, have written:

> Followers of Christ must avoid a tragic separation between faith and everyday life. They can neither shirk their earthly duties nor, as the Second Vatican Council declared, "immerse [them]selves in earthly activities as if these latter were utterly foreign to religion, and religion were nothing more than the fulfillment of acts of worship, and the observance of a few moral obligations."[29]

Gayraud Wilmore, a specialist in African-American religious studies, has stated: "Black [churches] have held historically that the church's responsibility for a just society *mandated* people to engage in political action from a Christian perspective."[30] The conservative Protestant Fundamentalist minister Jerry Falwell has written:

> We have tended to develop the attitude that our only obligation is to preach the Gospel and prepare men for heaven. We have forgotten that we are still our brother's keeper and that the same spiritual truths that prepare us to live in eternity are also essential in preparing us to live on this earth. . . . If we as moral Americans do not speak up on these essential moral issues, who then will? As Christians we need to exert our influence not only in the Church but also in our business life, home life, and social and community life as well.[31]

This commitment to a socially and politically relevant faith tends to find concrete expression in two forms. One is the creation of politically relevant points of view and certain distinctive public policy positions based on religious beliefs (positions on abortion, gay rights, school prayer, and pornography come to mind). A second form is direct action by organized groups of believers who create programs of education, relief, and social service. They thereby seek to deal directly, rather than through government, with social needs, as required by their faith. Weber noted "the enormous expansion and growth of religious organizations" and their involvement in running "day-care centers, retirement homes, hospitals, [and] schools at all levels."[32] In the same vein, Wald has noted:

> In the United States, churches are not merely buildings that provide places for worship; rather, they have become multi-purpose agencies providing an astonishing array of services, including formal education, social welfare, pastoral counseling, publishing, charitable fund-raising, recreational facilities, medical care, cemeteries, libraries, and summer camps. Several of the largest churches have become hubs for world-wide operations, complete with the organizational complexity of a major corporation.[33]

What is of crucial importance to recognize is that whatever form the living-out of one's faith takes, whether direct acts of help and service or attempts to influence public policy, for deeply religious persons, their faith compels them to take these steps. It is as much a part of their faith as kneeling in prayer or attending religious services. The significance of this point is hard to overstate. It has both theoretical and practical consequences.

Theoretically, this means that any actions that limit or discourage persons as they seek to live out their faith in the broader world is a serious violation of their freedom of religion, as serious a violation as actions that would limit or discourage them from praying or attending religious services.

Practically, when one combines the greater religious pluralism of the United States (noted in the previous section) with the greater social and political activism of the various religious traditions (noted in this section), the pluralism of the world of religiously motivated political activity and involvement stands out in bold relief. The day is gone when religiously oriented persons who were politically interested and active were almost totally limited to the mainline Protestant denominations. In those days, the political system had to deal with religiously rooted demands of a fairly homogeneous nature that was largely in keeping with societal consensus. Today, however, not only are more religious traditions seeking to have an impact on the political system, but they themselves are in disagreement on what they wish the political system to do.

All this fuels church-state questions and debates. As socially and politically active groups — both religiously and secularly based — differ on the appropriate relationship between church and state and on what public policies should be pursued, church-state issues and conflicts arise. In addition, as a variety of religious traditions seek to live out their faith by establishing schools, hospitals, adoption agencies, spouse abuse shelters, and more — all activities in which both government and private, secular agencies are also involved, additional questions are bound to arise.

We return to the church-state conundrum. U.S. society and legal theory alike support the separation of church and state, yet the two, as vital forces in society, cannot be kept in hermetically sealed compartments. However, there are no agreed-on principles to guide when and how the two are to intersect. That this conundrum is likely to grow increasingly serious is indicated by the expanding vitality, diversity, and political and social activism of religion and the expanding role of government in modern society. There are many points at which religion and government intersect, and those points of intersection are becoming more, not less, numerous and more, not less, intense. Moreover, superimposed on this situation is the increasing proportion of persons with no religious faith, who also are gaining in the self-confidence and vigor with which they seek to advance their views and defend their rights in the public realm. The answers — to the extent that there are answers — will not come easily, but will only be derived with careful thought and much discussion.

This book is an attempt to present a new way of thinking about church-state relations in the United States. Its basic thesis is that government must be neutral in regard to religion — neutral both among the wide variety religious perspectives in the United States and between religious and nonreligious perspectives, but that in order for it to be truly neutral, it must sometimes take certain positive steps to recognize or accommodate religion. A strict separation of religion and government will seldom, in actual practice, lead to a genuine neutrality. Thus, I refer to the position I am advocating as *positive neutrality*. I root this concept of positive neutrality in structural pluralist theory (see Chapter 4), thereby giving it a theoretical underpinning that helps both to defend and to define it.

I begin my argument in the next chapter, where I seek to document the legal and policy controversies and confusions that mark church-state relations today, and how they pose a threat to full religious freedom by not supporting a genuine, real-world governmental neutrality toward religion. Then Chapter 3 explores the historical assumptions that underlie current approaches to church-state issues and argues that basic flaws in these assumptions have given birth to the shortcomings in the current church-state approaches that Chapter 2 documents. (These flaws are only now coming to light because of recent societal developments.) The next chapter lays out alternative concepts and beliefs rooted in structural pluralism, followed by a chapter that applies these concepts and beliefs to the realm of church-state relations. It is there that I fully develop the concept of positive neutrality. The final chapter applies positive neutrality to current, concrete policy issues and debates.

NOTES

1. Quoted in Gerard V. Bradley, "Church Autonomy in the Constitutional Order: The End of Church and State," *Louisiana Law Review* 49 (1989): p. 1057.

2. Here and elsewhere in the book I follow the conventional U.S. practice of using the terms *church and state* or *church-state* to refer generically to religion in its various manifestations and traditions and to government in its various manifestations. Later, I make some important distinctions and introduce more precise terms. I will use those terms when precision is called for, but continue to use the more common church and state or church-state when the advantages of following common usage outweigh the need for precision.

3. *Edwards v. Aguillard*, 482 U.S. at 636 (1987).

4. Phillip E. Johnson, "Concepts and Compromise in First Amendment Religious Doctrine," *California Law Review* 72 (1984): p. 817.

5. The Williamsburg Charter Foundation, *The Williamsburg Charter Survey on Religion and Public Life* (Washington, DC: The Williamsburg Charter Foundation, 1988), p. 1.

6. Ibid., p. 14, and Appendix, Table 23.

7. Laurence H. Tribe, *American Constitutional Law* (Mineola, NY: Foundation Press, 1978), p. 822.

8. Laurence H. Tribe, *American Constitutional Law*, 2d ed. (Mineola, NY: Foundation Press, 1988), p. 1166.

9. On the significance of the rise of the comprehensive administrative state for church-state issues, see Paul J. Weber, "Excessive Entanglement: A Wavering First Amendment Standard," *Review of Politics* 46 (1984): pp. 488–491.

10. Ibid., p. 488.

11. Robert Booth Fowler, *Religion and Politics in America* (Metuchen, NJ: American Theological Library Association, 1985), p. 1.

12. See Alexis de Tocqueville, *Democracy in America*, trans. George Lawrence (New York: Doubleday, Anchor Books, 1969); and Robert Bellah, Richard Madsen, William M. Sullivan, Ann Swidler, and Steven M. Tipton, *Habits of the Heart* (New York: Harper & Row, Perennial Library, 1986).

13. George Gallup, Jr., and Jim Castelli, *The People's Religion* (New York: Macmillan, 1989), pp. 29, 31, 35–36.

14. Ibid., p. 20.

15. Ibid., p. 63; and Richard John Neuhaus, ed., *Unsecular America* (Grand Rapids, MI: Eerdmans, 1986), pp. 119, 120, 134.

16. Gallup and Castelli, *The People's Religion*, pp. 26–29, 92–119; and Dean Kelley, *Why Conservative Churches are Growing* (San Francisco, CA: Harper & Row, 1977).

17. Kenneth D. Wald, *Religion and Politics in the United States*, 2d ed. (Washington, DC: Congressional Quarterly, 1992), p. 9.

18. Everett Carll Ladd, "Secular and Religious America," in Neuhaus, *Unsecular America*, p. 16.

19. Theodore Caplow, Howard M. Bahr, Bruce A. Chadwick, Reuben Hill, and Margaret Holmes Williamson, *Middletown Families: Fifty Years of Change and Continuity* (Minneapolis: University of Minnesota Press, 1982), p. 259. Emphasis added.

20. Theodore Caplow, "Religion in Middletown," *The Public Interest*, no. 68 (Summer 1982): p. 85.

21. Quoted in Ari L. Goldman, "Broad New Study of America Confirms: 'In God We Trust,'" *International Herald-Tribune*, April 11, 1991, p. 1.

22. Mark A. Noll, "The Revolution, the Enlightenment, and Christian Higher Education in the Early Republic," in Joel A. Carpenter and Kenneth W. Shipps, eds., *Making Higher Education Christian* (St. Paul, MN: Christian University Press, 1987), p. 65.

23. Martin E. Marty, "The Twentieth Century: Protestants and Others," in Mark A. Noll, ed., *Religion and American Politics* (New York: Oxford University Press, 1990), p. 328.

24. See Richard John Neuhaus, *The Naked Public Square* (Grand Rapids, MI: Eerdmans, 1984), pp. 202–225.

25. Gallup and Castelli, *The People's Religion*, p. 23.

26. Ibid., pp. 17, 23–30.

27. There is no consensus on the best terms with which to refer to the wing of Protestantism that accepts the traditional, historical teachings of Christianity and the Bible in a literal, orthodox manner. I have chosen the term *conservative Protestant* and will use it consistently in this book to refer to the *theologically* conservative wing of Protestantism, not prejudging whether this wing is also marked by political conservatism. Within this wing of Protestantism there are at least three distinct groupings or traditions. First, there are the Fundamentalists, who take the Bible very literally, are suspicious of modern learning, and have a recent history of separation from the world. Their best-known leader is Jerry Falwell. Second, there are the charismatics, who are distinguished by an emphasis on the active work of the Holy Spirit in the world today, leading them to emphasize the reality of frequent miracles, speaking in tongues, and direct guidance by the Holy Spirit in the lives of individual believers. Their best-known leaders are Pat Robertson and Oral Roberts. Third, there are the evangelicals, who emphasize a thought-out, rational approach to Christian truth and historically have sought to engage those outside of evangelicalism in discussion and debate. Their

best-known leaders are the evangelist Billy Graham and the theologian Carl F. H. Henry. For a helpful discussion of some of these distinctions, see George Marsden, *Evangelicalism and Modern America* (Grand Rapids, MI: Eerdmans, 1984).

28.   Bellah, Madsen, Sullivan, Swidler, and Tipton, *Habits of the Heart*, p. 220.

29.   National Conference of Catholic Bishops, *Economic Justice for All* (Washington, DC: National Conference of Catholic Bishops, 1986), pp. vi–vii.

30.   Gayraud S. Wilmore, "The Black Experience," *Newsweek*, September 17, 1984, p. 31. Emphasis added.

31.   Jerry Falwell, *Listen, America!* (Garden City, NY: Doubleday, 1980), p. 262.

32.   Weber, "Excessive Entanglement," p. 489.

33.   Wald, *Religion and Politics*, p. 27.

2

The Present:
Church-State Theory and Practice

A basic contention of this book is that in the area of church-state relations, the United States — both as a political system and as a society — has lost its way. It is on the wrong path and existing maps are proving worthless. In order to find the way back, it is first crucial to recognize that the nation indeed is lost and that something fundamental is wrong. It is more than a matter of needing to shift a bit more to what is usually called the strict separationist position or to its opposite, the accommodationist position. Both are wrong: Neither deals at all adequately with the host of ways in which an increasingly pluralistic, vigorous religious realm interacts with an expanding comprehensive administrative state. This chapter looks, first, at Supreme Court church-state decisions and the reasoning underlying them, and then at fundamental societal perspectives and assumptions related to church-state relationships. In so doing I seek to demonstrate the exact position of the United States concerning church-state issues and how, in fundamental ways, it is indeed on the wrong path.

THE SUPREME COURT

"Congress shall make no law respecting the establishment of religion, or prohibiting the free exercise thereof." The Supreme Court has repeatedly been called on to interpret the meaning of these sixteen words, which lie at the heart of the constitutional provisions regarding church and state. To say that there is widespread dissatisfaction with the interpretations that the Supreme Court has developed is a gross understatement. Legal scholar Phillip Johnson wrote, "Doctrinally, first amendment religion law is a mess," and, in referring to a recent Supreme Court church-state decision, he stated that it "illustrates the conceptual chaos that pervades this area of the law."[1] He went on to explain, "Many areas of constitutional law are unsettled, of course, but in most areas the uncertainty concerns how far the Constitution requires us to go in a particular direction. In the religion clause area, even the general direction is often difficult to ascertain."[2] Political scientist A. James Reichley declared that "the Court has plunged boldly — some would say recklessly — into the thicket of complex relationships involving religion, civil society, and the individual. The result is a tangled body of law."[3] Law professor Stephen Pepper has argued "that first amendment doctrine protecting freedom of religious conduct is in significant disarray."[4] Yet another observer commented, "It is difficult to find anyone who is willing to come to the defense of the Supreme Court's record on questions of establishment of religion."[5] The Supreme Court itself is aware of the disorder and tension in its interpretations of the Constitution's religion language, as Justice Antonin Scalia's dissenting opinion (quoted in Chapter 1) illustrates. Chief Justice Warren Burger once, almost plaintively, declared, "The language of the Religion Clauses of the First Amendment is at best opaque."[6]

I share in a sense of discontent with the Supreme Court's interpretations of the religion provisions of the First Amendment. However, it is important to be more specific and to uncover more exactly what it is that has gone wrong. Only then can one hope to start formulating a better way. That is what this section seeks to do. In it, I contend that the heart of the problems in current interpretations lie in two assumptions that the Supreme Court has made: that the religion provisions of the First Amendment should be read as two distinct clauses with two distinct objectives, rather than one provision with one objective; and that governmental neutrality toward all religions and between religion and nonreligion is achieved if a wall of separation is maintained between church and state. In this section I seek to demonstrate that these two assumptions lie at the heart of what has gone wrong with Supreme Court interpretations of the religion language of the First Amendment. I do so, first, by summarizing Supreme Court rulings in relation to the two religion clauses, and then, at greater length, by critiquing them.

The Free Exercise of Religion

In understanding the Supreme Court's interpretations of the free exercise clause, it is first of all important to understand the Court's distinction between religious beliefs and practices. In the well-known 1879 case dealing with the Mormon practice of polygamy, *Reynolds v. United States*, the Court clearly held that it was beliefs, and not actions, that were protected: "Laws are made for the government of actions, and while they cannot interfere with mere religious beliefs and opinions, they may with practices."[7] The Court went on to argue that to hold otherwise, "would be to make the professed doctrines of religious belief superior to the law of the land, and in effect to permit every citizen to become a law unto himself."[8]

This dichotomy between belief and practice has, in turn, given rise to what has been termed the secular regulation rule. Political scientist C. Herman Pritchett clearly summarized this tenet: "Religious beliefs admittedly must have absolute protection, but actions, even though purporting to be taken for religious reasons or as part of religious observances, must conform with the regulations established by the community to protect public order, health, welfare, and morals."[9] As long as the government has a valid secular purpose in mind and otherwise has legal authority to engage in a certain form of regulation, the fact that it interferes with or hampers persons' free exercise of their religion is not a basis for them to escape the regulation. On this basis, the Supreme Court has upheld compulsory vaccinations, compulsory saluting of the flag by school children, mandatory Sunday closing laws that adversely affected Orthodox Jews, military regulations that forbade the wearing of a yarmulke, and the denial of unemployment compensation to Native Americans who had lost their jobs due to the use of peyote in their religious ceremonies.[10] In all these cases, since a legitimate secular purpose — such as public health, safety or order, military discipline, or national unity — underlay the law or regulation, the fact that it interfered with the exercise of one's religiously rooted beliefs was an insufficient basis to require exemptions. Religious dissenters must conform, even if doing so violates their religious beliefs, or suffer the consequences.

One may appropriately inquire at this point what is left of free exercise protections. If the free exercise clause only protects beliefs (which presumably would be protected by other provisions of the Constitution anyway) and not religious practices, and if any law with legitimate secular purposes can be enforced on religious groups irrespective of sincerely and deeply held religious beliefs underlying their practices, is there any protection given by the free exercise clause, which citizens would not enjoy anyway? One response notes that the Supreme Court has made it clear that it would hold any act that *intentionally* singles out a religious group for disadvantages or limitations to be a violation of free exercise rights. Laws under the secular intent rule must have a secular purpose, which applies indiscriminately to all, regardless of their religious beliefs or lack of them. In this sense, a law under the free exercise provision must be evenhanded or neutral — at least on its face. As far as I have been able to determine, however, the Supreme Court in actual practice has never decided a case in which it has invoked this principle.

The more difficult issue, one the Court has repeatedly faced, is a law that has a legitimate secular purpose and appears to be neutral in regard to religious groups, yet adversely affects certain ones. Must government make exemptions or accommodations for adherents of these religions so that they will not be penalized for acting in keeping with their religious beliefs? Not to allow exemptions often severely disadvantages certain religious groups, seemingly in violation of their free exercise rights. However, to make special exemptions for them could create severe practical problems in running secular programs of benefit to all society and would seem to violate the establishment provision by giving special consideration or advantages to religious groups.

The current Supreme Court is sharply divided on this issue. Beginning in the 1960s, the Court developed, and for a period of about twenty years a majority of the justices embraced, the compelling state interest test. This test modified the secular regulation rule and put some real teeth into the free exercise language of the First Amendment. Pepper summarized the compelling state interest principle in these terms: "In essence, if an otherwise valid legal provision or governmental action has the effect of significantly burdening an individual's exercise of his religion, the government must tailor its requirements to avoid the imposition unless it has an extraordinarily strong reason for not doing so."[11] This principle was utilized in a 1972 decision in which Chief Justice Burger, speaking for the Court, stated that for a state to compel actions in violation of religious beliefs, it must demonstrate "a state interest of sufficient magnitude to override the interest claiming protection under the Free Exercise Clause."[12] In the next paragraph, he wrote that "only those [state or societal] interests *of the highest order* and those not otherwise served can overbalance legitimate claims to the free exercise of religion."[13] On this basis the Court — with only one dissenting justice — ruled that Wisconsin could not force Old Order Amish parents to send their children to school beyond the eighth grade.

This same compelling state interest principle was used in three separate cases to protect persons' rights to receive state unemployment benefits after having quit or been fired from their jobs due to their religious scruples.[14] In one of these cases, the Supreme Court clearly expressed the free exercise principle at issue:

> Where the state conditions receipt of an important benefit upon conduct proscribed by a religious faith, or where it denies such a benefit because of conduct mandated by religious belief, thereby putting substantial pressure on an adherent to modify his behavior and to violate his beliefs, a burden upon religion exists. While the compulsion may be indirect, the infringement on free exercise is nonetheless substantial.[15]

The Court then went on to note that an infringement on free exercise of such a nature could only be justified if the state could demonstrate that its action "is the least restrictive means of achieving some compelling state interest."[16] In this case, the Court ruled that Indiana had not demonstrated a compelling interest and, therefore, it could not withhold unemployment benefits from a worker who had quit his job rather than work on military tanks in violation of his religious conscience. As recently as 1987, the Court reaffirmed the compelling state interest standard in a decision that required Florida to grant unemployment benefits to a worker who had lost her job for refusing to work on her Sabbath. It found that Florida's refusal to grant her unemployment benefits constituted an "infringement" of her free exercise rights which "must be subjected to strict scrutiny and could be justified only by proof by the State of a compelling interest."[17]

The compelling state interest standard, however, was never consistently or fully followed by the Court. In 1961 the Court rejected free exercise claims of Orthodox Jewish businesspersons to be free from a Sunday closing regulation; in 1982 it rejected those of an Old Order Amish employer and his Amish employees to be free from paying social security taxes that violated their religious beliefs; and in 1986, it rejected the request of an Orthodox Jewish air force psychologist to be free from air force regulations forbidding him to wear a yarmulke that his faith required him to wear.[18] In all these cases, the Court essentially followed the compelling state interest test but set a low threshold for meeting it, holding each time that, in fact, the government had demonstrated a compelling interest that overruled the claimed free exercise right.

More recently, the Supreme Court has virtually scuttled the compelling state interest test, leaving the secular regulation rule as the key guiding principle in free exercise cases. In 1981 Justice William Rehnquist, in a lone dissent, clearly stated his opposition to the standard itself: "Where, as here, a State has enacted a general statute, the purpose and effect of which is to advance the State's secular goals, the Free Exercise Clause does not in my view require the State to conform that statute to the dictates of religious conscience of any group."[19] Then, in two decisions in 1988 and 1990, the Court came close to simply doing away with the compelling state interest test. It ruled that as long as a government action has a legitimate secular goal that, on its face, is not intended to infringe on persons' free exercise of their religion, it meets the demands of the First Amendment free exercise provision. The 1988 case dealt with state plans to build a road through wilderness lands held sacred by Native American religion. The Court readily acknowledged, "It is undisputed that the Indian respondents' beliefs are sincere and that the Government's proposed actions will have severe adverse effects on the practice of their religion."[20] Later, the decision stated that the Court had "no reason to doubt" that "the logging and road-building projects at issue in this case could have devastating effects on traditional Indian religious practices."[21] Then, however, the Court distinguished between "coercion" and "incidental effects" and said that the compelling state interest test only applies in cases of outright coercion, not in cases of "indirect effects," even when those effects on Native American religious practice — by the Court's own admission — would be "severe" and possibly "devastating." It found that the free exercise provision does not mean "that incidental effects of government programs, which may make it more difficult to practice certain religions but which have no tendency to coerce individuals into acting contrary to their religious beliefs, require government to bring forward a compelling justification for its otherwise lawful actions."[22]

The 1990 case dealt with the use of peyote by Native Americans in religious ceremonies. Justice Scalia, writing for the Court, held that "an individual's religious beliefs [do not] excuse him from compliance with an otherwise valid law prohibiting conduct that the State is free to regulate."[23] What of the compelling state interest principle? It was left in tatters.

> The government's ability to enforce generally applicable prohibitions of socially harmful conduct, like its ability to carry out other aspects of public policy, "cannot depend on measuring the effects of a governmental action of a religious objector's spiritual development." To make an individual's obligation to obey such a law contingent upon the law's coincidence with his religious beliefs, except where the State's interest is "compelling[,]" . . . contradicts both constitutional tradition and common sense.[24]

What can one conclude in regard to Supreme Court interpretations and applications of the free exercise clause? Two observations are helpful at this point. The first is that the Supreme Court is deeply divided on free exercise issues and is not even agreed on the proper standards or principles that should be applied. The foundation for what developed into the compelling state interest standard was first articulated in a 1961 decision, and thirty years later, the Court still is deeply divided, not just on how the standard should be applied in any given case, but on whether the standard itself is valid.[25] *Employment Division v. Smith* (1990) is typical, with the Court going three different ways: A bare majority of five essentially rejected the compelling state interest standard, one justice accepted the standard but held that the government had demonstrated a compelling interest, and three justices also accepted the standard but held that the government had not demonstrated a compelling interest.

A second summary observation is that, taken as a whole, the free exercise clause has been made relatively weak. It has not been interpreted by the Supreme Court in a bold manner so as to assert clear-cut constitutional rights. With some notable exceptions, the Court has ruled against free exercise claims. The early distinction between beliefs and actions made in *Reynolds v. United States* viscerated the clause, and it was not until recent times that some life was breathed back into it by way of the compelling state interest standard. Now, however, that standard has been largely abandoned by a majority of the Court justices.

The weakness of the free exercise clause can also be seen in the tendency for the Court to avoid using it when it can defend an asserted free exercise claim on other grounds. In *West Virginia State Board of Education v. Barnette* (1943), the Supreme Court overruled a decision it had made only three years earlier and upheld the right of the children of Jehovah's Witnesses not to pledge allegiance to the flag in West Virginia schools. In doing so, the Court explicitly rejected deciding the case on religious grounds, but instead did so on general First Amendment grounds. In fact, the Court distinguished its decision in this case from its earlier one on the basis that, in the earlier case, "the Court only examined and rejected a claim based on religious beliefs," while the current case considers whether "that power exists in the State to impose the flag salute discipline upon school children in general."[26] Similarly, in *Widmar v. Vincent* the Court upheld the right of a religious student group to meet on the campus of a state university, but in doing so, it explicitly rejected deciding the case on the free exercise claims of the students and instead decided the case on free speech and association grounds.

> This case is different from cases in which religious groups claim that the denial of facilities not available to other groups deprives them of their rights under the Free Exercise Clause. Here, ... respondents' claim to use that forum does not rest solely on rights claimed under the Free Exercise Clause. Respondents' claim also implicates First Amendment rights of speech and association, and it is on the bases of speech and association that we decide the case.[27]

In both these cases, what the Court-weakened free exercise language was unable to accomplish, the other freedom of expression provisions of the First Amendment could accomplish.

One is left with a free exercise provision that protects religious beliefs and presumably would protect a religious group from governmental actions specifically and directly aimed at curtailing the practice of its religion, but offers little or no protections to religious groups whose religious practices are disadvantaged or penalized — even severely — as long as there is a genuine secular purpose for the governmental action. The contrast with the strength and vitality that the Supreme Court has pumped into the establishment clause is great.

No Establishment of Religion

Two Key Decisions

The other First Amendment provision dealing with religion is the establishment clause: "Congress shall make no law respecting the establishment of religion." Two key Supreme Court decisions have largely set the direction for how these words have been interpreted: *Everson v. Board of Education* (1947) and *Lemon v. Kurtzman* (1971). The first of these established two crucial precedents. One is that the First Amendment establishment clause, although originally written to serve as a limitation on the national government, has been incorporated into the Fourteenth Amendment and, thereby, made equally binding on the states. Second, it held that nonpreferential aid to religion generally was proscribed by the establishment clause:

> The "establishment of religion" clause of the First Amendment means at least this: Neither a state nor the Federal Government can set up a church. Neither can pass laws which aid one religion, *aid all religions*, or prefer one religion over another. . . . In the words of Jefferson, the clause against establishment of religion by law was intended to erect "a wall of separation between Church and State."[28]

It had long been assumed that laws that would aid or favor one religious group over others would be unconstitutional, but the enshrining in constitutional interpretation of the proscription of nondiscriminatory aid to religion generally and the Jeffersonian metaphor of a wall of separation between church and state (used by him in an 1802 letter to the Danbury Baptist Association), was new.

It was twenty-four years and numerous establishment cases later that the Supreme Court articulated three tests for whether an impermissible establishment had taken place. These three tests have been reiterated time and again in subsequent Court decisions. Writing for the Court majority in *Lemon v. Kurtzman*, Chief Justice Burger stated:

> Every analysis in this area [of religious establishment] must begin with consideration of the cumulative criteria developed by the Court over many years. Three such tests may be gleaned from our cases. First, the statute must have a secular legislative purpose; second, its principal or primary effect must be one that neither advances nor inhibits religion; finally, the statute must not foster "an excessive government entanglement with religion."[29]

The first of these tests is that "the statute must have a secular legislative purpose." Here the Supreme Court inquires concerning what purposes the legislators had in mind in enacting a challenged statute: Did they have a nonreligious, secular purpose in mind, or were they motivated by religious, sectarian goals? In *Edwards v. Aguillard* (1987), a case in which the Court ruled Louisiana's creation science law to be in violation of the establishment clause because it failed this "secular purpose" test, Justice William Brennan elaborated on the Court's position:

> Lemon's first prong focuses on the purpose that animated adoption of the Act. "The purpose prong of the Lemon test asks whether government's actual purpose is to endorse or disapprove religion." A governmental intention to promote religion is clear when the State enacts a law to serve a religious purpose. This intention may be evidenced by promotion of religion in general, or by advancement of a particular religious belief. . . . If the law was enacted for the purpose of endorsing religion, "no consideration of the second or third criteria [of *Lemon*] is necessary." In this case, the petitioners have identified no clear secular purpose for the Louisiana Act.[30]

Justice Brennan then went on to note explicitly the relevancy of the religious motivations of the bill's sponsor:

> The sponsor of the Creationism Act, Senator Keith, explained during the legislative hearings that his disdain for the theory of evolution resulted from the support that evolution supplied to views contrary to his own religious beliefs. . . . The legislation therefore sought to alter the science curriculum to reflect endorsement of a religious view that is antagonistic to the theory of evolution.[31]

In *Wallace v. Jaffree* (1985), which held Alabama's requirement of a "moment of silence" at the start of school days to be unconstitutional, the Supreme Court also looked into the motives of the law's chief sponsor, state Senator Donald Holmes. It noted that Holmes had testified that the purpose of the law was "to return voluntary prayer to public school," and "that he had 'no other purpose in mind.'"[32]

What is illustrated by the Court's opinions in these two cases is that intentions or motivations can be controlling. Determining whether a law was intended to serve "a religious purpose" can be crucial. This test thereby calls for the courts to unravel religious from nonreligious purposes and to conclude that if religious purposes predominate, the legislators who enacted the legislation were unconstitutionally motivated by religious goals.

This test has been used to find four state laws unconstitutional, all of which involved attempts to interject certain religiously related activities or teachings into public schools. The Court has struck down laws forbidding the teaching of evolution in the public schools and requiring the posting of the Ten Commandments in classrooms, and — as already seen — has also struck down laws requiring a moment of silent prayer or meditation at the start of the school day and "creation science" to be taught alongside evolution.[33]

The second *Lemon* test holds that to pass Constitutional challenge, "the law's principle or primary effect must be one that neither advances nor inhibits religion." This is the secular effect test. The effects of the questioned law must be neutral in regard to religion, neither helping nor hindering it. However, as the highly respected constitutional law scholar, Laurence Tribe, has pointed out, in practice, the primary effect standard has virtually become a no-aid standard:

> The constitutional requirement of "primary secular effect" has thus become a misnomer; while retaining the earlier label, the Court has transformed it into a *requirement that any non-secular effect be remote, indirect and incidental*. This shift is analytically significant, for the remote-indirect-and-incidental standard plainly compels a more searching inquiry, and comes closer to the absolutist no-aid approach to the establishment clause than the primary effect test did.[34]

A 1985 case — *Grand Rapids School District v. Ball* (1985) — dealing with nonreligious classes taught in nonpublic, religiously oriented schools by teachers paid with public funds, reveals that the secular effect test has indeed been made formidable. The Supreme Court acknowledged "that respondents adduced no evidence of specific incidents of religious indoctrination in this case."[35] If this was true, how could the program have an effect that advanced religion? The Court said nonetheless that there was a "substantial risk, overtly or subtly, [that] the religious message . . . will infuse the supposedly secular class."[36] Moreover, it referred to the importance of appearances: "An important concern of the effects test is whether the symbolic union of church and state effected by the challenged governmental action is sufficiently likely *to be perceived* by adherents of the controlling denominations as an endorsement, and by the non-adherents as a disapproval, of their individual religious choices."[37] To violate the test of governmental action not having the effect of advancing or inhibiting religion, there need not even be a demonstration of an actual effect, but only that there is a risk of such an effect or, in the absence of an actual cause and effect, that the symbolic link between religion and the government is likely to give some persons the impression of support or disapproval. The Court indicated its official position when, in 1963, it favorably quoted from an earlier dissent by Justice Wiley Rutledge stating that the First Amendment forbids *"every* form of public aid or support for religion."[38]

The Supreme Court has relied on this second of the three *Lemon* tests to outlaw a number of state attempts to support nonpublic, religiously based schools. It has held it impermissible for states, for example, to provide grants to religious schools for facilities and equipment, to loan religious schools instructional materials, to provide religious schools with teachers for auxiliary services, and to provide transportation for religious school field trips.[39] On the other hand, the Court has ruled that broad governmental programs that incidentally and indirectly provide aid to religious and nonreligious groups alike are permissible. Fire and police protection granted to both religious and secular organizations is an obvious example. In specific cases, the Supreme Court has held there was no impermissible advancement of religion by way of the loan of textbooks to children attending religiously oriented schools, the provision of diagnostic services to religious school students, the rendering of therapeutic help to religious school students if given off the premises of the school, and tax deductions to parents for their children's educational expenses, including children attending religious schools.[40] The sort of fine distinctions on which these decisions have turned can be seen in the majority opinion in *Wolman v. Walter* (1977):

> We recognize that, unlike the diagnostician, the therapist may establish a relationship with the pupil in which there might be opportunities to transmit ideological views. In *Meek* the Court acknowledged the danger that publicly employed personnel who provide services analogous to those at issue here might transmit religious instruction and advance religious beliefs in their activities. But . . . the Court emphasized that this danger arose from the fact that the services were performed in the pervasively sectarian atmosphere of the church-related school. . . . So long as these types of services are offered at truly religiously neutral locations, the danger perceived in *Meek* does not arise.[41]

The Court, in short, has made the secular effect part of the *Lemon* test into a formidable test, but not an insurmountable one. Some limited, carefully circumscribed aid to religious organizations can pass Supreme Court muster.

The third test outlined in the *Lemon* case is that there must be no "excessive government entanglement with religion." Subsequent cases have revealed three types of entanglement that may be "excessive." One that has seldom been used is what Tribe calls "vesting entanglement."[42] This occurs when government seeks to transfer certain discretionary governmental powers to a religious body. The one case in which the Supreme Court clearly relied on this form of entanglement to find a statute in violation of the establishment provision was *Larkin v. Grendel's Den* (1982). This case concerned a Massachusetts statute that permitted schools and churches to block the issuance of state liquor licenses to establishments located within 500 feet of their premises. The Court held that "few entanglements could be more offensive to the spirit of the Constitution" than this one, which "enmeshes churches in the processes of government."[43]

Of greater importance have been the other two types of excessive entanglements. One is administrative entanglement, which has been defined as "an intimate and continuing relationship between church and state." This quotation is from the *Lemon* case, in which the Supreme Court felt that conditions of entanglement would exist because state grants to religiously oriented schools would involve "comprehensive measures of surveillance and controls. . . . In particular the government's post-audit power to inspect and evaluate a church-related school's financial records and to determine which expenditures are religious and which are secular creates an intimate and continuing relationship between church and state."[44]

Violation of this administrative entanglement test played a prominent role in *Meek v. Pittenger* (1975), which invalidated a Pennsylvania act that sought to provide various auxiliary services and instructional materials to private school students, and in *Aguilar v. Felton* (1985), which invalidated a New York state–supported remedial program for children from low-income families in nonpublic schools. In this latter case, the Court stated:

> The supervisory system established by the City of New York inevitably results in the excessive entanglement of church and state, an Establishment Clause concern distinct from that addressed by the effects doctrine. Even where state aid to parochial institutions does not have the primary effect of advancing religion, the provision of such aid may nonetheless violate the Establishment Clause owing to the nature of the interaction of church and state in the administration of that aid.[45]

A third type of excessive entanglement is entanglement in the form of fostering political divisiveness. This religious divisiveness form of entanglement was first articulated and defended by Chief Justice Burger in the *Lemon* opinion:

> A broader base of entanglement of yet a different character is presented by the divisive political potential of these state

programs. . . . Ordinary political debate and division, however vigorous or even partisan, are normal and healthy manifestations of our democratic system of government, but political division along religious lines was one of the principal evils against which the First Amendment was intended to protect. The potential divisiveness of such conflict is a threat to the normal political process. To have States or communities divide on the issues presented by state aid to parochial schools would tend to confuse and obscure other issues of great urgency. We have an expanding array of vexing issues, local and national, domestic and international, to debate and divide on. It conflicts with our whole history and tradition to permit questions of the Religion Clauses to assume such importance in our legislatures and in our elections that they could divert attention from the myriad issues and problems that confront every level of government.[46]

The potential divisiveness of religion in political affairs has never been used by itself as a basis to invalidate an otherwise valid law, but it has occasionally been cited as a relevant consideration, and, as will be explained later, it helps throw light on the state of mind and value presuppositions with which some members of the Supreme Court approach church-state issues.

In spite of the wall of separation metaphor that the Supreme Court adopted as its own in the *Everson* case, the Court has not always upheld challenges to governmental practices based on alleged establishment violations. It has upheld prayers at the start of legislative sessions, governmental aid to religiously based colleges and universities, religious symbols in municipal Christmas and Hanukkah displays, tax exemptions for churches, and, as seen earlier, some limited forms of governmental aid to religious, nonpublic schools. In addition, it has indicated that it would approve a religious motto on coins and an acknowledgment of God's help in the pledge of allegiance to the flag.[47] It has occasionally done so simply by not applying the three-part *Lemon* test. As the Court stated in *Lynch v. Donnelly* (1984), "We have repeatedly emphasized our unwillingness to be confined to any single test or criterion in this sensitive area. In two cases, the Court did not even apply the *Lemon* 'test.'"[48] On other occasions the Court has claimed that ostensibly religious symbols or activities have been sufficiently secularized or that the benefits granted religion are sufficiently indirect and incidental that the no establishment burden no longer applies.

The Underlying Goal

The foregoing exploration of various tests or standards that the Supreme Court has used in interpreting the establishment provision of the First Amendment do not, in and by themselves, reveal a fundamental goal or aim that has largely animated those efforts of the Court. That aim or goal has, for the most part, been the concept of neutrality. Time and again, the Court has made it clear that the goal it was seeking to reach was that of complete neutrality of government, both among different religions and between religion and nonreligion. In the precedent-setting *Everson* case, the Court articulated its belief that neutrality was the basic concern of the First Amendment when it stated that the amendment "requires the state to be a neutral in its relations with groups of religious believers and nonbelievers; it does not require the state to be their adversary. State power is no more to be used so as to handicap religions, than it is to favor them."[49] In another case the Court referred to "the established principle that the government must pursue a course of complete neutrality toward religion."[50] The clearest statement of the neutrality goal came in a unanimous decision written by Justice Abe Fortas in *Epperson v. Arkansas* (1968):

> Government in our democracy, state and national, must be neutral in matters of religious theory, doctrine, and practice. It may not be hostile to any religion or to the advocacy of no-religion; and it may not aid, foster, or promote one religion or religious theory against another or even against the militant opposite. The First Amendment mandates governmental neutrality between religion and religion, and between religion and nonreligion.
>
> As early as 1872, this Court said: "The law knows no heresy, and is committed to the support of no dogma, the establishment of no sect." This has been the interpretation of the great First Amendment which this Court has applied in the many and subtle problems which the ferment of our national life has presented for decision within the Amendment's broad command.[51]

Thus, the Court's decisions seeking to establish a wall of separation between church and state, as well as its rulings against governmental acts with religious purposes or effects or that would entangle religion and government, should be seen as attempts at achieving the underlying goal of neutrality. The close conjunction of church-state separation and neutrality was made explicit in the famous *Abington* case of 1963. The Court majority wrote: "We have come to recognize through bitter experience that it is not within the power of government to invade that citadel [of religion], whether its purpose or effect be to aid or oppose, to advance or retard. In the relationship between man and religion, the State is firmly committed to a position of neutrality."[52] Similar statements are frequently found in Supreme Court church-state decisions. For example, Justice Thurgood Marshall wrote in a dissenting opinion: "The Establishment Clause of the First Amendment prohibits a State from subsidizing religious education, whether it does so directly or indirectly. In my view, this principle of neutrality forbids . . . any tax benefit . . . which subsidizes tuition payments to sectarian schools."[53]

The basic assumption is that if government would either support or oppose religion, neutrality would be lost. If it supported religion, it would be favoring one religion over another or religion as a whole over nonreligion; if it opposed religion, it would be favoring nonreligion over religion. The way to assure that neither eventuality occurs is to separate religion and politics, erecting a high wall of separation between the two. If government has nothing — or, at the least, as little as possible — to do with religion, it cannot help but be neutral. Common sense says this is obvious. However, I will shortly argue that it is also profoundly false.

Summary Observations

This, then, is how the establishment clause has been interpreted by the Supreme Court. At this point, three summary observations are in order. The first is that, in contrast to its interpretations of the free exercise clause, the Supreme Court has built the establishment clause into a powerful tool of constitutional discernment and enforcement. Numerous legislative initiatives — from prayer and other religious rituals in public schools to aid to religious schools and religiously oriented displays on public property — have been ruled in violation of the establishment clause. The contrasting weight that the Court attaches to free exercise claims as compared to no establishment claims was made explicit in a 1992 decision when the Court majority declared: "The principle that government *may* accommodate the free exercise of religion does not supersede the fundamental limitations *imposed* by the Establishment Clause."[54] Satisfying free exercise claims was couched in permissive terms; satisfying no establishment claims was couched in mandatory terms.

A second observation is that the Supreme Court's articulated doctrines of the establishment clause largely conform to the strict separationist position, which holds that there should be a complete separation between church and state.[55] In concluding that the establishment clause proscribes even nonpreferential aid to religion generally, and in setting forth and applying its three-part *Lemon* test, the Supreme Court has largely aligned itself with strict separationist reasoning. Admittedly, there have been decisions whose results have deviated from the strict separationist position, but when they have done so, the Court has almost always maintained strict separationist, neutrality-by-way-of-separation reasoning. The *Everson* case is a good example. As already explained, it articulated a strict separationist position. In fact, the majority opinion ended with ringing separationist words: "The First Amendment has erected a wall between church and state. That wall must be kept high and impregnable. We could not approve the slightest breach."[56] However, the irony is that in this case the Court approved the state of New Jersey's subsidizing the bus transportation of parochial school children. It allowed support or accommodation of religion, but in its opinion, the Court did not do so by reasoning that in this case, strict church-state separation did not apply. Instead, it reasoned that the transportation of children to parochial schools was simply a form of "public welfare legislation" that was available to all, "without regard to their religious beliefs."[57] One can argue whether the Court was breaching the wall of separation (the dissenting justices argued that it was), but there can be no doubt that the Court majority upheld a strict separation doctrine even while allowing a limited form of aid to children attending religiously based schools. This is the typical pattern: Even when the Supreme Court has allowed certain forms of cooperation or assistance to religiously based groups or organizations or has allowed some forms of religious expression in the public realm, it has developed reasoning that allows such cooperation or aid without abandoning its strict separation doctrine.

Thus, strict separationist scholar Leonard Levy is accurate when he concluded that "history has made the wall of separation real. The wall is not just a metaphor. It has constitutional existence."[58] Moreover, few questioned the person who is probably the nation's foremost advocate of the strict separationist position, Leo Pfeffer, when he wrote in 1984 that "pro-strict separationist decisions still stand intact."[59]

A third observation is that the phrase *separation of church and state*, despite its widespread popular usage, does not accurately encapsulate the Supreme Court's religion decisions. To the extent that the Court has followed the strict separationist position, the separation on which it has insisted has not been merely the separation of church and state in a technical sense, but the much more radical separation of religion and politics. The former action refers to separating religion in an organized, institutional sense from government in its institutionalized manifestations. The latter refers to separating the sphere of religion in its various forms and activities from the entire governing or policy-making and -implementation process. The dissenting justices in the *Everson* case wrote concerning the goal of the First Amendment: "But the object was broader than separating church and state in this narrow sense. It was to create a complete and permanent separation of the spheres of religious activity and civil authority by comprehensively forbidding every form of public aid or support for religion."[60] The fact that at times, the Supreme Court has appeared to have taken this stance has been noted by Reichley: "Since the 1940s the Court has sometimes seemed to interpret prohibition of establishment to mean not only that there should be no direct tie between government and the organized churches but also that the whole of civil society should be kept insulated against contact with religion."[61] The significance of all three of these summary observations will emerge as I proceed with my argument.

Evaluation and Critique

In this section I argue that the principles the Supreme Court has developed for interpreting the religion provisions of the First Amendment and the way in which it has applied them in concrete cases are fundamentally flawed and are having the effect of constricting the freedom of religion in the United States. It is important to note at the outset that the problem does not lie so much in a Supreme Court that has defied the rest of U.S. society and is forcing it down untenable paths against its will. Instead, the failures of the Court are also deeply rooted in U.S. society and its history. This is a major theme of this book. The reasons why I hold to this position and exactly what I mean by it will be developed more fully in the next section of this chapter and in the following chapter. Nevertheless, manifestations of the problems that inhere in U.S. society's approach to church-state relations reveal themselves in the Supreme Court's rulings and standards. It is to these that I now turn.

Original Intent Has Not Been Followed

The concept of original intent in its strict version holds that the Supreme Court should interpret the words of the Constitution exactly in keeping with what its original authors intended them to mean. This supposedly will keep the current justices from reading into the Constitution whatever their own personal policy preferences and predilections might be. Actually, however, this is a flawed concept that is saved by its own impossibility of being fully followed. If today we could know perfectly and fully, for every question of constitutional interpretation, exactly what the original drafters of the Constitution intended, and if we would always exactly follow that intention, the Constitution would be made into an inflexible, static document that would soon prove irrelevant to a society whose size, composition, and values are constantly evolving. Fortunately, today we do *not* have perfect insight into the intentions of the fifty-five authors of the Constitution, who have been dead since 1836. Moreover, as anyone who has participated in or closely observed a legislative body can testify, the intentions of the hundred or so persons voting for a certain provision in a new law, or even of the three or four persons who play a leading role in writing the language — working out the inevitable compromises and shepherding it through the legislature — will be veiled in the mists of mixed motives and tactical considerations that always accompany human endeavors. Thus, it is neither wise nor possible to base the exact interpretation of the religion clauses on a supposedly fully known original intent of their authors.

On the other hand, this is not to say that original intent is an irrelevant consideration. To the extent that the original intent of the authors of certain constitutional provisions can be fathomed — even if only the broad outlines of that intent, a greater certainty or predictability, and a keeping of Supreme Court decisions within certain bounds or channels are achieved. This is good. The Constitution should not be static, but neither should it be totally flexible, bending with every breeze that moves through society, for then it would become meaningless as a force for setting the rules of the political game or the protection of basic human rights. If the Constitution can be made to mean whatever today's majority forces wish it to mean, it will become meaningless. The concept of original intent can play a key role in achieving a meaningful, yet evolving, Constitution: it can serve as a fixed point of reference that slows overly rapid change — blocking attempts to respond to every passing fad, but its uncertainty and imprecision allow for an evolution or movement in interpretation.

The conclusion I reached is that the original intent of the authors of the First Amendment religion language is a relevant consideration that should be explored and weighed, but that one should not search for a clear-cut, fully knowable intent of the members of the First Congress, which adopted the Bill of Rights, and then try to use that intent as an unalterable guide to the precise meaning to be given the First Amendment today. Rather, what one should seek is the general outlines of the intent of the drafters of the relevant Constitutional provisions, and then one should seek to root today's interpretations in those intentions, even while allowing for adaptation to society's changing conditions. In this way, the religion language of the First Amendment will have a measure of fixed meaning and predictability, yet will also be able to evolve to meet this generation's needs and circumstances.

Even in light of this flexible standard, there are major problems in the Supreme Court's use of the original intent of the drafters of the First Amendment's religion language. Three especially crucial questions have come up in regard to original intent. One concerns whether the First Amendment's religion provisions are applicable only to the national government or to the state governments as well. No one disputes the fact that the original Bill of Rights, including the free exercise and establishment provisions, was intended to restrict only the newly created federal government, not the thirteen state governments: "*Congress* shall make no law . . ." (emphasis added). It is equally clear that the Fourteenth Amendment, adopted in 1868 following the Civil War, was intended to apply to the state governments: "No *state* shall ... deprive any person of life, liberty, or property, without due process of law; nor deny to any person within its jurisdiction the equal protection of the laws" (emphasis added). Gradually, by an evolving process of interpretation, the Supreme Court has held that almost all the Bill of Rights, including the religion provisions of the First Amendment, applies as fully to the states as to the national government. It has done so on the grounds that for a state to violate any of these provisions of the Bill of Rights, it would mean violating the provisions just quoted from the Fourteenth Amendment. This is the well-known concept of the incorporation of the Bill of Rights into the Fourteenth Amendment.

Occasionally persons will challenge the propriety of the incorporation of the free exercise and establishment language into the Fourteenth Amendment, arguing that this was never the intent of its authors. Such arguments are unpersuasive, however. While they are technically correct from a rigid perspective of original intent, they are irrelevant. The Constitution should be allowed to evolve and develop, and in a highly interdependent, nationalized society, there should be national constitutional protections safeguarding religious freedom.

A second question of original intent, however, raises more problems. It is the question of whether the original authors of the First Amendment intended the establishment clause to bar accommodations to, favorable recognition of, and support for religion generally without discriminating among religious beliefs and groups. Did they intend to erect a high, impenetrable wall of separation between church and state? The question of original intent in this form has engendered much continuing debate, both because it deals with a fundamental issue of the broad outlines of a constitutional provision and because the Supreme Court has, in fact, relied heavily on original intent arguments in defending the answer it has adopted to this question.

As seen earlier, the Supreme Court, in its 1947 *Everson v. Board of Education* decision, found that neither the federal government nor the state governments might "aid all religion," and that the *intent* of the authors of the First Amendment was "to erect 'a wall of separation between Church and State.'" The Court reached this conclusion with a minimum of historical analysis. It limited itself to looking at the adoption in 1786 of Virginia's Bill for Establishing Religious Liberty and the legislative debates surrounding it, especially weighing the role played by James Madison and Thomas Jefferson in its adoption. The Court argued "that the provisions of the First Amendment, in the drafting and adoption of which Madison and Jefferson played such leading roles, had the same objective and were intended to provide the same protection against governmental intrusion on religious liberty as the Virginia statute."[62] This was asserted by the Court without giving any historical evidence in support of it. Common sense at the least raises serious questions about it, since Jefferson was not even a member of the First Congress, which wrote the First Amendment, but rather was thousands of miles away in Paris as the ambassador of the new U.S. nation to France. James Madison was indeed a member of the First Congress and clearly played the leading role in the writing and adoption of the First Amendment. However, can one just assume, without looking at the debates and the various versions of language considered by the Congress, that whatever position Madison had taken three years earlier in the Virginia legislature was what he felt was needed for the new federal government (he originally believed that no Bill of Rights at all was needed to limit it), and that what Madison wanted, the Congress as a whole supported and intended? I think not.[63]

In fact, a look at congressional debates accompanying the drafting and adoption of the First Amendment reveals that Madison did not even try to get Congress to pass what he had advocated in Virginia. The initial version of the First Amendment that he drafted and introduced in Congress read, "The Civil Rights of none shall be abridged on account of religious belief or worship, nor shall any national religion be established, nor shall the full and equal rights of conscience be in any manner, nor on any pretext infringed."[64] Madison's language dealing with the establishment issue only called for the prohibition of a "national religion." That this was indeed Madison's basic intent was collaborated later in the debates, when a committee report recommended that the amendment simply read, "No religion shall be established by law, nor shall the equal rights of conscience be infringed." Some members of Congress objected to this language, apparently on the basis that they feared it would ban all direct and indirect assistance to religion generally. Was Madison's answer to this objection that this was precisely what he favored? No, Madison proposed that the word *national* be added, so the amendment would read, "No national religion shall be established. . . ." The point is that Madison was not fighting for the position of no general assistance to religion, which he had articulated in the earlier Virginia debates, to be incorporated into the federal Constitution, as the Supreme Court assumed was the case. Reichley accurately observed:

Madison's own description during the debate in the House on the objective of the part of the amendment dealing with establishment — "that Congress should not establish a religion, and enforce the legal observation of it by law" — indicates an idea of establishment much more narrow than that conceived by those who would interpret the clause to prohibit all forms of nondiscriminatory cooperation between government and religion.[65]

The Court has simply misread history. One scholar who has made one of the most thorough studies of the debates of the First Congress on the adoption of the religion language of the First Amendment concluded:

All of the speakers, except [Roger] Sherman [of Connecticut], agreed that the Bill of Rights should prohibit the new government from establishing a national religion. In addition, they did not want the government to have the power deliberately to favor one religion over another. But every one of them seemed to agree that the Bill of Rights should not prevent the federal government from giving nondiscriminatory assistance to religion. . . . Madison, even though he privately questioned the efficacy of governmental assistance to religion, accepted the . . . [nondiscriminatory assistance] view throughout the First Congress debates.[66]

This conclusion is supported by the fact that the very same Congress that adopted the First Amendment also appointed a paid chaplain to open its sessions with prayer and reenacted the Northwest Ordinance, which included the famous provision, "Religion, morality, and knowledge, being necessary to good government and the happiness of mankind, schools and the means of learning shall forever to encouraged."[67] It is inconceivable that the First Congress would take actions — with Madison's approval and support — that violated the very things it was intending to accomplish in the First Amendment.

Examination of the First Congress's debates and actions at the very least raise serious questions about the Supreme Court's facile assumption that what Madison had supported in the Virginia legislature in 1786 was what he wanted to be included in the national Bill of Rights, and that what Madison wanted in the Bill of Rights is what Congress as a whole, without compromise, adopted. The historical record does not support the claim that the drafters of the religion clauses of the First Amendment intended to enact a wall of separation between church and state, with government prohibited from supporting or accommodating itself to religion generally.

A third question of original intent concerns the Supreme Court's failure to consider original intent as it relates to the free exercise language of the First Amendment. Legal scholar Michael McConnell has pointed out that, in contrast to its establishment decisions, "The

Court made no effort in *Sherbert* or subsequent cases to support its holdings through evidence of the historical understanding of 'free exercise of religion' at the time of the framing and ratification of the first amendment."[68] The distinction between belief and practice and the use of the compelling state interest standard as a means to protect practice were not rooted in original intent. McConnell, in a carefully reasoned and well researched article, concluded that most of the available historical evidence indicates that the original authors of the First Amendment intended to include protection of religious practices or actions as well as religious beliefs within the free exercise provision. He concluded, "By using the term 'free exercise,' the first amendment extended the broader freedom of action to all believers. As noted, the freedom of religion was almost universally understood (with Jefferson being the prominent exception) to include conduct as well as belief."[69] Cutting free exercise interpretations off from original intent helps explain why the Court's free exercise decisions have vacillated between protecting religious beliefs only and also protecting practices by way of the compelling state interest standard.

As a result of this selective reading of history, the Supreme Court has failed to root its First Amendment interpretations of religion in even the broad outlines of the intentions of the First Amendment's authors. This would not cause overly serious problems for the political system and religious freedoms if the Supreme Court had substituted other guidelines or interpretations that now moor contemporary interpretations on principled standards, which protect a full, complete freedom of religion. However, this the Court has been unable to do. The standards that the Supreme Court has adopted are not rooted in principle, have not led to consistent, predictable results, and — most seriously — have compromised the freedoms and protections afforded religion. The following sections elaborate on and defend this conclusion.

The Weakness of Free Exercise Protections

In a 1991 public address, Justice Sandra Day O'Connor declared that she was "very worried about the future of the free exercise of religion" in the United States.[70] She is not alone. As noted earlier, the Supreme Court's interpretations of the free exercise language of the First Amendment have had the effect of severely restricting and weakening it. The basic direction of the Court's interpretations was set in its original distinction between religious beliefs and religious practices and the holding that free exercise rights protect belief but not practice. In making this distinction, the Court went against both the clear words of the First Amendment — since it refers to the free *exercise* of religion, not to the freedom of religious beliefs — and, as just noted, the apparent intent of the First Amendment authors. The negative results of this distinction for freedom of religion rests in the basic fact that in the real world religious belief and practices are inextricably linked. Governmental actions that limit religiously rooted practices necessarily affect persons in their deepest religious natures. As Tribe pointed out: "This belief-action dichotomy . . . is at best an oversimplification. Short of government mandated or state-immunized brainwashing[,] . . . the state does not directly attack citizens' religious beliefs. Rather, the state rewards or proscribes beliefs indirectly, by encouraging or discouraging actions that are based on those beliefs."[71] Thus, when the Court's belief-practice distinction leaves religiously rooted practices vulnerable, religious freedom as a whole is left vulnerable as well. The Supreme Court itself even recognized in a recent case that the governmental action it held to be constitutional might "virtually destroy the Indians' ability to practice their religion," but could not find in the free exercise provision "a principle that could justify upholding" the Native Americans' claim.[72]

The problem is not that the Court would approve governmental action that directly and purposely sought to restrict religious freedom. The problem rather is that the belief-practice distinction formed the basis for the Court's secular regulation rule, which holds that when otherwise legitimate secular programs or regulations of government adversely affect the practice of a religious group, free exercise rights cannot be used to limit the government. In the age of the comprehensive administrative state — where government's secular regulations and programs reach almost all facets of life, the danger to religious liberty is great. In particular, minority, non-mainstream religious groups are left vulnerable since they typically have difficulty defending themselves and their interests in the public policy-making arena.

Admittedly, sometimes the state needs to limit or flatly prohibit certain acts that are rooted in sincerely held religious beliefs in order to protect public health, safety, or order. Hypothetically, preventing some religious sect from engaging in human sacrifices or, more realistically, requiring the members of some other religious group to be vaccinated against infectious, communicable diseases in violation of their religious beliefs are clear examples of this need. Thus, the Supreme Court appropriately developed the compelling state interest standard discussed earlier. The government could prohibit or compel actions in violation of one's religious conscience only if it had a compelling interest, an interest (as the Court said in *Wisconsin v. Yoder*), of "the highest order." The big difficulty, however, is that the current Supreme Court is sharply divided on whether this standard should be applied. In the 1990 case *Employment Division v. Smith*, a Court majority of five justices rejected the compelling state interest standard in sweeping terms, while four justices indicated their continuing support for it. If the position of the majority prevails in the future, we will be returned to the sharp belief-practice distinction, with protection only afforded belief. Given the inseparable tie between religious belief and practice, such a position is a significant and troubling threat to religious freedom generally. As a group of four legal scholars wrote: "The prime function of the Free Exercise Clause is to enable religious communities to preserve their way of life in the face of hostile state power. After *Smith*, the protection is all but gone."[73]

If the Supreme Court persists in its abandonment of the compelling state interest principle in favor of the much weaker secular regulation principle, the resulting danger to small, non-mainstream religious groups, such as adherents of traditional Native American religion, is clear. Less frequently recognized are the negative implications of a constricted interpretation of the free exercise clause for religious freedom in general. To understand this latter point one must lay the weak interpretations the Supreme Court has given the free exercise language alongside the strong interpretations that it has given the establishment language of the First Amendment. This I will do shortly, after looking more carefully at the Court's interpretations of the establishment language.

The Wall of Separation and Neutrality

As seen earlier, the basic purpose or goal underlying the Supreme Court's interpretations of the establishment clause (aimed at separating government and religion) is to assure government's neutrality toward religion. By not supporting or favoring one religious doctrine or group over another, and by favoring neither religion nor nonreligion, neutrality or evenhandedness is presumably maintained. The Court, therefore, seeks as much as practicable to maintain a wall of separation between government and religion. Religion is removed from the public realm, and the public realm is removed from the affairs of religion.

However, this is not neutrality. Implicitly, it supports secularism. One of the foremost advocates of secularism in the nineteenth century defined it as "the doctrine that morality should be based solely in regard to the well-being of mankind in the present life, to the exclusion of all considerations drawn from belief in God or in future life."[74] If one removes all positive, supportive references to religion from all the wide-ranging programs of the comprehensive administrative state (from public schools, child-care services, sex education programs, drug rehabilitation programs, child foster-care services, and more), morality, values, and human goals are being considered and taught, either explicitly or implicitly, only in terms of the "well-being of mankind in the present life, to the exclusion of all considerations drawn from belief in God." Government is not being neutral between religion and an irreligious secularism; secularism is being favored and advanced over theistic religion. Reichley, therefore, was correct when he noted:

> Banishment of religion does not represent neutrality between religion and secularism; conduct of public institutions without any acknowledgment of religion *is* secularism. . . . A society that excludes religion totally from its public life, that seems to regard religion as something against which public life must be protected, is bound to foster the impression that religion is either irrelevant or harmful.[75]

In a 1963 dissenting opinion, Justice Potter Stewart saw this issue clearly:

> If religious exercises are held to be an impermissible activity in schools, religion is placed at an artificial and state-created disadvantage. Viewed in this light, permission of such exercises for those who want them is necessary if the schools are truly to be neutral in the matter of religion. And a refusal to permit religious exercises thus is seen, not as the realization of state neutrality, but rather as the establishment of a religion of secularism, or at the least, as government support of the beliefs of those who think that religious exercises should be conducted only in private.[76]

Sociologist James Davison Hunter of the University of Virginia wrote a perceptive essay that helps clarify what is at stake in the issue raised here. He noted the increasing proportion of secularists in U.S. society and raised the question of whether secularism (or humanism, as he usually refers to it) is a religion.[77] He concluded that in its formal, organized manifestation, humanism "clearly does fit certain sociological criteria of religion," but that the concept in this form is a minority, non-mainstream phenomenon with little cultural impact.[78] He then went on to make a crucial point:

> To the extent that secular humanism exists in the larger culture, it does not as a formal ideological system (in the sense that it is formalized in the humanist movement), nor as a religion. . . . Nevertheless, it is possible to speak of humanism as a latent moral ideology, a "folk" ideology or even a tacit faith. It is in this latent sense that the American social theorist, Talcott Parsons, spoke of secular humanism as America's fourth faith.[79]

Hunter referred to humanism in this form as a "cultural ethos" and suggested "that the structure of contemporary culture provides . . . a reinforcing cultural context, within which humanistic ideology, both formal and 'folk,' becomes credible if not 'commonsensical' to an increasing number of people."[80]

It is this secular, humanistic cultural ethos that remains once — under Supreme Court mandates — religion is removed from the public schools and other aspects of public life. This is the form of secularism that Reichley and Justice Stewart were identifying in today's United States. Hunter himself concluded:

> To describe [secular humanism] as a relatively diffuse moral ethos is not to say it is indistinct and culturally impotent. Quite the opposite. Indeed, the evidence points to the fact that it occupies much the same place in American public culture as nondenominational Protestantism in the nineteenth century. Because of its specific role in the contemporary public school curricula, it actually enjoys the status of a quasi establishment.[81]

The bottom line is that the Supreme Court's decisions are supportive of a secularized public sphere that is not neutral on religion and nonreligion. Those who seek to live out a religious faith in all walks of their lives (in the education of their children, in the public policies they advocate, and in the acts of charity and social responsibility they take) face insistent direct and indirect hindrances and discouragements. The free exercise of their religious faith has been compromised. Secularism as a diffuse cultural ethos is in a privileged position, implicitly endorsed and supported by various public practices and ceremonies. A leading secularist, Paul Blanshard, may have overstated the case — but not by much — when he wrote: "I think the most important factor moving us toward a secular society has been the educational factor. Our schools may not teach Johnny to read properly, but the fact that Johnny is in school until he is sixteen tends toward the elimination of religious superstition."[82] This is where the Supreme Court's neutrality-by-way-of-separation position has led: A secular cultural ethos is favored over theistic religion.

I note in passing that the way to correct for the nonneutrality of government-religion separation is not to put religion into a favored, advantaged position. Rather, the proper answer to the current quasi establishment of secularism to which Hunter refers is not to go back to the nineteenth-century quasi-establishment of Christian Protestantism (which the next chapter documents). What is needed is a new paradigm: a new way of thinking about religion-state relations. That is what I seek to develop in subsequent chapters.

The Wall of Separation and the Secularization of Religion

In most establishment cases, the Supreme Court has, in theory, embraced the strict separationist doctrine, yet (as noted previously) it has frequently permitted certain forms of governmental support for or accommodation to religious organizations and practices. One of the frequently invoked bases that the Court has used to justify such exceptions to the wall of separation theory has been the claim that the religious organizations or practices being supported or accommodated are in reality not religious at all. Religion is secularized and what appears to be support for religion is said to be support for just another nonreligious aspect of U.S. life. This is crucial. It means that the claimed neutrality of government on religion and secularism is violated even when government acknowledges or supports certain limited religiously rooted symbols or programs, for the only aspects of religion that it is allowed to acknowledge or support are ones that fit within a secular cultural ethos.

One way in which the Supreme Court has achieved this transformation is by simply declaring that certain manifestations of religion have lost all religious meaning. Justice Brennan, in a dissenting opinion joined by three other justices, declared:

> I would suggest that such practices as the designation of "In God We Trust" as our national motto, or the references to God contained in the Pledge of Allegiance to the flag can best be understood, in Dean Rostow's apt phrase, as a form of "ceremonial deism," protected from Establishment Clause scrutiny chiefly because they have lost through rote repetition any significant religious content. Moreover, these references are uniquely suited to serve such wholly secular purposes as solemnizing public occasions, or inspiring commitment to meet some national challenge in a manner that simply could not be fully served in our culture if government were limited to purely nonreligious phrases. . . . Their message is dominantly secular.[83]

By some reverse alchemy, references to God that many deeply religious citizens take as golden are debased into the lead of a "ceremonial deism," with no "significant religious content." Even more insulting to sensitive believers is the idea that references to God are good for the "secular" purpose of building support "to meet some national chal-lenge." To them, this is like calling a beautiful Claud Monet painting good because it is useful for covering up a crack in the wall! Religion, when safely defanged and declawed by "rote repetition," is permitted into the public realm to serve certain secular purposes.

The Supreme Court has handled in this same manner displays that some communities have wished to erect at Christmas and other religious holidays. The basic stance of the Court has been that public displays may commemorate these holidays if they are sufficiently secular in nature. *Lynch v. Donnelly* (1984) dealt with a municipal

Christmas display in Pawtucket, Rhode Island, which included a crèche. The crèche in this case passed establishment clause standards because it was surrounded by reindeer, a Santa Claus, and candy canes. It was therefore judged to have a secular purpose: "The crèche in the display depicts the historical origins of this traditional event long recognized as a National Holiday. . . . The display is sponsored by the city to celebrate the Holiday and to depict the origins of that Holiday. These are legitimate secular purposes."[84] However, five years later, a crèche in Pittsburgh's city hall failed the establishment clause standard because it was displayed by itself. ("Nothing in the context of the display detracts from the crèche message.")[85] Some poinsettias were not enough to do the trick; presumably, a Santa Claus and some reindeer or candy canes were needed to neutralize (secularize) the religious aspects of the display. Meanwhile, in the same case, a menorah commemorating Hanukkah passed establishment muster because a Christmas tree and a secular saying were also included in the display, thereby signaling that "both Christmas and Chanukah are part of the same winter holiday season, which has attained a secular status in our society."[86]

As I have written elsewhere, the problem here is that

> The price religion must pay for its admission to the public sphere is to deny its heart and soul — to deny the religious character of its actions and commitments and reduce itself to just another secularized aspect of American life. What to the devout Christian is a scene of the holiest and most profound of miracles of human history — Almighty God himself stooping to be born of a peasant girl in wretched circumstances thereby demonstrating the depths of God's love for his children — is allowed on public property only if it reduces itself to the level of reindeer with red bulbs for noses that flash on and off.[87]

What to the devout believer is the Pledge of Allegiance's affirmation that the nation exists under the benevolence and normative will of a sovereign God is only allowed into the public sphere on the assumption that "rote repetition" has secularized it. What to the devout Jew is a symbol of God's miraculous provision for the Jewish nation is allowed into a public place only because it is accompanied by a Christmas tree and because the holiday it commemorates allegedly has "a secular status." It is hard to disagree with Henry Siegman, executive director of the American Jewish Congress, when he reacted as follows: "We are unhappy that the Court strained to give the menorah a secular meaning. In a sense, this denudes the menorah of its truly religious significance."[88]

Attempts to secularize traditions, symbols, and phrases with obvious religious meaning has troubling implications for the Supreme

Court's goal of neutrality toward all religions and between religion and nonreligion. For one's religiously rooted beliefs and traditions to enter the public sphere, they must be debased into some secular aspect of U.S. life, or, at the least, into the soft sentiments of what church historian Martin Marty termed *religion-in-general*. Under religion-in-general, according to Marty, "Particularity is challenged by a blurry, generalizing religion; distinctive witness is confronted by amiable syncretism; theological content is often replaced by sentiments about religion."[89] If one insists (by one's actions or statements) that one's religious beliefs have a deeper, more specific religious meaning, one runs the risk that they may be banished from the public sphere. On the other hand, the beliefs of the confirmed secularist and of the adherent of a soft, sentimental religion-in-general are affirmed and welcomed into the public realm. It is the persons who take their particularistic religious beliefs seriously and literally who are excluded. They are free to exercise their beliefs in private, but must leave them at home when entering public life. This is not neutrality.

A second way in which religion has been secularized as a precondition to passing establishment clause muster is by making a clear-cut distinction between the religious and secular aspects of a single phenomenon, and then allowing the secular, but not the religious, aspects to pass establishment clause review. Church-related colleges and universities — founded and sometimes today still supported by deeply devout believers — are allowed to receive public aid on the basis that they are not "pervasively sectarian" and that the aid goes only to support their "secular aspects" (which presumably are kept isolated from the religious aspects).[90] In some instances, this secular nature of church-related colleges and universities is accurate; in others, it is no more than a convenient fiction. In such situations, religion is forced to deny its essence and parade in secular garb if it is to be allowed by the Supreme Court.

Also instructive is *Bowen v. Kendrick* (1988), which upheld the 1981 Adolescent Family Life Act, including a provision that made funds available to private charitable groups — nonreligious and religious alike — to teach teenagers sexual prudence in an attempt to reduce the incidence of teenage pregnancy. Again, the secular-religious dichotomy was important, with the majority opinion arguing that since the religious organizations receiving governmental aid were not "pervasively sectarian," there was the potential for them to segregate out the religious from the secular elements in their programs. If so, government would be constitutionally free to support the secular aspects. Thus, the Court remanded the case to the lower courts to determine whether, in fact, religious beliefs had crept into the teaching and counseling of the religious organizations receiving help. One news report on the decision reported that Justice Scalia in oral argument had observed that "a church-affiliated group could use the money to teach that premarital sex is 'wrong' but not that it is 'sin.'"[91] In such cases, religious organizations are being told that if they are to qualify for governmental financial aid, they must put aside their religious orientation and approach the task in the same way as a secular organization would do. Whether in fact they can do so — especially in as morally sensitive an area as sex and procreation — is, at the very least, open to question, as the dissenting opinion argued.

The problem is that the Court's doctrine seems to be saying that government and religion may act in partnership to deal with a severe social problem as long as religion — for the most part — ceases to be religious. Religion may enlist in the fight against social evils as long as it resembles any secular group or takes on the soft, broad characteristics of religion-in-general — or, perhaps, conspires to maintain the fiction that it has done so. Again, a secular cultural ethos is being favored over religion or, at the very most, religion-in-general is being favored over particularistic religions with a strong sense of a literal divine moral will that human beings are called to follow and respect. The secular or the religion-in-general institution can receive aid; however, the deeply religious cannot unless it gives up or constricts its religious tenets. An organization rooted in a particular, deeply religious tradition — whether a liberal arts college, a counseling agency, a homeless shelter, or some other such service agency — must either forego government aid that is available to every one else or deny and confine (in actuality or in legal fiction) its religious nature. In either case, government is not being truly neutral among all religions or between religion and nonreligion. Neutrality and therefore the free exercise of religion are violated.

In summary, the secularization of religion as its ticket into full participation in the public realm begins with the Supreme Court's adoption of the strict separation of religion and government as the sole means to achieve governmental neutrality. There is to be a wall of separation between them. However, religion is part of the warp and woof of U.S. life, so the Court finds it impossible in practice to maintain the wall. It allows religion and government to cooperate in some endeavors and government to give some recognition to the religious traditions held by many of its citizens. In order for this to happen, however, religion must be secularized and confined, stripped of that which makes it a force of power in many persons' lives; if not, the entire edifice of neutrality by way of separation will fall. The irony is that in the real world, neutrality and religious freedom are thereby violated. Religion in all its specific traditions and manifestations is disadvantaged and constricted. It is a secular cultural ethos and — at most — a soft, comfortable religion-in-general that are favored and advantaged.

The Wall of Separation and the Secular Purpose Test

As seen earlier, one test that the Supreme Court has used in determining whether a challenged governmental action meets establishment clause standards has been the secular purpose test, the first prong of the three-prong *Lemon* test. In applying this test, the Court has looked into the motivations of those who passed a law to determine if they perhaps were improperly motivated by religious concerns. Justice Scalia once described the test (even while disagreeing with it) as meaning "that legislation can be invalidated under the Establishment Clause on the basis of its motivation alone, without regard to its effects."[92]

Earlier we saw that the Supreme Court, in holding Louisiana's creation science and Alabama's moment of silence laws unconstitutional, relied on certain statements made by the laws' chief sponsors to demonstrate that religious purposes underlay the laws. In the Louisiana case, the Court argued that state Senator Bill Keith possessed religiously rooted views on creation and evolution that had motivated him to sponsor the law. However, what if he had been a totally nonreligious person who had been motivated to sponsor the same bill on the grounds of a belief that if creation science were required to be taught alongside evolution, it would look so weak and silly that converts in droves would be made for his secular outlook? Similarly, what if he had sponsored the same bill, but on the basis of his district's economic interests? (Perhaps a major employer in his district publishes a book on creation science that the schools might choose to use if his bill passes.) The logic of the Court's reasoning would indicate that the law would have had a better chance of being found constitutional under those conditions. Mark Tushnet wrote: "The secular purpose requirement . . . means that if enough people take religion seriously, they cannot enact their program, but if they favor the same program for other reasons, they can enact it. It seems fair to say that this rule does not accept the view that religion should play an important part in public life."[93]

Theoretically, even a law of an apparently obvious secular nature could be found in violation of the establishment clause if legislators supporting it were found to have had religious motivations. Tribe has written that this test

> Could in theory strike down laws whose application will be entirely secular. Legislators might increase aid to the poor because of religious convictions, or fund a public forum because they hope that it will be used mainly for religious events, or reduce taxes because they hope that most citizens will donate the money to churches. Although courts would not strike such statutes down, current doctrine could be construed

to require them to do so. As a consequence, some legislators may feel that they cannot voice whatever religious beliefs form the grounds for their political positions, lest they poison the relevant legislation. Constitutional doctrine should not be permitted to generate such a religious chill.[94]

As Tribe implied, the worst effect of the secular purpose standard is not that it will be used to undermine the constitutionality of a major civil rights law, an appropriations measure increasing payments for Aid for Families with Dependent Children (AFDC), or an endangered species act, if the sponsors of such acts — as indeed is often the case — can be shown to have been motivated by deeply held religious beliefs in passing these laws.[95] Instead, the bigger danger is that this standard presents a constant threat in cases in which an especially controversial or unpopular position is (in part or wholly) motivated by religious beliefs.

If legislators court trouble by espousing legislation because of their religious beliefs — as did State Senators Keith of Louisiana and Holmes of Alabama — while legislative colleagues of theirs can espouse similar legislation without the same risk if they do so on secular grounds, what has happened to the free exercise of religion? Clearly, it has been diminished. As pointed out in Chapter 1, religion in the United States today is not purely a private affair. Religious beliefs have social, political consequences in the lives of believers. Many religious persons believe, and many religious systems teach, that to be a faithful believer one must live out one's beliefs in society. Doing so is to exercise one's faith. However, the secular purpose test for no establishment of religion puts a damper on such an exercise. Legislators with a deeply felt, particularistic faith are told that they had best check their religious beliefs in with the legislature's sergeant-at-arms when they enter the legislative chambers.

The secular purpose test violates the Supreme Court's goal of religious neutrality. Religiously motivated legislators must be careful to shield those religious motivations. They cannot fully and openly lay out their deeply felt spiritual beliefs. However, legislators who are committed to secularism or to a soft religion-in-general can take their beliefs with them into the legislative arena and speak freely concerning what underlies the policy positions they are advocating. It is those with nonmainstream or particularistic religious beliefs who need to be careful. This is hardly neutrality. Again, the Supreme Court — while seeking to pursue neutrality by way of separation — has blundered into a nonneutral stance.

The secular purpose standard is also a case of the Supreme Court's reasoning bringing the free exercise clause and establishment clause into tension with each other. The free exercise clause of the First Amendment itself has a clearly nonsecular — that is, religious — purpose. Presumably, the members of the First Congress were motivated by religious concerns — a desire to protect religious beliefs and practices from repression — in enacting it. How, then, can one square this religiously motivated provision of the Constitution with the secular purpose test? The secular purpose test for no establishment ends up having a potential negative impact on legal provisions seeking, under free exercise concerns, to exempt adherents or certain religious groups from some legal requirements. As Justice O'Connor wrote in her concurring opinion in *Wallace v. Jaffree* (1985),

> A rigid application of the Lemon [secular purpose] test would invalidate legislation exempting religious observers from generally applicable government obligations. By definition, such legislation has a religious purpose and effect in promoting the free exercise of religion. . . . It is disinguous to look for a purely secular purpose when the manifest objective of a statute is to facilitate the free exercise of religion by lifting a government-imposed burden.[96]

Tribe made this same point when he noted that Title VII of the Civil Rights Act of 1964 stipulated that employers should make "reasonable accommodations" for the "religious observations and practices" of their employees. Clearly, Tribe argued, the act thereby possesses a religious purpose.[97] Should its constitutionality also be challenged?

The Supreme Court has wandered into an interpretative quagmire, where under its logic, even the writers of the First Amendment, who clearly had a religious purpose in mind in providing for the free exercise of religion, could be said to have acted unconstitutionally.

The Wall of Separation and the Religious Divisiveness Test

The religious divisiveness test is an aspect of the third prong of the *Lemon* excessive entanglement test. As quoted earlier, Chief Justice Burger stated that "political divisions along religious lines was one of the principal evils against which the First Amendment was intended to protect." He then went on to argue that such divisiveness is a threat to the "normal political process" and to imply that there are more important issues with which this process should be dealing.[98]

In an area of questionable constitutional interpretations, this is probably the most questionable of all. It cannot mean that religiously motivated activists are to be barred from political involvement. Justice Brennan wrote in a concurring opinion: "Religionists no less than members of any other group enjoy the full measure of protection afforded speech, association, and political activity generally."[99] In spite of protestations such as this, however, the Supreme Court has sometimes seen special dangers adhering in public policy conflicts that are rooted in religious beliefs, and thus in certain ill-defined instances it will more quickly hold an act to be an unconstitutional violation of the establishment clause if it believes it likely to stimulate public policy divisions along religious lines. This stance is not supported by the original intent of the framers of the First Amendment or by history, and it discourages the participation of religiously motivated persons and groups in the public policy arena. (I will take each of these points in turn.)

Political scientist Paul Weber wrote an excellent essay clearly refuting Chief Justice Burger's attempt to claim original intent as a basis for the religious divisiveness test.[100] As Weber pointed out, James Madison in *The Federalist* argued the exact opposite, writing that division along religious lines was one of the safeguards for freedom and democratic government, and not a threat. In *Federalist* No. 51 Madison argued that due to "the great variety of interests, parties and [religious] sects which it embraces, a coalition of the majority of the whole society could seldom take place on any other principles than those of justice and the general good."[101] Weber summarized Madison's position as follows:

> What is critical to a proper understanding of the text is to recognize the republican strategy by which religion is to be limited. It must occur *not* by limiting the access of religious leaders to the political process or building a "wall of separation" between religion and politics. On the contrary, the limitation comes precisely from eliminating all special privileges, coercions, or disabilities and forcing religious political activism into the political mainstream where the number of sects and extent of the country will provide safeguards, both for the religious groups and against factious spirits.[102]

However, the Supreme Court has argued as a point of historic fact that the writers of the Constitution tried to drum religious groups and their contributions to public debate out of the public arena on grounds they were "one of the principal evils against which the First Amendment was intended to protect."[103]

Neither does history uphold the Court's claim that religious divisions are "a threat to the normal political process" and "tend to confuse and obscure other issues of great urgency," or that they conflict "with our whole history and traditions."[104] These patronizing words imply that public policy debates rooted in differing religious perspectives are abnormal and trivialize otherwise significant and weighty debates. This is nonsense. Religion has played major — and, many people are convinced, positive — roles in policy debates throughout U.S. history, from the separation of the thirteen colonies from England in the seventeenth century to the abolition of slavery in the eighteenth century and the protection of black civil rights in the twentieth.[105] Would the painful journey from Jim Crow to legal racial equality have been less divisive and more peaceful without the influence of the Reverend Martin Luther King, Jr., and the Southern Christian Leadership Council, with their philosophy of nonviolence? To ask the question is to answer it. Worldwide, have the most bitter divisions, wars, and cold wars of the twentieth century been caused by secular movements such as fascism, communism, and nationalism, or by religious disputes and fissures? There have been conflicts in Northern Ireland, Lebanon, and the Iran of radical Islam, but the woes they have wreaked on humankind nowhere match the woes wreaked by such thoroughly secularized persons as Adolf Hitler and Joseph Stalin. Within the United States, there is no basis to suppose that disputes rooted in religiously inspired differences are, or are likely to be, more bitter than those inspired by differences in social class, race, economic self-interest, or other such secular divisions.

The use of the alleged divisiveness of religion as a basis for holding certain laws in violation of the establishment clause discourages deeply religious persons from participating in the public realm on the basis of their religious faith. It thereby raises problems of neutrality and free exercise. If divisions based on religious principles are to be kept out of the public realm, what happens to persons whose free exercise of their religion demands social and political involvement? They are disadvantaged as compared with those whose beliefs are secularly based or are rooted in a gentle religion-in-general that makes few demands on its adherents for social and political involvement. As a consequence, the divisiveness standard threatens the free exercise of religious beliefs that have a strong, societal relevance — and perhaps a countercultural or prophetic edge — to them.

In the context of both the religious divisiveness and secular purpose standards, Tribe suggested that free exercise problems arise when religiously motivated persons are discouraged from participating in politics. He went on to explain: "Marxists, Republicans, ecologists, and members of other groups may voice their deep-seated beliefs during political debates without self-censorship; religious believers deserve no less. Indeed, under the free exercise clause they may deserve more, when religious doctrine itself requires active political involvement."[106] To paint religion into a shrunken corner of citizens' lives, forbidding the full play of religiously rooted motivations and perspectives in the public policy arena, is to abandon neutrality and discriminate against religion.

Free Exercise and No Establishment:
Light Protections, Heavy Burdens

When the religion language of the First Amendment is read as two separate clauses with two separate purposes, religion is placed in a favored, protected position by the free exercise clause and in a burdened, restricted position by the establishment clause. Conflict is, therefore, inevitable. Pepper has pointed out the tension — perhaps even conflict — that is created when the First Amendment is read as guaranteeing two separate religious freedoms:

> The Free Exercise Clause, on its face, prefers religion, favoring it as no other activity is favored. There is no parallel constitutional protection for free exercise of tourism, boating, hiking, beer drinking, or environmentalism. To the extent the Establishment Clause is read as a blanket prohibition upon governmental preference for religion, the Free Exercise Clause is therefore itself a violation. Approached from the opposite perspective, the Establishment Clause may be seen as a discrimination against religion and a burden upon religion, and therefore, arguably, a Free Exercise Clause violation. There are no parallel clauses preventing the establishment of science, philosophy or speech. Thus, the clauses thrust in conflicting directions.[107]

Pepper is right: free exercise, taken by itself, implies that religion is to be put in an elevated position of constitutional protection, safeguarding certain religiously inspired practices, which, if not religiously inspired, could be illegal. On the other hand, the establishment clause, read by itself, implies that religion bears a special constitutional burden, that certain forms of governmental assistance, if given to a religious organization or in support of religiously inspired activities, would be unconstitutional, while, if given to non-religious organizations or activities, they would be fully constitutional. In this perspective the free exercise clause demands what the establishment clause forbids.

Justice Potter Stewart pointed out this conflict in his concurring opinion in *Sherbert v. Verner* (1963), which expanded free exercise protections by holding that South Carolina had to grant unemployment benefits to a worker who had lost her job due to her religious scruples:

> To require South Carolina to so administer its laws as to pay public money to the appellant under the circumstances of this case is thus clearly to require the State to violate the Establishment Clause as construed by this Court. . . . [The majority

opinion of the Court] holds that the State must prefer a religious over a secular ground for being unavailable for work — that state financial support of the appellant's religion is constitutionally required to carry out "the governmental obligation of neutrality in the face of religious differences. . . ." Yet in cases decided under the Establishment Clause the Court has decreed otherwise. It has decreed that government must blind itself to the differing religious beliefs and traditions of the people. With all respect, I think it is the Court's duty to face up to the dilemma posed by the conflict between the Free Exercise Clause of the Constitution and the Establishment Clause as interpreted by the Court.[108]

In light of the conflict between the two clauses as they have been interpreted by the Supreme Court, it is highly significant that, as seen earlier, the Court has pumped power and strength into the establishment clause, asserting that religion and government must be kept separate and allowing only limited and carefully circumscribed exceptions. Meanwhile, the free exercise clause (which is intended to protect religion and even to elevate it to a higher level of protection than secularly based beliefs and organizations) has been left in a position of reduced power and effect. As currently interpreted, the establishment clause burdens on religion outweigh the free exercise protections of religion. Potentially, the free exercise clause could be used by religious groups to protect themselves and their activities from the vigorous imposition of establishment clause burdens. Unfortunately, this has proven extremely difficult to do. Free exercise claims as a defense against no establishment burdens have routinely been rejected, when they have even been raised by religious groups in the first place.[109]

The potential for conflict between the free exercise and establishment clauses and the problems posed by allowing no establishment burdens to overwhelm free exercise protections are highlighted by considering the problem of defining religion.[110] The Supreme Court has adopted, in several free exercise cases, increasingly broad definitions of religion. In *Torcaso v. Watkins* (1961), the Court struck down a Maryland constitutional provision requiring public officials to declare a belief in God. In doing so, the Court made reference to "religions founded on different beliefs" than a belief in the existence of God, and in a footnote it went on to say "religions in this country which do not teach what would generally be considered a belief in the existence of God," and "Buddhism, Taoism, Ethical Culture, and Secular Humanism and others."[111] During the Vietnam War era, the Supreme Court was called upon to interpret the selective service act, which exempted from military combat any man whose "religious training and belief" made him conscientiously opposed to participation in war in any form. The act then went on to define religious training and belief as "an individual's belief in relation to a Supreme Being involving duties superior to those arising from any human relation, but [not including] essentially political, sociological or philosophical views or a merely personal code."[112] In interpreting this language, the Court held that the congressional use of the term *Supreme Being* in defining religious training and belief includes a "belief that is sincere and meaningful and occupies a place in the life of its possessor parallel to that filled by the orthodox belief in God of one who clearly qualifies for the exemption."[113] The Court thereby broadened the definition of religion to include nontheistic religions and even nontheistic beliefs that fulfill functions in persons' lives that are similar to those fulfilled by traditional religion.

This broadening has the commendable effect of recognizing the broad plurality of beliefs present in contemporary U.S. society and laying the groundwork for their constitutional protection, as the ideal of a free, open society would mandate. However, when combined with the Court's very broad interpretations of the establishment clause, enormous problems emerge. If various secular belief structures — such as humanism, nationalism, and self-actualization — and other sincerely held ethical or moral principles are to be considered religions, and if the establishment clause excludes religion from the public schools and prohibits various forms of public recognition and support of religion, all values and ideologies will, in effect, be driven from the public realm. Combining the broad definition of religion that the Supreme Court has developed in some free exercise cases with the establishment clause's broad rejection of religion in the public realm, much of what is taken for granted in public education and other facets of public life is suddenly called into question. Can even the value of honesty be taught in the public schools? After all, it is one of the Ten Commandments of the Judeo-Christian religion, and somewhere one can find a "religion" that would claim it stifles one's creative freedoms.

This problem has led some to propose that there be two different definitions given religion as it appears in the First Amendment, one, a broad one, as applied to the free exercise clause, and the other, a narrow one, as applied to the establishment clause.[114] Although this would solve the immediate practical problem, it would do violence to the plain words of the Constitution, since two different interpretations would be given to a word that appears only once.

This issue of definition demonstrates the depth of the dilemma into which the Supreme Court has wandered. A narrow definition of religion would rescue the value of honesty in the schools from the broad concept of no establishment, but the same narrow definition limits the protections of the free exercise clause. The two clauses are thus played off against each other. The net result of the clashing of the two religion clauses (with the establishment clause usually coming out the winner) is the repeated violation of religious neutrality. The Supreme Court itself said in a free exercise case, "Government may . . . [not] penalize or discriminate against individuals or groups because they hold religious views."[115] However, in actual practice, repeatedly, religion — and especially religion of a deeply felt, more literal nature — is disadvantaged as compared to a secular cultural ethos or a broadly consensual religion-in-general.

Concluding Observations

In this section of the chapter, which has explored the Supreme Court's interpretations of the First Amendment's religion provisions, I have argued that these interpretations have significantly reduced full, genuine freedom of religion in two ways: by separating the free exercise and establishment clauses and then favoring no establishment burdens on religion over free exercise protections of religion; and by assuming that religion-government separation leads to the neutrality of government toward religion, when in fact it leads rather to a favoring of a secular cultural ethos and a soft, cultural religion-in-general over more particularistic faiths.

There are three concluding observations that help put the above two conclusions in perspective. The first points to the serious impact that the current abridgment of religious freedom poses for the U.S. political system and U.S. society as a whole. As I have stated, the religion that is disadvantaged by the Supreme Court's interpretations is not religion-in-general. Instead, three other categories of religion have been disadvantaged. One includes a variety of small, minority, nonmainstream faiths: Native Americans, Orthodox Jews, Old Order Amish, and a variety of other minority, or so-called fringe religions. The problems posed by current Supreme Court interpretations are often severe for these groups, especially due to the weak interpretations given the free exercise clause. A second group is the Catholics, especially those within the Catholic Church who take their faith seriously and seek to follow it daily out in society. Due to the Catholic Church's adoption of basic Christian teachings in a literal, authoritative manner, due to its view of its teachings as profoundly affecting all aspects of life, including the social and political, and due to its tendency to be at odds with the U.S. religion-in-general, it is often in tension — if not outright conflict — with prevailing social and political beliefs and practices. This has led Catholics to establish their own schools and other social service agencies and to take clear-cut stands that sometimes go against prevailing societal opinion on such issues as abortion, gay rights, family planning, and nuclear war.

The third group to be particularly disadvantaged by current Supreme Court religion decisions is that of conservative Protestants, including the Fundamentalist, evangelical, and charismatic wings. As with Catholics, this is a religious grouping that accepts basic Christian teachings in a literal, authoritative manner. For a period of time it was marked by a withdrawal from the world, but recently it is perceiving a social and political relevance to its faith. It is often at odds with the prevailing secular or religion-in-general attitudes toward such issues as religion in the public schools, the teaching of evolutionary explanations for human origins, and — increasingly — issues such as pornography, abortion, and gay rights.

If one goes through the various cases on religious freedom that have come before the Supreme Court in the past fifty years, almost every one has dealt with defining the role of the state in relation to one of these three groupings. To the extent — and, I have argued, the extent is substantial — that the Supreme Court's decisions have limited the freedom of religion in the United States, it is largely the religious freedom of persons in these three groupings that have suffered. The fact that Catholics constitute about 28 percent of the population and conservative Protestants, using a restricted measure, about 20 percent, and assuming that minority, nonmainstream groups come to over 2 percent of the population, more than half the people of the United States are experiencing a substantial threat to their full, genuine freedom of religion.[116] No one should minimize the problem that U.S. society is facing in regard to the preservation and extension of full, genuine freedom of religion.

A second observation is that the appropriate answer to the favoring of secularism and religion-in-general over minority, nonmainstream faiths, Catholicism, and conservative Protestantism is not to return to putting Christianity or any other religion into a favored position. I do not call for a return to the semiestablishment of the Protestant Christianity that was prevalent in the nineteenth century (see next chapter). Nor should the Court's tilt toward no establishment burdens on religion over free exercise protections of religion mean that the Court should now lean in the other direction. To frame the issue in terms of tilting either toward secularism or toward Christianity or some other religion — either toward less strict no establishment burdens or toward more free exercise protections — is to frame the issue improperly. The problem runs deeper. What is needed is a new framework with which to view and react to religion-state issues. That is what I seek to develop in subsequent chapters.

A third and final observation is that I do not see the difficulties and dilemmas into which the Supreme Court has stumbled as being due to having wrong-headed or obtuse persons on the Court. The appropriate conclusion is not that we have had a deficient Supreme Court and that with justices of greater integrity, intelligence, or determination all problems would be resolved. Again, the problem runs deeper. The botch that able, committed, hard-working justices have made of the interpretation of the religion provisions of the First Amendment suggests there is something wrong with the basic assumptions and perspectives with which they approach their task. Moreover, these assumptions and perspectives are not theirs alone, but rather are those of U.S. society as a whole. The Supreme Court has not stood alone in coming up with inappropriate answers to wrongly put questions. In so doing it has reflected U.S. society and its history and traditions, especially those of its social and political elites. It is to the broader U.S. society and its perceptions and beliefs in regard to church-state relations that I now turn.

U.S. SOCIETY

Just as the Supreme Court is repeatedly called on to interpret the religion provisions of the Bill of Rights, so, also, U.S. society more broadly is called on to do the same on a daily basis. By the statements of its politicians, the actions of its public officials, the opinions of its editorial writers, and the beliefs of its populace, U.S. society on a daily basis defines what is proper and improper in relations between church and state. The Supreme Court's legally binding, formal interpretations and applications of the First Amendment's religion language are certainly important; equally important are the underlying societal perspectives and assumptions that collectively define church-state relations. Some observers would even contend that they are more important, for they set the societal bounds and context within which the Supreme Court makes its determinations. It is to these underlying societal attitudes that this section of the chapter turns.

The Separation of Church and State

Various studies have noted that the U.S. public gives near unanimous support for certain basic civil liberties such as free speech, freedom of the press, and a right to trial by jury, although support for applications of these principles sometimes wavers in specific circumstances.[117] This is also true of the separation of church and state. When given a choice between two statements — "The government should take special steps to protect the Judeo-Christian heritage" and "There should be a high wall of separation between church and state," 51 percent of the general public chose the "high wall" response and only 32 percent, the "special steps" response (18 percent had no preference).[118] A slender majority (and a wide plurality) of the general public committed itself to a position of strict church-state separation. However, when it came to questions that the same poll asked regarding more specific applications of the strict separation concept, majorities of the public were willing to support a variety of accommodations between church and state, many of which the Supreme Court has declared unconstitutional. Some 64 percent agreed that it is good for Congress to start its sessions with prayer, 59 percent supported prayer before public school sporting events, 80 percent supported manger scenes put up by city governments, 79 percent supported candles put up by city governments for "a Jewish religious celebration," and 77 percent supported public schools setting aside a moment of silence each day for student prayer. When asked to choose between two other statements — "The government should not supply any support to any religions" and "The government should support all religions equally," a 52 percent majority chose "help all religions equally," while 44 percent chose the "no support" alternative. As the authors of the study concluded, "The average American gives rhetorical assent to the strict separation of church and state, yet frequently approves of policies which involve considerable cooperation between church and state."[119]

Equally important, the same poll also questioned national samples of academics (a random sample of 155 university faculty members of Ph.D.-granting departments of political science, sociology, history, and English), media leaders (a random sample of 100 consisting of radio and television news directors who are members of the Radio and Television News Directors Association and newspaper editors in cities of over 100,000 population), and government elites (a random sample of 106 high-level federal executive-branch political appointees). These political and social elites tended to support strict separation more consistently than did the general public. Among the academics, 92 percent chose the "high wall of separation" response, as did 79 percent of the media leaders and 77 percent of the government elites.[120] In addition, as Table 1 shows, the leadership groups also tended to favor the strict separationist position to a greater degree than did the general public when presented with specific applications of the general principle. The sample of academics was especially consistent in its support of strict separation applications. In response to the question concerning whether the government "should support all religions equally" or not give "any support to any religion," the leadership groups also took a stricter separationist position than did the public, with 87 percent of the academics, 78 percent of the media leaders, and 64 percent of the government officials taking the "no support" position (compared to 44 percent of the public).[121] Given the disproportionate influence of the leadership groups as molders of cultural values and perspectives, the strict separation position taken by the leadership groups is especially significant, and it generally coincides with that of the legal doctrines taken by the Supreme Court in its establishment clause

TABLE 1
Elite Opinion on Applications of the
Separation of Church and State
(percent taking the strict separation position)

	Congress prayer	Sports events prayer	City manger scenes	City Jewish candles	Silent school prayer
Academics	57	73	54	55	68
Media	36	62	32	35	46
Government	25	49	25	24	43
Public	25	30	13	15	19

Source: The Williamsburg Charter Foundation, *The Williamsburg Charter Survey on Religion and Public Life* (Washington, DC: The Williamsburg Charter Foundation, 1988), Tables 28, 29, 30, 31, and 34.

interpretations. This leaves, however, the more important question of exactly what attitudes, assumptions, and perspectives underlie and help explain these more specific conclusions on religion-state relations. It is to these that I now turn.

Religion as Private Belief

In this and the following two sections I seek to gain an understanding of the underlying beliefs and perspectives that animate the "street-level" leaders of U.S. cultural attitudes, such as journalists, politicians, op-ed writers, and other popular opinion leaders. My goal is to attain a sense of the values, assumptions, and perspectives to which popular culture and its leaders hold in regard to church-state relations. By *popular culture* I mean something midway between the off-the-cuff opinion of the citizen caught in a national survey or "person-on-the-street" interview and the ideologically inspired, theoretical position of the academician. It is the beliefs and perspectives of popular culture that are most important in giving shape and meaning the church-state relations in the actual, ongoing world of public policy debates and struggles. There is no *Baedeker's* guide to these beliefs and perspectives. Thus, I have largely relied on a limited number of relevant opinion polls, statements made by elected public officials and candidates for public office, editorial and opinion columns in major newspapers, and news reports (often mixed with opinion) found in *Time* and *Newsweek* magazines. From extensive readings in these sources, one can distill three key perspectives that play major roles in shaping U.S. society's approach to church-state relations. These three perspectives crop up repeatedly. The first one is considered here and the other two are examined in the following sections.

The 1984 presidential race between then President Ronald Reagan and challenger Walter Mondale was marked by much discussion of the role of religion in public life. Following what many perceived to be an improper interjection of religion into the campaign by Reagan, Mondale gave a crucial rebuttal before the International Convention of B'nai B'rith. A reading of that speech reveals that it was essentially founded on Mondale's belief that religion should be a private affair between persons and their God and should not intrude into public affairs. "I believe in an America . . . where religion is a private matter between individuals and God, between families and their churches and synagogues, with no room for politicians in between."[122] *Newsweek* interpreted Mondale's theme as being "simple: religion and faith were private matters."[123]

This same privatization of religion can be seen in a 1984 editorial in the strict separationist magazine, *Church and State*, which is the official organ published by Americans United for the Separation of Church and State:

> The political behavior sought by the Catholic hierarchy challenges the very basis of church-state separation by declaring that there can be no division between sectarian morality and public policy. On the contrary, American candidates and officials generally have recognized that personal religious convictions, unique to their faiths, cannot be enforced by political might.[124]

Put in these terms, this position seems to be self-evidently correct, but one must pause to recognize what this editorial is saying in less loaded terms. It appears to argue that the "very basis of church-state separation" is the splitting of religiously based morality from public policy debates. The second sentence quoted would seem to qualify the more sweeping language contained in the first sentence when it states that it is "personal religious convictions, unique to their faiths" that ought not to be politically enforced. However, the context of this statement shows that this was not intended to be taken literally, since the specific policy position of the Catholic bishops against which this editorial was largely reacting was the bishops' antiabortion position, a position shared by Catholics, most conservative Protestants, many Orthodox Jews, and even some modern-day secularists such as Nat Hentoff, editor of the *Village Voice*. An antiabortion position is not unique to the Catholic faith but rather is shared by at least some members of all four mentioned faiths (counting secularism as a faith). One can only interpret the position of the editors of *Church and State* as being that the phrase "personal religious convictions" is, in their view, a redundancy.

Such attempts to read religion out of presidential politics were not limited to the 1984 campaign. Back in 1960, John Kennedy's basic response to charges that a Catholic should not be president was that he would not be subservient to the Pope and others in the Catholic hierarchy and that he would act "in the public interest, without regard to my private faith."[125] In 1988 the archdiocese of Democratic presidential candidate Michael Dukakis's church — the Greek Orthodox Church — responded to questions raised concerning whether Dukakis was a member in good standing by this statement: "With regret, we have observed recent attempts being made to inject religion into the political life of this nation, in direct contradiction to the First Amendment, and we will not become party to this effort."[126]

Hugh Sidey, columnist for *Time* magazine, expressed nervousness with President Jimmy Carter because he made "political decisions on the results" of his religious faith. Sidey went on to explain: "I simply don't want Mormons, or Episcopalians, or Jews or Adventists running this nation. It is surely okay to have American politicians who happen to be Mormons, or Episcopalians, or Jews or Adventists. I would like a president who, when he feels his pancreas jump, consults his physician and not his archbishop."[127] Sidey's point is clear: It is fine to have deeply religious presidents as long as their faith is strictly a personal, private affair that is sealed off in a separate compartment of their lives from the part involved in serving as president.

The fact that this privatization of religious faith has become an integral part of U.S. culture is revealed by two further examples. One is a brief spat that arose in 1989 in the California Parks and Recreation Society. Several writers in a symposium in the organization's magazine had called for greater cooperation between public parks and recreation organizations, on the one hand, and church-related recreation programs, on the other. This symposium released a fire storm of criticism, including calls by a California legislator for the governor to fire one of the symposium authors, the state Parks and Recreation director. A professor in the Department of Leisure Studies and Recreation in one of the California state universities criticized the suggestions that had been made in part on the basis that "religion has its place in our *individual* lives, and that place has been well defined by the Supreme Court."[128] Most constitutional law scholars would be surprised to learn about the "well defined" nature of the Supreme Court's limiting of religion to citizens' individual lives, but clearly, to a significant degree, the debate was turning on the belief that religion is a personal, individual matter.

A final example also demonstrates how the privatization of religion has seeped into U.S. culture. Richard Baer, professor in Cornell University's Department of Natural Resources, tells it this way in a chapel talk he gave at Cornell:

> For over five years I attended a weekly Cornell graduate student/faculty seminar that focussed on issues of science, technology, and public policy. Perhaps every third or fourth week, I would make a comment or two based on my knowledge of Bible, theology, or Christian ethics. . . . But again and again I would get the same kind of response. No one agreed with me, no one disagreed. To put it rather crudely, but very accurately, it was as if I had farted. And when someone farts in public, no one applauds, no one boos. They simply act as if it hadn't happened. Someone violated a social taboo, and the best way to deal with the embarrassment is to go on to the next item of business as quickly and unobtrusively as possible.[129]

The point is that religion is considered irrelevant to the public realm of ideas and public policy, and to bring up religion caused embarrassment and a desire quickly to move on to more appropriate comments. It is felt that religion should be left behind in church or in the privacy of one's own home.

The Religion–Public Policy Dichotomy

Closely related to, and a natural outgrowth of, the privatization of religion is a more focused rejection of religion as a legitimate basis for public policy positions. This rejection is clearly seen in the reactions of the well-known political columnist Anthony Lewis to a speech that Ronald Reagan gave in 1983 to the National Association of Evangelicals. Lewis described the speech as "outrageous" and "primitive," even while acknowledging that "any President is entitled to give uplifting talks about moral or spiritual questions."[130] Lewis appeared to be saying that a little piety is fine in presidents as long as it conforms to the generalities of religion-in-general or a civil religion, with no one taking it too seriously.[131] What was Reagan doing that so aroused Lewis? "He was purporting to apply religious concepts to the contentious technical particulars of arms programs." Later, Lewis charged Reagan with making "a political speech identifying himself with a particular sectarian view." In other words, instead of making some general, religiously neutral references in support of agreed-on policy goals ("Mom and apple pie"), he was using specific, nonconsensual religious beliefs to support specific, nonconsensual public policy positions. This, as seen by Lewis, was a violation of the U.S. system, which "has lasted nearly 200 years." A careful reading of the Reagan speech reveals what I personally would consider bad theology and bad reasoning in support of some unwise public policy positions.[132] However, this is beside the point, which is that Lewis did not even try to show that Reagan was drawing improper conclusions from a distorted use of Christian teachings (if that indeed was what he was doing). No, Lewis rejected the legitimacy of Reagan — and presumably, any president or any other public official — explicitly using specific, religiously rooted beliefs to explain, defend, and seek to build support for his public policy positions.

Similarly, the *New York Times* editorial writers a year later excoriated Reagan for a speech he gave that had heavy religious overtones: "You don't have to be a secular humanist to take offense at that display of what, in America, should be private piety, . . . Americans ask piety in Presidents, not displays of religious preference. Mr. Reagan uttered not just an ecumenical summons to the spirit. He was pandering to the Christian right that helped to propel his national political career."[133] Stripped of its rhetorical flourishes, the editorial was saying that it is fine if presidents display a generic piety that matches the confines of religion-in-general, but they are not to use their religious beliefs to explicate and support specific policy programs. Similarly, in Mondale's campaign speech mentioned earlier, he declared, "No president should attempt to transform policy debates into theological disputes."[134] The separation of church and state is translated into a separation of religious values and policy debates.

Also informative is the degree to which Reagan was criticized when he tried explicitly to defend the bringing of religious values into policy considerations. In a 1984 campaign appearance before a Dallas prayer breakfast, he gave this defense: "The truth is, politics and morality are inseparable. And as morality's foundation is religion, religion and politics are necessarily related. We need religion as a guide. . . . All are free to believe or not to believe, all are free to practice a faith or not. But those who believe must be free to speak of and act on their belief, to apply moral teaching to public questions."[135] Reagan saw religion and morality as being linked and believed that if the link were denied, religious belief, translated into "moral teaching," would be unable to affect public policy questions. The *Sun* of Baltimore editorialized about this position: "But ever since the president offered the dubious thesis that government needs the church as a guide and that politics and religion are necessarily related, the nation has been reverberating. Most Americans know instinctively when the wall separating church and state is under assault, and they don't like it."[136]

The reason underlying a rejection of religion as contributing to public policy debates is revealed in an article by Joseph Conn, managing editor of *Church and State*. This article summarized the argument taken by Americans United in its amicus curiae brief in *Webster v. Reproductive Health Services* (1989). Quoting from the brief, he stated:

[The] concern [of Americans United] . . . is directed to what we believe to be theologically-derived legislative findings by the Missouri legislature that personhood begins at the moment of conception. Such an inherently theological, but controversial, determination violates a core purpose of the Establishment Clause of the First Amendment — that is, the absolute prohibition against government preference of one religious sect or denomination over another and the placing of the state's imprimatur on a particular religious dogma.[137]

Conn went on to quote Rabbi David Saperstein, a spokesperson for a coalition of prochoice religious groups: "It is precisely because religious faiths hold widely divergent views about when human life begins that we believe that the government must respect religious diversity and remain neutral, respecting the right of every woman to act in accordance with her conscience — religious or secular. Separation of church and state requires nothing less!"[138]

The logic of the argument being advanced here is that if religious beliefs are used to support specific public policy positions, for government to choose one of the positions would be a form of establishing the supremacy of one among several contending religious beliefs. This argument is closely related to the secular purpose prong of the *Lemon* test (discussed earlier). Secular, not religious, grounds must support public policies. That is the only way that government can remain neutral among contending religious and nonreligious points of view, so the reasoning goes.

Although there is a surface plausibility to this position and although neutrality is a commendable goal, the very real problem it raises is that ultimately *all* public policy positions are rooted in values and beliefs derived from religion or secularly based moral-philosophical systems. Whether one supports, for example, wider availability of government-supported child care in licensed child-care centers will depend on one's views of the family (its nature, origins, and ideal embodiment), gender-specific roles (their nature, origins, and consequences), and child development (its nature and healthy manifestations). Necessarily (whether explicitly or implicitly) one's religious or moral-philosophical predispositions and beliefs are going to enter in. If the government legislates *any* position on this and a myriad of other issues, it is going to be legislating some persons' and some groups' religious-philosophical beliefs and assumptions. *Every* position on child care, nuclear proliferation, civil rights, drug abuse, abortion, or health care, if adopted, cannot be a violation of the separation of church and state. James Wall, the editor of the *Christian Century*, once wrote that to speak of a "'religious' president is redundant, since all presidents have some belief system that guide their decision-making."[139] What is true of presidents is also true of members of Congress, cabinet officers, and all other public policy-makers. The position that Conn and many others have advanced makes sense only if religious beliefs are assumed to be purely private and personal with no wider sociopolitical reverberations, a clearly false assumption.

If U.S. society dictates that religious beliefs and public policy issues should be kept in separate compartments, is there any way at all that they can be allowed to mix? Three answers have been suggested. One is to separate morality and religion. The *Hartford Courant*, in a 1984 editorial, made this separation: "It's perfectly fitting — in fact praiseworthy — for political candidates to talk about morals. It's better when officeholders talk about it, and admirable when they act accordingly. Morality is indeed the foundation of good government. But morality and religion can be separated, and so can — and should — religion and politics."[140] Politics must be rooted in morality, and the morality of various public policy options can be debated, but, the editorial was saying, religion and morality are capable of separation, and indeed should be.

To separate morality and religion and then admit morality but not religion into the public sphere is to separate the inseparable. One's sense of morality (one's ethics), invariably is rooted in one's responses to life's ultimate questions, namely, in one's religion.[141] In practice, trying to enforce a religion-morality separation is likely to result in religious persons having to take their religiously rooted moral principles into the public arena divorced from the fundamental religious beliefs that gave birth to them in the first place. To drive persons' religious beliefs underground would impoverish our national debate and cloud an understanding of the real values and issues at stake. To require this is also to violate governmental neutrality and the free exercise of religion. Secularists could present and argue their public policy positions on the basis of their true underlying beliefs, while devout believers would have to hide their real motives and try to defend their positions on a contrived secular basis.

A second response was adopted by Mario Cuomo in a thoughtful speech that he delivered as a Catholic public official at Notre Dame University in 1984. He argued, "The values derived from religious belief will not — and should not — be accepted as part of the public morality unless they are shared by the pluralistic community at large, by consensus."[142] Cuomo thereby was ready to allow religious beliefs to enter public debate, but only if there was consensus on them. If society disagrees, say, on when life begins, such beliefs are then relegated to the realm of private beliefs and ought not to play a role in the arena of policy debates. The only alternative that he presented to this position is the "Christian nation" concept, in which the religious-political views of a dominant Christian segment of the population are imposed on the rest of society.

However, most of the religiously rooted principles that history has demonstrated were worth fighting for — such as the abolition of slavery in the nineteenth century and the equality of all races in the twentieth — sparked enormous controversy when they were first put forward. This approach works to create what Weber called in the case of the Supreme Court's divisiveness test a "heckler's veto."[143] My right to bring the moral power of my religious beliefs into the political sphere is dependent on someone else not opposing me. In all likelihood this would limit religion's explicit role in public affairs to the bland, consensual "pep talks" of civil religion or religion-in-general. By definition, public policy debates deal with controversy and divided opinions. The religiously rooted beliefs and values informing different policy positions are also likely to be nonconsensual. Thus, allowing only consensual religious beliefs into the public sphere leads right back to the stifling of free debate and the free exercise problem of not allowing particularistic religious beliefs on the same terms as beliefs rooted in secularism or religion-in-general.

A third way in which religious belief could be allowed to enter the public policy arena is based on a distinction that Senator Edward Kennedy made in a speech at Liberty Baptist College (now Liberty University). He made a fundamental distinction between personal and public morality:

The real transgression occurs when religion wants government to tell citizens how to live uniquely personal parts of their lives. The failure of prohibition proves the futility of such an attempt when a majority or even a substantial minority happens to disagree. Some questions may be inherently individual ones or people may be sharply divided about whether they are. In such cases — cases like prohibition and abortion — the proper role of religion is to appeal to the conscience of the individual, not the coercive power of the state. But there are other questions which are inherently public in nature, which we must decide together as a nation, and where religion and religious values can and should speak to our common conscience. The issue of nuclear war is a compelling example. It is a moral issue; it will be decided by government, not by each individual; and to give any effect to the moral values of their creed, people of faith must speak directly about public policy. The Catholic bishops and the Reverend Billy Graham have every right to stand for the nuclear freeze — and Dr. Falwell has every right to stand against it.[144]

There is much merit in what Kennedy suggested, but the major unresolved problem is how to distinguish between personal and public morality. What does one do when there is disagreement over whether an asserted moral principle is public or private? This is not a trivial question. A key distinguishing mark of those on the two sides of the abortion debate is whether abortion is a matter of public or private morality. Kennedy seems to suggest that as long as there is dispute over whether a question is private or public, it should be kept out of the public sphere. In the portion of his speech quoted earlier, he said, "Some questions may be inherently individual ones *or people may be sharply divided about whether they are.* In such cases . . . the proper role of religion is to appeal to the conscience of the individual, not the coercive power of the state" (emphasis added). However, this position returns us the problem of the "heckler's veto": If one's claim that an issue is one of public morality is disputed by others, that issue is excluded from the public realm. My free exercise of religion is made dependent on others accepting my claims.

Both this section and the previous one have demonstrated popular culture's assumption that a basic dichotomy exists between religious beliefs, which are viewed as being purely personal or private in nature, and political or public policy stances, which are viewed as being largely and appropriately secular in nature. The two are to be kept in separate compartments, or, at the most, some broadly consensual religiously based beliefs can be allowed into the public arena under some limited circumstances. This assumption closely parallels Supreme Court doctrines and approaches to church-state issues discussed earlier in this chapter. It can be seen most clearly in the Court's secular purpose and religious divisiveness standards, both of which raise obstacles to bringing specific, particularistic religious beliefs to bear on public policy questions.[145] Religion is assumed to be an individual, private affair. Thus, keeping it out of the public arena really does no harm to one's ability freely to exercise one's religious beliefs. Similarly, the Supreme Court's neutrality-by-way-of-separation position is supported by the same assumption. Strictly separating religion and government poses no threat to religious freedom since religion really has nothing to do with the public realm anyway. In this view, governmental neutrality toward religion is not violated by keeping it out of the realm of government and public policies since it properly belongs elsewhere.

Assumptions that view religion as a purely private matter, however, fly in the face of reality, and thus, efforts to keep religion out of the public realm are not neutral, but rather violate many persons' full freedom of religion. As Chapter 1 made clear, time and again religion has spoken insistently on public policy questions of war and peace, capital punishment, racial justice, economic opportunities, environmental degradation, and much more. To try to force adherents of religious faiths that have public facets into a purely private mold is to limit their ability to fully live out the dictates of their religious faiths. Moreover, to remove religiously based positions and arguments from the arena of policy debates and issues results in a "naked public square," clothed only in nonreligious, secular garb.[146] This is not neutrality. Adherents of faiths without a social-political dimension or of faiths of a diffuse religion-in-general character are favored over adherents of particularistic faiths with a social-political dimension, and a secular cultural ethos is favored over religiously informed perspectives.

The basic problem is that politically relevant religious traditions and beliefs thereby collide with perspectives and frames of reference that are deeply ingrained in the U.S. experience. U.S. culture simply has no theoretical framework or paradigm with which to deal with socially and politically relevant religious faiths. Confusion and uncertainty result, both in Supreme Court decisions and in culturally dominant attitudes, and full religious freedom is the casualty.

An Antireligious Bias

Most Americans instinctively recoil from the claim that there is an antireligious bias running through the underlying assumptions with which their society approaches church-state issues. However, there is persuasive evidence that among some influential segments of the population, there is a very real antireligious strain. This strain does not react against religion-in-general but rather against particularistic religions whose adherents take their faith seriously as an authoritative, literal force in their lives. Catholics and conservative Protestants, plus some nonmainstream, minority groups, seem especially to raise these fears. The evidence in support of this proposition is not systematic, but it is pervasive.

The clearest evidence suggesting at least a degree of bias against religion is found in the widespread assumption that religious differences and disputes are particularly divisive, leading to intolerance and a bitterness that is normally absent from U.S. society. The influential, well-known scholar Leonard Levy wrote on the very first page of the preface to a recent book:

> Given the extraordinary religious diversity of our nation, the establishment clause functions to depoliticize religion; it thereby helps to defuse a potentially explosive situation. . . . The establishment clause separates government and religion so that we can maintain civility between believers and unbelievers as well as among the several hundred denominations, sects, and cults that thrive in our nation.[147]

Levy here presents religious differences as being uniquely dangerous ("potentially explosive") without even an attempt to demonstrate this claim from U.S. history. Similarly, political scientists Herbert McClosky and Alida Brill made the following unsupported claim: "Although tolerance is in all spheres difficult to achieve, it has been particularly difficult to achieve in the sphere of religion. . . . No other form of intolerance has been as ubiquitous as religious persecution."[148] As I suggested earlier, to see the falseness of such claims of religion's especially great divisiveness in the U.S. experience, all one needs to do is weigh the divisiveness, bitterness, and bloodshed that U.S. history has featured due to religious differences against what was caused by regional, racial, economic, and social class differences.

Nevertheless, examples of the belief in the dangerous divisiveness of religion abound. The *Sacramento Bee* raised the horror of religious divisiveness in opposing a bill that would simply allow student-initiated religious clubs to meet on school property during noninstructional hours on the same basis as secularly-based clubs are allowed to meet: "The equal access bill opens a Pandora's box of problems, including . . . the . . . prospect of religiously motivated hostility and ostracism."[149] Mondale, in the speech from which I quoted earlier, also raised the specter of religious divisiveness: "But the yearning for traditional values is not a simple tide. It has undertows. And in the hands of those who would exploit it, this legitimate search for moral strength can become a force of social divisiveness and a threat to individual freedom."[150] A brochure from the Adult Learning Satellite Service of the Public Broadcasting Service (PBS), which recently came across my desk, begins an advertisement for a PBS program on church and state with: "Religion and war: for centuries one has too often led to the other." The accuracy of this claim is so little questioned in U.S. culture that even an advertising brochure can state it as a self-evident truth.

As noted earlier, this same fear of the divisiveness of religion has been a part of the Supreme Court's excessive entanglement test. Law professor Michael Smith has suggested that perhaps an underlying antipathy to religion may help explain this emphasis of the Court Justices on religion's divisiveness in the face of contrary evidence:

The Justices' fear of religious divisiveness was greatly disproportionate both to the evidence on which they relied and to the reality. There is strong reason to doubt that recent government action concerning religion is especially apt to cause social strife. What little evidence the Justices have adduced, mainly the religious history of Europe and America before 1791, is scarcely pertinent now. An underlying distaste for corporate religion may have caused their special sensitivity to religious disputes.[151]

McClosky and Brill's explanation for the divisiveness of religion that they perceive helps reveal the sort of prejudices that underlie this mind-set:

> The tendency for the faithful of one religion to display intolerance toward the followers of another arises, in part, out of the nature of religion itself, which is usually based on some form of "revealed" truth. As the product of revelation, it is distinguished from more inductively derived scientific or secular "truths." Whereas the latter are, in principle, "open" and subject to challenge, refutation, and proof, a revealed truth, by its very nature, can be neither refuted nor confirmed — and its devotees are unreceptive to challenge or disagreement.[152]

McClosky and Brill thereby tried to show that the very nature of religion causes believers to be rigid and intolerant of others. It is on this basis that the California writer quoted earlier who objected to public and religious recreation organizations working cooperatively said at one point: "But we must avoid substituting religious dogma for scholarly discussions of ethical issues."[153] The assumption is that religious dogma — or, more neutrally, religious beliefs — and scholarly discussions are mutually exclusive. This sort of bias crops up repeatedly; it permeates U.S. culture. A recent essay in *Time* magazine, dealing with the changing world scene at the beginning of the 1990s, used the word *theology* as a synonym for *outdated*. It concluded: "Nations are rarely given the opportunity to prepare in tranquility for a looming threat. We must not sacrifice that opportunity to the theologies of arms control and cold war thinking."[154] The use of language can speak volumes about underlying assumptions and prejudices.

Ignored in all this is the indisputable fact that, in point of fact, even deeply religious movements and religiously based beliefs constantly change and evolve. The mainline Protestant denominations have, for the most part, accommodated themselves to the findings of modern science and biblical higher criticism; Vatican II graphically illustrated the ability of the Catholic Church to change; and, under the proddings of the Reverend Jerry Falwell and others, the Fundamentalist wing of conservative Protestantism has moved from a position of separation from the world to attempts to change it. To paint religious persons and movements as invariably and uniformly rigid and unchanging is factually inaccurate. Conversely, to assume that nonreligious persons and movements are models of openness and flexibility is equally misleading. One would be hard-pressed to choose between the National Conference of Catholic Bishops and the National Organization of Women as to which is more flexible and open-minded on the question of abortion.

What helps explain the flexibility and openness that often marks religious organizations or movements is the fact that almost all religious traditions emphasize certain fundamental truths whose meaning and implications must then be worked out anew by each generation and — in some traditions — each individual. As the Catholic bishops (whom many would consider to represent the most authoritarian church structure in the United States) stated at the beginning of a pastoral letter on nuclear arms:

> We recognize that the Church's teaching authority does not carry the same force when it deals with technical solutions involving particular means as it does when it speaks of principles or ends. People may agree in abhorring an injustice, for instance, yet sincerely disagree as to what practical approach will achieve justice. Religious groups are as entitled as others to their opinion in such cases, but they should not claim that their opinions are the only ones that people of good will may hold.[155]

History and experience, in short, demonstrate that religious organizations and movements are not (contrary to what McClosky, Brill, and others have contended) uniquely rigid and inflexible. The fact that they are nevertheless often seen to be suggests an antireligious bias on the part of their detractors.

More controversial and open to question is the sometimes asserted claim that there is a strong antipathy to Catholicism among a certain influential segment of U.S. intellectuals. Smith, after exhaustive research into the Supreme Court Justices' attitudes toward religion, drew the following conclusions about two justices who played key roles in moving the Court toward the strict separationist position: "The views of corporate religion of Justices Black and Douglas were unusually explicit. They thought that much of corporate religion is socially harmful. It is apt to be greedy, totalitarian, and politically and scientifically backward. These observations applied especially to the Catholic Church."[156] This prejudice can be seen in a concurring opinion written by Justice William Douglas in which Justice Hugo Black joined. In a footnote, they quoted a caricature of Catholic education as though it were an accurate picture:

> The whole education of the child is filled with propaganda. That, of course, is the very purpose of such schools, the very reason for going to all of the work and expense of maintaining a dual school system. Their purpose is not so much to educate, but to indoctrinate and train, not to teach Scripture truths and Americanism, but to make loyal Roman Catholics. The children are regimented, and are told what to wear, what to do, and what to think.[157]

With a quotation such as this in mind, one can understand why Smith went on to conclude: "Characteristically, foes of aid to religion outside the Supreme Court were quite hostile to the most rigorous of the large corporate religions, the Catholic Church."[158]

An influential book by Paul Blanshard, an attorney and writer, is illustrative of the anti-Catholicism, especially as it relates to Catholic schools, that has marked U.S. society. One scholar noted that Blanshard's rhetoric "verges on absurdity."[159] Typical in terms of Blanshard's content and tone is the following:

> My own conviction is that the outcome of the struggle between American democracy and the Catholic hierarchy depends upon the survival and expansion of the public school. Even if the differential Catholic birth rate should soar in the United States[,] . . . the Catholic hierarchy could never make the United States into a clerical state unless it captured the public-school system or regimented a majority of American children into its own parochial-school system.[160]

This brief quotation illustrates that Blanshard saw U.S. democracy and the Catholic church structure as mutually exclusive opposites, with the Catholic hierarchy wishing to make the United States over into a clerical state and Catholic schools specializing in regimenting their students. If Blanshard were a lonely voice of prejudice and distortion, it would not be worth citing his work, but his book was highly popular, selling a quarter of a million copies.[161] As political scientist Booth Fowler pointed out, "His popularity and the considerable respect he obtained among some educated people was a mark . . . of the deep uneasiness about Catholicism in the American psyche."[162] Blanshard was also a leading figure in Protestants United for the Separation of Church and State, now known as Americans United for the Separation of Church and State, which is probably the foremost organized group advocating a strict separationist position.[163] The very fact of this organization's name change indicates that in its origins it saw itself as a Protestant bulwark against a Catholic threat. That Blanshard played a leading role in its affairs indicates that it was indeed comfortable with his brand of anti-Catholic hostility and that such beliefs, especially in terms of Catholic schools, may have been a factor in the development of both societal attitudes and Supreme Court decisions in the church-state area.

Although more evidence of an anti-Catholic prejudice among some societal leaders could be cited, there is also contrary evidence. The extent and exact nature of this prejudice is admittedly speculative. What cannot be denied is that the prejudicial view of religion as being uniquely divisive is clearly present and has found its way into Supreme Court decisions. Both it and more general sentiments against particularistic, authoritative religion may very well have influenced positions adopted by the Supreme Court and have acted as an independent force discouraging devout persons from explicitly acting on the basis of their faith in the public realm. To whatever extent this has happened, full religious freedom has thereby been diminished.

A Christian Nation

Although the commitment to religion-state separation and the three perspectives underlying this commitment that were just described are culturally dominant in U.S. society, to complete the picture of how society views the interrelationship of religion and government, it is helpful briefly to explore the major alternative to the wall of separation concept. This is the Christian nation concept.

President Woodrow Wilson once wrote, "America was born a Christian nation for the purpose of exemplifying to the nations of the world the principles of righteousness found in the Word of God."[164] In 1892 the Supreme Court stated that "our [American] civilization and our institutions are emphatically Christian."[165] The well-known contemporary fundamentalist, Jerry Falwell, has written, "Any diligent student of American history finds that our great nation was founded by godly men upon godly principles to be a Christian nation."[166] In 1990 Pat Robertson, a conservative Protestant from the charismatic wing and a candidate for the Republican presidential nomination in 1988, launched a new Christian political organization called the Christian Coalition. Its executive director explained the new organization's goals: "What Christians have got to do is take back this country, one precinct at a time, one neighborhood at a time, and one state at a time. I honestly believe that in my lifetime we will see a country once again governed by Christians . . . and Christian values."[167]

Different persons can mean different things when they refer to the United States as a Christian nation, but they seem almost always to start out by stressing that the United States was founded by strong, committed Christians and that its Constitution and laws are rooted in Christian beliefs. From this, some conclude that God has singled out the United States for his special blessings and has put the United States under his special providential care, much as he did for the Israelites in biblical times. Senator Jesse Helms of North Carolina has given voice to this belief:

I pray every day for a rebirth of the spiritual values that made us a nation in the first place. If the Spirit of God were to rouse 200 million Americans to action, there is no describing the greatness and glory in store for this country, or the blessings forthcoming to nations now held captive if and when, once again, the United States rededicates itself to the cause of freedom under God's law.[168]

Other individuals conclude, since the key features of U.S. economic, social, and political life are uniquely Christian, that Christian beliefs, practices, symbols, and moral standards should be accommodated by all of society and supported by government. Christianity would thereby become in practice, even though not in legal form, the semiestablished religion of the nation. Prayers and Bible readings would be reintroduced into the public schools, Christian holidays would be recognized and accommodated by the schools and by government more broadly, and government in various ways would cooperate with and give assistance to Christian groups. In this view, adherents of other religions and nonbelievers are, of course, free to practice their faith or lack of faith, but they must understand that they are in the minority and should expect to accommodate themselves to the dominant Christian practices and assumptions.

The freedom of religion problems in the Christian nation concept are easy to demonstrate. As soon as the government supports and accommodates itself to Christianity — even to a "nonsectarian" Christianity that does not distinguish among the various Christian traditions, it is favoring one religion over another. A semiestablishment of religion is taking place. This is true in both an obvious and a less obvious sense. In the obvious sense, it favors Christianity over Judaism, Islam, New Age beliefs, nonbelief, and other religious-philosophical systems of thought. Is Christmas to be recognized and accommodated, but not Ramadan? Are prayers to a personal, hearing God to be offered up in public settings, but no time given for meditation and the reaching of one's inner resources? The favoring of one religion over others violates the norm of neutrality and necessarily interferes with the free exercise of those other religions. The Christian nation concept, by elevating Christianity to a favored status, does exactly this.

A more subtle free exercise problem emerges from the fact that the Christian nation concept is usually supportive of a generic, religion-in-general Christianity, or even the broad Judeo-Christian tradition. It seeks to include Unitarians and fundamentalist Baptists, Catholics and mainline Protestants, Mormons and the Eastern Orthodox — and sometimes even Judaism — under one umbrella. However, the Christianity that thereby emerges and is being advanced by the Christian nation concept is a watered-down, lowest-common-denominator Christianity. To recognize this, one need only to recall the innocuous (some would say insipid) New York State

Regents' prayer, which was found unconstitutional in *Engel v. Vitale* (1962): "Almighty God, we acknowledge our dependence upon Thee, and we beg Thy blessings upon us, our parents, our teachers and our Country."[169] Compare this prayer to the deeply moving beauty of a centuries-old Eastern Orthodox mass, the prophetic thunderings of a black preacher calling on God's justice in an unjust society, or a myriad of other specific, distinctive manifestations of Christianity or other religions. The free exercise rights of a Hasidic Jew, a deeply religious evangelical Protestant, or a devout Catholic are not fulfilled by a lowest-common-denominator, religion-in-general prayer. The religious faith being recognized and accommodated is supposed to be everyone's, but in reality is no one's. The religion one is left free to exercise (or, in some situations, pressured to exercise) in the public square is not one's own, meaningful faith, but a generic, watered-down version. One must leave one's real faith at home.

There is a dilemma here. To the extent that the semiestablishment of religion of the Christian nation approach resembles traditional Christianity (or even Protestantism, as will be seen in the next chapter was the case during most of the nineteenth and early twentieth centuries), the free exercise of those who are not adherents of this faith are violated; to the extent that one avoids this horn of the dilemma by making the semiestablished religion generic, the free exercise rights of no one are being respected — all are being forced to take part in or support a religion that is not their own.

If the Christian nation approach was ever tenable, it certainly is becoming increasingly less so as the religious diversity of U.S. society noted in Chapter 1 continues to increase. Both Catholics and conservative Protestants are increasing in number and both are increasingly seeing the political relevance of their faith and becoming willing to act on this basis. Similarly, African-American churches are becoming increasingly self-confident and assertive. All three traditions are breaking the more genteel consensus over which mainline Protestantism will preside. Added to this are the increasing numbers of non-Christian religions such as Islam and Eastern religions, as well as those who are committed to a nontheistic view of the world. These trends are likely to continue. All this means that the semiestablishment of Christianity that is implicit in the Christian nation approach to church-state relations will likely become violative of the free exercise rights of increasing numbers of persons.

One is left with a situation in which current Supreme Court positions and culturally dominant attitudes are not neutral, but rather tend to favor a secular cultural ethos over religion. However, the Christian nation alternative to this approach also is not neutral, because it favors Christianity over non-Christianity or a generic, lowest-common-denominator religion over specific, particularistic manifestations of religious faith. To find a way out of this morass, one needs first to understand more exactly how and why U.S. society and its government came to arrive at this position. That is the story to be told in Chapter 3.

NOTES

1. Phillip E. Johnson, "Concepts and Compromise in First Amendment Religion Doctrine," *California Law Review* 72 (1984): pp. 819, 839.

2. Ibid., p. 819.

3. A. James Reichley, *Religion in American Public Life* (Washington, DC: Brookings, 1985), p. 117.

4. See Stephen L. Pepper, "The Conundrum of the Free Exercise Clause — Some Reflections on Recent Cases," *Northern Kentucky Law Review* 9 (1982): p. 303.

5. Wayne R. Swanson, *The Christ Child Goes to Court* (Philadelphia: Temple University Press, 1990), p. 185.

6. *Lemon v. Kurtzman*, 403 U.S. at 612 (1971).

7. *Reynolds v. United States*, 98 U.S. at 166 (1879).

8. Ibid., p. 167.

9. C. Herman Pritchett, *The American Constitution*, 3d ed. (New York: McGraw-Hill, 1977), p. 392.

10. *Jacobson v. Massachusetts*, 197 U.S. at 11 (1905); *Minersville School District v. Gobitis*, 310 U.S. at 586 (1940); *Braunfeld v. Brown*, 366 U.S. at 599 (1961); *Goldman v. Weinberger*, 475 U.S. at 503 (1986); and *Employment Division v. Smith*, 58 U.S.L.W. at 4433 (1990).

11. Pepper, "The Conundrum of the Free Exercise Clause," pp. 266–267.

12. *Wisconsin v. Yoder*, 406 U.S. at 214 (1972).

13. Ibid., p. 215. Emphasis added.

14. *Sherbert v. Verner*, 374 U.S. at 398 (1963); *Thomas v. Review Board*, 450 U.S. at 707 (1981); and *Hobbie v. Unemployment Appeals Commission*, 480 U.S. at 136 (1987).

15. *Thomas v. Review Board*, 450 U.S. at 717–718 (1981).

16. Ibid., p. 718.

17. *Hobbie v. Unemployment Appeals Commission*, 480 U.S. at 141 (1987).

18. *Braunfeld v. Brown*, 366 U.S. at 599 (1961); *United States v. Lee*, 285 U.S. at 252 (1982); and *Goldman v. Weinberger*, 475 U.S. at 503 (1986).

19. *Thomas v. Review Board*, 450 U.S. at 723 (1981).

20. *Lyng v. Northwest Indian Cemetery Protective Association*, 485 U.S. at 447 (1988).

21. Ibid., p. 451.

22. Ibid., pp. 450–451.

23. *Employment Division v. Smith*, 58 U.S.L.W. at 4435 (1990).

24. Ibid., p. 4437. The quoted material is from *Lyng v. Northwest Indian Cemetery Protective Association*, 485 U.S. at 451 (1988).

25. See *Braunfeld v. Brown*, 366 U.S. at 599 (1961).

26. *West Virginia State Board of Education v. Barnette*, 319 U.S. at 635 (1943).

27. *Widmar v. Vincent*, 454 U.S. at 273 (1981).

28. *Everson v. Board of Education*, 330 U.S. at 15–16 (1947). Emphasis added.

29. *Lemon v. Kurtzman*, 403 U.S. at 612–613 (1971). The quoted material is from *Walz v. Tax Commission*, 397 U.S. at 674 (1970).

30. *Edwards v. Aguillard*, 482 U.S. at 585 (1987). The material quoted first is from Justice O'Connor's concurring opinion in *Lynch v. Donnelly*, 465 U.S. at 690

(1984); and the material quoted second is from *Wallace v. Jaffree*, 472 U.S. at 56 (1985).

31. *Edwards v. Aguillard*, 482 U.S. at 592–593 (1987).

32. *Wallace v. Jaffree*, 472 U.S. at 57 (1985).

33. *Epperson v. Arkansas*, 393 U.S. at 97 (1968); *Stone v. Graham*, 449 U.S. at 39 (1980); *Wallace v. Jaffree*, 472 U.S. at 38 (1985); and *Edwards v. Aguillard*, 482 U.S. at 578 (1987).

34. Laurence H. Tribe, *American Constitutional Law*, 2d ed. (Mineola, NY: Foundation Press, 1988), pp. 1215–1216. Tribe's emphasis.

35. *Grand Rapids School District v. Ball*, 473 U.S. at 388 (1985).

36. Ibid., p. 387.

37. Ibid., p. 390. Emphasis added.

38. *Abington School District v. Schempp*, 374 U.S. at 217 (1963). Emphasis added.

39. *Committee for Public Education and Religious Liberty v. Nyquist*, 413 U.S. at 756 (1973); *Meek v. Pittenger*, 421 U.S. at 349 (1975); and *Wolman v. Walter*, 433 U.S. at 229 (1977).

40. *Board of Education v. Allen*, 392 U.S. at 236 (1968); *Wolman v. Walter*, 433 U.S. at 229 (1977); and *Mueller v. Allen*, 463 U.S. at 388 (1983).

41. *Wolman v. Walter*, 433 U.S. at 247 (1977).

42. See Tribe, *American Constitutional Law*, pp. 1228–1229.

43. *Larkin v. Grendel's Den*, 459 U.S. at 127 (1982).

44. *Lemon v. Kurtzman*, 403 U.S. at 621–622 (1971).

45. *Aguilar v. Felton*, 473 U.S. at 409 (1985).

46. *Lemon v. Kurtzman*, 403 U.S. at 622 (1971).

47. *Marsh v. Chambers*, 463 U.S. at 783 (1983); *Tilton v. Richardson*, 403 U.S. at 672 (1971); *Hunt v. McNair*, 413 U.S. at 734 (1973); *Roemer v. Board of Public Works*, 426 U.S. at 736 (1976); *Lynch v. Donnelly*, 465 U.S. at 668 (1984); *County of Allegheny v. American Civil Liberties Union*, 109 S.Ct. at 3086 (1989); and *Walz v. Tax Commission*, 397 U.S. at 664 (1970).

48. *Lynch v. Donnelly*, 465 U.S. at 668 (1984).

49. *Everson v. Board of Education*, 330 U.S. at 18 (1947).

50. *Wallace v. Jaffree*, 472 U.S. at 60 (1985).

51. *Epperson v. Arkansas*, 393 U.S. at 103–104 (1968).

52. *Abington School District v. Schempp*, 374 U.S. at 226 (1963).

53. *Mueller v. Allen*, 463 U.S. at 404 (1983).

54. *Lee v. Weisman*, 60 U.S.L.W. at 4725 (1992). Emphasis added.

55. For two articulate defenses of the strict separationist position, see Leonard W. Levy, *The Establishment Clause: Religion and the First Amendment* (New York: Macmillan, 1986); and Leo Pfeffer, *Church, State and Freedom*, rev. ed. (Boston: Beacon Press, 1967).

56. *Everson v. Board of Education*, 330 U.S. at 18 (1947).

57. Ibid., p. 16.

58. Levy, *The Establishment Clause*, p. 185.

59. Leo Pfeffer, *Religion, State and the Burger Court* (Buffalo, NY: Prometheus Books, 1984), p. xiv.

60. *Everson v. Board of Education*, 330 U.S. at 31–32 (1947).

61. Reichley, *Religion in American Public Life*, p. 158.

62. *Everson v. Board of Education*, 330 U.S. at 13 (1947).

63. Some of the leading works that have shown the problems in the *Everson* case's reading of the intent of the authors of the First Amendment are Michael J. Malbin, *Religion and Politics: The Intentions of the Authors of the First Amendment* (Washington, DC: American Enterprise Institute, 1978); Walter Berns, *The First Amendment and the Future of American Democracy* (New York:

Basic Books, 1970); Robert L. Cord, *Separation of Church and State* (New York: Lambeth, 1982); A. James Reichley, *Religion in American Public Life* (Washington, DC: Brookings, 1985), ch. 3; and Jack R. Van Der Slik, "Respecting an Establishment of Religion in America," *Christian Scholar's Review* 13 (1984): pp. 217–235. Also see the excellent summary of the available historical evidence in the dissenting opinion of Justice William Rehnquist in *Wallace v. Jaffree*, 472 U.S. at 91 (1985). For contrary positions, see Levy, *The Establishment Clause* and Justice David Souter's concurring opinion in *Lee v. Weisman*, 60 U.S.L.W. at 4731 (1992).

64.   This and the following quotations of differing versions of the First Amendment considered by the Congress are from Malbin, *Religion and Politics*, pp. 4–9.

65.   Reichley, *Religion in American Public Life*, p. 112.

66.   Malbin, *Religion and Politics*, p. 9.

67.   Quoted in Reichley, *Religion in American Public Life*, p. 112.

68.   Michael W. McConnell, "The Origins and Historical Understanding of Free Exercise of Religion," *Harvard Law Review* 103 (1990): p. 1413.

69.   Ibid., p. 1490.

70.   Quoted in "Is the Free Exercise of Religion Now in Doubt?" *Public Justice Report* 14 (July-August 1991): p. 1.

71.   Tribe, *American Constitutional Law*, p. 1184.

72.   *Lyng v. Northwest Indian Cemetery Protective Association*, 485 U.S. at 451–452 (1988).

73.   W. Cole Durham, Jr., Edward McGlynn Gaffney, Douglas Laycock, and Michael W. McConnell, "For the Religious Freedom Restoration Act," *First Things*, no. 21 (March 1992): p. 44.

74.   The quotation is from G. J. Holyoake, as quoted in Leroy E. Loemker, "The Nature of Secularism," in J. Richard Spann, *The Christian Faith and Secularism* (New York: Abingdon-Cokesbury, 1948), p. 12.

75.   Reichley, *Religion in American Public Life*, p. 165 (Reichley's emphasis). Others have made the same observation. For example, Michael McConnell wrote: "If the public school day and all its teaching is strictly secular, the child is likely to learn the lesson that religion is irrelevant to the significant things of this world, or at least that the spiritual realm is radically separate and distinct from the temporal. However unintended, these are lessons about religion. They are not 'neutral.'" Michael W. McConnell, "Neutrality under the Religion Clauses," *Northwestern University Law Review* 81 (1986): p. 162.

76.   *Abington School District v. Schempp*, 374 U.S. at 313 (1963).

77.   See James Davison Hunter, "Religious Freedom and the Challenge of Modern Pluralism," in James Davison Hunter and Os Guinness, eds., *Articles of Faith, Articles of Peace* (Washington, DC: Brookings, 1990), pp. 54–73. Hunter, as do I, largely uses *secularist* or *humanist* and *secularism* or *humanism* interchangeably (and sometimes together, as in *secular humanist*). Hunter quotes (in a footnote) a leading contemporary U.S. humanist, Paul Kurtz, who has put forth two key characteristics of humanists: "First, humanists reject any supernatural conception of the universe; they are sympathetic to one form or another of atheism, agnosticism, or skepticism. Second, humanists affirm that ethical values do not have a supernatural source and have no meaning independent of human experience; humanism is an ethical philosophy in which human beings are central." Quoted in Hunter, "The Challenge of Modern Pluralism," p. 154 n. 24. Note that this definition has exactly the same elements as Holyoake's definition of secularism, quoted earlier.

78.   Hunter, "The Challenge of Modern Pluralism," p. 65. Later, in Chapter 4, in presenting my own approach to church-state issues, I develop a definition of

religion that includes nontheistic faiths that rely on the supernatural but excludes secular philosophies and mind-sets.

79. Ibid., p. 66.

80. Ibid., p. 68.

81. Ibid., p. 71. The same contention is also made by Peter L. Berger, "Religion in Post-Protestant America," in Janet Podell, ed., *Religion in American Life* (New York: H. W. Wilson, 1987), pp. 27–39.

82. Quoted in Hunter, "The Challenge of Modern Pluralism," p. 70. Originally from Paul Blanshard, "Three Cheers for Our Secular State," *The Humanist*, March-April 1976, pp. 17–25.

83. *Lynch v. Donnelly*, 465 U.S. at 716–717 (1984). Although a Court minority of four supported this dissent, a fifth justice, Sandra O'Connor, supported essentially the same position in a concurring opinion in this case; moreover, the same position was also articulated by Justice Brennan in an earlier concurring opinion: *Abington School District v. Schempp*, 374 U.S. at 203 (1963). All these claims have been made without explicit challenge from other justices.

84. *Lynch v. Donnelly*, 465 U.S. at 680–681 (1984).

85. *Allegheny County v. American Civil Liberties Union*, 492 U.S. at 598 (1989).

86. Ibid., p. 616.

87. Stephen V. Monsma, "The Neutrality Principle and a Pluralist Concept of Accommodation," in Paul J. Weber, ed., *Equal Separation: Understanding the Religion Clauses of the First Amendment* (New York: Greenwood, 1990), p. 81.

88. Quoted by Ari Goldman, "Displeasure with Decision Voiced by Religious Groups," *New York Times*, July 4, 1989, p. 12.

89. Martin Marty, *The New Shape of American Religion* (New York: Harper & Row, 1958), p. 2. Also see pp. 31–44.

90. *Tilton v. Richardson*, 403 U.S. at 672 (1971); *Hunt v. McNair*, 413 U.S. at 734 (1973); and *Roemer v. Board of Public Works*, 426 U.S. at 736 (1976).

91. See David G. Savage, "Court Signals Change on Religion Cases," *Los Angeles Times*, July 10, 1988, p. 23.

92. Dissenting opinion in *Edwards v. Aguillard*, 482 U.S. at 610 (1987).

93. Mark Tushnet, "The Constitution of Religion," *Connecticut Law Review* 18 (1986), p. 70. On this point, also see Johnson, "Concepts and Compromise," p. 827.

94. Tribe, *American Constitutional Law*, p. 1277.

95. See Peter L. Benson and Dorothy I. Williams, *Religion on Capitol Hill: Myths and Realities* (New York: Harper & Row, 1982), and, in regard to the 1964 Civil Rights Act, William A. Carroll, "The Constitution, the Supreme Court, and Religion," *American Political Science Review* 61 (1967): p. 662.

96. *Wallace v. Jaffree*, 472 U.S. at 82–83 (1985).

97. See Tribe, *American Constitutional Law*, pp. 1211–1212.

98. *Lemon v. Kurtzman*, 403 U.S. at 622–623 (1971).

99. *McDaniel v. Paty*, 435 U.S. at 641 (1978).

100. Paul J. Weber, "Excessive Entanglement: A Wavering First Amendment Standard," *Journal of Politics* 46 (October 1984): pp. 483–501.

101. *The Federalist* (New York: Modern Library, n.d.), pp. 340–341.

102. Weber, "Excessive Entanglement," p. 495. Weber's emphasis.

103. *Lemon v. Kurtzman*, 403 U.S. at 622 (1971).

104. Ibid., pp. 622–623.

105. For two excellent essays on the positive role that religion has played, and continues to play, in the U.S. polity, see Reichley, *Religion in American Public Life*, ch 7; and Glenn Tinder, "Can We Be Good without God?" *Atlantic Monthly*, December 1989, pp. 69–85.

106. Tribe, *American Constitutional Law*, p. 1280.

107.   Pepper, "The Conundrum of the Free Exercise Clause," pp. 293–294.
108.   *Sherbert v. Verner*, 374 U.S. at 415–416 (1963).
109.   See, for example, *Abington School District v. Schempp*, 374 U.S. at 203 (1963).
110.   On this issue, see Jesse H. Chopper, "Defining 'Religion' in the First Amendment," *University of Illinois Law Review* 1982 (1982): pp. 579–613.
111.   *Torcaso v. Watkins*, 367 U.S. at 495 (1961).
112.   Quoted in *United States v. Seeger*, 380 U.S. at 165 (1965).
113.   Ibid., p. 166.
114.   See Tribe, *American Constitutional Law*, pp. 1186–1187.
115.   *Sherbert v. Verner*, 374 U.S. at 402 (1963).
116.   On these figures see George Gallup, Jr., and Jim Castelli, *The People's Religion* (New York: Macmillan, 1989), pp. 13, 27.
117.   See Herbert McClosky and Alida Brill, *Dimensions of Tolerance: What Americans Believe about Civil Liberties* (New York: Russell Sage Foundation, 1983).
118.   These and the following figures in this paragraph are from The Williamsburg Charter Foundation, *The Williamsburg Charter Survey on Religion and Public Life* (Washington, DC: Williamsburg Charter Foundation, 1988), Appendix, Tables 23, 25, 28, 29, 30, 31, 34.
119.   Ibid., p. 36.
120.   Ibid., Appendix, Table 23.
121.   Ibid., Appendix, Table 25.
122.   Walter Mondale, "Religion Is a Private Matter," *Church and State*, October 1984, p. 205.
123.   *Newsweek*, September 17, 1984, p. 26.
124.   "The Bishops' Statement on Politics . . . and Why It's Wrong," *Church and State*, September 1984, p. 185.
125.   From a speech that Kennedy made to the American Society of Newspaper Editors, April 21, 1960. See *U.S. News and World Report*, May 2, 1960, p. 91.
126.   See "Dukakis and Religion," *New York Times*, June 2, 1988, p. D24.
127.   Hugh Sidey, letter to the editor, *Washington Post*, October 7, 1986, p. A-16. © The *Washington Post*.
128.   John J. Bullaro, "Religion and Recreation: A Dangerous Liaison for CPRS," *California Parks and Recreation* 45 (Winter 1989): p. 9 (emphasis added). Also see Mark Gladstone, "Bane Urges Deukmejian to Fire Park Director over Statement," *Los Angeles Times*, September 8, 1989, p. I-31. I believe there is a basis on which to object to some of the comments made by the director of the state Department of Parks and Recreation, but the statement that religion must be limited to "our individual lives" is not one of them.
129.   Richard A. Baer, Jr., "Cornell as a Sectarian University" (unpublished talk given in Sage Chapel at Cornell University, Ithaca, NY, February 26, 1984), p. 4.
130.   This and the following quotations are from Anthony Lewis, "Onward, Christian Soldiers," *New York Times*, March 10, 1983, p. A27.
131.   On civil religion, see Robert N. Bellah, "Civil Religion in America," *Daedalus* 96 (Winter 1967): pp. 1–21. Religion-in-general, as referred to by Martin Marty (*The New Shape of American Religion*), and civil religion, as referred to by Robert Bellah ("Civil Religion in America"), are closely related, but distinguishable, concepts. Compare Bellah's article with Marty's work. What they have in common is an emphasis on broad, generalized, consensual beliefs. As such, they reflect and affirm U.S. cultural attitudes and expectations and can be distinguished from particularistic, authoritative religious faiths whose adherents feel bound by the religious truths they profess even if their beliefs lead them to

oppose certain features of the U.S. societal consensus. I see the terms as distinguishable in that civil religion deals more specifically than religion-in-general with national identity and consensual public policy goals (e.g., freedom and equality of opportunity). Thus, I conceive of civil religion as a more specific version or subset of religion-in-general.

132. For Reagan's speech, see "Excerpts from President's Speech to National Association of Evangelicals," *New York Times*, March 9, 1983, p. A18.

133. "Sermon on the Stump," *New York Times*, February 3, 1984, p. A28. Demonstrating that the Supreme Court is not alone in taking confusing positions on church-state issues is another *New York Times* editorial which appeared seven months later and stated, "There's plenty of religion in politics — and ought to be. People in a democracy should act on their social values, whether derived from their religious faith or from secular sources." *New York Times*, September 9, 1984, p. 24E.

134. Mondale, "Religion Is a Private Matter," p. 206.

135. Ronald Reagan, "Religion and Politics Are Necessarily Related," *Church and State*, October 1984, p. 203.

136. Baltimore *Sun*, September 7, 1984. Reprinted in *Editorials on File* 15 (1984): p. 992.

137. Joseph L. Conn, "Church, State and Abortion," *Church and State* 42 (May 1989): p. 100.

138. Quoted in ibid., p. 102.

139. James M. Wall, "Why the Charge that Religion Makes Carter Weak?" *Detroit Free Press*, March 8, 1979, p. 9A.

140. *Hartford Courant*, July 12, 1989. Reprinted in *Editorials on File* 20 (1989): p. 778.

141. Later in Chapter 4 I define religion in terms of its ability to provide answers to ultimate questions through a reliance on the supernatural.

142. Mario M. Cuomo, "Religious Belief and Public Morality," *New York Review*, October 25, 1984, p. 32.

143. Weber, "Excessive Entanglement," pp. 495–496.

144. Edward M. Kennedy, "Tolerance and Truth in America" (unpublished remarks of Senator Edward M. Kennedy, Liberty Baptist College, Lynchburg, VA, October 3, 1983), p. 3.

145. All this is not meant to imply that, given the wide diversity of religious beliefs in U.S. society, bringing particularistic religious beliefs into the policy arena poses no problems. My key point is that simply trying to exclude religiously inspired positions from the public policy arena is surely no answer. For three able discussions of this issue, see Clarke E. Cochran, *Religion in Public and Private Life* (New York: Routledge, 1990); Kent Greenawalt, *Religious Conviction and Political Choice* (New York: Oxford University Press, 1988); and George M. Marsden, "Are Secularists the Threat? Is Religion the Solution?" in Richard John Neuhaus, ed. *Unsecular America* (Grand Rapids, MI: Eerdmans, 1986), pp. 31–51.

146. See Richard John Neuhaus, *The Naked Public Square* (Grand Rapids, MI: Eerdmans, 1984).

147. Levy, *The Establishment Clause*, p. ix.

148. McClosky and Brill, *Dimensions of Tolerance*, p. 103.

149. *Sacramento Bee*, August 4, 1984. Reprinted in *Editorials on File* 15 (August 1–15, 1984): p. 86.

150. Mondale, "Religion Is a Private Affair," p. 207.

151. Michael E. Smith, "The Special Place of Religion in the Constitution," in Philip B. Kurland, Gerhard Casper, and Dennis J. Hutchinson, eds., *The Supreme Court Review, 1983* (Chicago: University of Chicago Press, 1984), p. 107.

152. McClosky and Brill, *Dimensions of Tolerance*, p. 103.

153. Bullaro, "Religion and Recreation," p. 9.

154. Charles Krauthammer, "Why Arms Control is Obsolete," *Time*, August 5, 1991, p. 68.

155. National Conference of Catholic Bishops, *The Challenge of Peace: God's Promise and Our Response* (Washington, DC: U.S. Catholic Conference, 1983), p. 87.

156. Smith, "The Special Place of Religion," p. 105. Later, Smith notes that along with Justices Black and Douglas, Justices Rutledge and Felix Frankfurter also tended to see corporate religion as "socially harmful." See p. 110.

157. *Lemon v. Kurtzman*, 403 U.S. footnote 20 at 635 (1971). One needs to keep in mind that, as Chapter 6 later demonstrates, empirical evidence indicates that today's Catholic schools are, in fact, doing a *better* job of educating children than are the public schools.

158. Smith, "The Special Place of Religion," p. 105.

159. Barbara Welter, "From Maria Monk to Paul Blanshard: A Century of Protestant Anti-Catholicism," in Robert N. Bellah and Frederick E. Greenspahn, eds., *Uncivil Religion: Interreligious Hostility in America* (New York: Crossroad, 1987), p. 54.

160. Paul Blanshard, *American Freedom and Catholic Power*, 2d ed. (Boston: Beacon, 1958), p. 323.

161. Ibid., biographical sketch facing the title page.

162. Robert Booth Fowler, *Religion and Politics in America* (Metuchen, NJ: American Theological Library Association, 1985), p. 249.

163. See ibid., p. 249.

164. Quoted in Nathan O. Hatch, Mark A. Noll, and John D. Woodbridge, *The Gospel in America* (Grand Rapids, MI: Zondervan, 1979), p. 207.

165. *Church of the Holy Trinity v. United States*, 143 U.S. at 471 (1892).

166. Jerry Falwell, *Listen, America!* (Garden City, NY: Doubleday, 1980), p. 29.

167. Quoted in Russell Chandler, "Robertson Moves to Fill Christian Right Vacuum," *Los Angeles Times*, May 15, 1990, p. A5.

168. Jesse Helms, "A Nation Adrift," in Nancy Leigh DeMoss, ed., *The Rebirth of America* (Philadelphia: Arthur S. DeMoss Foundation, 1986), p. 79.

169. *Engel v. Vitale*, 370 U.S. at 422 (1962).

3

The Past as Prologue: The Development of Church-State Theory and Practice

Shakespeare's aphorism, "What's past is prologue," is surely accurate in the case of U.S. theory and practice concerning church-state relations. Only as one understands the past can one understand the positions that have come to characterize the Supreme Court and U.S. society (as described in Chapter 2). The origins of today's confusing church-state doctrines and assumptions, with their resulting restrictions on religious freedom, are rooted in theories and practices of the past. We need to start in the eighteenth century with the basic framework for religious disestablishment that U.S. society developed and accepted at the time. That framework was flawed at the outset, but the flaws were ignored at the time and covered over during the nineteenth century. Only in the twentieth century are they coming to light. It is like a fault line existing far below the surface of the earth, unknown and benign for decades, but then, under the pressures of shifting tectonic plates, suddenly giving rise to a major earthquake. This chapter tells the story of that fault line: how it developed, why it remained submerged throughout the nineteenth century, and how it has come to light in a major earthquake in the twentieth.

This chapter first considers two major movements that were formative in the eighteenth-century disestablishment of religion. It considers next how the concepts underlying this disestablishment developed and were applied in the nineteenth century, and finally how the twentieth century has revealed their limitations and inadequacies.

THE EIGHTEENTH CENTURY: THE FIRST DISESTABLISHMENT

This section focuses on how two key eighteenth-century movements — the Enlightenment and the Great Awakening — interacted with existing colonial practice to form the underpinnings of the U.S. concept of religious freedom and the separation of church and state. Both these movements were powerful, pervasive forces in the United States of the eighteenth century, and both need to be understood for the purpose of this volume.

Before exploring them, however, it is important to note that from the founding of the colonies to the end of the eighteenth century, there was no true separation of church and state and only limited religious freedom in almost all the thirteen colonies. Even those colonists who came seeking freedom from religious persecution came seeking it for themselves but had no intention of extending the same freedom to others. The prevailing pattern and assumptions were those that had prevailed in Christendom since the fourth century: Societal and political unity depends on the existence of only one true church in any given society or political jurisdiction. This concept had developed during the long centuries of Christian unity in Western Europe and had survived the fracturing of that unity by the Protestant Reformation. To the mind of that age, it was impossible to conceive of the coexistence of religious diversity and political and social unity.

Thus, the English Puritans in New England, the Dutch Reformed in New Amsterdam, the Anglicans in Virginia, and other colonists elsewhere assumed that "the pattern of religious uniformity would of necessity be transplanted and perpetuated in the colonies."[1] The norm was legally established churches, with favored churches receiving tax support, dissenters subjected to punishments of varying severity, and civil authorities exercising control over certain ecclesiastical matters. Nevertheless, by the end of the century, almost all this had been swept away. The establishment of religion had been done away with (or soon would be), and full religious freedom was firmly in place. This was revolutionary stuff, reversing over a thousand years of practice in Christendom. This section explores what lay behind this dramatic move to religious freedom and the ideas that came to underlie it.

The Enlightenment in the New World

The well-known historian Crane Brinton has suggested that the key to the eighteenth-century Enlightenment is the belief that humankind can attain a level of perfection and happiness on earth, here and now, that previous generations had believed could only be attained in a future lif.[2] This is a very broad concept of the Enlightenment, but its vision of human, earthly progress captures its animating ideal. In the New World context, Enlighten-ment thought, which came to play a dominant role among key leadership figures, saw human development rooted in a rational understanding of nature and in the validity and power of insights rooted in common sense and human intuition.[3] In regard to nature and reason, colonial Enlightenment thinkers were especially inspired by the scientific work of Sir Isaac Newton and others to believe that what they called nature was comprehensible by way of individual reason. Robert Handy has expressed it well:

> Impelled by the brilliant advances in the science of its time, which seemed to be sweeping mystery from the world, and repelled by the brutality and destructiveness of the terrible religious wars, Enlightenment thinkers proposed to discover the truth about God and the world by utilizing their rational faculties in the examination of Nature.[4]

Nature, as understood by the New World Enlightenment, was not simply what we today would call the natural environment, but was the world external to the individual, including the broad sweep of human history and human patterns of belief and behavior. This does not mean that the colonial Enlightenment was marked by rationalism in the sense of putting its faith in abstract reasoning. Instead, reason was to be applied to the real world of empirical observations and to be guided by the clear conclusions to which an intuitive common sense pointed. Thomas Jefferson reflected a widespread consensus when he penned his famous words: "We hold these truths to be *self-evident*: That all men. . . ."

Where did all this leave religion and God? Clearly the God of traditional, organized religion — the God supernaturally revealed in the Bible and defined in church creeds and doctrines — was excluded. The Enlightenment's emphasis on discovering truth by applying reason and common sense in observing nature precluded it from accepting the claims of traditional Christianity. Most of the New World Enlightenment thinkers were deists (in practice, if not always in theory), but whether or not fully deists, they certainly were outside the mainstream of traditional Christianity of their day. They tended to be religious, to believe in the existence of God, to make numerous references to him, and to base their arguments on religiously rooted concepts, but their religious beliefs were based not in organized, supernaturally revealed religion, with its creeds and doctrines, but in their bringing of reason and common sense to bear in observing nature. In this sense, theirs was a natural religion, in contrast to the revealed religion of traditional Christianity.

Finally, it is important to note that Enlightenment thinking was strongly individualistic in nature. It was individuals — not a select few with special training or abilities nor human beings jointly in the form of some collectivity — who were to discover truth through their own, individual use of reason and common sense in studying and reflecting on nature. The Enlightenment thereby proclaimed the autonomy of the individual: One could discover truth for one's self.

This Enlightenment faith was never a mass movement in the colonies, but it was dominant among the educated, leadership echelon in the last half of the eighteenth century, and certain aspects seeped into the thinking and perspectives of society more generally. The political leaders who led the fight for independence from England, who worked to disestablish the churches, and who wrote the Constitution and battled for its ratification (such as Thomas Jefferson, Thomas Paine, George Washington, Benjamin Franklin, James Madison, and John Adams) were men of the Enlightenment. All varied in their specific beliefs; yet all relied on individual reason and commonsense observation and understanding of nature as a direct, accessible path to human betterment. All favored this path over a reliance on traditional religion and supernatural revelation as the path to an other-worldly salvation.

To obtain a better insight into Enlightenment thinking in the New World, I will explore three especially influential representatives of this movement — Thomas Jefferson, Benjamin Franklin, and James Madison — and then draw some conclusions concerning what they contributed to the concepts underlying freedom of religion and religious disestablishment as they developed in the early United States.

Thomas Jefferson

President John Kennedy once remarked at a White House dinner in honor of Nobel Prize winners that this was the greatest assembly of talent and intelligence that the White House had ever seen . . . except for the night when Thomas Jefferson had dined alone![5] The facts of Jefferson's life and the reach of his accomplishments indicate that Kennedy's remarks were not too great an exaggeration. Author of the Declaration of Independence at the age of thirty-three, ambassador to France, leader in Virginia's struggles to disestablish the Anglican church, inventor, architect, author, and third president of the United States: his accomplishments and fame were enormous; his continuing influence hard to overstate. He, more than any other of the Enlightenment-molded Founding Fathers helped shape U.S. thinking about social and political issues, especially concerning the relationship between religion and government. Our consideration begins with Jefferson.

Fundamental to Jefferson's thinking were three underlying perspectives or points of departure. I will examine them first and then look at three more concrete applications of them. First, Jefferson's thought was marked by a strong individualism. He took the free, autonomous individual, unbridled by restraints, as his starting point. One team of scholars sees Jefferson's concept of society as consisting of free individuals in this way:

His picture of humanity was the Stoic ideal of a homogeneous, universal species of free, rational individuals. Those individuals were free to create a universal voluntary association with a set of common moral principals at its core and a government whose authority would be derived from the sovereignty of the individuals as a freely associating people.[6]

One searches Jefferson's speeches and writings in vain for clear concepts of collectivities such as society, the state, or the church. Instead, the autonomous individual freed from the restraints of superstitions and traditions was the focus of his thinking. Thus, Thomas Buckley noted of Jefferson: "He had copied from Locke the statement that the church is a 'voluntary society' of people who come together to worship God as they choose, but Jefferson was more concerned for the person than for the group or collectivity."[7]

A second key to Jefferson's thinking is a commonsense rationalism. There is an intended tension in this term: Jefferson was not a rationalist in the strict sense of the word, nor did he give full faith to intuitive common sense by itself. It was out of the interplay of human reason, applied and checked by the empirical world and an inborn intuitive moral sense, that he saw human advancement and the correction of error arising. One can see Jefferson's reliance on human reason when he wrote, "Reason and free inquiry are the only effectual agents against error. Give a loose to them, they will support true religion, by bringing every false one to their tribunal, to the test of their investigation. They are the natural enemies of error, and of error only."[8] Again, he wrote to his nephew, Peter Carr, advising him to "Fix reason firmly in her seat, and call to her tribunal every fact, every opinion."[9]

This does not mean, however, that Jefferson put his faith in abstract reasoning. He did not see reason, in the sense of complex philosophical constructs, as being a source of truth or a correcter of error. In the same letter to Peter Carr just quoted, he also wrote: "State a moral case to a ploughman and a professor. The former will decide it as well, and often better than the latter, because he has not been led astray by artificial rules."[10] David Little pointed out that, according to Jefferson,

The essentials of morality and religion are directly perceivable by a kind of sixth sense, closer in character to the normal sense than to the operations of reason. Just as the "sense of right and wrong . . . is as much a part of [human] nature as the sense of hearing, seeing, feeling, . . . as much a part of man as his leg or arm . . . ," so, for Jefferson, the true god is "nature's God," as referred to in the Declaration of

Independence, a deity to be discovered by direct sense experience, and not by tortuous theological speculation.[11]

Thus it was that Jefferson wrote in 1809, "The practice of morality being necessary for the well-being of society, he [God] has taken care to impress its precepts so indelibly on our hearts that they shall not be effaced by the subtleties of our brain."[12] Buckley properly noted that Jefferson's view of morality was rooted neither simply in reason nor in human instinct: "Morality is not the product of unaided instinct, therefore, but of reason and instinct working together."[13] In adhering to a commonsense rationalism, Jefferson — as will be shortly seen was also the case with James Madison — was heavily influenced by Scottish Common Sense philosophy.[14]

It was out of this commonsense rationalism that Jefferson's third underlying perspective, a belief in natural law and natural rights, emerged. Jefferson, in his famous words of the Declaration of Independence, gave voice to the concept of natural rights as follows: "We hold these truths to be self-evident: That all men are created equal; that they are endowed by their Creator with certain inalienable rights; that among these are life, liberty, and the pursuit of happiness." Even more explicitly, Jefferson wrote in his famous "Bill for Establishing Religious Freedom" that "the rights hereby asserted are of the natural rights of mankind and that if any act shall be hereafter passed to repeal the present, or to narrow its operation, such act will be an infringement of natural right."[15] What Jefferson's reason, observations, and intuitive common sense told him was that all human beings had been created by God and given rights that were inalienable because they were humankind's natural, inherent possession.

From out of these three basic perspectives or beliefs, Jefferson made three applications that are especially important for understanding his conception of religious freedom. The first is that he made a division between what is particular and what is universal in religion. Here is where Jefferson's individualism and commonsense rationalism came to the fore. At first glance, Jefferson seemed to have held contradictory positions in regard to religion. On the one hand, he was a member of the Anglican church and regularly supported it with his contributions. In his second inaugural address he asked for the nation's prayers to God:

I shall need, too, the favor of that Being in whose hands we are, who led our fathers, as Israel of old, for their native land and planted them in a country flowing with all the necessaries and comforts of life; who has covered our infancy with His Providence and our riper years with His wisdom and power, and to whose goodness I ask you to join in supplications with me.[16]

The God to whom Jefferson was appealing here is not merely the cold, "absentee landlord" God of deism.

On the other hand, Jefferson could be cavalier toward religion, as when he noted "the happy discovery, that the way to silence religious disputes, is to take no notice of them."[17] He seemed to treat Christian beliefs lightly when he wrote, "But it does me no injury for my neighbor to say there are twenty Gods, or no God. It neither picks my pocket nor breaks my leg."[18] Jefferson appeared to be hostile to religion when he wrote disapprovingly of "the Mountebanks calling themselves the priests of Jesus" and "the power and the profit of the priests. Sweep away their gossamer fabrics of factitious religion, and they would catch no more flies. We should all then, like the Quakers, live without an order of priests, moralize for ourselves, follow the oracle of conscience, and say nothing about what no man can understand, nor therefore believe."[19]

The key to understanding what could be construed to be contradictory positions is to recognize that Jefferson was personally a religious person and often utilized religiously rooted arguments, but that his religion was a very individualistic faith appropriated by him personally through reason and common sense. This approach led Little to conclude:

> Among the religious traditions, including Judaism, with which Jefferson was acquainted, Christianity was by far the most appealing to him; but this was so only after Jefferson had abstracted the true, simple message of Jesus "from the rubbish in which it is buried, easily distinguishable by its lustre from the dross of His biographers, and as separable from that as the diamond from the dunghill." This meant, for example, sifting through the New Testament so as to feature "the most sublime morality which has ever fallen from the lips of man" by excising all "inferior" theological and theoretical materials. Jefferson was absolutely sure that he was able to avoid all the difficult problems of exegesis and interpretation of Christian Scriptures, as of all Sacred Scriptures, because he had the sure guide of common sense at his disposal.[20]

Clergy, church tradition, doctrinal statements, scholarly research: All were not only unnecessary, but positive evils, since they worked to bind individuals and force them into molds not of their own making.

From such reasoning, Jefferson made a fundamental distinction that has influenced much of what has come after: a distinction between the beliefs and practices that are peculiar to a particular religious faith or group, which he believed were unimportant and rooted in superstitions and dead doctrines, and the beliefs and practices that were held in common by all religious faiths and groups, which were crucial to a sense of morality and civility, on which, in turn, social and political unity and progress depended. Here was the answer to those who for centuries had assumed that religious pluralism would inevitably lead to social disunity and decay. There could be religious diversity because, in the final analysis, the differences on which the plurality of religious groups were based did not matter. All persons of common sense and good will would arrive at the same basic sense of morality anyway, and that is all that is needed for social and political unity and progress.

Jefferson could not have expressed this position any more clearly than he did in a letter to James Fishback in 1809:

> Reading, reflection and time have convinced me that the interests of society require the observation of those moral precepts only in which all religions agree (for all forbid us to murder, steal, plunder, or bear false witness) and that we should not intermeddle with the particular dogmas in which all religions differ, and which are totally unconnected with morality.[21]

On the basis of this distinction Jefferson had earlier argued that religious diversity posed no problem for social unity and order.

> Our sister States of Pennsylvania and New York, however, have long subsisted without any establishment [of religion] at all. The experiment was new and doubtful when they made it. It has answered beyond conception. They flourish infinitely. Religion is well supported; of various kinds, indeed, but all good enough; all sufficient to preserve peace and order.[22]

In other words, the existence of various religious groups did not matter since all religions possessed a common core of beliefs "good enough" to "preserve peace and order."

A corollary of this position, and Jefferson's second application of his basic principles, was the privatization of religion in its particular manifestations.

> Jefferson considered theological statements, whether made by church councils, creeds, or individuals, to be simply "opinion," based not on reason, but on revelations unacceptable to a thoughtful man. Churches define themselves on the basis of these differences, but they do not affect the public sphere. Whether you are Calvinist or Arminian, Trinitarian or Unitarian, pray in church or shout under the trees, sprinkle children over the font or dip adults in the creek, it does not touch your life as a citizen. In the Jeffersonian scheme of

things, the religious dimension of personal belief was private, absolutely. He repeated it in a multitude of ways.[23]

This belief that religious doctrines and discussions were irrelevant to the world of public policies and issues was central to Jefferson's concept of religious freedom and the separation of church and state. Since religious beliefs and public affairs were two totally separate spheres, sealing them off from each other would work to the detriment of neither. Little aptly expressed this crucial conclusion in these words:

> Now we can begin to understand why Jefferson dismissed and discounted as irrelevant distractions all beliefs, opinions, doctrines, and theories that did not pass the test of the sure, simple standard of common sense. And it is because all such beliefs were finally irrelevant and unimportant to Jefferson that he believed they should be set apart and fenced off from the world of action, the world of civil responsibility, by a "wall of separation."[24]

A final application of Jefferson's basic beliefs was his contribution to the development of a national faith or civil religion, which, building on what he saw as the common elements in all religions, helped define and unite the people of the United States. Buckley has listed three elements of this national faith: (1) a sense of shared beginnings, rooted in English experiences and expressed in common colonial experiences and struggles for independence; (2) a belief in natural rights, derived from a Creator; and (3) acknowledgment of dependence on a divine providence overseeing the new American nation.[25] In the portion of his second inaugural address already quoted, Jefferson made reference to the origins of the United States in biblical terms and compared the early colonial settlers with the people of ancient Israel. He once even suggested that a depiction of Moses leading the Israelites through the Red Sea be used on the Great Seal of the United States.[26]

Benjamin Franklin

Benjamin Franklin, with his genial wit and widely read writings, had a significant influence in the latter half of the eighteenth century as a popularizer of ideals and ways of thinking that were then dominant among the colonial political and educational leadership. While not contributing to the development of political, social, and religious thought as Jefferson did, his widespread popularity indicates that he was an important figure in the development of the U.S. belief system as it relates to religion and the state.

Franklin was a typical man of eighteenth-century New World Enlightenment thinking. He did not look to traditional religion and its doctrines for wisdom and insight, but to persons' own individual observations and conclusions. His scientific experimental bent — which led to ground-breaking work on the nature of electricity and many practical inventions — can also be seen in his approach to questions of religion and philosophy, where he put strong emphasis on results and deeds. Already at age twenty-two he wrote his parents the following in regard to theological doctrines.

> I make such Distinctions very little my Study; I think vital Religion has always suffer'd, when Orthodoxy is more regarded than Virtue. And the Scripture assures me, that at the last Day, we shall not be examin'd what we *thought*, but what we *did*; and our Recommendation will not be that we said *Lord, Lord*, but that we did GOOD to our Fellow Creatures.[27]

Two more specific attitudes of Franklin deserve special mention. One is his strong agreement with Jefferson and others of his day in making a clear distinction between what is particular and what is universal in religion. Franklin clearly thought that the differences in doctrine and practice that divided religious groups were unimportant and inconsequential. What was important in religion were those moral truths all religions held in common.

> I had been religiously educated as a Presbyterian; and though some of the dogmas of that persuasion, such as the *eternal decrees of God, election, reprobation, etc.,* appeared to me unintelligible, others doubtful, and I early absented myself from the public assemblies of the sect, Sunday being my studying day, I never was without some religious principles. I never doubted, for instance, the existence of the Deity; that he made the world, and govern'd it by his Providence; that the most acceptable service of God was the doing of good to men; that our souls are immortal; and that all crime will be punished, and virtue rewarded, either here or hereafter. These I esteemed the essentials of every religion; and, being to be found in all the religions we had in our country, I respected them all, though with different degrees of respect, as I found them more or less mixed with other articles, which, without any tendency to inspire, promote, or confirm morality, served principally to divide us, and make us unfriendly to one another. This respect to all, with an opinion that the worst had some good effects, induced me to avoid all discourse that might tend to lessen the good opinion another might have of his own religion; and as our province increased in people, and new places of worship were continually wanted, and generally erected by voluntary contribution, my mite for such purpose, whatever might be the sect, was never refused.[28]

This is vintage Franklin. He shows his disdain for the distinctive doctrines of specific religious groups, yet he also shows respect for and acknowledges his support for religion generally. What is universal in religion is useful "to inspire, promote, or confirm morality." Elsewhere, Franklin wrote of the large number of persons "who have need of the motives of religion to restrain them from vice"[29] and to the question of the divinity of Jesus, he responded that he could see no harm in its belief "if that Belief has the good Consequence, as probably it has, of making his Doctrines more respected and better observed."[30] Franklin was in full agreement with Jefferson's position that the specifics of different religious groups were irrelevant for public life. In fact, they posed the danger of dividing and making persons "unfriendly" to each other. It was only the sense of morality and the basic beliefs that religious groups held in common that were important and needed to be of concern.

A second, more specific, emphasis of Franklin was not a matter of belief but of style. He used his wit, originality, and cleverness to take a cavalier, slightly irreverent, deflating approach to what others considered religious questions of serious moment. Even today one cannot help but chuckle at many of his sayings and responses to religious issues. On the question of the divinity of Jesus, to which he responded only a month before his death, he wrote, in addition to the portion already quoted: "It is a question I do not dogmatize upon, having never studied it, and think it needless to busy myself with it now, when I expect soon an Opportunity of knowing the Truth with less Trouble."[31] This style contributed as much as his actual beliefs to the propagation of the belief that the religious differences about which wars had been fought, endless words had been written, and legislative establishment debates had turned need not, after all, be taken that seriously.

James Madison

Few have challenged Norman Cousins' observation that "if Franklin and Jefferson were the philosophers of the [constitutional] period, and Washington its overseer, then Madison was the chief engineer and foreman."[32] Madison was concerned with translating basic concepts and goals into actual, effective political practices and structures. It is not that he was unfamiliar with or ill at ease in the realm of ideas and ideals. In fact, as a reading of *The Federalist* indicates, he thought long, hard, and creatively about the theoretical underpinning of the new government that he worked to shape. Madison's influence in thought and action was sufficiently great in the formative years of the United States that it is essential to take a closer look at his perspectives and beliefs. In this section I first look at several underlying characteristics of Madison's thought and then at three more specific features of Madison's perspective on religion-state relations.

Madison shared with Jefferson a strong commitment to common-sense rationalism. Ralph Ketcham wrote: "Two sources stand out as preeminent in the intellectual background of Madison's religious views. First [was], the overall rationalism that saturated the theology of the eighteenth century and second, the rather rough-hewn Scottish 'Common Sense' philosophy."[33] The rationalism of Madison — a quality Jefferson shared — was strongly conditioned by empirical observation and the intuitive grasp of truth stressed by Common Sense philosophy. Madison attended the College of New Jersey (later Princeton University) and there became close to John Witherspoon, who introduced him to Common Sense philosophy, with its emphasis on the insight of intuition or one's own heart as the way to truth over abstract reasoning or complex philosophical systems. Its influence can be seen throughout the rest of Madison's life.[34]

A second underlying characteristic of Madison's thinking that is important for his understanding was his commitment to the concept of natural, inalienable rights as the key basis for religious freedom. As with Jefferson and other Enlightenment leaders of his day, Madison accepted the existence of natural rights that are inherent in all humankind and therefore inalienable. This concept plays a crucial role in all of Madison's thinking, and especially in his defense of freedom of conscience. As he stated in the opening of his famous "Memorial and Remonstrance":

> Because we hold it for a fundamental and undeniable truth, "that Religion or the duty which we owe our Creator and the Manner of discharging it, can be directed only by reason and conviction, not by force of violence." The Religion then of every man must be left to the conviction and conscience of every man; and it is the right of every man to exercise it as these may dictate. This right is in its nature an unalienable right.[35]

Later, Madison went on to write:

> If "all men are by nature equally free and independent," all men are to be considered as entering into Society on equal conditions; as relinquishing no more, and therefore retaining no less, one than another, of their natural rights. Above all are they to be considered as retaining an *equal* title to the free exercise of Religion according to the dictates of conscience."[36]

A third underlying characteristic of Madison's thinking was a basic commitment to the free, autonomous individual. As was the case with the other Enlightenment thinkers, Madison had a very weak concept of the collectivity; he thought in terms of the individual and individual rights. This needs emphasis because Madison, more than the other founders of the new nation, developed a defense of the newly written Constitution on the basis of factions. In this sense, his political philosophy did take cognizance of groups. Madison's concept of factions, however, actually helps demonstrate his individualism. He defined factions in a purely negative light; he could not conceive of a good faction, dedicated to the common good. In his famous *Federalist No. 10*, Madison made clear the negative nature of factions: "By a faction, I understand a number of citizens, whether amounting to a majority or minority of the whole, who are united and actuated by some common impulse of passion, or of interest, adverse to the rights of other citizens, or to the permanent and aggregate interests of the community."[37] The point of Madison's essay is to show how the negative effects of factions could be controlled in a large republic such as the new Constitution would create. Implicit in this is the virtue of the free, autonomous individual.

A final underlying characteristic of Madison's thinking, and one which distinguished him from Jefferson and Franklin, was a genuine respect for traditional Christianity. In Madison one finds none of the cavalier poking fun of the religious groups of his day as with Franklin and none of Jefferson's clear rejection of basic Christian teachings or clear antipathy to organized religion. One ought not to make too strong a distinction here, since Madison never joined a church (although he regularly attended the Episcopal Church in his home county in Virginia), and he clearly was a man of the Enlightenment in elevating individual reason and intuition over the doctrines of organized religion. Nevertheless, his detailed study of religion, his close association with John Witherspoon, and the lack of cavalier attacks even on organized religion all indicate a more genuine, deeper respect for Christianity than marked either Jefferson or Franklin.

Out of these four underlying characteristics of Madison's thought emerged three especially important applications that Madison made in regard to the relationship between government and religion. One is a strong, lifelong commitment to religious freedom and the separation of church and state. Early in his career, at twenty-four years of age, Madison wrote a letter in which one can feel the sense of disgust with which he reacted to religious persecution:

There are at this time in the adjacent county not less than five or six well-meaning men in close jail for publishing their religious sentiments, which in the main are very orthodox. I have neither patience to hear, talk, or think of anything relative to this matter; for I have squabbled and scolded, abused and ridiculed, so long about it to little purpose, that I am without common patience. So I must beg you to pity me, and pray for liberty of conscience to all.[38]

Almost sixty years later, the elder statesman Madison wrote that he favored "an entire abstinence of the Government from interference in any way whatever, beyond the necessity of preserving public order, and protecting each sect against trespasses on its legal rights by others."[39] Ketcham is correct when he observed, "There is no principle in all of Madison's wide range of private opinions and long public career to which he held with greater vigor and tenacity than this one of religious liberty."[40]

In defending religious liberty, and church-state separation as the means to attain it, Madison consistently argued that such separation would be good for religion as well as for government. This concern for the health of religion seems to be genuine, and not based on tactical advantage. In an 1819 letter he looked back and wrote with a sense of satisfaction concerning how well religion had prospered in Virginia under church-state separation: "On a general comparison of the present and former times, the balance is certainly and vastly on the side of the present, as to the number of religious teachers and the zeal which actuates them, the purity of their lives, and the attendance of the people on their instructions."[41]

Second, Madison viewed religion as being important for order and peace in society, although he did not make the distinction between what is particular and what is universal in religion as explicitly or as frequently as did Jefferson and Franklin. His greater respect for religion apparently led him not to so casually dismiss as inconsequential the differences that separate religious groups. On the other hand, neither did he clearly contradict or argue against the position of Jefferson and Franklin. Moreover, his beliefs meshed with those of Jefferson and Franklin in that he saw religion as important to good order and morality in society. In an 1825 letter he referred to "the belief in a God All Powerful wise and good" which was "essential to the moral order of the World and to the happiness of man."[42]

Finally, and perhaps most distinctively, Madison, ever the political engineer, believed religious freedom would lead to a multiplicity of religious groups, which in turn, would help assure religious freedom. In the 1788 Virginia ratifying convention, he stated:

If there were a majority of one sect, a bill of rights would be poor protection for liberty. Happily for the states, they enjoy the utmost freedom of religion. This freedom arises from that multiplicity of sects, which pervades America, and which is the best and only security for religious liberty in any society. For where there is such a variety of sects, there cannot be a majority of any one sect to oppress and persecute the rest.[43]

As Madison argued in regard to political factions, so he argued in regard to religious organizations as well: in numbers and diversity there is safety, since no one can dominate.

Conclusions

What, then, can be concluded in regard to the New World Enlightenment leaders, as exemplified by Jefferson, Franklin, and Madison? What did they contribute to the U.S. understanding of religious freedom and church-state relations? There are three especially important summary observations. The first is that Enlightenment thought bifurcated religious beliefs and practices between those that were perceived as common to all religions and in keeping with nature, on the one hand, and those that were perceived as characteristic of particular religious sects or groups and resting in revelation or tradition, on the other. This bifurcation was fundamental to the eighteenth-century Enlightenment in the United States and has been fundamental to all thinking in regard to church-state issues since then. This distinction was used to answer what, up until then, had been the prevailing assumption: that religious unity was needed in order to have social and political peace and order. Reason and nature would lead all open-minded persons of good will to embrace the basic, self-evident truths contained within all religions, and public unity and order could be built on the belief in those truths. The distinctive beliefs of the various religious groups — including even such theologically important beliefs as the unitarian versus the trinitarian nature of God — were irrelevant to the public realm. They were issues that petty, crabbed clerics argued over, but really were of no great moment and certainly had no place in the public sphere. Persons' tendency to be concerned about them and to put great stock in them was a weakness that could be indulged, for they would be safely sealed off from the public realm and would be purely private.

This division resulted in what Mead has called "the particularistic theological notions of the sects and the cosmopolitan, universal theology of the Republic."[44] The former was read out of the public arena; the latter became the foundation for the civil religion of the United States. As Robert Bellah wrote:

> But the civil religion was not, in the minds of Franklin, Washington, Jefferson, or other leaders . . . ever felt to be a substitute for Christianity. There was an implicit but quite clear division of function between the civil religion and Christianity. Under the doctrine of religious liberty, an exceptionally wide sphere of personal piety and voluntary social action was left to the churches. But the churches were neither to control the state nor to be controlled by it. The national magistrate, whatever his private religious views, operates under the

rubrics of the civil religion as long as he is in his official capacity.[45]

This basic bifurcation has provided a powerful theoretical base for church-state separation ever since and can be seen today in both the Supreme Court's and the broader society's belief (documented in Chapter 2) that religious beliefs outside the broad, consensual platitudes of religion-in-general or civil religion should be kept out of the public sphere. Since religion in its particular manifestations is a personal and private matter, and irrelevant to the political realm, segregating it from public affairs does no harm to freedom of religion. Eighteenth-century Enlightenment thinking thereby bequeathed to subsequent generations the basic notion that disestablishment and church-state separation equate with freedom of religion. As Bellah wrote in reference to the situation today: "The principle of separation of church and state guarantees the freedom of religious belief and association, but at the same time clearly segregates the religious sphere, which is considered to be essentially private, from the political one."[46]

A second basic observation that can be made concerning the eighteenth-century Enlightenment concerns the strong individualism present in its perspectives on religion, society, and government. Jefferson, Franklin, and Madison — and others of their day — lacked a clear theory of the collectivity. It was free, autonomous individuals using their reason, observations of nature, and intuitive common sense that were both the discoverers of truth and the key actors in public affairs. This is why someone such as Franklin never missed an opportunity to stick a knife into what he saw as the pretentiousness of organized religion and why the Enlightenment in general was out of step with the organized churches and their leaders. Religious truth could be discovered by anyone, using common sense and observations to read God's truth in nature, that is, in the world around them. This was natural religion — simple, direct, and self-evident — in contrast to the complexities, supernaturalism, and authoritarianism of traditional Christianity.

This second observation leads to a third: Enlightenment thought placed a strong emphasis on the importance of protecting government and society from the machinations of organized religion. The Enlightenment's distrust of organized religion, with its frequent attempts to gain establishment status and financial assistance for itself, led it to see the key church-state issue as being that of disestablishment. The biggest threat to religious freedom was establishment, which the Enlightenment saw as helping to perpetuate in power narrow-minded clerics who would stifle the spread of true, natural religion. Mark DeWolfe Howe has made reference to the "Jeffersonian fear that if it [the First Amendment] were not enacted the federal government would aid religion and thus advance the interest of impious clerks."[47] Religious freedom thereby translated into no establishment of religion.

Again, the impact of these last two observations has proven to be powerful and long-lasting. They can still be seen in present-day Supreme Court rulings and societal attitudes. The tendency of the Supreme Court to read the two religion clauses of the first amendment separately and to favor no-establishment burdens on religion over free exercise protections of religion can be traced back to the Enlightenment's distrust of organized religion and its belief that the key threat to religious freedom arose from its establishment. Enlightenment thinkers believed that if persons were to be truly free, they must be freed from the superstitions and controls of a state-assisted religious establishment so that they could discover religious truth for themselves. In the process, government and society would be spared the bitter religious divisions that had racked Europe and the early colonies. Today, this same position is reflected in an emphasis on blocking any form of governmental support for religion as the key path to freedom of religion. Government and society are to be protected from religion, not the other way around.

Although the Enlightenment leaders discussed here were highly influential in the founding of the United States and setting the initial terms of political (especially church-state) discourse, they did not represent the only vital force in eighteenth-century colonial society. In fact, in terms of numbers they represented more of an intellectual and political elite than a mass movement. The Great Awakening, in contrast, was a mass movement and a second vital force in colonial society at the time of the founding of the republic. I consider it next.

The Great Awakening

The first stirrings of religious awakening occurred in 1719 when a revival moved through the Dutch Reformed churches in New Jersey's Raritan Valley. In 1734 there were further stirrings by way of the preaching of Jonathan Edwards in Northampton, Massachusetts, and then in the first half of the 1740s the religious revival known as the Great Awakening swept through New England, emerging the following years at various points in the other colonies. "Throughout the 1740's and into the 1750's revival crackled, exploded, and burned out in one place after another throughout the colonies."[48] The Great Awakening reacted against the formalism and perceived dead orthodoxy of the existing churches. It was typically marked by itinerant preachers who attracted large crowds and stirred a depth of religious emotion previously not experienced, followed by a renewal of fervor and dedication on the part of the regular ministers.

It is hard, 250 years later, to catch the full force and depth of the series of revivals that affected almost all thirteen colonies. Richard Bushman pointed out that to understand the full impact of the Great Awakening, one must recognize that it was at the center of eighteenth-century culture, not peripheral to it.

> We inevitably will underestimate the effect of the Awakening on eighteenth-century society if we compare it to revivals today. The Awakening was more like the civil rights demonstrations, the campus disturbances, and the urban riots of the 1960s combined. All together these may approach, though certainly not surpass, the Awakening in their impact on national life.[49]

Although the Great Awakening itself had died down by the last quarter of the eighteenth century, its aftereffects continued to be a major force in colonial society. They played a major role — along with Enlightenment thinking — in shaping the concept of church and state that gained ascendancy at the end of the century. In this section, I first explore four characteristics of the Great Awakening and then examine its influences on religious freedom and on church-state relations generally.

It is difficult to describe the Great Awakening in terms of several key characteristics that accurately portray all aspects of it, for it was a diverse, multifaceted movement, spread over vast distances and as much as three decades. What may be true of the Awakening in New England in the early 1740s may not be true of its characteristics in Tidewater Virginia in the late 1750s. Nevertheless, at the risk of missing some nuances, I highlight four underlying characteristics that tended to mark the Great Awakening in most of its facets and that throw light on its subsequent influence on the development of U.S. church-state relations.

First, the Great Awakening had a distinct lower-class flavor to it. It was the masses, not the urban elite, who responded to George Whitefield, Jonathan Edwards, Gilbert Tennent, Samuel Davies, and a host of other preachers and itinerant revivalists. The educated, well-established classes used the terms *enthusiasm* and *enthusiasts* in a disparaging manner to refer to preachers and converts of the Great Awakening. "From the sixteenth century well into the nineteenth, *enthusiasm* bore usually a pejorative connotation, and Englishmen on both sides of the Atlantic used it to damn religious extremists who stepped across orthodox lines and claimed a close, warm, emotional relationship with God."[50] The shouting, swooning, and other evidences of emotion that often accompanied Great Awakening revivals embarrassed and outraged the polite, genteel society of cosmopolitan areas such as Boston and Philadelphia and the old, traditional — often established — church structures of the day. However, the common farmers, merchants, laborers, and even slaves responded by the thousands to the emphasis on emotion and experience over dry doctrine and deference to traditional church hierarchies. The Great Awakening was a people's movement. As such, it also had certain antiauthority aspects to it, but this point must not be carried too far. Revivalists such as Jonathan Edwards and George Whitefield were hardly antiauthority rabble-rousers. However, in the Awakening's rejection of existing traditional church leaders and patterns of behavior and its direct contact with the people — out in the open fields if no church would welcome its itinerant revivalists, there naturally was an undercurrent of rejection of existing authorities in favor of the moving of the Holy Spirit in individual lives. The point is especially significant since many of the traditional churches of the time were formally established and closely allied with existing governmental authorities.

Second, it is important to note that the Great Awakening was highly controversial. It provoked strong opposition and heated condemnations from the majority of the religious and social leaders of the day. Polite society was scandalized by what it saw as the excesses of the movement and used argumentation and sometimes repressive legal means in attempts to thwart it. The contempt in which the Great Awakening was held by a certain segment of society is seen in the words used by Timothy Cutler, an Anglican priest and former rector of Yale, to describe the preaching of Gilbert Tennent: "People wallowed in snow, night and day, for the benefit of his beastly brayings." Similarly, the Boston clergyman Charles Chauncy once referred to revivalism as "properly a disease, a sort of madness."[51] The scorn of Great Awakening preachers for what they saw as dead churches was equally great. For example, David Lovejoy referred to "the Revival's affront to the established clergy, who were often looked upon with contempt, and whose offices and duties were frequently disregarded when itinerants swooped down on likely spots and congregations flocked to them."[52]

The very real tensions between Great Awakening preachers and converts and the older, traditional churches and their congregations were largely rooted — in addition to a basis in the class differences already noted — in the tendency of the Great Awakening to ignore denominational lines and the natural jealousies, rivalries, and hurt feelings of the traditional churches toward the enormously successful Great Awakening preachers. Lovejoy reported that "these religious carryings on and their popularity among the lesser folk were direct threats to the established and privileged Anglican Church."[53] The differences in temperament that no doubt underlay much of the antipathy is described well by Henry May:

Thus, the partisans of order, of intellect, of rationality — those to whom colonial life was steadily growing more civilized, more English, more pleasant, those who loved Addison and admired Pope — could not help taking alarm. . . . Not only were the revivalists destroying church order and social seemliness, they were making nonsense of the rational and moral teachings of modern Christianity. . . . Not far beneath the counterattacks of Boston Arminians, Old Side Philadelphia Presbyterians, or Virginia Episcopalians were quite obvious feelings of class; the revivalists were stirring up the ignorant rabble, to the prejudice of social as well as moral order.[54]

To someone brought up in, and a leader of, a traditional church — characterized by set routines and proper decorum and accustomed to accepting the heritage and importance of one's own denomination — to suddenly have some outsider descend on one's community, claiming by word and action that denominational lines are unimportant and drawing crowds of which one's old church could only dream, anger and jealousy were natural reactions.

Although many of the existing churches were caught up in the Great Awakening as revival swept through them, those that were not attacked it and its "enthusiasm" by the written and spoken word. "Books, tracts, sermons, letters, and newspapers condemned the 'New Way' and spoke of the ignorant, the rabble, the 'admiring Vulgar,' and Negroes, all of whom revival ministers and exhorters aroused and made restless and kept from their callings."[55] Legal restrictions were put on new churches that emerged out of the Great Awakening and on existing churches that were newly "awakened." In 1742 Connecticut enacted restrictions on itinerant preachers, a major means by which the Awakening was being spread, in "An Act for regulating Abuses and correcting Disorders in Ecclesiastical Affairs." It, in part, provided:

That if any person whatsoever, that is not a settled and ordained minister, shall go into any parish and (without the express desire and invitation of the settled minister of such parish . . .) publickly preach and exhort the people, shall for every such offence, upon complaint made thereof to any assistant or justice of the peace, be bound to his peaceable and good behaviour . . . by said assistant or justice of the peace, in the penal sum of one hundred pounds lawful money.[56]

Earlier we noted Madison's condemnation and disgust in 1774 at the imprisonment of several Baptist clergy in Virginia. These were Separatist Baptists whose roots went directly back to the Great Awakening in New England.[57] Similarly, Baptist and other separatist churches experienced legal restrictions and persecution throughout the colonies. In short, controversy, tensions, and opposition accompanied the Great Awakening wherever it went.

A third characteristic of the Great Awakening was its pietistic tendencies. The Great Awakening was rooted in orthodox Christianity, largely in the Calvinist tradition, and most of the older, existing churches did not differ greatly in this regard. Where the Awakening departed from previous Calvinist theology and practice was in its strong pietistic tendency. Sydney Ahlstrom has described pietism as "a movement of revival, aimed at making man's relation to God experientially and morally meaningful as well as socially relevant. It stressed the feelings of the heart."[58] Christianity to the pietist is not primarily a matter of intellectual assent to certain formal church doctrines or formal membership in some church; it is experiential. It is a matter of personal, inner conviction and feeling. This personal — even individual — emotional experience of the conviction of sin and assurance of forgiveness was central to the Great Awakening. The emphasis on personal, emotional experience is what led to charges of "enthusiasm" and to opposition from many of the church structures of the day.

The pietism of the Great Awakening was especially important for church-state relations because it overshadowed an earlier Puritan emphasis on a more systematic application of Christianity to the broader social and political worlds. Mead has indicated that for the early New England Puritans, "the sovereignty of God could be made manifest on earth only by full incarnation in social, political, and economic as well as ecclesiastical institutions."[59] For the seventeenth-century Puritans, Christianity had implications for society as a whole and for one's relation to it and to issues affecting all society, such as political authority, economic relations, and the role of the government in relation to ecclesiastical matters. However, by the time of Jonathan Edwards — probably the most influential of the Great Awakening preachers, a fundamental change had occurred.

> The fact is that neither the casual reader nor the assiduous student of Edwards will find much in his life or writings that concerns the political order or the tenure of kings and magistrates. Early Puritans had been involved in the definition of church and civil government and their relationship under God, and they wrote about these questions at length. But except for the occasional piece, like a funeral sermon for a magistrate, Edwards writes as though almost totally preoccupied with "things of religion," civil matters neither constituting a real problem nor possessing vital interest.[60]

Pietism in its purest form involves more of a withdrawal from the world in order to cultivate the inner life of personal piety, than an engagement with the world. Although Edwards and the Great Awakening generally were not completely pietistic in nature, they did have strong tendencies in that direction.[61] As Herbert Schneider wrote:

> For in New England ... religion had been an objective social institution, preoccupied with public concerns; Edwards, however, transformed it into an inner discipline of the emotions. The gospel of the divine sovereignty, of election, of predestination, and of the Covenant of Grace, which the New England Puritans had constructed into a social and political philosophy, was now transformed to the inner life of the soul.[62]

A consequence of the pietistic tendencies of Edwards and the Great Awakening can be seen in the observation of Alan Heimert that "in the quarter century or so after the Awakening" its leaders were not disposed to "pulpit politics" and that in 1750 Jonathan "Edwards was reminding his Northampton congregation that the 'mutual concerns of ministers and their people' were of infinitely greater moment 'than any of the temporal concerns of men, whether private or public' — of more importance indeed than the fate of the greatest 'earthly monarchs, and their kingdoms or empires.'"[63]

Religion emerged out of the Great Awakening as a greatly strengthened, revitalized force, but it also emerged as a more limited, privatized one. The conclusion is aptly stated by Mead: "The revivalists' almost exclusive emphasis on personal religious experience as the only basis for 'assurance,' drove a wedge between the convert's ultimate concern ('salvation') and his concern for the fate of his society."[64]

This third characteristic of the Great Awakening existed in tension with a fourth one, namely, a millennial orientation. To obtain a full picture of the Awakening, both its pietistic and its millennial tendencies must be recognized and given their due. Millenarianism in Christian thought refers to a thousand-year period of time when God's kingdom of peace, healing, and progress will abound on earth. The lamb will lie down with the lion and swords will be beaten into plows. Christians have differed, however, in the extent to which this millennium vision is interpreted literally and on whether they see it occurring before Christ returns to earth at the culmination of history or after Christ returns amid cataclysmic events to rescue and take home his church. Christians who believe that the millennium is to occur before Christ returns look for a glorious improvement in human affairs and a period of peace and progress, which could occur at any time; while Christians who believe that the millennium is to occur after Christ returns expect human affairs to degenerate increasingly as the return of Christ and the millennium come closer.

Depending on one's view of the millennium, one would have quite different beliefs about the possibilities for human progress and one's responsibility to help bring it about.

It is therefore significant that the Great Awakening had strong tendencies to take the millennium prophecies literally and to believe that Christ was to return to earth *after* the glorious, peaceful, thousand-year period. The Great Awakening and its spectacular and — even to its leaders — surprising successes gave rise to the thought that perhaps the millennium was close at hand. H. Richard Niebuhr expressed it well:

> The reality and surprising scope of these experiences now brought a great surmise and hope to the leaders. What if this movement were itself the coming of the kingdom in power? It is remarkable how under the influence of the Great Awakening the millenarian expectations flourished in America. [Samuel] Hopkins [a disciple of Edwards] remarks that few writers in the seventeenth century said anything about this doctrine but "in the present century there has been more attention to it." To Edwards the surprising conversions indicated that "it is not unlikely that this work of God's Spirit, so extraordinary and wonderful, is the dawning, or at least a prelude of that glorious work of God, so often foretold in Scripture, which, in the progress and issue of it, shall renew the world of mankind." He gave various reasons why "we cannot reasonably think otherwise, than that the beginning of this great work of God must be near. And there are many things that make it probable that this work will begin in America."[65]

Later Niebuhr went on to highlight the importance of the Great Awakening in U.S. millenarian thinking: "Many efforts have been made to account for the prevalence in American Christianity of the millenarian tendency. . . . Yet the Awakening and the revivals seem above all to have made it the common and vital possession of American Christians. They brought the remote possibility very near."[66]

There is a tension between the pietist vision of the inner workings of the Holy Spirit, converting and purifying the hearts of individuals, and the millennial vision of God's kingdom of peace coming to earth here and now. Is the true vision one of individual Christians of pure hearts called out of a world of sin and hate to live as redeemed individuals, or is it one of Christians transforming society as a whole into a kingdom of peace? Edwards is representative of the Awakening when he resolved this tension by seeing the millennial kingdom coming by way of individual Christians with changed hearts so infusing society with their love and ideals that God's kingdom is brought to earth. As Heimert wrote: "The millennium was to come neither by a reconstruction of the temple [the institutions and structures of this world] nor through its destruction, but as a renewal of the nature of those who dwell within."[67]

To Edwards and other Great Awakening leaders, God's new millennial kingdom was at hand, but it was a kingdom to be brought about not by the implementation of a thought-out Christian political philosophy, rather, it was to emerge as a natural consequence of hearts of individual men and women being wondrously touched, warmed, and changed by the Spirit of the living God.

The Great Awakening, in summary, was a powerful force, permeating and energizing eighteenth-century U.S. religion. It also tended to limit or restrict religion to the private, inner life of the believer. Personal, experiential knowledge was elevated; theoretical thinking was played down. At the same time, the vision of a bountiful, Christianized nation marked by peace and progress was maintained. These are themes to which I will shortly return, because their implications for church-state relations were great.

The Strange Coalition: Enlightenment Elites and Great Awakening Pietists

In achieving religious freedom, a "strange coalition" — to use Sidney Mead's term — developed between Enlightenment elites and heirs of the Great Awakening, especially those who formed dissenting churches.[68] At the outset it must be stressed this was largely a convergence born of certain limited, immediate goals, not a convergence rooted in a common theoretical base. As Edwin Gaustad pointed out, the two movements differed fundamentally:

The Enlightenment . . . was a movement and mood which in several ways and to varying degrees lauded the capacity of men's minds to reason and to know. Pietism . . . was a movement and mood which in several ways and to varying degrees affirmed the capacity of men's hearts to feel and to believe. Broadly — and therefore to a degree inaccurately — speaking, the former recalled Greece and the renaissance, the latter, Judea and the reformation. Whereas the Enlightenment was anthropocentric, pietism was theocentric; the first embraced common sense and what was "natural" in religion and morality, while the second spoke of a sense of the heart and asserted revealed religion and supernaturally sanctioned morality. One was utilitarian, prudential; the other absolutist and committed. The Enlightenment assumed man's nobility and prowess, pietism built upon God's goodness and power.[69]

Nevertheless, most scholars agree with the conclusion reached by Robert Bellah and his colleagues: "It was undoubtedly pressure from the dissenting sects, with their large popular following, on the one hand, and from that significant portion of the educated and politically effective elite influenced by Enlightenment thought on the other, that finally led to the disestablishment of religion in the United States."[70] This was especially true in the crucial, precedent-setting events in Virginia which led to its 1784 rejection of the General Assessment Bill and the 1786 passage of the Bill for Establishing Religious Freedom authored by Thomas Jefferson. Most of the rationale for these historic actions by the Virginia legislature at the time was articulated by Enlightenment leaders, such as Madison and Jefferson, and subsequently, it surely has been their writings and argumentation that have been most prominent. However, at the time, much — or, many would persuasively argue, most — of the actual impetus for these actions arose from the Baptist and Presbyterian dissenters, the Virginia heirs of the Great Awakening. It was a convergence or coalition between these two dissimilar movements that played the crucial role in disestablishing religion in Virginia. Elsewhere, the Great Awakening, in conjunction with Enlightenment thought, also acted to weaken religious establishments — as the role played by someone such as the Massachusetts Baptist Isaac Backus in New England indicates — but it was in Virginia where this combination of forces proved crucial.[71] Much of what has occurred subsequently in regard to religion-state relations can be traced directly back to the nature and conditions of this coalition. In this section I first look at the importance of the dissenting churches in the disestablishment movement and at the basis for the dissenters' support for complete disestablishment of religion. Next I explore the nature of the convergence of the Enlightenment and Great Awakening movements in supporting disestablishment, noting their similarities and differences.

Religious Dissenters and Disestablishment

Thomas Buckley has compared the relative impact of the religious dissenters and the Enlightenment elite in providing the impetus for the crucial events in Virginia in the 1780s:

> But the role of Madison and Jefferson and the liberal elements who gathered under their banner can be overplayed, just as the significance of the "Memorial and Remonstrance" as representative of the sentiments of the Virginians can be overemphasized. To do so is to distort the meaning of what happened. Despite the best efforts of Madison's allies to circulate the memorial, less than one fifth of those who signed petitions against the assessment in 1785 put their names beneath his

composition. The key to understanding the nature of the religious settlement in Virginia rests with the dissenters, the members of the evangelical churches, for they wrote and signed the overwhelming majority of the memorials which engulfed the legislature that year; and their representatives provided the votes in the Assembly which determined the outcome. Had the evangelicals, and particularly the Presbyterians, opted for the assessment bill, Virginia would have had a multiple establishment of religion instead of Jefferson's bill.[72]

Rhys Isaac has stated flatly that the religious dissenters were crucial in the passage of Jefferson's 1786 religious freedom bill.[73] The dissenters as a mass movement had the numbers plus the fervor and commitment needed to create a ground swell of popular support that the Enlightenment elite could never have mustered.

A basic motivation of the dissenters in supporting disestablishment was their very practical desire for complete religious freedom. Here, the bitter opposition of the established churches to the Great Awakening, noted earlier, is relevant. Naturally, those who had been denounced and sometimes fined or imprisoned under various forms of establishment would tend to oppose it. Their own freedom fully to exercise their religious faith depended on disestablishment.

That cannot be the full story, however, for the evangelical dissenters might have worked simply for toleration, that is, for their own freedom of religion, along with the continuation of established churches. This was a pattern that had been used elsewhere. The fact that they did not, but rather insisted on disestablishment and full religious freedom, can probably be traced back to two interrelated thoughts or themes that tended to mark eighteenth-century dissenters' writings and proclamations: a concept of Christian voluntarism and a belief in the corrupting power of government on religion. Both these views sprang from a concern for the health and spread of Christianity. These were revivalists who in their lifetime had witnessed the dramatic spread of faith by way of preaching, not coercive measures. Thus, William McLoughlin makes reference to the principle of voluntarism when he refers to Isaac Backus as "quoting Biblical texts that he construed to ordain voluntarism and insisting that since Christ's kingdom was not of this world all man-made laws governing ecclesiastical affairs were contrary to divine laws."[74] Buckley summarizes the voluntarism argument made by the Virginia Baptist and Presbyterian dissenters this way: "Every man had to be free to respond in faith and worship as God would draw him. The intervention of the state in any fashion hindered the purity of that relationship and was unwarranted interference in God's work."[75]

When the ideal of Christian voluntarism was linked with the vision of an imminent millennium, a powerful concept was born: the reign of Christian peace and societal advancement based on religion's freedom from government controls. The dissenters saw both the established church and government as barriers to the free flow of the gospel in all its power in the lives of persons, which in turn they expected would usher in the millennium. Buckley has expressed it well when he argued that the evangelicals in Virginia "were concerned about the future of the church, and wanted it separated from the state precisely so that it might freely influence society and permeate it with the Gospel message."[76]

One ought not to conclude from this, however, that these themes in the dissenters' writings resulted in a thought-out theory of religious freedom or church-state separation. The pietism of the Great Awakening left its heirs in a poor position to develop sophisticated justifications or defenses for the church-state separation positions that they took. Their pietism stressed individual, experiential religion, leaving little ground for the development of theories dealing with the social or political implications of their faith. That had been left behind in the seventeenth century. Thus, much of the theoretical initiative passed by default to the Enlightenment wing of the coalition. Mead did not overstate the case when he wrote: "American Protestantism has never developed any full-blown theoretical justification for its most distinctive practice. It was the [Enlightenment] rationalists who articulated the original defense."[77] Thomas Sanders reached a similar conclusion: "Despite the cooperation of revivalist and rationalist in the actual struggle for separation of religion from the state, the former group did not contribute significantly to the theory of separation in Virginia and the United States, which is based on a patently rationalist philosophy."[78] It is hard to exaggerate the importance of this fact.

Religious Dissenters and Enlightenment Rationalists: Convergence and Divergence

It is important, first, to explore the nature of the convergences that brought Enlightenment rationalists and religious dissenters together in the 1780s in a surprising coalition of dissimilar movements. One obvious, and probably the key, basis for their coming together was the very pragmatic, immediate goal of disestablishment, which they both desired. "Politics," as the old saying goes, "makes strange bedfellows." The reason why it does is that often a shared, practical goal will bring otherwise dissimilar persons and movements together. This was so in the 1780s in the newly freed colonies.

In addition to the Enlightenment leaders and the "awakened" evangelical dissenters agreeing on the immediate, practical goal of disestablishment, there was a second, more subtle factor that also helped make their cooperation possible. In spite of their obvious differences, there were also some less obvious — but no less real — similarities or parallels in thought or approach between the heirs of the Enlightenment and the heirs of the Great Awakening. In some surprising ways they possessed a similar mind-set. Earlier I noted the influence that Scottish Common Sense philosophy had on Enlightenment figures such as Jefferson and Madison. This philosophy also influenced the heirs of the Great Awakening — and especially those who left the traditional churches to form their own dissenting churches. This influence became even clearer several decades later in the early nineteenth century, but seeds of it can already be seen in the eighteenth century in a tendency to trust direct, personal experience as a way to truth.[79] Historians Alan Heimert and Perry Miller may have overstated the case somewhat, but they certainly were picking up on what was a real strain in the Awakening when they wrote:

> But it was not so much a doctrinal revolution that the Awakening introduced as a profound shift in the very character, the perspective and focus, of religious thought and discourse. . . . The spokesmen of evangelical religion . . . stressed the "beauty" of the gospel that was revealed to the gracious eye and mind as the inner meaning of the Testaments. . . . [Evangelicals] had come out of the Awakening to argue, ultimately, from Nature — the nature of the universe, of man, and of society.[80]

For the heirs of both the Enlightenment and the Great Awakening, nature — in the sense of the real world of human experience and history — was a dependable source of truth and insight. Thus, McLoughlin could write concerning the dissenter Isaac Backus, "In many ways he displayed a striking sensibility to the new scientific, empirical, and pragmatic way of looking at things. Always ready to learn by the trial and error of the experimental method, he had a favorite phrase for it: 'we experimentally saw' what would work."[81] Both the Enlightenment and the Awakening emphasized individuals and their ability to comprehend truth for themselves without the intervention of institutional authorities or complex theoretical constructs. Mead pointed out that Awakening pietists had a concept of human autonomy rooted in the individual believer's ability to comprehend truth by his or her own personal experience of God's grace.[82] Perhaps most important, Great Awakening pietism emphasized the importance of individual religious experience and salvation to the near exclusion of theories which would link Christian beliefs to social and political questions. As a result there was a tendency for the dissenters to move in the direction of privatizing their faith, to relating it primarily to questions of individual salvation and morality, not questions of social relations and public morality. Thus, Isaac has concluded: "Jefferson's system proclaimed individual judgment as sacred, sacred against the pressures of collective coercions; the evangelicals did the same for private conscience. Having created a private sanctuary in the mind, or heart, both could view the public domain as secular — a region where law and contract prevailed."[83]

These similarities or parallels in mind-set seem to have dulled the dissenters' sensitivity to fundamental differences with the Enlightenment leaders of the drive for disestablishment. In particular, the dissenters' emphasis on personal, experiential salvation over the social, political implications of their faith allowed them to enter into a coalition without developing their own principled theories of church-state separation. One has a hard time imagining the early Puritans working closely with Enlightenment leaders on disestablishment — even if they had agreed on the immediate goal — without having a thought-out, theoretical basis for doing so rooted in a conception of the complementary roles of church and state in God's ordering of human society. However, the pietism of the Awakening tended to deprecate the importance of such constructs, and its emphasis on individual, personal religious experience and faith had — on a superficial basis — a similarity to the Enlightenment's emphasis on individual autonomy and commonsense reasoning. Thus, warning signs pointing to fundamental differences between them and Enlightenment thought, which they were, to some degree, implicitly accepting, seem never to have emerged. Many basic questions were left unanswered. Most persist to this day and can be seen in the contradictions and problems in church-state relations described in Chapter 2.

The key unanswered question was the rival emphases on religious freedom rooted in a desire to protect religion from government versus religious freedom rooted in a desire to protect government from the interference of religion. Although the two parties participating in the coalition occupied the same ground, they were facing in opposite directions. Sanders has drawn the contrasting views well: "Whereas the revivalists tended to favor church-state separation because they feared the intrusion of the state into religious life, and their religious convictions forbade their supporting a religion with which they did not agree, the rationalists acted out of an opposite concern, fear of religious intrusion into political and economic life."[84] The two partners in the coalition were motivated by different concerns. The heirs of the Great Awakening who supported church-state separation were clearly doing so in order to safeguard the freedom of religion to recruit new believers and grow and develop as an influence in society. For example, Howe referred to "the evangelical hope that private conscience and autonomous churches, working together and in freedom, would extend the rule of truth."[85]

The religious dissenters did not, however, support a separation of church and state such as the Enlightenment leaders had in mind. They just assumed that the United States was a Christian nation and that its laws would reflect that fact. "The intent of the evangelicals was not a complete separation of church and state in rationalist terms nor the total privatization of religion. In contrast to Jefferson and Madison, they did not envision or desire a secular state."[86] In point of fact, they advocated a variety of laws aimed at punishing practices that they considered immoral.[87] This explains why the strong supporter of disestablishment in New England, Isaac Backus, saw no problem in advocating laws to enforce Christian morality, such as laws against gambling, card playing, dancing, and theater-going.[88] McLoughlin reported that the dissenting Baptists of New England insisted "that a true government must be a Christian government in which there was a 'sweet harmony' between church and state."[89] In the dissenters' view, the church should be protected from interference by the government but should be free to influence society. The millenarian vision spawned by the Great Awakening encouraged its heirs to enshrine Christian morals in society and even in law, thereby helping to bring on the thousand-year reign of peace and morality. They never saw disestablishment implying that a wall of separation was to be erected between Christianity and the state. Christianity, in their view, was to play a permeating role in society and to be supported by the state.

The Enlightenment thinkers had, of course, a quite different vision. "Believing that religion was a strictly private affair, the rationalists wanted the state, and by implication society at large, separated from the churches' influence."[90] Their fear was, as seen earlier, that religious sects, with their doctrinal differences and narrow moral codes, would seek to use the government to impose their beliefs onto all of society to its detriment. Government — and society — must be protected from the machinations of narrow-minded clerics, so that free, autonomous individuals could map their own course by the light of their observations, reason, and common sense. Disestablishment of religion was their means to achieve this goal.

This was a fundamental difference between the Enlightenment leaders and the religious dissenters, and one that has never been resolved. We saw it in Chapter 2 in the way in which the Supreme Court has taken the two religion clauses of the First Amendment separately and has been unable to resolve the clear tension thereby created between them. Due to the sophisticated church-state theory of the Enlightenment elite and the dissenters' lack of an articulated countertheory with which to engage and challenge it, it is the

Enlightenment's vision that has tended to dominate U.S. thinking and in recent years has led to the strict separation position largely followed by the Supreme Court and U.S. social and political elites.

The dissenters never developed and articulated a clear challenge to the idea that matters of religion, outside a very broad consensus on general morality that is needed for social order, were irrelevant to the political realm. They did not put forward an alternative construct, even though they were clearly operating from the quite different assumption of Christianity that was permeating all of society. Implicitly — by their silence — they accepted the Enlightenment leaders' position. As a result, Mead has accurately observed:

> It is hard to escape the conclusion that each religious group accepted, by implication, the responsibility to teach that its peculiar doctrines, which made it distinct from other sects and gave it its only reason for separate existence, were either irrelevant for the general welfare of the nation-community, or at most, possessed only an indirect and instrumental value for it. It is no wonder that a sense of irrelevance has haunted religious leaders in America ever since.[91]

The crucial differences between Enlightenment thought and the eighteenth-century evangelical dissenters were fundamental, present, and consequential; they were also ignored. They constitute the fault line that ever since has underlain U.S. church-state relations. What happened to this fault line in the nineteenth century is the next part of our story.

THE NINETEENTH CENTURY: THE REESTABLISHMENT OF RELIGION

At the end of the eighteenth century and the beginning of the nineteenth, the future of religion — at least traditional, biblical Christianity — appeared none too bright. The closing days of the eighteenth century had seen the disestablishment of the churches (either as an accomplished fact or shortly to be accomplished). The nineteenth century began with the so-called "infidel" Thomas Jefferson being elected president over the objections of most of the traditional religious leaders of the day. Robert Handy has pointed out that in 1800, less than 10 percent of the population of the United States were church members and the "picture was not very promising" for the churches.[92] However, within in a few decades, all this had changed. Historian Timothy Smith wrote:

> Could Thomas Paine, the free-thinking pamphleteer of the American and French revolutions, have visited Broadway in

1865, he would have been amazed to find that the nation conceived in rational liberty was at last fulfilling its democratic promise in the power of evangelical faith. The emancipating glory of the great awakenings had made Christian liberty, Christian equality and Christian fraternity the passion of the land. The treasured gospel of the elect few passed into the hands of the baptized many. Common grace, not common sense, was the keynote of the age. The Calvinist idea of foreordination, rejected as far as it concerned individuals, was now transferred to a grander object — the manifest destiny of a Christianized America.... Religious doctrines which Paine, in his book *The Age of Reason*, had discarded as the tattered vestment of an outworn aristocracy, became the wedding garb of a democratized church.[93]

The phenomenal growth and vitality of Christianity during the nineteenth century is a story that has often been told and one it is important to keep in mind. During the opening decades of the century, the Second Great Awakening moved through the young nation and "did more to Christianize American society than anything before or since."[94] The growth of the Methodists and Baptists in particular was phenomenal. Methodists grew from only a handful of adherents in the latter part of the eighteenth century to 250,000 by 1820, 500,000 by 1830, and 1 million by 1845. The number of Baptists increased tenfold in the thirty years following the War for Independence; the number of Baptist churches increased fivefold. From 1775 to 1845, in spite of massive population growth, the number of ministers per capita more than tripled, from 1 minister per 1,500 persons to 1 per 500.[95] The exciting, fluid, revolutionary nature of the time in religious terms is shown by the sudden appearance and upsurge of many new religious groups. Nathan Hatch reported that in 1843, as compared to 1775:

Twice the number of denominations competed for adherents, and insurgent groups enjoyed the upper hand. For example, an upstart church such as the Freewill Baptists had almost as many preachers in the early republic as did the Episcopalians. Antimission Baptist preachers far outnumbered both Roman Catholic priests and Lutheran pastors. One new denominational cluster, the Christians and the Disciples of Christ, had an estimated four thousand preachers, equalling the number of clergy serving Presbyterian denominations. The Congregationalists, which had twice the clergy of any other American church in 1775, could not muster one-tenth the preaching force of the Methodists in 1845.[96]

That this vitality and growth was not limited to the early decades of the nineteenth century, but rather continued throughout most of it, was indicated by Smith, who described the major revivals that swept through many of the cities in the middle decades,[97] and by Handy, who noted that the churches continued to grow and expand in the last half of the century.[98]

It is this growing, robust Christianity that gave shape and meaning to the concept of church-state separation and religious freedom as they were actually put into place. This story is crucial for understanding the development of religious freedom in the United States and where U.S. church-state relations are today. In this section I first characterize nineteenth-century Christianity more fully, then explore the de facto establishment of Protestant Christianity which emerged, and last consider the theories underlying nineteenth-century church-state relations.

Nineteenth-Century Christianity

A greater understanding of the nature of nineteenth-century Christianity can be gained by recognizing five features of Christianity as it developed during the Second Great Awakening and the subsequent decades prior to the Civil War.[99] These decades set the pattern for the rest of the century. One feature is that the churches of that era were united in a basic commitment to orthodox, historic Christianity. Once disestablishment had been accomplished, the old division between traditional, established churches and the pietistic, revival-oriented dissenting churches disappeared almost overnight. The new religious division in society was between the revealed religion of historic Christianity and the natural religion of Enlightenment thinking. The terms *infidels* and *infidelity* were coined and widely used by the churches to describe and discredit the Enlightenment leaders and their way of thinking. Mead has pointed out, "Once disestablishment finally came, the realignment of [the Christian] sectarian-pietist with [the Christian] traditionalist against [the Enlightenment] rationalist immediately took place."[100] The Christianity that emerged at the start of the nineteenth century was committed to the basic, traditional doctrines of Christianity as revealed in the Bible. It thereby put itself in the tradition of Puritan Calvinism and the First Great Awakening. There were, of course, certain doctrinal differences among the various Protestant denominations, and in particular, the vigorous, fast-growing Methodists and Baptists differed from an earlier Calvinism in giving a greater emphasis to the "free will" of the individual believer and in not giving as great a primacy to God's sovereignty. However, such differences should not overshadow the fact that on the basic teachings of historic Christianity, they were in agreement.

Paradoxically, a second characteristic of early-nineteenth-century Christianity was its tendency — even while opposing Enlightenment infidels — to be itself influenced by Common Sense rationalism, which also heavily influenced the U.S. heirs of the Enlightenment.[101] This led to a certain blurring of the differences between Christian and Enlightenment thinking. George Marsden wrote that in nineteenth-century society, "Two premises were absolutely fundamental — that God's truth was a single unified order and that all persons of common sense were capable of knowing that truth."[102] Later he went on to point out: "The Bible, of course, revealed the moral law; but the faculty of common sense, which agreed with Scripture, was a universal standard. According to Common Sense philosophy, one can intuitively know the first principles of morality as certainly as one can apprehend other essential aspects of reality."[103] This mindset played down the corrupting influence of original sin on human reasoning and insight and deprecated the need for complex theological or philosophical constructs. Richard Hughes and Leonard Allen have pointed out that both the Enlightenment and nineteenth-century Christianity sought after the *primordium*: the simple truth, unencumbered by the accretions of human traditions and conventions accumulated over the centuries.[104] The Enlightenment looked to nature and sought to find within it truths and guiding principles that were self-evident and discernible to individuals, while Christianity looked to personal religious experience and the New Testament church as recorded in the Bible for the unencumbered truth which was discernible to any sensitive, reasonable individual.

One must be careful not to exaggerate the parallels between nineteenth-century Christianity and Enlightenment thought, for there were fundamental differences. Nevertheless, there is abundant evidence to suggest that the nineteenth-century churches were influenced by the Enlightenment to move in a direction that depreciated tradition and theological formulations and elevated personal, commonsensical insight and understanding. It was the individual who was supreme in matters of religion. These parallels in Enlightenment and Christian thinking probably worked to desensitize the Protestant leaders of the nineteenth century to the dangers and problems posed by the major differences between their practices and assumptions concerning the Christianization of society and the still-prevalent Enlightenment-inspired theories of church-state separation.

Third, Christianity of the early nineteenth century was revivalistic in nature, as the First Great Awakening had been. Its explosive growth and permeation of society relied heavily upon itinerant preachers and lay evangelists who converted sinners and brought them into the churches by way of mass meetings and emotional appeals. Periodic revivals would sweep through whole regions and cities, resulting in an upsurge in church membership and hundreds or thousands of lives changed. It is important to note that revivalism tended to simplify Christianity and to stress intense, emotional experience over a carefully thought out, systematic approach to the Christian faith. However, under the influence of Common Sense thinking, it was thought to be unnecessary anyway. Again, theology suffered.

A fourth feature of early-nineteenth-century Christianity was a millenarian outlook. Here, also, the Second Great Awakening was a direct descendant of the First. Christ's earthly kingdom of peace and morality was seen as being imminent, with the preaching of the word and the gathering in of the saints as its forerunners. For example, Alexander Campbell (leader of the Disciples of Christ, the largest nineteenth-century indigenous Protestant group), in 1830 named his journal the *Millennial Harbinger*.[105] A millenarian outlook can readily be recognized in a statement adopted in 1815 by the Presbyterian General Assembly:

> We have the happiness to live in a day, Brethren, when the Captain of our Salvation, in a distinguishing manner, is marshalling his *mighty host*, and preparing for the moral conquest of the *world*. The grand contest that has been so long conducting, is drawing rapidly towards a termination, that shall be infinitely honourable both to our glorious leaders, and to those who have fought under his banner. Not a finger shall be lifted, nor shall a devout aspiration heave the bosom of a single son or daughter of man, to contribute to the advancement, or plead for the glory of the kingdom of the Messiah, that shall not be met with the smiles and crowned with the blessing of God.[106]

This sort of optimism, which was rooted in the expectation of a soon-to-be-realized era of Christian dominance, morality, and harmony, gave nineteenth-century Christianity much of its drive and vigor, especially in its social and political aspects. I will discuss this in greater detail later in this chapter.

Fifth, the Christianity of the early nineteenth century was strongly democratic or populist in spirit and organization. It was a populist religion of the masses. Hatch has referred to *populist saints* who "were radically innovative in reaching and organizing people" and whose "alienation from the established order matched their aptitude for mobilizing people."[107] These populist saints built new religious movements from the ground up and gathered in phenomenal numbers of new believers. The leaders built on an

> Explosive conjunction of evangelical fervor and popular sovereignty. . . . Christianity was effectively reshaped by ordinary

people who molded it in their own image and threw themselves into expanding its influence. Increasingly, assertive common people wanted their leaders unpretentious, their doctrines self-evident and down-to-earth, their music lively and singable, their churches in local hands. It was this upsurge of democratic hope that characterized so many religious cultures in the early republic and brought Baptists, Methodists, Disciples, and a host of other insurgent groups to the fore. The rise of evangelical Christianity in the early republic is, in some measure, a story of the success of common people in shaping the culture after their own priorities rather than the priorities outlined by gentlemen, such as the Founding Fathers.[108]

The Christianity of the early nineteenth century was a religion of the people, not of the clergy; it found its expression in newly created structures and forms of worship, not in traditional churches and liturgies. It was democratic and populist.

In summary, there was a lack of intellectual pursuits and of a sense of history in the Christianity that developed in the early nineteenth century. It was a commonsense, populist, mass movement based in emotional, experiential revivals, and had little time or patience for theologizing. It was certainly orthodox in its belief in basic, historic Christianity, but it was almost a source of pride not to go beyond this. A "no creed but Christ" emphasis and an attempt to restore a primitive Christianity of the New Testament church led to a loss of a sense of history which — implicitly or explicitly — asserted that between the early church of the New Testament and that day, there was nothing of religious significance from which one needed to learn.[109] One could discover for one's self the truth of Christianity by looking to the Bible and embracing the teachings and patterns for living laid bare there for all to see. A reliance in ordinary persons' common sense over the formulations of theologians and historians emerged. The churches lived in the here and now of revivals, personal morality, and church building.

This lack of interest in intellectual pursuits meant that the Christian attacks on Enlightenment thinking of the eighteenth century — or infidelity as it was labeled — were devoid of intellectual, theological argumentation, even though they were highly successful in a popular sense. Mead wrote:

The most effective argument used against infidelity was moral and political, not theological. It was . . . the vivid assertion that infidel thinking led . . . to personal immorality and social chaos while Christianity was the only sure foundation for good morals and sound government, and that men must choose between these two. The success of this approach in gaining popular support in the attack on infidelity meant that the crucial issue between natural [Enlightenment] religion and revealed [Christian] religion was seldom discussed on the theological level.[110]

Mead concluded that the weaknesses inherent in this approach and the Christian alignment that had supported it "effectively scuttled much of the intellectual structure of Protestantism."[111] Even though the nineteenth century was the "great century" of U.S. Protestantism — when it reached its zenith of cultural penetration and power — it produced no theologian who, one hundred years later, is still read and discussed.[112] Intellectually, theologically it was a barren era.

The De Facto Establishment of Protestantism

In 1888, James Bryce, the perceptive and thoughtful English commentator on U.S. society and government, noted that "the National Government and the State governments do give to Christianity a species of recognition inconsistent with the view that civil government should be absolutely neutral in religious matters." He went on to give examples of ways in which Christianity is acknowledged and supported by the government, such as laws against profanity and "forbidding trade or labours on the Sabbath," as well as Bible reading in "State-supported schools." He then concluded, "The matter may be summed up by saying that Christianity is in fact understood to be, though not the legally established religion, yet the national religion."[113] In the 1830s a Czech visitor to the United States, Francis Grund, observed that

> The religious habits of the Americans form not only the basis of their private and public morals, but have become so thoroughly interwoven with their whole course of legislation that it would be impossible to change them without affecting the very essence of their government. Religion presides over their councils, aids in the execution of the laws, and adds to the dignity of the judges.[114]

It is not an exaggeration to say that in spite of the legal disestablishment of Christianity and the widespread acceptance of the "separation of church and state," throughout the nineteenth century Protestant Christianity was the de facto, quasi-established religion of the United States.

The Christian influence in U.S. society of the nineteenth century included a generalized Christian impact on cultural values and outlooks, but it was more than this. It extended to legally enacted measures and other governmental actions. Handy noted that "as the evangelicals saw it, when persuasion failed, the 'wise and good' might resort to pressure through public opinion and the law."[115] For example, Timothy Smith made reference to "Stephen Colwell, Philadelphia Presbyterian and reformer," who, in 1854, "declared that statutes requiring observance of the Sabbath, proclamations calling the nation to prayer, state laws against blasphemy, court rulings in church cases, oath swearing on the Bible and the maintenance of chaplains in legislative halls and the armed services all proved that evangelical Protestantism was indeed 'legally recognized as the popular religion of the country.'"[116] For example, in 1851 New Orleans was the only city in the United States that allowed omnibuses to operate on Sunday.[117]

The establishment of Protestantism can be seen even more clearly in the public schools as they came into being in the nineteenth century. Smith's careful study led him to conclude: "The school systems of cities both large and small were in fact instruments of an informal Protestant establishment. In a society weighted so heavily toward the Protestant side in wealth and numbers and traditions, little conscious effort was required to make them so."[118] He argued that one of the factors encouraging the creation of a public school system was the general belief that such schools would be rooted in a consensual Protestantism: "An evangelical consensus of faith and ethics had come so to dominate the national culture that a majority of Protestants were now [in 1840] willing to entrust the state with the task of educating children, confident that education would be 'religious' still."[119]

The mind-set that prevailed in regard to the informal establishment of Christianity was clearly summarized and testified to by Bela Bates Edwards, a nineteenth-century seminary professor and editor of several religious periodicals, when he wrote:

> Perfect religious liberty does not imply that government of the country is not a Christian government. The Christian Sabbath is here recognized by the civil authorities in a great variety of forms. Most, if not all, of our constitutions of government proceed on the basis of the truth of the Christian religion. Christianity has been affirmed to be part and parcel of the law of the land. The Bible is practically, however much opposition there may be theoretically, *read* daily, in one form or another, in a large proportion of the common schools supported by the State. There is convincing evidence to show that this real, though indirect, connection between the State and Christianity is every year acquiring additional strength, is attended with less and less of exception and remonstrance.[120]

That this establishment was Protestant and not Catholic is revealed by the strong anti-Catholic statements made by many leading Protestant figures of the era. Typical is the remark of one Daniel Dorchester: "We believe that the Roman Catholic Church is inimical to the best progress of society, and in direct antagonism to the historic religion of the nation — the religion of the Holy Scriptures."[121] In 1831, public financial aid was denied a Catholic orphanage in New York City for its education program even though public aid was being given to similar Protestant agencies.[122] In 1836, a runaway best-seller entitled *Awful Disclosures of the Hotel Dieu Nunnery of Montreal* swept the nation and went through many printings in subsequent years. It was a claimed exposé of Catholic teachings and practices, which "combined concern for undemocratic practices with a discussion of the immorality and lewd activities practiced in the convents."[123] Its extreme popularity, in spite of its wild exaggerations and outright falsehoods, indicates that it accurately reflected the state of public suspicions and fears.

Disestablishment at the end of the eighteenth century had been rooted in a separation — some would say, a strict separation — between church and state. A few years later, an interlocking of church and state had developed that was as strong or stronger than Virginia or New England had had under religious establishment. How did this come to be? Three considerations are important. One is that the de facto establishment of Protestant Christianity was simply a carrying forward of the assumptions and beliefs of eighteenth-century Christians, even those who had supported disestablishment. As seen earlier, Christian dissenters who supported disestablishment never saw their support as resting on a clear separation between church and state. They supported disestablishment as a means to protect religion from the negative influences of government. Disestablishment cut the financial tie between government and religion but left in place the belief that religion — Protestant Christianity, to be exact — was crucial for the health of society and thereby had a mission to improve and uplift its morals. In fact, disestablishment was seen as unleashing the power of Christianity to have a revitalizing, civilizing impact on society. Handy aptly put it this way:

> With varying degrees of articulation and in slightly varying details, Protestant leaders from many denominations operated on the assumption that American civilization would remain a Christian one, and that its Christian (which for them always mean Protestant) character would become even more pronounced. The Christian character of the nation was to be maintained by voluntary means since the patterns of establishment had proved to be unacceptable and inadequate.

Indeed, it was widely asserted that now that civilization in America had been freed of the corruptions of established ecclesiasticism, it could become more Christian than it had ever been. Churches had been disestablished and separated from the state, but the idea of a Christian society certainly had not disappeared. True Christian churches (i.e., evangelical Protestant churches) and Christian civilization with its developing patterns of freedom and democracy would go on from strength to strength together, mutually reinforcing one another.[124]

As noted earlier, even a strong disestablishment leader such as Isaac Backus simply assumed that laws enforcing standards of Christian morality were needed and proper. McLoughlin reported that at the end of the eighteenth century, "The Baptists, while denying the need for religious taxes, nevertheless insisted as much as the Trinitarian or evangelical 'theocrats' like Jedidiah Morse, Timothy Dwight, and later Lyman Beecher, upon the necessity for strict enforcement of the Puritan blue laws and Sabbatarian restrictions."[125] No doubt one factor helping bring together the Christian dissenters and the pro-establishment Christian traditionalists almost immediately after disestablishment was their agreement on the vision of a society Christianized in morals, outlook, and law.

The famous Congregational minister Lyman Beecher fought against disestablishment in his home state of Connecticut, and when it passed in spite of his opposition he called it "as dark a day as ever I saw." Later, however, he admitted he had been wrong and called it the "best thing that ever happened in the State of Connecticut."[126] Why did Beecher experience a total change of opinion? Was he converted to a strict church-state separation position? This was hardly the case. Rather, as Sanders pointed out: "He and others saw that the will of God could mold society just as effectively without legal associations, through the prestige and exertion of the churches."[127]

In short, with disestablishment there came no lessening of the Christian millenarian vision of remolding society in keeping with God's will. The only change was that establishment came to be seen as unnecessary to the goal; the goal, however, remained. The nineteenth-century evangelical Protestant never saw any contradiction between supporting disestablishment on the one hand and promoting a Christian nation by the joint action of church and state on the other.

A second consideration which explains why the de facto establishment of Protestantism developed in the nineteenth century is the sheer size, strength, and vitality of Protestantism. Smith, in the statement quoted earlier, perceptively pointed out concerning the nation's schools that the sheer weight of numbers and social power tended naturally, without any grand strategy, to make the schools profoundly Protestant: "In a society weighted so heavily toward the Protestant side in wealth and numbers and traditions, little conscious effort was required to make them so." Protestant Christianity, with its dramatically increasing numbers and its vigorous institutionalized forms, was at the center of nineteenth-century society and culture. Its adherents dominated strategic points of influence such as the universities, the newspapers and magazines, large business firms, and many public boards and commissions. Its influence in government and society flowed naturally from this dominance.

Another aspect of this second consideration (apart from the sheer size and vitality of the churches) was the development of a host of voluntary associations. These were organizations of Christians, cutting across denominational lines, who came together to promote certain specific causes. Winthrop Hudson described them well:

> At the turn of the century, local societies for the promotion of a host of causes — mission, education, peace, temperance, Sabbath observance, tract distribution, manual labor institutes — had begun to appear, and within a relatively brief period the local, state, and regional societies were replaced by organizations national in scope, such as the American Bible Society (1816), the American Colonization Society (1817), the American Sunday School Union (1824), the American Temperance Society (1826), the American Home Missionary Society (1826), the American Education Society (1827), the American Peace Society (1828), the American Seamen's Friend Society (1828), the American Tract Society (1828), the American Anti-Slavery Society (1833), and others too numerous to mention.[128]

Few historians would dissent from a letter sent to Lyman Beecher in 1830 which claimed: "One thing is becoming daily more evident," namely, "that the grand influence by which the church has been advancing with matchless success and triumph in the last forty years" was due to the "voluntary associations of Christians."[129]

A final consideration explaining the emergence of a Christian establishment is the absence of any thought out theory of church-state relations. There was a lack of theoretical reflection which blinded nineteenth-century Christians to the contradictions present in embracing a religious freedom based on Enlightenment-rooted theories of church-state separation and at the same time supporting various forms of Protestant establishment. They never really analyzed what they were doing. Thus, "the overtones of religious establishment implicit in much of what they did then was not clear to them, because as they developed new ways they did not realize how much of the old patterns they carried over the wall of separation between church and state into their new vision of Christian civilization."[130] This point is important enough that I will develop it more fully in the following section.

The Absence of Church-State Theories

There were no systematic attempts to develop or elaborate a theory of church-state relations to support nineteenth-century church-state developments. The church-state positions developed at the close of the eighteenth century were rooted in certain Enlightenment beliefs concerning the nature of government, religion, and society. These beliefs led to religious freedom of conscience and action being rooted in a separation — even a strict separation or wall of separation — between religion and government. Each had its own sphere of activity and neither was to be (or had need to be) concerned with the other. Society was, thereby, to be spared the divisiveness, intolerance, and pettiness that the Enlightenment associated with revealed religion. Even though the nineteenth century at numerous points in practice contradicted this theory, there were no serious attempts to develop new theoretical underpinnings for the new religion-government relations that developed. Protestant Christianity and government were closely linked in mutually supportive relationships, compromising the religious freedoms of Jews, Catholic, and nonbelievers — or anyone other than evangelical Protestants, for that matter. Separationist theory and establishment practice existed side by side with no felt need to reconcile them.

Two nineteenth-century episodes related to church-state issues vividly illustrate the extent to which Enlightenment theory coexisted with Christian establishment practice. One occurred in 1831 in New York City. The common council voted to fund the educational efforts of a Catholic orphanage. The public was outraged and the elected council members — as do all good politicians when faced with a public outburst — appointed a study commission to come up with recommendations. This commission recommended that the Catholic orphanage not be funded. Its reasoning was based on typically strict separationist rationale straight from eighteenth-century Enlightenment thinking: "If religion be taught in a school, it strips it of one of the characteristics of a common school, as all *religious* and *sectarian* studies have a direct reference to a future state, and *are not necessary* to prepare a child for the mechanical or any other business."[131] Religion was assumed to be a private concern, irrelevant to the worlds of business and commerce. The irony is that this report was made at a time when overtly religious exercises were a regular part of the common school curriculum. The Bible was read daily and exercises stressed that "God always sees you" and that students were to "remember your Creator in the days of your youth" because it was "written in the Holy Bible."[132] Rockne McCarthy and his associates were correct when they wrote: "While a just majority of Protestants in the city would *not* have agreed that religion was irrelevant to everyday life, they were content to support a supposedly neutral, nonreligious, 'secular' argument if it meant that Catholics would be excluded from participating in the common school fund."[133] When the Protestant majority of New York City wished to exclude Catholic schools from receiving public money, the only theoretical arguments they could come up with were those of strict separation Enlightenment thought, even when they did not fit the facts of the case.

An 1854 court case in Maine illustrates the same point. Catholics in Maine had challenged the reading of the King James version of the Bible in the schools. The Maine Supreme Court's decision first gave an eloquent, Enlightenment-inspired defense of religious liberty and church-state separation when it said government "knows no religion" and "regards the Pagan and the Mormon, the Brahmin and the Jew, the Swedenborgian and the Buddhist, the Catholic and the Quaker, as all possessing equal rights."[134] Then, however, the Court went on to make a typically nineteenth-century, "Christian nation" decision. As Loren Beth described it, "After such a ringing pronouncement of the separation doctrine, the court's decision is a study in contrast, for it upheld the reading of the King James Version of the Bible in the Public schools against a Catholic protest! The grounds were that the Bible was used merely for reading instruction, just as a book on Greek mythology might be used."[135] A fiction had to be created in order to reach the result the culture of the day demanded because no theory of religious freedom and church-state separation had been developed other than the one left over from the eighteenth-century Enlightenment, and that theory clearly contradicted the practice. Theory and practice were often in direct conflict in the United States of the nineteenth century, but no one seemed to care as long as the outcome was what the Protestant consensus desired.

Given the blatant disparities between theory and practice that these two examples illustrate, it is surprising that the culturally dominant, self-confident Protestant majority felt no need to develop a theory to support the reigning practice. I suspect that this was the case, first, because the dominant Protestants were never pressed to develop a theoretical justification for their practice. Their position was the overwhelming consensus in society to such a degree that they never were forced into developing a rationale for it. This, however, can only be a part of the story. The explanation for the Protestant failure to develop a church-state theory that was supportive of prevailing practice also lies within the nature of nineteenth-century Protestantism itself. Theoretical thinking, as noted earlier, went against the mood or spirit of the nineteenth-century churches. Common sense and direct experiential knowledge were all that were thought necessary. In large part, the failure to develop new theoretical underpinnings for church-state relations was part of a broader pattern of eschewing theoretical constructs.

As a result, a certain pragmatism replaced more careful, theoretical thinking in nineteenth-century Christians' approach to church-state issues. Mead pointed out, as noted earlier, that at the start of the century, the pietist-traditional Christian alliance won out over the infidels not by responding to their theoretical arguments but by a pragmatic assertion that Christian influence in society and government was essential to good order and safety. Common sense and daily observation made this clear to the nineteenth-century Protestant. Mead concluded that "eminent men who were finally persuaded and began to insist that Christianity 'was absolutely necessary to good Government, liberty and safety' were not necessarily convinced that revealed religion was true and natural religion was false. There is considerable evidence to indicate that they may have been convinced only that the choice was more expedient."[136]

In short, the Enlightenment theoretical explanations and defense of religious freedom based on strict church-state separation were never effectively challenged in the period when Protestant Christians were culturally dominant. They were seeking to create a Christianized nation, while the only thought-out theory of church-state relations in existence denied the very legitimacy of what they were doing. In the twentieth century the consequences of their neglect came home to roost.

THE TWENTIETH CENTURY:
THE SECOND DISESTABLISHMENT

During the twentieth century, a second disestablishment took place: the disestablishment of the nineteenth-century informal de facto Protestant establishment. The decade of the 1920s was pivotal. Essentially, it saw a collapse of the Protestant hegemony in U.S. society. Hudson pointed out that this collapse was not primarily a matter of Protestantism experiencing a precipitous drop in members or other contrasting religious traditions experiencing a surge in members.[137.] Instead, it was a matter of Protestantism losing the position of cultural dominance it had enjoyed throughout the nineteenth century. Suddenly, Protestant Christians and their clergy were no longer dominant figures in the educational, literary, and political worlds. Ahlstrom reported that in the 1920s, "the churches tended to lose their capacity to shape and inform American opinion" and that a "greatly diminished hold on the country's intellectual and literary leadership was another important sign of change."[138] Hudson reported that "religion, which had been one of the principal subjects of serious and intelligent discussion in the literary monthlies and quarterlies, now became conspicuous by its absence, and was usually resurrected only to serve as a target for the satirical shafts of a Mencken."[139] Similarly, he also suggested that

> The most vivid illustration of the change which had taken place is to be found in the colleges and universities. Throughout the nineteenth century the president of almost every important college and university was a clergyman, but by the fourth decade of the twentieth century no clergyman occupied the presidential chair of any leading institution of learning. . . . The predominance of ministers on college faculties disappeared with equal suddenness, and distinctly religious concerns were relegated to the periphery of campus life.[140]

Since World War II most of the laws that gave substance to the Protestant establishment of the nineteenth century have been repealed, are simply ignored, or have been found unconstitutional by the Supreme Court. Sunday closing laws are rare, prohibition was repealed, "no fault" divorce is common, most abortion restrictions have been declared unconstitutional, and Bible reading, prayer, and religious exercises have been removed from the public schools. Furthermore, when was the last time someone was prosecuted for profanity or adultery, even though many states still have statutes on the books outlawing such actions? Indeed, a second disestablishment has taken place.

Why did this occur? Why did a hundred-year tradition of Christian cultural hegemony and a Christian quasi-establishment suddenly disappear in not much more than a single generation? Three reasons suggest themselves. First, and probably most important, the loss of Protestant Christianity's cultural hegemony in the early decades of the twentieth century can be explained as a result of certain weaknesses that had developed in Protestantism. The picture of an internally weakened Protestantism giving up its cultural leadership role by default is more accurate than one of its cultural influence being wrestled away from a strong, vibrant faith. Protestantism in the latter half of the nineteenth century was already showing signs of weakness. It was not, for example, keeping up with the growth of the cities. By 1890, Protestant churches had only half as many members in large cities relative to the total population compared to 1840.[141] As the nineteenth century ended and the twentieth began, the United States was becoming increasingly an urban nation, with the rapidly growing cities becoming key in terms of cultural influence. Protestantism, however, was increasingly becoming the religion of small towns and rural areas. As the nineteenth century waned, the churches also seemed to become increasingly complacent, marked more by accommodation to cultural trends than by a transformation of culture. There was a general secularization or acculturation of the churches. "Instead of the church having Christianized civilization, they [several Protestant leaders] found that the civilization had captured the church."[142] By the 1920s, the vigor and sense of dedication that had marked Protestantism since the Second Great Awakening was clearly dwindling. The Student Volunteer Movement, for example, was a potent force for recruiting missionaries. In 1920, some 2,700 students had volunteered for foreign mission work; in 1928 only 252 did so. Similarly, the peak year for contributing to foreign missions was 1921, and after that year it steadily declined.[143] There were also declines in Sunday school enrollments and many churches were abandoning Sunday evening services due to low attendance.[144] The picture is one of a weakened, complacent Protestantism.

Also weakening the churches was a basic division between those who held to New Theology (a liberal vision of religion that sought to harmonize traditional Christian teachings with higher criticism of the Bible and the Darwinian concept of naturalistic evolution) and those who held firmly to orthodox Christianity (which developed into the fundamentalist movement in the 1920s).[145] The churches turned inward as they struggled with deep and bitter divisions over biblical interpretation and how to react to scientific discoveries that seemed to challenge historic teachings.

A second key factor leading to the disestablishment of Protestantism in the twentieth century was the rise of competing religious groups. Throughout the nineteenth century, U.S. Protestantism had not faced a situation of real pluralism. Rather, it faced few challenges. As the twentieth century got underway, this changed, and by mid-century, it had changed dramatically. As already demonstrated in Chapter 1, Catholics grew in numbers and influence. Changing immigration patterns, which shifted in the late nineteenth and early twentieth centuries, brought in many more immigrants from predominantly Catholic countries, and now the rise in educational levels and social status of second- and third-generation Catholics became crucial in the rise of Catholic influence. After World War II, both the black and the conservative Protestant churches experienced a surge of strength and vitality. Moreover, nonbelievers became more numerous and quicker to speak out openly and publicly.

All through the nineteenth century, Protestant Christianity had been in a position of cultural dominance. The United States was a Christian (that is, Protestant) nation. However, as seen earlier, the Protestants during their period of hegemony never developed a self-conscious theory of church-state relations. This is the third cause of the twentieth century's Protestant disestablishment. As a result, when a Protestantism that was divided and had lost much of its vitality faced a rising pluralism, it had no basis on which to define and defend — either to itself or to the broader society — its political and cultural roles. It emphasized certain specific causes, such as prohibition and the defeat of the Catholic Al Smith for president in 1928, but it did not have an integrated theory to defend and explicate what its social and political role was all about and how it fit into an increasingly pluralistic society. Decline — and even collapse — were the results. A weakened Protestantism simply did not have the intellectual and theoretical tools with which to define or defend its role in society and politics. Even today, those in society and on the Supreme Court who favor religion playing a greater role in the public life of the nation have no consistent theory by which to defend this position and square it with the vision of full religious freedom for all.

Meanwhile, the Enlightenment construct that defined religious freedom in terms of a strict separation between church and state was still alive and well. It had been overwhelmed in the nineteenth century by a Protestant consensus; theory and practice diverged. However, when the Protestant cultural hegemony that had undergirded the practice collapsed, Enlightenment separationism was still there to insist that religion's role in the public sphere was illegitimate. The new cultural elite, with a religion-in-general or outright secular outlook, eagerly seized the assumptions and conclusions of the eighteenth-century wall of separation theory, a theory that had continued to receive lip service in the nineteenth century. The unseen fault line gave way to a major earthquake, and Protestantism and particularistic religion as a whole were largely expelled from the public realm. This resulted the church-state situation — and confusions — described in Chapter 2.

NOTES

1. Sidney E. Mead, *The Lively Experiment* (New York: Harper & Row, 1963), p. 17.

2. Crane Brinton, *Ideas and Men: The Story of Western Thought* (New York: Prentice-Hall, 1950), p. 369.

3. On the Enlightenment in the United States, see Henry A. May, *The Enlightenment in America* (New York: Oxford University Press, 1976), and Donald H. Meyer, *The Democratic Enlightenment* (New York: G. P. Putnam's Sons, 1976).

4. Robert T. Handy, *A Christian America: Protestant Hopes and Historical Realities* (New York: Oxford University Press, 1984), p. 15.

5. Bill Adler, ed., *Presidential Wit from Washington to Johnson* (New York: Trident, 1966), p. 219.

6. Rockne M. McCarthy, James W. Skillen, and William A. Harper, *Disestablishment a Second Time* (Washington, DC: Christian University Press, 1982), p. 32.

7. Thomas E. Buckley, "The Political Theology of Thomas Jefferson," in Merrill D. Peterson and Robert C. Vaughan, eds., *The Virginia Statute for Religious Freedom* (Cambridge: Cambridge University Press, 1988), p. 103 n.64. Buckley's emphasis.

8. Thomas Jefferson, "Republican Notes on Religion and an Act Establishing Religious Freedom, Passed in the Assembly of Virginia, in the Year 1786," in Norman Cousins, ed., *In God We Trust: The Religious Beliefs and Ideas of the American Founding Fathers* (New York: Harper & Brothers, 1958), p. 123.

9. Thomas Jefferson, "Letter to Peter Carr, August 10, 1787," in Cousins, ed., *In God We Trust*, p. 128.

10. Ibid., p. 127.

11. David Little, "Religion and Civil Virtue in America: Jefferson's Statute Reconsidered," in Peterson and Vaughan, eds., *The Virginia Statute*, p. 240. The quoted material is from Jefferson.

12. Thomas Jefferson, "Letter to James Fishback, September 27, 1809," in Cousins, ed., *In God We Trust*, p. 138.

13. Buckley, "The Political Theology of Thomas Jefferson," p. 87.

14. On Scottish Common Sense philosophy and its wide-ranging impact in America, see Sydney E. Ahlstrom, "The Scottish Philosophy and American Theology," *Current History* 24 (1955): pp. 257–272; and May, *The Enlightenment in America*, pp. 337–350.

15. Thomas Jefferson, "Bill for Establishing Religious Freedom," in Robert S. Alley, ed., *The Supreme Court on Church and State* (New York: Oxford University Press, 1988), p. 26.

16. Thomas Jefferson, "Second Inaugural Address," in Joint Congressional Committee on Inaugural Ceremonies, *Inaugural Addresses of the Presidents of the United States* (Washington, DC: Government Printing Office, 1989), pp. 22–23.

17. Jefferson, "Republican Notes on Religion and an Act Establishing Religious Freedom," p. 125.

18. Ibid., p. 123.

19. Quoted in William G. McLoughlin, "Isaac Backus and the Separation of Church and State in America," *American Historical Review* 73 (1968): p. 1402 n.27.

20. David Little, "Thomas Jefferson's Religious Views and Their Influence on the Supreme Court's Interpretation of the First Amendment," *Catholic University Law Review* 26 (1976): p. 61. The quoted material is from Jefferson.

21. Jefferson, "Letter to James Fishback," p. 138.

22. Jefferson, "Republican Notes on Religion and an Act Establishing Religious Freedom," p. 124.

23. Buckley, "The Political Theology of Thomas Jefferson," p. 90.

24. Little, "Thomas Jefferson's Religious Views," p. 64.

25. See Buckley, "The Political Theology of Thomas Jefferson," p. 80; and the discussion in Robert Bellah, *The Broken Covenant: American Civil Religion in Time of Trial* (New York: Seabury, 1975), pp. 1–35.

26. Bellah, *The Broken Covenant*, p. 24.

27. Quoted in May, *The Enlightenment in America*, p. 126. Franklin's emphasis.

28. Benjamin Franklin, *Autobiography*, in Cousins, ed., *In God We Trust*, pp. 25–26. Franklin's emphasis.

29. Quoted in Mead, *The Lively Experiment*, p. 44.

30. Benjamin Franklin, "Letter to Ezra Stiles, March 9, 1790," in Cousins, ed., *In God We Trust*, p. 42.

31. Ibid.

32. Norman Cousins, "James Madison," in Cousins, ed., *In God We Trust*, p. 295.

33.   Ralph L. Ketcham, "James Madison and Religion: A New Hypothesis," in Robert S. Alley, ed., *James Madison on Religious Liberty* (Buffalo, NY: Prometheus, 1985), p. 177.

34.   See May, *The Enlightenment in America*, p. 96.

35.   James Madison, "Memorial and Remonstrance against Religious Assessments," in Robert A. Rutland and William M. E. Rachel, eds., *The Papers of James Madison*, vol. 8 (Chicago: University of Chicago Press, 1973), p. 299. The quoted material is from the Virginia Declaration of Rights of 1776, Article 16.

36.   Ibid., p. 300. Madison's emphasis. The quoted material is from the Virginia Declaration of Rights of 1776, Articles 1 and 16.

37.   *The Federalist* (New York: Modern Library, n.d.), p. 54.

38.   James Madison, "Letter to William Bradford, Jr., January 24, 1774," in Cousins, ed., *In God We Trust*, p. 299.

39.   James Madison, "Letter to the Reverend Adams, 1832," in Cousins, ed., *In God We Trust*, p. 325.

40.   Ketcham, "James Madison and Religion," p. 187.

41.   James Madison, "Letter to Robert Walsh, March 2, 1819," in Cousins, ed., *In God We Trust*, p. 320.

42.   James Madison, "Letter to Frederick Beasley, November 20, 1825," in Cousins, ed., *In God We Trust*, p. 321.

43.   Quoted by Neal Riemer in "Religious Liberty and Creative Breakthrough: The Contributions of Roger Williams and James Madison," in Charles W. Dunn, ed., *Religion in American Politics* (Washington, DC: Congressional Quarterly Press, 1989), p. 22.

44.   Sidney E. Mead, *The Nation with the Soul of a Church* (New York: Harper & Row, 1975), p. 69.

45.   Robert N. Bellah, "Civil Religion in America," *Daedalus*, 96 (Winter 1967): p. 8.

46.   Ibid., p. 3. It is important to note that although the Enlightenment leaders personally favored separation between church and state and saw this as the way to achieve religious freedom, their commitment to church-state separation was a qualified one. First, they believed it was appropriate for government to encourage or acknowledge the broad beliefs that all religious groups possessed in common, since it was on these beliefs that the unity and order of society rested. Jefferson's Declaration of Independence and Madison's "Memorial and Remonstrance," of course, abound in references to the Creator, God, and the "Supreme Lawgiver of the Universe." Second, they sometimes were willing, as was the case with Madison in the congressional debates on the adoption of the First Amendment, to modify their separationist position for tactical political considerations. The First Amendment was even phrased, with Madison's concurrence, so as to assure that states with religious establishments would be able to keep them.

47.   Mark DeWolfe Howe, *The Garden and the Wilderness: Religion and Government in American Constitutional History* (Chicago: University Press, 1965), p. 19.

48.   May, *The Enlightenment in America*, p. 42. For a good historical summary of the events and key personalities of the Great Awakening, see Sydney E. Ahlstrom, *A Religious History of the American People* (New Haven, CT: Yale University Press, 1972), pp. 280–329.

49.   Richard L. Bushman, ed., *The Great Awakening: Documents on the Revival of Religion, 1740–1745* (New York: Atheneum, 1970), p. xi.

50.   David S. Lovejoy, *Religious Enthusiasm in the New World: Heresy to Revolution* (Cambridge, MA: Harvard University Press, 1985), p. 1.

51.   Both quotations are from A. James Reichley, *Religion in American Public Life* (Washington, DC: Brookings, 1985), pp. 72–73.

52. Lovejoy, *Religious Enthusiasm in the New World*, p. 186.

53. Ibid., p. 219.

54. May, *The Enlightenment in America*, p. 55.

55. Lovejoy, *Religious Enthusiasm in the New World*, p. 195.

56. "An Act for Regulating Abuses," from Bushman, ed., *The Great Awakening*, p. 59.

57. On Separatist Baptists in Virginia, see Ahlstrom, *A Religious History*, pp. 318–320.

58. Ibid., p. 236.

59. Sidney E. Mead, *The Old Religion in the Brave New World* (Berkeley: University of California Press, 1977), p. 50.

60. Gerhard T. Alexis, "Jonathan Edwards and the Theocratic Ideal," *Church History* 35 (1966): p. 329.

61. One must be careful not to overstate Edwards' pietism. It was a strong, important tendency, not a fixed, thoroughgoing characteristic. Edwards saw his New England society as "a city set on a hill" and as the object of God's special blessings and providential care. His pietism was not completely individualistic in nature. Harry Stout has shown that especially at times of crisis, such as when New England was engaged in fighting against the French, Edwards invoked the picture of a God who was deeply concerned with the affairs of nations. However, this is not the same as saying that Edwards or other Great Awakening leaders had a self-conscious, well worked out concept of Christian engagement with social and governmental affairs. See Harry Stout, "The Puritans and Edwards," in Nathan O. Hatch and Harry S. Stout, eds., *Jonathan Edwards and the American Experience* (New York: Oxford University Press, 1988), pp. 142–159.

62. Herbert Wallace Schneider, *The Puritan Mind* (London: Constable and Company, 1931), p. 106.

63. Alan Heimert, *Religion and the American Mind from the Great Awakening to the Revolution* (Cambridge, MA: Harvard University Press, 1966), p. 15. The quoted material is from one of Edwards' sermons.

64. Mead, *The Old Religion in the Brave New World*, p. 54.

65. H. Richard Niebuhr, *The Kingdom of God in America* (Hamden, CT: Shoe String Press, 1956; originally published by Harper & Brothers, 1935), p. 141. The same basic point has been made by Heimert in *Religion and the American Mind*, pp. 61–84.

66. Niebuhr, *The Kingdom of God in America*, p. 143.

67. Heimert, *Religion and the American Mind*, p. 64.

68. Mead, *The Lively Experiment*, p. 35. Similarly, Thomas Sanders wrote, "One could hardly imagine a more unlikely coalition than revivalists and rationalists." Thomas G. Sanders, *Protestant Concepts of Church and State* (New York: Holt, Rinehart and Winston, 1964), p. 187.

69. Edwin Scott Gaustad, *The Great Awakening in New England* (Gloucester, MA: Peter Smith, 1965), pp. 2–3.

70. Robert N. Bellah, Richard Madsen, William M. Sullivan, Ann Swidler, and Steven M. Tipton, *Habits of the Heart: Individualism and Commitment in American Life* (New York: Harper & Row, 1985), pp. 221–222.

71. See McLoughlin, "Isaac Backus"; and William G. McLoughlin, *Isaac Backus and the American Pietistic Tradition* (Boston: Little, Brown, 1967).

72. Thomas E. Buckley, *Church and State in Revolutionary Virginia, 1776–1787* (Charlottesville: University Press of Virginia, 1977), p. 175.

73. Rhys Isaac, "'The Rage of Malice of the Old Serpent Devil': The Dissenters and the Making and Remaking of the Virginia Statute for Religious Freedom," in Peterson and Vaughan, eds., *The Virginia Statute for Religious Freedom*, p. 139.

74. McLoughlin, "Isaac Backus," p. 1405.
75. Buckley, *Church and State in Revolutionary Virginia*, p. 178.
76. Ibid., p. 180.
77. Mead, *The Lively Experiment*, pp. 55–56.
78. Sanders, *Protestant Concepts of Church and State*, p. 189.
79. See Ahlstrom, "The Scottish Philosophy and American Theology."
80. Alan Heimert and Perry Miller, eds., *The Great Awakening: Documents Illustrating the Crisis and Its Consequences* (Indianapolis, IN: Bobbs-Merrill, 1967), p. xliii.
81. McLoughlin, *Isaac Backus and the Pietistic Tradition*, p. 187.
82. Mead, *The Lively Experiment*, pp. 61–62.
83. Isaac, "'The Rage of Malice of the Old Serpent Devil,'" p. 161.
84. Sanders, *Protestant Concepts of Church and State*, p. 186. This contrast is also clearly drawn by Buckley, *Church and State in Revolutionary Virginia*, pp. 180–182; and Howe, *The Garden and the Wilderness*, pp. 18–20.
85. Howe, *The Garden and the Wilderness*, p. 19.
86. Buckley, *Church and State in Revolutionary Virginia*, p. 180.
87. Ibid., p. 181.
88. See McLoughlin, "Isaac Backus," pp. 1407–1413.
89. Ibid., p. 1408.
90. Buckley, *Church and State in Revolutionary Virginia*, p. 180.
91. Mead, *The Lively Experiment*, p. 66.
92. Handy, *A Christian America*, pp. 24–25.
93. Timothy L. Smith, *Revivalism and Social Reform in Mid-Nineteenth-Century America* (New York: Abingdon, 1957), p. 7.
94. Nathan O. Hatch, "The Democratization of Christianity and the Character of American Politics," in Mark A. Noll, ed., *Religion and American Politics* (New York: Oxford University Press, 1990), p. 97.
95. These figures are from Nathan O. Hatch, "The Democratization of Christianity and the Character of American Politics," pp. 97–98; and Nathan O. Hatch, *The Democratization of American Christianity* (New Haven, CT: Yale University Press, 1989), pp. 4, 220.
96. Hatch, *Democratization of American Christianity*, p. 4.
97. Smith, *Revivalism and Social Reform*.
98. See Handy, *A Christian America*, p. 69.
99. For general information on the Second Great Awakening, see Ahlstrom, *A Religious History of the American People*, pp. 415–454.
100. Mead, *The Lively Experiment*, p. 52.
101. Many scholars have noted this tendency. See, for example, Ahlstrom, "The Scottish Philosophy and American Theology," and Theodore Dwight Bozeman, *Protestants in an Age of Science* (Chapel Hill: University of North Carolina Press, 1977).
102. George M. Marsden, *Fundamentalism and American Culture* (New York: Oxford University Press, 1980), p. 14.
103. Ibid., p. 15.
104. Richard T. Hughes and C. Leonard Allen, *Illusions of Innocence: Protestant Primitivism in America, 1630–1875* (Chicago: University of Chicago Press, 1988), pp. 13–22.
105. Handy, *A Christian America*, p. 30.
106. Quoted in ibid., p. 30.
107. Hatch, "The Democratization of Christianity", pp. 98–99.
108. Ibid., p. 95.
109. This point was made by Mead in *The Lively Experiment*, pp. 108–113.
110. Ibid., pp. 52–53.

111. Ibid., p. 54.

112. The term *the great century*, to describe the vigor and strength of nineteenth-century U.S. Christianity, was used in a chapter title by Winthrop S. Hudson in *The Great Tradition of the American Churches* (New York: Harper & Brothers, 1953), p. 80.

113. James Bryce, *The American Commonwealth*, rev. ed., vol. 2 (New York: Macmillan, 1911), pp. 769–770.

114. Quoted in Hudson, *The Great Tradition of the American Churches*, p. 39.

115. Handy, *A Christian America*, p. 50.

116. Smith, *Revivalism and Social Reform*, p. 34.

117. Ibid., p. 37.

118. Timothy L. Smith, "Religion, Schools, and the Community of Values," in Carol Friedley Griffith, ed., *Christianity and Politics: Catholic and Protestant Perspectives* (Washington, DC: Ethics and Public Policy Center, 1981), p. 99.

119. Timothy L. Smith, "Protestant Schooling and American Nationality, 1800–1850," *Journal of American History* 53 (1966–67): p. 687.

120. Quoted in Handy, *A Christian America*, p. 49. Edwards' emphasis.

121. Quoted in Handy, *A Christian America*, p. 89.

122. See McCarthy, Skillen, and Harper, *Disestablishment a Second Time*, pp. 60–65.

123. Barbara Welter, "From Maria Monk to Paul Blanshard: A Century of Protestant Anti-Catholicism," in Robert N. Bellah and Frederick E. Greenspahn, eds., *Uncivil Religion: Interreligious Hostility in America* (New York: Crossroad, 1987), p. 55.

124. Handy, *A Christian America*, p. 27.

125. McLoughlin, *Isaac Backus and the American Pietistic Tradition*, p. 212.

126. Quoted in Sander, *Protestant Concepts of Church and State*, p. 249.

127. Ibid.

128. Hudson, *The Great Tradition of the American Churches*, p. 72.

129. Quoted in Ibid.

130. Handy, *A Christian America*, p. 35.

131. Quoted in W. M. Oland Bourne, *History of the Public School Society of the City of New York* (New York: W. M. Wood and Co., 1870), p. 136. The commission's emphasis. Cited in McCarthy, Skillen, and Harper, *Disestablishment a Second Time*, p. 64. For a summary account of this controversy, see pp. 60–65.

132. These are quotations from exercises contained in a teacher's manual put out by the board of trustees of the New York Public School Society. See McCarthy, Skillen, and Harper, *Disestablishment a Second Time*, p. 65.

133. Ibid., p. 64. Authors' emphasis.

134. Quoted in Loren Beth, *The American Theory of Church and State* (Gainesville: University of Florida Press, 1958), p. 84. For an account of this incident, see pp. 84–85.

135. Ibid., p. 84.

136. Mead, *The Lively Experiment*, p. 53.

137. Winthrop Hudson, "The Passing of the Protestant Era in America," in John F. Wilson and Donald L. Drakeman, eds., *Church and State in American History*, 2d ed. (Boston: Beacon, 1987), p. 148.

138. Ahlstrom, *A Religious History of the American People*, p. 915.

139. Hudson, *The Great Tradition of the American Churches*, p. 196.

140. Ibid., p. 197. On this trend also see George Marsden and Bradley Longfield, eds., *The Secularization of the Academy* (New York: Oxford University Press, 1992).

141. Hudson, *The Great Tradition of the American Churches*, p. 199.

142. Handy, *A Christian America*, p. 182.

143. On these figures, see ibid., p. 174.

144. Ibid.

145. On the division between "New Theology," or theological liberalism, and orthodoxy, or fundamentalism, in Protestantism, see Ahlstrom, *A Religious History of the American People*, pp. 905–915; Hudson, *The Great Tradition of the American Churches*, pp. 160–169; and Marsden, *Fundamentalism and American Culture*, pp. 17–26.

4

Back to Basics: The Pluralist Understanding of Society

To develop a new perspective on church-state issues it is necessary to go back to the basics of the nature and makeup of society. Only then can one ask how religion and government relate to society and what relationship they have — and should have — to each other. If church-state relations are to bear fruit in full religious freedom in a truly free society, they must be rooted in a theoretically sound understanding of the nature of society and of the roles that religion and government play in it.

Pluralism in a normative, structural sense has a rich history in political and social thought and offers a helpful way of understanding the basics of society, government, and religion.[1] Especially among a wide range of European Christian theorists, pluralism has served as a basis for thinking about society and government and about the role of religion in relationship to them. These theorists have often used pluralism as a basis for constructing political theories in response to or in contrast to both the individualism of eighteenth-century liberal Enlightenment thought and the collectivism of nineteenth- and twentieth-century socialist and nationalist thought. It is found in the Roman Catholic concept of subsidiarity and its underpinnings as they have been developed and articulated by the Catholic Church and a variety of continental European thinkers. However, it is not simply a Catholic perspective. Dutch Protestants have built a political theory on a pluralist vision of society, the early twentieth century saw a school of pluralism develop in the Church of England, and the Christian Democratic parties of Western Europe are rooted in a pluralist view of society.

However, this rich vein of thought, which has done much to shape thinking about church and state and other sociopolitical relations in most of the liberal democracies of Western Europe, has received little systematic attention in the United States and has done little to shape U.S. church-state views. Political scientist Henry Kariel once noted,

"In the United States, no systematic theoretical defense of political pluralism has ever been formulated."[2] Nevertheless, I am convinced that pluralism has much to offer the U.S. scene as well as the potential to lead us out of the blind alleys into which U.S. church-state relations have wandered.

This chapter lays the groundwork for using pluralism as a means to enlighten U.S. church-state issues by looking carefully at pluralism as it has been developed and conceived by a wide range of thinkers.[3] It does so, first, by defining and developing the concept of pluralism itself, and then by considering how religion and government fit into the pluralist understanding of society.

PLURALISM

Political pluralism is anything but a unified, neatly packaged theoretical construct. It contains thinkers who are usually perceived as coming from antagonistic, mutually exclusive traditions. It includes popes and Catholic social philosophers such as Jacques Maritain (1882–1973) and Yves Simon (1903–1961). However, it also includes Abraham Kuyper (1837–1920), a Dutch Protestant in the strict Calvinist tradition. The Englishman John N. Figgis (1866–1919) was an Anglican clergyman who also espoused a version of political pluralism and heavily influenced the socialist G. D. H. Cole and others. As already mentioned, today's Christian Democratic parties are rooted in a pluralist interpretation of government and society. This breadth of political pluralism demonstrates its wide influence and suggests that it may provide valuable insights into today's church-state issues; it does not make its description and analysis easy. Especially in their theological and philosophical underpinnings, the various pluralist theorists and the national and religious traditions that they represent exhibit significant differences. Nevertheless, wide reading in the various strains within pluralism and commentaries on them reveals a surprisingly large amount of common ground. If one focuses on the more concrete observations concerning society and government and conclusions to be drawn from them, the areas of agreement are larger than those of disagreement.

In this section of the chapter I first need to establish the ground rules, so to speak, of the following discussion by defining several key terms. Then I consider two fundamental beliefs or perspectives pluralists hold in common.

Definitions

There are five key terms which, once clarified, will be helpful in considering the pluralist vision of government and church in society.

The concepts contained in the definitions that I present here for these five terms reappear frequently in the writings of a wide variety of pluralist thinkers, but the diverse traditions understandably use a wondrous variety of terms to denote these concepts. Thus, to establish some common ground I define five terms that are fundamental to pluralist thought.[4] More ought not to be made of these definitions than I intend. They are working definitions, designed to do no more than establish a common mode of discourse in order to explicate and understand pluralist thought.

The first, and perhaps most basic, is *community*. A community is a collectivity of people bound together by shared, affective ties that lead them to identify themselves as members of a distinct collectivity. Communities are groupings that are not called into being by a formal, legal agreement for a specific, instrumental purpose. Instead, they grow or develop much as does a living tree. They are based on shared traditions and common backgrounds, out of which feelings of identity with and affection for the collectivity or grouping — a sense of community — develop un-self-consciously and gradually. Usually, but not always, community ties develop in a person at a young age as part of the socialization process and are retained throughout his or her lifetime. Examples of communities include family, kinship, ethnic, religious, linguistic, and neighborhood or village groupings.

A second key term is that of *nation*, which is a particular type of community. A nation is a community that includes all or almost all the persons living in a defined geographic area and that aspires to have its own state or government. Nations are rooted in affective feelings, shared traditions, and self-identification as a distinct people. To qualify as a nation, there also has to be a longing or desire for statehood. I will define the state or government shortly, but it, of course, has reference to an independent political existence. One should consider, for example, the Flemish and the Walloons in Belgium as separate communities based on distinct languages and traditions, but not as separate nations, since there is no significant aspiration for independent statehood. The Kurds, who are presently included within several states, would be considered a nation since they possess shared traditions, loyalties, and feelings of identity, plus the aspiration for statehood. This distinction between nation and community means that normally communities are groupings found within the larger, more inclusive nation and — where a nation is also a state — within the state.

Association is a third term in need of definition. An association is a collectivity of persons formally, intentionally organized for the achievement of one or more specific, chosen purposes. There are two key elements in this definition that distinguish between associations and communities. First, an association is a formal organization: it has a formal structure, resulting from a self-conscious decision and usually provided for in an express, written form. Second, associations are instrumental: they are created in order to achieve certain self-conscious goals. Businesses, lobbying organizations, trade unions, and universities are all examples of associations. In contrast, communities rest on feelings of identity and affection that evolve or develop, usually in an un-self-conscious manner. Communities are organic, un-self-conscious, and affective; associations are purposeful, self-conscious, and goal-oriented or instrumental.

Communities and associations may or may not coincide. Some communities are also associations, but there can also be associations that are not communities and communities that are not associations. Take the example of a neighborhood in a large city. A neighborhood should be considered a community if it is united by feelings of solidarity and pride, which may be based on common ethnic and religious roots or long-term relationships built up over years of living nearby and sharing experiences. However, that neighborhood might very well not be an association if there is no formal organization but only ties of friendship, sharing, and common experiences. On the other hand, a neighborhood might be an association as well as a community. In this case, at some point the neighborhood would have established a formal neighborhood organization, adopting bylaws, electing officers, and setting goals. One might also find a neighborhood association without a community, as when some residents or perhaps an outside organizer forms a neighborhood organization to work for certain objectives in the absence of any real sense of community solidarity and pride. In such a situation the leaders of the association might hope that in time, a sense of community may develop. I use the terms *structure* or *social structure* to refer to both communities and associations without distinguishing between them.

A fourth term needing to be defined is the *state* or *government*. A state or a government — I use the terms interchangeably — is to a nation what an association is to a community. A state is a formal, purposeful organization which exercises authority over all persons in a defined geographic area on a continuing basis. Three key facets of this definition are (1) the formal, purposeful nature of the state, (2) its exercise of authority, and (3) its doing so among all persons in a geographic area and on a continuing basis. The government is a formal structure, established for certain articulated or widely understood purposes. Thus, it is instrumental or goal-oriented.

The government also exercises authority; that is, it has the right to command the obedience of its citizens and they have an obligation to obey it. The source of this authority can be located in God's will for human society, which is what most Christians do, or in learned patterns of behavior and certain traditions, as most secularists would. In either case, authority is crucial to the state. Governmental authority is backed up by coercion, but distinguishable from it. The state has at its disposal coercive instruments such as imprisonment and fines, but if that were the distinguishing mark of the state, it would be no different than a thief robbing a victim at knife-point. The state is defined by the relationship of authority between government and governed which leads to obedience being willingly given out of a sense of rightness and obligation. In the same breath, one must emphasize that authority is, by its very nature, limited. Whether looked at in a factual, empirical sense or in a normative fashion, government's authority is hardly limitless. It has boundaries beyond which it can not and should not go. This is a crucial, central contention of pluralism, as will be seen later.

Moreover, government exercises its authority on a continuing basis and over all persons in a certain geographic area. The state's authority is not episodic — of a temporary, hit-and-miss nature — but rather is ongoing. Furthermore, its authority is limited, but in a geographic sense, it is inclusive. Although there are other distinctions between associations and government, this distinguishes them most clearly. Associations usually possess authority, but that authority is limited by their membership, while a government or state exercises authority over all persons in a geographic area.

As with associations and communities, a government and a nation may coincide, or there can be a nation that is not a state or a state that is not a nation. The Kurds in the Middle East are a clear example of a nation that presently is not a state. The United States today is an example of a nation-state, where a single state and a single nation coincide. However, in 1789 the United States was a state with, at best, a poorly developed sense of nationhood. Some African governments today, such as Nigeria, are states with several competing nations within them due to tribal divisions.

A final term in need of definition is that of a *polity*, which is a nation and its government or state taken together. Another term I use synonymously with *polity* is the *body politic*. Both terms bring together the formal, purposeful concept of the state and the organic, affective concept of the nation. Finally, I should note that I use the term *society* in its commonsense, nontechnical, dictionary meaning of "a community, nation, or broad grouping of people having common traditions, institutions, and collective activities and interests."[5] When a more specific meaning is called for, I will use one of the previous five more precisely defined terms.

These terms help define the terrain we will be traversing. Equipped with them, we are now in a position to consider and understand how pluralists look at society and the body politic.

The Presence and Vital Role of Communities and Associations in the Polity

In spite of the diverse traditions out of which pluralist thinkers have come, all are agreed that communities and associations are both intrinsic and indispensable to modern societies. By nature every polity or society is composed of a host of communities and associations, and without them, society would disintegrate and the individual would be left alone and vulnerable. Typically, pluralists see this emphasis on social structures as a corrective both to an individualism that atomizes society and leaves the individual alone in a mass of other individuals and to a collectivism that submerges the freedom of persons in the anonymity of the polity as a whole. In making these points, pluralists start out with a concept usually called personalism and from there move to the structural nature of society.

Personalism

Fundamental to pluralist thinking is personalism, which pluralists see as distinguishing their thought from that of the individualism of the eighteenth-century liberal Enlightenment. Pluralists see personalism, first, as being holistic, as taking into account the whole person in his or her material, social, spiritual, and other facets. Individualism, in contrast, is seen as only focusing on the material facet of human existence to the exclusion of other equally important facets. R. E. M. Irving, in describing the political theory of the Christian Democratic parties of Western Europe, wrote, "The essence of personalism is its strong emphasis on the importance of the development of *all* dimensions of human personality, social as well as individual and spiritual as well as material."[6] The French Catholic theorist, Jacques Maritain, saw individuality as a purely material concept, based on an unconnected "fragment of a species."[7] Abraham Kuyper, a Dutch Protestant theologian, party leader, and prime minister, condemned the individualism of the French Revolution and its liberalism for reducing human beings to the material, "earthly things," creating "a sphere of lower pressures in which money was the standard of value, and everything was sacrificed for money."[8] As historian Dirk Jellema put it, Kuyper believed, "Christianity, in contrast [to the French Revolution and the Enlightenment], means that people must be treated as *persons* rather than as 'machines of flesh.'"[9]

This first aspect of personalism leads to a second: an emphasis on the importance of social relations. Irving put it clearly: "Personalism differs from liberalism in two important respects: first, in its emphasis on the spiritual side of life[,] . . . and secondly, in its contention that the individual can only reach fulfillment within the 'natural social structures' of society, such as the family, the community or the place of work."[10] The link between an emphasis on persons or personality and men and women as social beings is made explicitly by Maritain: "By the very fact that each of us is a person and expresses himself to himself, each of us requires communication with *other* and *the others* in the order of knowledge and love."[11] The Belgian Christian Democratic official Paul Dabin wrote: "A fundamental element of Christian-Democratic political philosophy is 'communitarian personalism.' ... According to communitarian personalism, human beings, conceived as persons, and society, conceived as a community of persons, are bound up together and cannot be separated, not even conceptually."[12] Elsewhere he noted that "the human being as a person and the society as a community of people belong together and are conceptually indivisible."[13] Jellema described Kuyper's social program and then concluded, "Basic to it is the insistence on man as a *person* who can find true freedom only in *organic* social ties."[14] Pluralists see personalism — in contrast to individualism — as stressing the whole person in all of his or her facets, and persons, as necessary, integral parts of a broader human society.

The Intrinsic Nature of Communities and Associations

Pluralists believe that since persons in their deepest nature are social beings, society necessarily and naturally is composed of a variety of social structures. This is a basic, observable fact. Communities, and sometimes associations as well, are seen by pluralists as a necessary expression of the inherent, created nature of human beings and as part of the warp and woof of society. This perspective on human beings and society all pluralists return to again and again.

More specifically, pluralists frequently stress three interrelated perspectives. One of these perspectives views society as a living, naturally arising network of persons based on their nature as social beings in need of each other, and not as a mere collection of individuals coming together for mutual convenience or advantage. A society has the character of a community or nation, not an association. Kuyper said it well when he wrote "that our national society is . . . 'not a heap of souls on a piece of ground,' but rather a God-willed *community*, a living, human organism."[15] In another place he stated: "Human life . . . is so constituted that the individual can exist only within the group and can come to full expression only in community."[16]

The same perspective as that of Kuyper is found in almost all pluralist thinkers, who typically see society emerging out of the social nature of humankind. Human beings were made to live in community with other human beings, and it is only in conjunction with others that persons can attain their full meaning as persons. "Man is a social person, who achieves his perfection only in society," as the Catholic writer R. E. Malcahy put it.[17] Maritain went back to Aristotle's famous contention that human beings are political animals in order to make this same point in greater detail:

> Here the question is not only of his material needs, of bread, clothes and shelter, for which man requires the help of his fellowmen, but also, and above all, of the help which he ought to be given to do the work of reason and virtue, which responds to the specific feature of his being. To reach a certain degree of elevation in knowledge as well as a certain degree of perfection in moral life, man needs an education and the help of other men. In this sense, Aristotle's statement that man is by nature a political animal holds with great exactitude: man is a political animal because he is a rational animal, because reason requires development through character training, education and the cooperation of other men, and because society is thus indispensable to the accomplishment of human dignity.[18]

Political scientist David Koyzis, after a lengthy comparative study of Herman Dooyeweerd (1894–1977), a Dutch Calvinist political philosopher, and Yves Simon, a Catholic social theorist, concluded that "there is at least one issue on which Dooyeweerd and Simon are at one. This is the fact that man is a social being, i.e., a creature meant for life in community and in association with his fellow man."[19]

The social nature of human beings does not lead pluralists to see society as composed of an undifferentiated mass of men and women joined in a homogenized society. This would be the German Volk of Naziism. Instead, a second perspective that pluralists consistently hold is that of society by its very nature consisting of a plurality of distinct social structures. Franz Mueller traced this perspective back to Thomas Aquinas:

> It is the nature of the [Thomistic] organismic analogy that society is not regarded as a homogeneous mass but as an articulated whole. Accordingly, the individual members are conceived as being incorporated into the large social bodies not directly, but through the medium of intermediate associations. Therefore, society is, properly speaking, not a mere aggregation of single human beings, but an ordered unity of associations, more specifically, a system of social organizations disposed organically in ranks and orders, each subordinate to the one above it.[20]

Maritain made a similar point:

> But the body politic also contains in its superior unity the
> family units, whose essential rights and freedoms are anterior
> to itself, and a multiplicity of other particular societies which
> proceed from the free initiative of citizens and should be as
> autonomous as possible. Such is the element of pluralism
> inherent in every truly political society. Family, economic,
> cultural, educational, religious life matter as much as does
> political life to the very existence and prosperity of the body
> politic.[21]

Protestant pluralists have expressed similar points of view. The
Anglican pluralist John Figgis said in regard to society: "What do we
find as a fact? Not, surely, a sandheap of individuals, all equal and
undifferentiated, unrelated except to the State, but an ascending
hierarchy of groups, family, school, town, county, union, Church,
&c., &c."[22] He also wrote:

> Now the State did not create the family, nor did it create the
> Churches; nor even in any real sense can it be said to have
> created the club or the trade unions; nor in the Middle Ages
> the guild or the religious order, hardly even the universities or
> the colleges within the universities: they have all arisen out of
> the natural associative instincts of mankind, and should all be
> treated by the supreme authority as having a life original and
> guaranteed.[23]

Henry Magid has described Figgis' position in this way: "Man, whose
personality is social, develops that personality in numerous groups
that cannot be said to be derived from the state and yet are obviously
not private."[24] Jellema summarized Kuyper's view in this way:
"Society is made up of social groups, related organically, rather than
of individuals related impersonally. These groups, or spheres,
received their sovereignty from God, not from the state. They are
prior to the state."[25] Concerning the theory of today's Christian
Democratic parties, Irving stated that "the 'natural social structures,' such as trade unions, family associations and regional bodies,
must be given full rein to play their part in this new-style democracy,
because they are the vehicle through which the individual can
develop his full personality."[26]

The key point made by all these pluralists is that these social
structures are an intrinsic part of human society, prior to and in a
real sense independent of the state. This independence will be more
fully discussed shortly, but here it is important to note that in
pluralist thought, social structures are not something optional,

created by a conscious act of will of humankind or government. Rather, they are a natural, necessary, and intrinsic fact of human existence.

Pluralists stress not only the social nature of humankind and the necessary, intrinsic nature of social structures within the polity, but, as a third perspective, they also view social structures as playing a crucial role in promoting a stable, viable society. Running through pluralist thought is the idea that communities and associations are crucial for a healthy polity and that they offer an alternative to the individualism of a laissez-faire liberalism and the collectivism of socialism and nationalism. Henry Kariel, thinking largely in terms of English pluralists such as Figgis, summarized it well: "Poised between the individual and the state, a newly vindicated cluster of groups might enable man to develop his true potentialities, to find himself, and to be himself. Intermediary associations would provide a sense of community while shielding their members against undue state power."[27] Magid pointed out that Figgis saw communities as crucial in being able to give "the individual the opportunity for self-development." Magid then went on to note that Figgis believed "that it is chiefly in groups such as churches that individuals realize themselves."[28] In the contemporary U.S. context, Peter Berger and Richard John Neuhaus have argued that four "mediating structures," as they term them — the family, church, neighborhood, and voluntary association — are essential for a vital democratic society and can be useful in providing an effective means to achieve public policy goals in U.S. society.[29]

In summary, pluralist thought emphasizes the social nature of human beings, the necessary, intrinsic nature of communities and associations in society, and the vital contributions communities and associations make to society.

Quasi-Sovereign Social Structures

In addition to pluralists' emphasis on the presence and vital role of communities and associations in the polity, there is a second element that is fundamental to their thinking. This element, however, is hard to uncover and to grasp with a certainty which enables its exact contours to be laid out. For some pluralists it is more implicit than explicit; others state it boldly but explicate it poorly. For all, however, it is key to understanding pluralism's view of government and its role in society.

The Basic Concept

Pluralism asserts the quasi-sovereignty or quasi-autonomy of society's various communities and associations in their respective realms or spheres of human endeavor.[30] This quasi-sovereignty is theirs as a necessary, inalienable right; they do not possess it at the sufferance of the state or some other institution. Two separable points are contained in this statement: first, that each of society's various social structures has a sphere or area of activity and responsibility in which it possesses a qualified sovereignty or freedom to develop and act; and, second, that social structures possess these spheres in which they possess a quasi-sovereignty as an inherent, God-ordained possession. Thus families have a natural realm of competence in which they are free or sovereign — within certain limits — to function. They exercise this sovereignty not at the sufferance of government, but as a right. Just as no government or constitution creates the dignity of the human being, but can only recognize and make allowance for what the Creator implanted in all persons, so also the family's right to raise children in a certain manner and to establish certain wife-husband relationships is inherent, God-given, and inalienable. A totalitarian state may seek to abrogate such rights and a democratic state may honor them, but in either case, they exist, because they are inherent, natural, and inalienable, not made or created by human beings. What persons have not given, persons cannot take away.

This perspective is clearly seen in Dutch Protestant thinkers such as Kuyper:

> In a Calvinist sense we understand hereby, that the family, the business, science, art and so forth are all social spheres, which do not owe their existence to the state, and which do not derive the law of their life from the superiority of the state, but obey a high authority within their own bosom; an authority which rules, by the grace of God, just as the sovereignty of the state does.
> . . .
> These different developments of social life have *nothing above themselves but God[;]* . . . the State cannot intrude here, and has nothing to command in their domain.[31]

Later Kuyper went on to explain that "each of these spheres or corporations is conscious of the power of exclusive independent judgment and authoritative action, within its proper sphere of operation."[32]

This is Kuyper's concept of *sphere sovereignty*, which asserted there are a variety of realms or spheres within each of which there exists social structures that exercise a sovereign power. A U.S. follower of Kuyper, theologian Henry Meeter, further explicated this position:

> As each of these spheres has been authorized and commissioned by God to carry on its specific task, it has therefore

sovereign rights within its own domain. No outside influence, whether of State or Church or other social unit, may interfere with the proper pursuance of this task by the group itself, without thereby infringing upon the authority which God has delegated to that group. This is what is known as the sovereignty of the spheres of society.[33]

The spheres Kuyper had in mind included "in the narrow sense, such things as family, town, province, church, school, occupational groups; and, in the wider sense, such things as science, literature, art, ideology."[34]

A present-day official in the Dutch Christian Democratic Party, Arie Oostlander, neatly summarized this concept of quasi-sovereign spheres: "Every sphere of life has its own objective, its own character, its own autonomy and its own rights. Precisely this is what is meant by the idea of a 'pluralist society.'"[35]

The concept of quasi-sovereign realms or spheres can be found in all forms of pluralist thought. It is present in the Catholic doctrine of subsidiarity, which is rooted in the concept of structures in society exercising a quasi-autonomy or quasi-sovereignty. Pope Pius XI articulated the principle of subsidiarity in his 1931 encyclical, *Quadragesimo Anno*:

> The state should therefore leave to smaller groups the settlement of business of minor importance, which otherwise would greatly distract it; it will thus carry out with greater freedom, power and success the tasks belonging to it alone, because it alone can effectively accomplish these: directing, watching, stimulating, restraining, as circumstances suggest and necessity demands. Let those in power, therefore, be convinced that the more faithfully this principle of subsidiary function be followed, and a graded hierarchical order exist between various associations, the greater will be both social authority and social efficiency, and the happier and more prosperous the condition of the commonwealth.[36]

Subsidiarity contains a clear limitation on the right of the state to intervene in the affairs of other structures in society, based on the nature of the state and the social structures. Arthur Utz wrote that the subsidiarity principle "is primarily a principle constraining and delimiting social and political interference with the fundamental rights of the individual and the lesser groupings."[37] What Utz emphasized is that both individuals and social structures have basic rights that must not be violated by other social structures. This results in the various social structures having "the right and even the duty of being autonomous."[38] Mueller made this point explicitly when he wrote that the subsidiarity "principle presupposes and postulates the existence of a sphere of subsidiary activity proper to each of the various supplemental social groups and institutions."[39]

Maritain placed a strong emphasis on the importance and independence of social structures when he criticized Jean-Jacques Rousseau's concept of the "sovereignty of the people" on the basis that it "excluded the possibility of any particular bodies or organizations of citizens enjoying in the State any kind of autonomy."[40] Later he argued that under the absolute sovereignty of the state, "the pluralist ideal is not only disregarded, but rejected by necessity or principle. Centralism, not pluralism, is required. It is at the price of a patent self-contradiction that the sovereign States will reluctantly accept the smallest amount of autonomy for particular agencies and associations born out of freedom."[41] The English pluralist Figgis also developed a strong sense of the state and social structures as having autonomous spheres of authority and activity. He emphasized that social structures do not receive their authority from the state, but possess it as a right.

> It is, in a word, a real life and personality which those bodies [associations and communities] are forced to claim, which we believe that they possess by the nature of the case, and not by the arbitrary grant of the sovereign. To deny this real life is to be false to the facts of social existence, and is of the same nature as that denial of human personality which we call slavery, and is always in its nature unjust and tyrannical.[42]

In the quotations of both Maritain and Figgis the concept of social structures possessing a necessary, inherent independence of action — a quasi-sovereignty — is clearly, if implicitly, present.

All these positions — Protestant and Catholic, Continental European and English — have in common the belief that social structures possess spheres of competence or responsibility within which they by right exercise a certain autonomy. Michael Fogarty described the Dutch Protestant concept of sphere sovereignty and then went on to compare it to the Catholic position in this way:

> The Catholic phrasing stresses rather the inclusion of these small units of society in greater wholes, within which however they have a sphere of autonomy on which they have a right to insist. But in practice the two conceptions come to much the same thing. . . . Every social unit or group has a sphere of work which it can do efficiently in the interests not only of its members but of society as a whole, and this sphere must be defined and reserved for it.[43]

Finally, it is helpful to note that within such spheres as the family, religion, government, and education, pluralists recognize a multitude of specific, concrete communities and associations. Thus, the family is a sphere possessing a quasi-sovereignty in pluralist thought. In actual practice, of course, the family is composed of millions of individual family units. Similarly, religion is a sphere of human endeavor within which a host of specific, concrete faith communities, denominations, and individual congregations exist and act. Even the political sphere includes in the United States over 80,000 separate governments on the state, local, and national levels. In making use of pluralism to guide thinking in regard to concrete actions and limitations, I find it helpful to think both in terms of the spheres or realms of human endeavor whose quasi-sovereignty must be protected and the myriad of concrete communities and associations within those spheres whose rights to a quasi-sovereignty must be recognized and respected in the carrying out of their responsibilities. The quasi-sovereignty of a sphere is recognized and respected by recognizing and respecting the quasi-sovereignty of the myriad of specific, concrete embodiments of that sphere.

The Question of Hierarchy

This leaves two key questions in regard to the pluralists' emphasis on quasi-sovereign spheres in the body politic. First, is the question of whether the spheres and social structures that possess a quasi-autonomy are hierarchical in nature, with some of them superior to and more inclusive than others, or whether they are different but without that difference implying a ranking. Catholic thinkers and English pluralists tended to take the former view and the Dutch Protestants, the latter. In a passage quoted earlier, Figgis referred to "an ascending hierarchy of groups, family, school, town, county, union, Church, &c., &c." Pope Pius XI, in the encyclical quoted earlier, spoke of a "hierarchical order," and Mueller noted the hierarchical nature of the Catholic concept of social structures when he emphasized Aquinas' view of society as "an ordered unity of associations, more specifically, a system of social organizations disposed organically in ranks and orders, each subordinate to the one above it."[44] In contrast, Kuyper and other Dutch pluralists insisted that social structures are not to be seen as being hierarchical in nature, and particularly that neither the state nor the church is at the apex of a hierarchy of social structures. Rather, both church and state were seen as simply two structures along with all the others, all of which receive their mandates or "sovereignty in its sphere" directly from God.

The difference, however, is more apparent than real. Kuyper and other Dutch pluralists would not, of course, argue that the various spheres of human endeavor, with their specific structural manifestations, exist in isolation from each other, existing side by side, but not interacting with each other. Art, for example, comments on and holds up a mirror to all aspects of human existence: family life, religious life, political life, and more. Similarly, it would be a mistake to see Kuyper as privatizing religion, sealing it off in its own separate sphere where it is active, but leaving the other, "secular spheres" alone. Instead, Kuyper's Calvinism possessed a *Weltanschauung* that impregnated all aspects of life with Christianity. When invited in 1898 to give a series of lectures at Princeton, Kuyper's lead-off lecture was entitled, "Calvinism as a Life-System," and in it he referred to his Calvinism as possessing "a peculiar principle dominating *the whole of life.*"[45]

This does not yet imply a hierarchy, with various spheres or social structures in subordinate and superior orders and ranks. However, in writing about the state, the hierarchy that Dutch Protestants denied in theory tends to reappear. Meeter, in typical Dutch Protestant fashion, first argued, "It [the state] has not the duty to take over the work of these spheres, as is the tendency in a totalitarian or collectivist state." However, then he went on to give the other side of the coin:

> Nor may the Government allow them to operate unrestrained according to their sinful desires, as the laissez-faire policy of the Liberals would demand. That would be to shirk a great part of the duty which the State is called upon to perform in a sinful society, namely, to administer justice. It is rather the business of the State, negatively, to counteract whatever forces would tend to break down the normal operation of the several spheres of society in their God-given task; and, positively, to promote such conditions and relations as will be helpful to them in the pursuance of their cultural tasks.[46]

If the government is to promote justice among the various social structures — to regulate relations among them and help empower them to fulfill their tasks — what has happened to the non-hierarchical nature of the spheres? Government has been assigned a broad coordinating role, which affects and conditions the other social structures and their activities. Kuyper himself once wrote that the "state must . . . keep each sphere within its proper limits. . . . The sovereignty of the state, therefore, rises high above all the other spheres by enjoining justice and utilizing force justly."[47] Koyzis made this point in regard to the thought of Dooyeweerd: "By allowing that the state's task includes protecting the integrity of the various societal spheres and enabling them to fulfill their respective normative tasks, it would certainly appear that Dooyeweerd is conceiving the state as something of an overarching hierarchical institution."[48]

While Dutch pluralists allowed elements of hierarchy to enter their theorizing, Catholic thinkers such as Mueller made the crucial point that although the concept of subsidiarity in Catholic thinking has a hierarchical framework, "the relative worth of the lower body is not merely a derivative one, but of an original nature, based on the respective common good to be accomplished."[49] Even the lower social structures have a worth and possess rights not at the sufferance of higher structures — the state in particular — but of their own right. Mueller favorably quoted the medieval historian Otto Gierke as saying: "The social life which these groups enjoy is not bestowed on them by the State; it is a life which proceeds from themselves. . . . They have therefore rights of their own which belong inviolably to them in their own particular area, even if their inclusion in a greater whole involves a number of limitations upon their freedom."[50] Koyzis, after an extensive study of the Protestant Dooyeweerd and the Catholic Simon, concluded that the difference in their views on the hierarchical nature of society's structures or spheres is, in practice, more apparent than real:

> We have noted throughout the course of this study that a principal difference between Simon's and Dooyeweerd's political theories is the element of hierarchy. Whereas Simon is willing to concede to the state the status of hierarchical superiority over other communities, Dooyeweerd is definitely not. This difference between the two is very evident at the foundational philosophical level. Yet on the level of practice, it would appear that the distance between the two is not that great.[51]

Because an element of hierarchy exists — explicitly or implicitly — in almost all pluralist thought, especially with the state playing some sort of an overarching or coordinating role, and because all the spheres help to condition the context within which all the other spheres pursue their endeavors, I prefer to speak of quasi-sovereign or quasi-autonomous spheres and social structures rather than sovereign or autonomous spheres, as some pluralists do.

Determining the Proper Responsibilities of the Spheres

A second question concerns how one determines the specific role or responsibility of a particular sphere or realm such as the family or the political sphere. This is a question to which pluralism in and by itself does not offer a clear answer. Oswald von Nell-Breuning has made the needed point: "It is completely erroneous to try to delimit the spheres of operation of diverse social groupings, that are not related as member to whole, with the aid of the principle of subsidiarity."[52] Similarly, Leicester Webb pointed out in regard to Figgis: "He talks of the State as 'an ascending hierarchy of groups' and of groups as having functions 'which are of the nature of government,' without facing the difficulties inherent in such phrases. How, for instance, does one delimit the respective spheres of authority of State and group?"[53] Figgis had no really clear answer. He advocated a strong role for government, seeing the prime duty of the state as being the regulation of relations among groups, between individuals and groups, and among individuals. However, Figgis was weak in developing a principled basis for that role in relation to other social structures.

Pluralism as a concept is not itself equipped — and does not claim to be equipped — to designate the exact responsibilities of the various spheres over which they exercise a quasi-sovereignty. Thus, the exact boundaries of the various societal realms are often in question. What is the nature of the family's responsibilities? Where do they begin and end? How can one know when a family has exceeded its sphere of responsibility and taken on duties that it should not? Pluralism defines these as important, highly relevant questions — and that is no small achievement, but it does not within itself supply the answers.

To answer questions such as these, one must turn elsewhere: to observation; to political, social and religious thought; and to common sense. Nell-Breuning and a number of other Catholic theorists, for example, have turned to the concept of the common good for answers. "The sphere of operation of each social grouping is determined by its specific *bonum commune*; and insofar as spheres overlap (e.g., functions that fall to the competence of both Church and State), the delimitation is made not with the aid of the principle of subsidiarity, but has to be referred back to the comprehensive *bonum commune* that embraces both."[54] One determines the distinctive responsibilities of the spheres by what will best promote the common good. The Protestant Dooyeweerd developed a complex scheme whereby each sphere is assigned a specific task (e.g., the state, justice; the religious, faith; the economic, stewardship) based on the nature of its existence and what he saw as its fundamental aspect, or *modality* as he termed it.[55] Webb cited a passage by the nineteenth-century commentator Richard Simpson as containing a theme that reappeared in Figgis' thought: "The true aim of politics is to harmonise the three elements of the State — the free individual, the free corporation, and the free State — in such stability of equilibrium as shall leave to each the greatest amount of free scope that is possible without injury to others."[56] Responsibilities should be distributed among the spheres so as to increase their freedom of action.

All three of these suggested approaches to delineating the responsibilities of the various spheres, and thereby to delineating the boundaries between them, are helpful — but also deficient. They give direction in finding answers that are crucial for our purposes, but fall short of giving the answers themselves. Later in this chapter, I suggest an approach to understanding the roles or responsibilities of the two key spheres with which this book deals: the religious and the political.

Pluralism in the U.S. Tradition

The preceding section is largely rooted in European thought that is heavy with religious overtones. This raises the question of whether perhaps structural, normative pluralism is a perspective appropriate for the European setting, with its particular history and social institutions, but with little relevance to the U.S. scene. Pluralism, however, is far from being at odds with the U.S. experience and U.S. patterns of thought. In fact, it has several parallels in U.S. thought and several factors suggest that its time for playing a major role in U.S. thinking may have come.

More specifically, I wish to highlight three theoretical perspectives on the U.S political scene that are related to the structural, normative pluralism described in this chapter. The first of these perspectives has been articulated most clearly by a number of sociologists, particularly Robert MacIver (1822–1970). MacIver wrote of the "multi-group society" and noted that "human beings are everywhere members of groups. They are utterly dependent on their relations with one another within these groups, dependent for their nurture, their modes of living, their economic and spiritual sustenance, and the continuance of their species."[57] MacIver distinguished among social groups, the state, and the individual, each of which has a distinct role to play that must be respected. Leon Bramson described this aspect of MacIver's thinking: "In clarifying the relationship between individual and society, it also declares the partial autonomy of the individual. In analyzing the nature of the state, it also prescribes the limits of the power of the state. In dissecting the nature of the multigroup society, it also makes a commitment to democracy and to pluralism."[58]

In short, aspects of structural pluralism can be seen in MacIver's sense of the fundamental, pervasive nature of a wide variety of groups and associations in society, and in his seeking to protect the freedom of action for social groups and individuals. Having acknowledged this, one must also note MacIver's differences with the pluralism presented in this chapter. His concept of societal spheres and their autonomy is incomplete and underdeveloped. Plus, he is more descriptive and analytic than normative. His analyses and descriptions contain normative implications — and one suspects his strong Scotch Presbyterian upbringing informs more of his work than even he himself was fully aware — yet he sought to develop a theory supporting an alternative to the omnipotent state, not out of overtly normative concerns, but (in his own words) in order to "frame a conception more adequate to social reality."[59] Nevertheless, MacIver and others who have followed his approach to the issues of society and government represent a strain within U.S. thought that is compatible with the broad contours of structural pluralism.

What has been labeled the communitarian school of thought comes close to the basic ideas and concepts of structural, normative pluralism. Communitarians have a very strong emphasis — as their name itself implies — on the existence of a wide variety of communities that are essential for a healthy, vital body politic due to the values and responsibilities that are taught and lived out within them.[60] The opening words of the official platform of the communitarian journal, *The Responsive Community*, are very similar to statements made by the structural pluralists noted earlier:

> American men, women, and children are members of many communities — families; neighborhoods; innumerable social, religious, ethnic, work place, and professional associations; and the body politic itself. Neither human existence nor individual liberty can be sustained for long outside the interdependent and overlapping communities to which all of us belong.[61]

In this emphasis on communities, communitarianism is critical — as is pluralism — of the emphasis on individual autonomy of traditional liberal thought.

Communitarians also share some limited common ground with pluralism's view of the various communities and associations as possessing a quasi-sovereignty. This perspective of the pluralists is often hinted at or implied by communitarians, but not fully or explicitly embraced. The lead editorial in the inaugural issue of the most important communitarian journal states: "The community has a moral standing coequal to that of the individual."[62] The community is here clearly seen as having an ontological status and therefore, by implication, certain rights or a stature in its own right. At one point the official communitarian platform sounds a note very similar to the Catholic teaching of subsidiarity: "Generally, no social task should be assigned to an institution that is larger than necessary to do the job. What can be done by families, should not be assigned to an intermediate group — school etc. What can be done at the local level should not be passed on to the state or federal level, and so on."[63] Again, one gets a sense that communitarians see communities as possessing certain inherent rights and responsibilities. One description of the communitarian movement states: "The emergent theme is . . . that communities should have *the right* to promote standards and values."[64]

The communitarian movement thereby shares with structural, normative pluralism a view of communities and associations as an inherent, necessary part of a healthy polity. It also shares a view of communities and associations as possessing certain basic rights, but this aspect of communitarian thought is less well developed than it is under pluralism's concept of the quasi-sovereignty of the societal spheres. Nevertheless, the communitarian movement thinks in similar or parallel terms to those of normative, structural pluralism, thereby adding credence to the proposition that pluralism is indeed applicable and relevant to the U.S. experience.

Among the theorists who are usually thought of as being communitarians, one deserves special mention: Michael Walzer. He has used pluralist-type categories and concepts in analyzing the nature of equality and distributive justice. He distinguishes between simple and complex equality, with simple equality consisting of the wide distribution of advantages within a supposedly undifferentiated society. Complex equality, Walzer argued, more closely matches reality in that it posits a plurality of distributive spheres, with equality or justice being achieved as long as a person's gaining of advantages in one sphere does not mean that he or she will also gain advantages in other spheres. "To convert one good [gained in one sphere] into another [good gained in some other sphere], when there is no intrinsic connection between the two, is to invade the sphere where another company of men and women properly rules."[65] Walzer thinks in terms of spheres such as economics, politics, education, family, and religion. At one point he used a helpful example:

> There is nothing wrong, for example, with the grip that persuasive and helpful men and women (politicians) establish on political power. But the use of political power to gain access to other goods [in other spheres] is a tyrannical use. Thus, an old description of tyranny is generalized: princes become tyrants, according to medieval writers, when they seize the property or invade the family of their subjects.[66]

Walzer thereby asserted the illegitimacy of persons with power in one sphere using that power to gain power in another. Social spheres exist and their boundaries must be respected if tyranny and injustices are to be avoided. Implicit in this is a sense of the autonomy of the various spheres. At several points Walzer made explicit what is usually implicit in his thought. In regard to the sphere of religion, he wrote: "Here is perhaps the clearest example in our culture of an autonomous sphere."[67] Elsewhere he wrote: "The autonomy of spheres will make for a greater sharing of social goods than will any other conceivable arrangement."[68]

In all this Walzer comes close to the pluralism presented earlier in this chapter. He has a sense for the existence of spheres of human endeavor and for the achieving of justice and the prevention of tyranny depending upon respecting the boundaries between and the autonomy of these spheres. He does not have the same clear emphasis on the existence and importance of communities and associations within the life of the body politic, however, and his theorizing does not have the same normative thrust as that of the structural pluralists. His argument is secularly based rather than based on a religious worldview. However, it is significant that a theorist such as Walzer, relying on observations and reason, arrived at a position as close to that of structural pluralism as he did. It helps to demonstrate that the pluralism described in this chapter — although emerging out of Western European Christian thought — is not at odds with either experience or secularly based values that are widely shared in the U.S. polity.

Nevertheless, it is surprising that structural, normative pluralism, which has gained wide currency in Europe, has not been more prominent in U.S. thinking. This can in part be explained on the basis of the largely continental European roots of pluralist theory. Although there has been an English school of pluralism, it has been much more prominent in Continental European thinking. Pluralism's weakness in Anglo-Saxon political theory may have handicapped its ability to be readily disseminated and accepted in the United States. Probably more important, its roots in European Christendom mean that its most likely supporters on the U.S. scene would have been those with clear Christian commitments. However, as seen in the previous chapter, nineteenth-century Protestants did very little theorizing, and the conservative Protestants of the twentieth century have until recently been too weak, torn by internal struggles, and separate from the world to have had much impact. Catholics would have been the most likely bearers of a normative pluralism in the United States, since it has been a part of their intellectual heritage, but up until World War II — and perhaps up until the 1960s, with the Second Vatican Council and the election of John Kennedy as president — U.S. Catholics had not come into their own as a cultural force to be reckoned with. Prior to very recent years, Catholics tended to have an immigrant, minority mentality that limited their cultural impact in the United States.[69]

At the close of the twentieth century — with Catholics coming into their own as a major cultural force, with conservative Protestants gaining greater strength and self-confidence, and with communitarians winning increasing notice — the time may now be ripe for structural pluralism to develop into a major force for interpreting, understanding, and guiding the U.S. polity. Moreover, the need for its doing so has never been greater. Chapter 1 took note of the increasing religious diversity of the United States. Structural pluralism says that its perspectives are as relevant to a religiously homogeneous as to a religiously heterogeneous society. Nevertheless, the breaking of the nineteenth-century's Protestant cultural dominance and the increasing religious diversity in the United States have revealed the inadequacies of existing theories and categories. If full religious freedom is to exist in a religiously pluralistic society, the freedom of the plurality of faith communities and religious associations — as well as those of no religious faith — must be protected. Structural, normative pluralism, with its concern for the autonomy of all social structures, has a basis for defining and protecting the freedom of a diversity of religious faiths that more individualistic theories, which ignore a diversity of societal structures, lack.

RELIGION AND GOVERNMENT
IN A PLURALISTIC SOCIETY

Thus far, this chapter has talked in terms of theoretic constructs and broad views of society in its wholeness and its pluralism. It is time to become more specific. In this section I consider the basic roles played by religion and government in society. These are the roles that define the spheres within which, pluralism insists, governments and religious structures must possess a quasi-sovereignty. Once these roles have been outlined, the following chapter can become even more specific, delineating the contours of a church-state theory rooted in pluralism's understanding of society.

Religion: Definitions

If I am to consider the nature and place of religion in society, I must first define what I mean by religion. This is no easy task. As a pluralist I must be careful not to define religion in terms of any one religious tradition, yet an overly broad, inclusive definition would lose meaning by including almost all aspects of human society and in the process make guarantees of religious freedom meaningless.

The French sociologist Emile Durkheim offered a particularly insightful definition of religion: "A religion is a unified system of beliefs and practices relative to sacred things, that is to say, things set apart and forbidden — beliefs and practices which unite into one single moral community called a Church, all those who adhere to them."[70] There are several elements in this definition that are of special help. First, religion is "a unified system of beliefs and practices." Religion deals with both beliefs and practice. It is not merely a system of abstract, theoretical beliefs, but rather consists of beliefs linked to and translated into practice. Religion is practical, something one lives as well as believes. It is also a *system* of belief and practice. It is not necessarily a highly structured, thoroughly thought-out system, but neither is it only a few scattered, unconnected beliefs and practices. There needs to be an order or interconnectedness — however limited or primitive — to religion's beliefs and practices.

Second, religion is social or communal ("one single moral community"); it does not refer to isolated individuals and wholly private beliefs. Here Durkheim differed from William James and some other thinkers who defined religion in terms of individual beliefs. James defined religion as "the feelings, acts, and experiences of individual men in their solitude, so far as they apprehend themselves to stand in relation to whatever they may consider the divine."[71] However, this will not do. In the pluralist scheme, religion by nature is shared, communal. To include totally personal beliefs and practices of single individuals as "religion" would be to broaden the term to an extent that it loses much of its meaning.

The point at which Durkheim's definition becomes more problematic is in his reference to "sacred things" as the object of religious beliefs and practices. In his discussion, he identified "sacred" as the opposite of profane. However, this introduces an element into the definition that is almost tautological. Defining sacred as "things set apart and forbidden," as he did in his definition itself, is hardly delimiting at all. I would suggest that introducing the idea of the supernatural rather than the sacred as the object of religious belief would give a greater specificity to the definition and, in an appropriate manner, would distinguish the religious from the nonreligious.

Therefore, I would define religion as unified systems of beliefs and practices that give answers to ultimate questions by reliance on the supernatural and that unite their adherents into moral communities. This definition has a number of points in common with Durkheim's definition, specifically in its emphasis on beliefs and practices and on moral communities. It differs, first, in its emphasis on the supernatural as a delimiting element rather than "the sacred."[72] *Supernatural* is being used here in its ordinary dictionary meaning of that which is beyond the observable, physical world. The supernatural may include a God or gods, but not necessarily. Another new element in this definition borrows from Sidney Mead's definition — as well as from the definitions that others have formulated — to emphasize that religion deals with questions of ultimate matters, or in Mead's words, of "cosmic significance."[73] Religion deals with such questions as the purpose and meaning of human life, nature, and the universe. This definition includes nontheistic religions that recognize a reality transcending the observable, physical world and otherwise meet the terms of the definition. Pantheism and Buddhism are examples. My definition does not include purely secular, nonsupernatural philosophies or mind-sets, such as Marxism or secular humanism, even though they seek to give answers to ultimate questions, since they do not rely on the supernatural in seeking to do so. They should be considered as functional equivalents of religions for many of their adherents, but not as religions.

One additional note is that religion, as I will be dealing with and discussing it in this book, manifests itself in the form of communities and associations. A religious association is an association as defined earlier ("a collectivity of persons formally, purposefully organized for the achievement of a specific, chosen purpose") that has been organized for such purposes as developing, propagating, affirming, and living out persons' religious beliefs and practices. It is an organization with designated leaders, a formal structure, specified purposes, and a defined membership. An organized church or synagogue is the most common example in the U.S. setting, but a religiously based hospital, drug treatment center, school, retirement home, and a host of other religiously based service agencies are also examples.

One can think of religion not only in terms of formal associations, but also in terms of religious communities or, perhaps less confusingly, of faith communities. A religious or faith community is a community as defined earlier ("persons bound together by organic, affective ties which lead them to identify themselves as members of a distinct collectivity") whose ties that bind its members together are religious in nature. The concept of faith communities is less precise than that of religious associations. It can be difficult to know exactly what faith communities to identify and label as such in society. Some Presbyterians, for example, no doubt strongly identify with the Presbyterian denomination, and they should be considered part of a Presbyterian faith community. Others no doubt only identify with their local congregation, and are barely conscious, and certainly not loyal to the broader denomination. For them, their faith community is the local church. The faith community of others may be that of Christianity generally, having not made any distinctions among denominations or theological traditions and identifying simply with fellow Christian believers generally. Others may have joined the church much as one would join a country club, for reasons of business contacts, social pressure, or sociability, and not be part of any faith community at all even though they are part of a religious association. When necessary, I will make clear in subsequent discussions whether I have in mind religious associations, faith communities, both, or some combination of the two.

Religion's Fundamental Roles

Chapter 1 noted the continuing strength and vitality of religion in U.S. society. In terms of formal membership, participation in religious practices such as prayer and Bible reading, financial giving, and many other aspects of religion, Americans' religious commitments are stronger than those of almost any other aspect of social life. However, all this does not yet say what functions or roles are the distinguishing marks of religion. Here I outline four basic roles or functions that are vital to the very nature of religion. If religion is to be religion, these are the roles it must be free to pursue. These define the sphere or realm of religion, the one in which religious associations and faith communities, by right, possess a quasi-sovereignty.

All faith communities and religious associations cultivate, nurture, and develop their core beliefs in the lives of their adherents. This first role involves developing, shaping, interpreting, and affirming a religion's basic answers to ultimate questions (in distinction from making applications or following through on the implications of these basic answers). This is where religion is most purely "religious" in the traditional U.S. mind-set. It is also where religion is most inward-looking, yet it is foundational to the other three, more outward-looking of religion's roles. Churches, synagogues, mosques, and other religious associations develop and affirm their core beliefs through their religious services and rituals, educational programs, and informal group activities. Theological seminaries engage in this sort of explication and development through classroom instruction and publishing activities of their professors. Seminars, book and magazine publishing, and radio and television programs often also play a role. These activities may be organized along the lines of religious associations (such as churches, mosques, synagogues, and denominations), but they may also run along the lines of faith communities. In the latter case, these faith communities may either coincide with certain associations, reinforcing and making more compelling the association's message, or they may cross religious association lines, as with a television ministry such as that of the Reverend Robert Schuller of California's Crystal Cathedral, who appeals to persons belonging to a wide variety of churches (that is, religious associations).

A second role that religion plays is shaping members' behavior and attitudes in keeping with certain ethical standards or norms. All religious traditions have strong ethical dimensions. Both the existence of religiously inspired ethical standards and their integral connection to most religious traditions is readily recognized by almost all persons.

What is sometimes less readily recognized is that these ethical standards and religion's attempts to mold their members' behavior and attitudes have enormous social and political dimensions and consequences. Religion exists in society and its teachings and ethical standards affect the broader society of which it is a part. The

importance of these effects is hard to overstate. In the early nineteenth century, the famous French observer Alexis de Tocqueville
made this point clearly: "In the United States religion exercises but
little influence upon the laws and upon the details of public opinion;
but it directs the customs of the community, and, by regulating
domestic life, it regulates the state."[74] A little later he went on to
explain further: "Religion in America takes no direct part in the
government of society, but it must be regarded as the first of their
political institutions; for if it does not impart a taste for freedom, it
facilitates the use of it."[75] According to de Tocqueville, religion
profoundly shapes and influences society and politics, not by a direct
influence, but indirectly by shaping the sense of morality which
conditions all else. Thus, religion was "the first of [the Americans']
political institutions." Jumping ahead 160 years, to 1990, the
Reverend Vaclav Maly, a Czechoslovakian Catholic priest who was
active in the movement to topple the communist regime in his
homeland, explained his withdrawal from direct, active politics:
"Party politics is 'not my task,' Father Maly said in an interview. He
said he was trying to instill in people 'trust, hope, and mutual help,
forgiveness, sacrifice' and other virtues that he called essential for
political life."[76] The present day observer who has probably made this
point most clearly is political scientist A. James Reichley, who has
written:

> Republican government depends for its health on values that
> over the not-so-long run must come from religion. Through
> theist-humanism, human rights are rooted in the moral worth
> with which a loving Creator has endowed each human soul,
> and social authority is legitimized by making it answerable to
> transcendent moral law. In a highly mobile and heteroge-
> neous society like the United States, these values based on
> religion are even more essential to democracy than they may
> be in more traditional societies, where respect for freedom,
> order, and justice may be maintained for some time through
> social inertia or custom.[77]

The key point to remember in all this is that religion's efforts in
shaping members' attitudes and behavior is integral to religion. For
religion truly to be religion, it needs to be free to shape members'
attitudes and behavior, including their socially and politically
relevant attitudes and behaviors.

Religion's third role lies near the heart of most religious
traditions: directly providing a wide variety of services to members
and others in society. Religious associations such as churches,
synagogues, and mosques provide their members in the normal
course of activities with counseling, support, and material help. A

moment's reflection, however, reveals a startling array of additional programs and services that churches and other religiously rooted associations provide. Hospitals, K-12 schools, and colleges and universities are the oldest and best-known examples of what I have in mind. As important as these programs are, they are only the beginnings of the list. There are a host of social service agencies with deep religious roots: food banks, thrift stores, adoption agencies, drug rehabilitation centers, family counseling centers, runaway shelters, ex-offenders' halfway and support agencies, and on and on. The services that religious associations thereby provide go to both the members of the religious tradition sponsoring them and, frequently, to the community at large.

What needs to be emphasized in regard to religiously based service programs is that in most religious traditions, they are not optional or ancillary to what religion is really all about. As Chapter 1 pointed out, these acts of service are in many religious traditions — and certainly in the Judeo-Christian tradition — as much a part of religion as kneeling in prayer or attending religious services. For most segments of the U.S. populace, taking part in providing a wide range of services is an integral part of their faith. To remove that function would be to rip the heart out of their religion.

A fourth key role that marks religion is participation in society's public policy-making process, broadly conceived. Religious associations fulfill this role, first, through direct attempts to influence the policy-making process by adopting resolutions, issuing position papers, and lobbying decision makers. Almost all religious denominations adopt statements dealing with such issues as world hunger, war and peace, liquor sales on Sunday, gambling, pornography, abortion, and euthanasia. Political scientist Allen Hertzke has written ably concerning the role and influence of lobbying by organized religious groups in Washington, D.C.[78] Religious associations such as the United States Catholic Conference, the Israeli-American Public Affairs Committee, and the Christian Legal Society are respected, influential players on the Washington scene.

Of greater importance to religious associations and faith communities than entering the policy-making fray is the influence they exert — often inadvertently — over their adherents on public policy issues. Different faith communities, such as the Catholic, evangelical, and Jewish, have sharply different attitudes on certain issues (as well as agreement on others). Pollsters George Gallup, Jr., and Jim Castelli noted the large amount of agreement on public policy issues across religious lines, but went on to state that "the many and often sharp differences in views held by different religious groups are dramatic."[79] They concluded that some of these differences are due to different life situations rather than differences in religious beliefs, yet "strong differences persist among major religious groups that appear to be linked to a general worldview rather than a particular situation. Members of different religious groups often live in very different mental worlds — they hold different views of key issues, have different priorities, different heroes, different values."[80] On the level of political leaders, researchers Peter Benson and Dorothy Williams, after a methodologically rigorous study of members of Congress, labeled as a myth the belief that "religion bears little relationship to voting decisions."[81] They went on to conclude that although religious beliefs are not necessarily the most important force affecting congressional roll call voting, yet they "should join some of the more commonly recognized factors, like party affiliation and constituent pressure, as forces that bear on political behavior. . . . For many voting issues, knowing how members scored on three or four of the religious themes can tell us as much or more about how they will vote than knowing whether they are Republican or Democrat."[82]

What needs to be kept in mind is the fact that, as Chapter 1 noted, for most religious traditions, speaking out on public policy issues and molding their members' politically relevant attitudes are an integral part of their faith. For an Isaiah in ancient Israel to keep silent in the face of oppression, a Dietrich Bonhoeffer in the face of Nazi tyranny, or a Martin Luther King in the face of racial injustice would — in terms of their religious beliefs — be wrong. The faith of these men *required* them to speak out. The same holds true of the more numerous, less prominent ordinary believers of various religious traditions. Religion by its very nature involves — directly or indirectly — participation in the policy-making process.

The conclusion is that religion plays a number of vital roles that define what it is and what it means to be religious. All four of the roles discussed here lie at religion's heart: they are not ancillary or incidental to it. For religious associations and faith communities to give up any one of these roles would mean that they would cease to be what they by nature are.

Government's Fundamental Roles

Earlier I defined the state or government as the formal, purposeful organization that exercises authority over all persons in a defined geographic area on a continuing basis. It is this exercise of authority that is the defining role of government, that which makes it a state. The chief additional point that needs to be made is that in the exercise of its authority government is to meet the demands of justice, the common good, or some other such norm. The possession and exercise of authority are not ends in themselves; rather, authority is to be exercised in the pursuit of some normatively defined goal. Justice and the common good are the two most frequently cited. The important thing for the pluralist is that the normative goal must be defined in terms of protecting, coordinating, respecting, and empowering the other spheres in society. Individual persons are to be given their due, but so are neighborhoods, religious associations, faith communities, business enterprises, universities, labor unions, families, and so on. They and government are sovereign in their appropriate realms or spheres.

With this in mind, it is helpful to think in terms of four more specific areas in which government exercises its authority in society. One is the area of national security. In the modern nation-state, the government protects the independence and integrity of the nation from foreign conquest, domination, or intimidation. It thereby protects the autonomy of the nation — and of the various spheres of human endeavor within it. The second area of governmental authority is that of public safety. The state has the responsibility or role to protect society from harm and danger arising from threats that are internal to society. Public safety and peace are thereby assured. In the modern world, this role must be seen in a very broad light to include protection not only from traditional criminal activity, but also from such forces as environmental pollution and unscrupulous, fraudulent schemes — whether from business enterprises or television evangelists. In doing so, government's differences from religion are especially clear due to the coercion and sanctions at the disposal of government and because government is dealing with overt behavior, not motives and inner values. Jesus said that those who hate their fellow human beings have already committed murder in their hearts — and such hate is of concern to churches, but the government could not care less, as long as that hate does not lead to the actual deed. Government thereby plays an empowering, freeing role by protecting society and its spheres of human endeavor from those who would reduce freedom and opportunity through violence, fraud, and other means of endangering others.

A third area in which government exercises its authority is that of the economy. Government seeks to promote justice or some other vision of the common good by promoting economic stability and opportunities. Here, also, government is acting in an enabling, empowering fashion. A fourth area of governmental authority is that of providing a vast array of needed services to society, including services as diverse as education, roads, welfare, health care, pensions, postal service, safe drinking water, parks, and so forth. The judgment has been made that government can provide certain services better than can the private sector. Debates often emerge over whether government is providing services that the individual could better provide for him- or herself, but that is an improper way of framing the question. In pluralist thinking, it should be framed in terms of whether government or some other social structure could better provide the service in question. Rarely does an individual provide a needed service for him- or herself in isolation from other persons. Pluralism suggests that government should be the provider of last resort and that when it does provide services, it should do so in such a way as to empower and enhance other vital social structures, not undercut them. In that way, the autonomy of the other areas of human endeavor is respected.

In describing the role that government plays in society and the four key areas in which it plays this role, the great power and overarching nature of the state's authority in society come clear. However, pluralism sees government as being quasi-sovereign in its area of competence, just as the other social structures are in theirs. Economic, family, artistic, and religious life are of as much inherent importance as political life. They are different, and politics by its very nature involves great power and a broadly coordinating role in relation to the other social structures, yet this does not make government sovereign in any absolute sense or even relatively more autonomous or sovereign. All societal spheres have a sovereignty that is limited by an area of competence in which it is to be exercised and by norms defining how it is to be exercised.

SUMMARY

Douglas Pike once quoted one of the clearest summaries of the structural, normative pluralism presented in this chapter:

> The heart of the pluralistic thesis is the conviction that government must recognize that it is not the sole possessor of sovereignty, and that private groups within the community are entitled to lead their own free lives and exercise within the area of their competence an authority so effective as to justify labeling it a sovereign authority. To make this assertion is to suggest that private groups have liberties similar to those of individuals and that those liberties, as such, are to be secured by law from governmental infringement.[83]

The key point of pluralism is that associations and communities are a natural, integral, necessary part of any society, and have positive, valuable roles to play in society, which are normatively defined and circumscribed. This means that all social structures possess, by right, a certain sovereignty or autonomy in their proper spheres or realms of responsibility and competence. Government and religious associations are particularly important examples of such structures. Each possesses a distinct sovereignty in its realm which must be recognized and respected if society is to be stable, prosperous, and free.

This perspective differs — not totally, but in some significant ways — from the liberal Enlightenment thought bequeathed to the United States by Thomas Jefferson, Benjamin Franklin, and their compatriots. Liberal thought essentially thinks in terms of individual rights and freedom as a negative concept. Individual rights and the freedom that they assure are achieved by legal restrictions on what government can do. Under this scheme, religion especially is individualized and privatized. Religion — in all its particularity and specificity, in contrast to its broad, consensual contours — is seen as a divisive, disruptive force to be isolated away from the body politic. Thereby, individual religious freedom is preserved and the polity is spared the divisiveness of religion while reaping the benefits of its broad, consensual tenets.

This perspective fails to recognize that typically, persons' religion is not merely a matter of individual worship of God apart from the other facets of one's life. Religion is communal, not individual, and it relates to the whole person, not one aspect of existence. Persons are social beings who live their lives as whole persons, not as segmented pieces.

The key question that all this poses is how to respect the inalienable right of a wide diversity of religious associations and faith communities to be fully free in developing and practicing their core beliefs, molding behavior and attitudes, providing services, and participating in the public policy-making process — and how to do so without violating the rights of nonbelievers. To the conventional U.S. mind-set, this question poses an unresolvable dilemma. We have been taught that if religion is allowed into the political arena, divisiveness and a favoring of one religion over another or of religion over nonbelief will result. Moreover, politicized religion will be a weaker, less vibrant religion, drawn into the political maelstrom and reduced to a dead formalism due to a dependence on government. The other horn of the dilemma is that to privatize religion — to ignore it and hold it irrelevant in relation to the public life of the nation — is to favor nonbelief over belief and to make it more difficult for religion to play roles that define its very nature. In pluralist terms, the state would be intruding into the sphere of religion to restrict and limit. The quasi-sovereignty of religion in its sphere of competence would be violated and religious freedom would be compromised.

The next chapters seeks to apply in concrete terms the pluralistic concept of society, religion, and government to this question and the presumed church-state dilemma. I believe that it offers the basis for a way out of that dilemma, which gives religion, nonbelief, the state, and society as a whole each their due.

NOTES

1. The type of pluralism to which I make reference here is structural in the sense that it takes into account the observable, demonstrable nature of society as composed of distinct social structures, that is, associations and communities (to be defined shortly); it is normative in the sense that it assigns value and ontological status to these social structures. I am not using pluralism here, as is sometimes done, to describe the process of public policies emerging from the competition and interplay of numerous interest groups. Nor am I using pluralism to refer to *cultural* pluralism, that is, a situation in which a society is marked by a diversity of groupings based on such factors as ethnicity, language, or religion. Even culturally homogeneous societies are marked by pluralism in a structural sense. Cultural pluralism and structural, normative pluralism are distinguishable concepts, even though they are related in that structural pluralism establishes a framework with which to recognize and accommodate a diversity of cultural — including religious — traditions.

2. Henry S. Kariel, "Pluralism," in David L. Shils, ed., *International Encyclopedia of the Social Sciences*, vol. 12 (New York: Macmillan and the Free Press, 1968), p. 168. Although this statement was true in 1968 when Kariel wrote it, a communitarian school of thought with distinct pluralist characteristics has recently developed. Thus, Kariel's statement must now be qualified.

3. I make no attempt to give full explications of the theoretical systems constructed by the various theorists I mention. That would take us far beyond the scope of this book. Instead, I highlight several fundamental features of pluralist thought that are relevant to the topic of church-state relations and cite representative theorists and movements to demonstrate their support for these features and to give a flavor for their perspectives. As a result, I lose a number of fine distinctions which, while important for a full, nuanced understanding of various pluralist theorists, are not necessary for the purposes of this study.

4. Although I have followed no one person in developing these definitions, I have found the formulations of Jacques Maritain especially helpful, and the following definitions, in greater or lesser degree, reflect my debt to him. See Jacques Maritain, *Man and the State* (Chicago: University of Chicago Press, 1951), pp. 1–19.

5. *Webster's New Collegiate Dictionary* (Springfield, MA: G. & C. Merriam, 1976).

6. R. E. M. Irving, *The Christian Democratic Parties of Western Europe* (London: George Allen & Unwin, 1979), p. 31. Irving's emphasis.

7. Jacques Maritain, *The Person and the Common Good*, trans. John J. Fitzgerald (Notre Dame, IN: University of Notre Dame Press, 1966), p. 38.

8. Abraham Kuyper, *The Problem of Poverty*, ed. James Skillen (Grand Rapids, MI: Baker, 1991), p. 45. Although Kuyper is not well known in the United States, his stature as a theorist was attested to by Ernest Troeltsch when he wrote, "In his historical, theoretical, and political writings Kuyper has made an intelligent and even brilliant study of this type of Neo-Calvinism." See Ernest Troeltsch, *The Social Teaching of the Christian Churches*, vol. 2, trans. Olive Wyon (New York: Harper & Row, 1960), p. 685. Michael Fogarty, in his comprehensive study of Christian Democracy, called Kuyper "the greatest leader whom Dutch Protestantism in modern times has produced." See Michael P. Fogarty, *Christian Democracy in Western Europe, 1820–1953* (London: Routledge & Kegan Paul, 1957), p. 172. On the life of Abraham Kuyper, see McKendree R. Langley, *The Practice of Political Spirituality* (Jordan Station, Ont., Can.: Paideia Press, 1984), and Justis M. van der Kroef, "Abraham Kuyper and the Rise of Neo-Calvinism in the Netherlands," *Church History* 17 (1948): pp. 316–334.

9. Dirk Jellema, "Abraham Kuyper's Attack on Liberalism," *Review of Politics* 19 (1957): p. 481. Jellema's emphasis.

10. Irving, *The Christian Democratic Parties*, p. 31.

11. Maritain, *The Person and the Common Good*, pp. 41–42. Maritain's emphasis.

12. Paul Dabin, "The Search for the Intellectual Basis of Christian-Democracy," in European People's Party, *Efforts to Define a Christian Democratic "Doctrine"* (Brussels: Parliamentary Group of the European People's Party, Occasional Papers No. 2, 1989), p. 20.

13. Quoted in Clay Clemens, *Christian Democracy: The Different Dimensions of a Modern Movement* (Brussels: Parliamentary Group of the European People's Party, Occasional Papers No. 1, 1989), p. 10.

14. Jellema, "Abraham Kuyper's Attack on Liberalism," p. 484. Jellema's emphasis.

15. Kuyper, *The Problem of Poverty*, p. 51. Kuyper's emphasis. The quoted phrase is from the Portuguese statesman, Antonio de Costa Cabral (1803–1889).

16. Quoted in Gordon Spykman, "Sphere-Sovereignty in Calvin and the Calvinist Tradition," in David E. Holwerda, ed., *Exploring the Heritage of John Calvin* (Grand Rapids, MI: Baker Book House, 1976), pp. 182–183.

17. R. E. Mulcahy, "Subsidiarity," in Catholic University of America, *New Catholic Encyclopedia*, vol. 13 (New York: McGraw-Hill, 1967), p. 762.

18. Maritain, *The Person and the Common Good*, pp. 48–49.

19. David T. Koyzis, *Towards a Christian Democratic Pluralism: A Comparative Study of Neothomist and Neocalvinist Political Theories* (Ann Arbor, MI: University Microfilms International, 1986), p. 336.

20. Franz H. Mueller, "The Principle of Subsidiarity in the Christian Tradition," *The American Catholic Sociological Review* 4 (1943): p. 147.

21. Maritain, *Man and the State*, p. 11.

22. John N. Figgis, *Churches in the Modern State*, 2d ed. (New York: Russell and Russell, 1914), p. 87.

23. Ibid., p. 47.

24. Henry Meyer Magid, *English Political Pluralism* (New York: Columbia University Press, 1941), p. 16.

25. Jellema, "Abraham Kuyper's Attack on Liberalism," p. 482.

26. Irving, *The Christian Democratic Parties*, p. 42.

27. Kariel, "Pluralism," p. 164.

28. Magid, *English Political Pluralism*, pp. 11, 12.

29. Peter L. Berger and Richard John Neuhaus, *To Empower People: The Role of Mediating Structures in Public Policy* (Washington, DC: American Enterprise Institute, 1977).

30. Here and throughout this section I make reference to the quasi-sovereignty or quasi-autonomy of society's various spheres, not their sovereignty or autonomy, as do most pluralist thinkers. Later I will explain why I do so.

31. Abraham Kuyper, *Calvinism: Six Stone Foundation Lectures* (Grand Rapids, MI: Eerdmans, 1943), pp. 9–91. Kuyper's emphasis. This quotation is from one of six lectures given at Princeton University in 1898.

32. Kuyper, *Calvinism*, p. 96.

33. H. Henry Meeter, *The Basic Ideas of Calvinism*, 5th ed. (Grand Rapids, MI: Baker Book House, 1956), p. 159.

34. Jellema, "Abraham Kuyper's Attack on Liberalism," p. 482.

35. Arie Oostlander, "Politics Based on Christian Consciousness," in European People's Party, *Efforts to Define a Christian Democratic "Doctrine,"* p. 29.

36. Quoted in Jean-Yves Calvez and Jacques Perrin, *The Church and Social Justice: The Social Teachings of the Popes from Leo XIII to Pius XII*, trans. J. R. Kirwan (London: Burns & Oates, 1961), p. 333.

37. Arthur Utz, "The Principle of Subsidiarity and Contemporary Natural Law," *Natural Law Forum* 3 (1958): p. 177.

38. Ibid.

39. Mueller, "The Principle of Subsidiarity in the Christian Tradition," p. 144–145.

40. Maritain, *Man and the State*, p. 47.

41. Ibid., p. 51.

42. Figgis, *Churches in the Modern State*, p. 42.

43. Fogarty, *Christian Democracy in Western Europe*, p. 41.

44. Mueller, "The Principle of Subsidiarity in the Christian Tradition," p. 147.

45. Kuyper, *Calvinism*, p. 38. Emphasis added.

46. Meeter, *The Basic Ideas of Calvinism*, p. 163.

47. Abraham Kuyper, "The Antirevolutionary Program," in James W. Skillen and Rockne M. McCarthy, eds., *Political Order and the Plural Structure of Society* (Atlanta, GA: Scholars Press, 1991), p. 260.

48. Koyzis, *Towards a Christian Democratic Pluralism*, p. 366.

49. Mueller, "The Principle of Subsidiarity in the Christian Tradition," p. 151.

50. Ibid., pp. 155–156.

51. Koyzis, *Towards a Christian Democratic Pluralism*, p. 366.

52. Oswald von Nell-Breuning, "Subsidiarity," in Karl Rahner, ed., *Sacramentum Mundi: An Encyclopedia of Theology*, vol. 6 (New York: Herder and Herder, 1970), p. 115.

53. Leicester C. Webb, "Corporate Personality and Political Pluralism," in Leicester C. Webb, ed., *Legal Personality and Political Pluralism* (Melbourne, Australia: Melbourne University Press, 1958), p. 55.

54. Nell-Breuning, "Subsidiarity," p. 115.

55. See Herman Dooyeweerd, *Roots of Western Culture: Pagan, Secular and Christian Options* (Toronto, Ont., Can.: Wedge, 1979). For a summary of Dooyeweerd's thought on this point, see Koyzis, *Towards a Christian Democratic Pluralism*, pp. 189–196, 253–259; James W. Skillen and Rockne M. McCarthy, "Herman Dooyeweerd," in Skillen and McCarthy, eds., *Political Order and the Plural Structure of Society*, pp. 265–270.

56. Webb, "Corporate Personality and Political Pluralism," p. 47.

57. Robert M. MacIver, *The Web of Government* (New York: Macmillan, 1947), pp. 421, 410.

58. Leon Bramson, "Introduction," in Robert MacIver, *On Community, Society, and Power* (Chicago: University of Chicago Press, 1970), pp. 23–24.

59. MacIver, *The Web of Government*, p. 421.

60. On the communitarians, see Clarke E. Cochran, "The Thin Theory of Community: The Communitarians and Their Critics," *Political Studies* 37 (1989): pp. 422–435; Robert Booth Fowler, *The Dance with Community* (Lawrence: University of Kansas Press, 1991); Fred Strasser, "Searching for a Middle Ground," *The National Law Journal* 14 (February 3, 1992): pp. 1, 28–29; and "The Responsive Communitarian Platform: Rights and Responsibilities," *The Responsive Community* 2 (Winter 1991/92): pp. 4–20.

61. "The Responsive Communitarian Platform," p. 4.

62. "The Responsive Community, Rights and Responsibilities," *The Responsive Community* 1 (Winter, 1990/91): p. 2.

63. "The Responsive Communitarian Platform," p. 11.

64. Strasser, "Searching for a Middle Ground," p. 28. Emphasis added.

65. Michael Walzer, *Spheres of Justice* (New York: Basic Books, 1983), p. 19.

66. Ibid.

67. Ibid., p. 244.

68. Ibid., p. 321.

69. See Kenneth D. Wald, *Religion and Politics*, 2d ed. (Washington, DC: Congressional Quarterly, 1992), pp. 280–294.

70. Emile Durkheim, *The Elementary Forms of the Religious Life*, trans. Joseph Ward Swain (Glencoe, IL: Free Press, 1947), p. 47.

71. William James, *The Varieties of Religious Experience* (New York: Modern Library, 1902), pp. 31–32.

72. Other theorists have used the supernatural as a key delimiting element in the definition of religion. See Peter L. Benson and Dorothy L. Williams, *Religion on Capitol Hill: Myths and Realities* (San Francisco, CA: Harper & Row, 1982), pp. 12–13; Clarke E. Cochran, *Religion in Public and Private Life* (New York: Routledge, 1990), pp. 7–11.

73. Mead wrote: "When we speak of the 'religion' of an individual or of a community we mean to point to whatever constellation of ideas and standards does in fact give cosmic significance and hence purpose to his or its way of life." See Sidney E. Mead, *The Old Religion in the Brave New World* (Berkeley: University of California Press, 1977), p. 63.

74. Alexis de Tocqueville, *Democracy in America*, vol. 1 (New York: Knopf, 1963), p. 304.

75. Ibid., p. 305.

76. Peter Steinfels, "Prague Priest Worries How Churches Will Use Liberty," *New York Times*, July 31, 1990, p. A4.

77. A. James Reichley, *Religion in American Public Life* (Washington, DC: Brookings, 1985), p. 348.

78. Allen Hertzke, *Representing God in Washington: The Role of Religious Lobbies in the American Polity* (Knoxville: Tennessee University Press, 1988).

79. George Gallup, Jr., and Jim Castelli, *The People's Religion: American Faith in the 90's* (New York: Macmillan, 1989), p. 215.

80. Ibid., p. 217.

81. Benson and Williams, *Religion on Capitol Hill*, p. 164.

82. Ibid., pp. 164–165.

83. Douglas Pike, "Churches and the Modern State," in Webb, ed., *Legal Personality and Political Pluralism*, p. 143. Pike cited the source of the quotation as the U.S. Supreme Court case of *Poulos v. New Hampshire*, 345 U.S. 395 (1953), but I could not find it anywhere in this case. Apparently, the quotation is miscited and, since Pike is now deceased, must remain anonymous.

5

Positive Neutrality: Religious Freedom in a Free Society

It was a cloudy January day when I visited the U.S. military cemetery near Florence, Italy, and walked among the row upon row of stone monuments marking the graves of over 4,000 U.S. citizens who were killed in World War II. It was an impressive, moving experience, but as I walked among the graves and reflected on the sacrifice that many had made, it also struck me that the military had handled a sensitive church-state issue more appropriately than is often done. If ever one's religious faith comes to the fore, it is in the presence of the ultimate fact of death. Thus, cemeteries are typically filled with religious symbolism. However, this was a government cemetery I was visiting: built and, even today, maintained by U.S. tax dollars. Is it appropriate — is it a constitutionally permitted breach in the wall of separation between church and state — for the government to purchase, erect, and maintain overtly religious symbols? (Remember the Christmas displays that have failed or barely managed to pass constitutional muster.) In addition, most of the men and women killed were Christians (defining "Christian" very broadly), but some, of course, were Jews. If religious symbolism is to be permitted, should it be distinctively Christian?

One solution to this situation — and one on which the Supreme Court and U.S. society have insisted in some parallel settings — would have been to ban all religious symbols and to develop a stone monument for the graves that is purely secular. A supposed neutrality among all religions and between religion and nonreligion would have been maintained. Another solution, one some have favored in parallel settings, would have been to provide Christian crosses for all, and if a family objected, its loved one would be buried off to the side and the family could purchase a marker of its choosing. Happily, the military has chosen another course of action. Thus, the cemetery is filled with the most common, powerful symbol of Christianity: the cross, which symbolizes the sacrificial death of Jesus Christ.

However, scattered throughout the cemetery, one also sees powerful symbols of the ancient Jewish faith — Stars of David — marking the graves of Jewish Americans who had made the ultimate sacrifice. In following this practice, the military, no doubt unwittingly, has moved in the direction of adopting a solution to this church-state issue that is in keeping with structural pluralism, an approach that I have termed *positive neutrality*.

Under positive neutrality, government is *neutral* in that it does not recognize or favor any one religion or religious group over any other, nor does it favor or recognize religious groups or religion as a whole over secular groups or secular philosophies and mind-sets as a whole.[1] It is evenhanded. Government takes a position of *positive* neutrality by recognizing that in practice, neutrality is often not achieved by government simply failing to do something. Positive neutrality insists that genuine religious freedom is not a negative freedom: it does not spontaneously spring into being in the absence of governmental regulations or programs. Sometimes government will have to take certain positive steps if it is to be truly neutral in the sense of assuring equal freedoms and equal opportunities for all religious persons and groups and for religious and irreligious persons and groups alike.

Thus, in the example of the military cemetery, government is neutral in that neither Christian nor Jewish religious symbols are uniformly placed onto the graves of all those who were killed in action. It is following positive neutrality in that neutrality is not gained by stripping the governmentally owned and operated cemetery of all religious symbols, but by the active, positive use of religious symbols corresponding to the religious faiths of the fallen men and women. Religion is recognized and given its due. If positive neutrality were to be more fully followed in this example, the military ought — especially in today's United States — to develop appropriate Islamic and secular symbols so that the graves of those of the Muslim faith or of no religious faith could also have their graves appropriately marked. Such an approach would break up the uniformity of rows and columns of crosses interspersed with a few Stars of David, but structural pluralism accepts and even celebrates pluralism over uniformity and diversity over conformity, even when things appear a bit messy as a result.

This chapter develops the implications for church-state relations of structural, normative pluralism (discussed in the previous chapter) and describes how it leads to the principle of positive neutrality. In the process, it demonstrates why structural pluralism supports the use of crosses and Stars of David and other appropriate religious or secular symbols in military cemeteries and how it can guide church-state relations in much more complex and controversial areas. In doing so I make use of the fundamental concepts and principles of the pluralist tradition explored in Chapter 4, but I do not seek simply to capture the thinking on church-state relations of that tradition and then apply it rigidly to the United States. To do so would be unduly limiting, since most theorists in the pluralist tradition have written for specific times and societies that, in significant ways, differ from those of the United States at the end of the twentieth century. In what follows I rely on the basic concepts and approaches of pluralism; the working out of their implications and applications to the present day U.S. setting are largely my own. I do so, first, by considering a new mind-set to which structural, normative pluralism leads; next, by considering the more specific content of the principle of positive neutrality; then, by contrasting positive neutrality with several other approaches to church-state questions; and last, by linking this principle to interpretations of the First Amendment.

It is important to be clear at the outset that positive neutrality and structural pluralism, which underlies it, do not produce a magical formula that will give clear-cut answers to church-state questions in a mechanical fashion. It will not yield a software program that, once loaded into a computer, spits out answers to any and all church-state issues. What pluralism does is, first, to provide a mind-set or perspective with which to view church-state questions that differs sharply from the one now dominant in the U.S. polity, and second, to form the basis for the principle of positive neutrality that, in turn, can give much-needed guidance in finding one's way through the thicket of church-state relations. This principle still needs to be applied in a creative, sensitive manner in order to yield just, balanced, and principled results. I will provide more on this last point in the next chapter.

PLURALISM AND A NEW MIND-SET

As described in Chapter 2, the current mind-set dominant within the Supreme Court and among the leaders of popular U.S. culture tends to see religion — at least in its particularistic manifestations, as distinct from religion-in-general — as having only a private, person-al relevance and lacking a real social or political impact. In fact, it views religion, when wedded to issues of social and political import, as a divisive, intolerant, and dangerous force.

Pluralism, in contrast, leads to a quite different perspective with which to approach church-state issues. This mind-set colors everything else, and thus is crucial in setting the context from which the more specific, concrete standard of positive neutrality emerges. Two features of this mind-set are especially important: a positive outlook on the contributions of religion in U.S. society and an unwavering commitment to full freedom of religion.

The first feature of pluralism's mind-set regarding religion and society is its perception that it is natural, healthy, and proper for the people of the United States to adhere to a great variety of faith communities and to join a wide range of churches and other religious associations, and for some to adhere to no religious faith at all. This is seen as an appropriate consequence of a free society. Structural pluralism welcomes religion in its various manifestations and in its various activities as a legitimate, contributing, integral part of U.S. society, including its political aspects. Not merely religion-in-general but also particularistic religion, whose adherents take it as an authoritative force in their lives, is respected and accepted as a part of the life of the U.S. polity. Moreover, it is not merely the individual in his or her religious dimension that pluralism accepts and honors; it is the religious structures of society — faith communities and religious associations — that are accepted and honored *as religious structures.* Catholic parochial schools, inner-city church-sponsored homeless shelters, Jewish senior citizen centers, evangelical Protestant colleges, Mormon nursing homes, Nation of Islam mosques, and those who identify with and have a close attachment to New Age thinking: all these and more are accepted and respected — including their politically relevant aspects. In dealing with them, the pluralist creatively seeks to develop political processes and public policies that will not merely tolerate faith communities and associations and their individual members, but will integrate them fully — as religious structures and persons — into the life of the body politic.

This is an enormously important shift from the mind-set that is prevalent today (as described and illustrated previously). That mind-set sees religion largely in individual, not structural, terms, and sees particularistic religion as a force that is largely irrelevant to the realm of politics and public policies and thus with little to contribute. Religious individuals should, of course, be tolerated, and their freedom of religion should not be denied, but their religious beliefs are seen as essentially private beliefs, relevant to individuals' personal lives but irrelevant to the affairs of state. Even worse, religious diversity is seen as socially divisive, and thus a danger when allowed into the political realm. Thus, erecting a wall of separation between religion and the state does no harm to religion and benefits the body politic. Religious structures — as religious structures — must be kept out of the political realm, or, at the most, allowed in in a carefully circumscribed, limited manner. This is held to be especially true of particularistic religious groups such as conservative Protestantism, Roman Catholicism, and Mormonism. Religious structures and individuals with potentially important religiously motivated political goals and insights are thereby finessed and squeezed onto the sidelines. Structural pluralism objects to this, seeing it as a form of religious intolerance and discrimination.

A second basic feature marking the mind-set fostered by pluralism is a commitment to full religious freedom for all faith communities and religious associations — and for persons and structures of no faith as well. Its goal is simple: full, complete freedom of religion. Pluralism has an expansive view of this freedom. It extends to believers in all religious traditions; the wide diversity of Christian religious associations and communities should have full religious freedom, but so also should native American religions, Islam, New Age beliefs, Hinduism, and more. Similarly, persons of no religious faith should have their freedom respected and guaranteed as fully as do persons of deeply held faith. In addition, religious freedom should extend not only to the development and practice of a religious structure's core religious beliefs, but also to the development and practice of the other three roles of religious associations and communities discussed in Chapter 4: molding their members' behavior and attitudes, providing an array of services, and influencing the policy-making process. These roles define the appropriate sphere of religion, and pluralism says that if religious associations and faith communities are to be truly, fully free, their freedom of action in their sphere must be assured. Also, religious freedom should extend to the religious beliefs and practices of churches, synagogues, and other such religious associations, but should also include the beliefs and activities of religiously based agencies such as schools, child-care centers, and other service or advocacy associations. A Jewish counseling center should have as full protection for its freedom to act on the basis of its distinctive Jewish character and beliefs as a synagogue. Pluralism insists that the tent of religious freedom be broad enough to encompass all these forms. Otherwise, the freedom of religious structures and their members will be thwarted.

It is important to note that pluralism also recognizes that religious associations and faith communities have certain obligations to other religious associations and faith communities, to the state, and to the rest of society. Full religious freedom does not mean that religious structures can do whatever they want, wherever and whenever they want to. I will develop this idea more fully as my argument progresses.

Current U.S. thinking does not hesitate to proclaim and protect full religious freedom as long as it is kept on the level of private, individual belief. Thus, a privatized religion is granted full religious freedom, but when religion moves from individual to corporate manifestations, from religion-in-general to particularistic religion, from beliefs to practice, or from a private, personal faith to one with social and political dimensions, trouble often arises. For example, the U.S. public and the U.S. legal system are fully comfortable with individual native Americans following their traditional religion in the quiet of their communities, but when that religion begins to move from individual observances to a tribal or area-wide movement, from beliefs to practices such as the use of peyote, and from private beliefs to social implications (such as questioning white society's continued use of traditionally sacred lands), doubts, fears, and challenges quickly surface. Structural pluralism has a broader, more inclusive, more expansive view of freedom of religion.

Conventional U.S. thinking on church and state tends to see pluralism's twin goals of full religious freedom and full involvement of a wide variety of religious structures in the polity as posing an unresolvable dilemma. To the conventional mind-set, religious freedom implies governmental neutrality toward religion and neutrality implies church-state separation. After all, if government accedes to one religion's demands for certain public policies, financially supports one religious group's drug rehabilitation center, or places the symbol of one religious group in front of city hall at the time of its major religious holiday, is not the state favoring and supporting that religion, thereby compromising the religious freedom of all other religious groups and of non-believers? On the other hand, structural pluralism argues that by discouraging religiously based groups from influencing public policy debates, by refusing assistance to religiously based social service agencies when it is being given to all others, and by ignoring the civic contributions of religious but not secular groups, freedom of religion is also being violated. In either case, it appears impossible to have full religious freedom. Either religious freedom is violated by denying religion equal access to or equal recognition in the public realm, or it is violated by favoring one religion over another or religion over secularism.

Structural, normative pluralism and the principle of positive neutrality, which it spawns, show this dilemma to be apparent, not real. There is another way that avoids being impaled on either horn of the dilemma and does not follow an unprincipled, messy middle ground. Religious structures can be given their full due, without favoring one religion over another or religion over secularism. However, to find this new way, old categories and assumptions must be laid aside and replaced by fresh ones. I have hinted at and described in general terms what new categories and assumptions I have in mind. The time has come to be more specific.

A PLURALIST FRAMEWORK FOR CHURCH-STATE ISSUES

Positive neutrality and structural pluralism begin their approach to church-state issues by recognizing and respecting the quasi-sovereignty that both religious structures and the state possess in their proper spheres of activity. Neither the one nor the other grants certain rights or imposes obligations on the other; rather, each possesses certain rights and obligations inherently. The Second Vatican Council could not have stated it more clearly: "The political community and the Church are autonomous and independent of each other in their own fields."[2] The Dutch Protestant Abraham Kuyper expressed it this way: "The sovereignty of the State and the sovereignty of the Church exist side by side, and they mutually limit each other."[3] The position of the Church of England pluralist John Figgis has been described as being rooted in "a recognition by the State of the sphere of authority of the churches [which] involved a reciprocal recognition by churches of the State's sphere of authority."[4] Moreover, the French Catholic Jacques Maritain wrote that "the body politic is autonomous and independent within its own sphere."[5] He also stressed the parallel freedom of the church, which is rooted in its inherent, inalienable rights: "Freedom of the Church appears as grounded on the very rights of God and as identical with His own freedom in the face of any human institution. . . . As a result, the first general principle to be stated, with respect to the problems we are examining, is *the freedom of the Church to teach and preach and worship, the freedom of the Gospel, the freedom of the word of God.*"[6]

Pluralism's belief in the quasi-autonomy of both the religious and political spheres means that in order to develop a pluralist perspective on church-state issues, it is crucial to explore the basic nature of the religious sphere within which specific, concrete religious associations and faith communities possess a quasi-autonomy and the nature of the political sphere within which specific, concrete governments possess the same feature. After doing so, we can then inquire how the two spheres relate to each other.

Religion as a Quasi-Sovereign Sphere

If religious structures are to possess an actual quasi-autonomy or quasi-sovereignty in their proper realm of endeavor, there are certain rights that they possess and that the rest of society (especially government) needs to honor and respect. However, this is not simply a one-way street. There are also certain responsibilities that religious structures have toward both the state and such societal spheres as that of the family, science, commerce, and the arts. This section explores both the rights and the obligations or responsibilities possessed by religion. Before doing so, however, it is important to specify more exactly what is meant by religion as a possessor of both rights and responsibilities.

Religious Structures

Religion manifests itself in three types of religious structures. First, there are religious associations that develop and teach the core teachings of a religious faith and provide a forum for their observance. In the Christian tradition, formally organized churches, whether on the local congregational or the national denominational levels, are prime examples of this first type of religious association. Synagogues, temples, mosques, and other such centers are formal associations that are the equivalent to churches within Christianity. What they all have in common is that they are religious in the sense that they possess a unified system of beliefs and practices that answer ultimate questions by reliance on the supernatural. (See Chapter 4 and the definition of religion introduced there.) They are associations in that they are formal organizations, with explicit, formal structures and, usually, written statements of faith or purpose. Another distinction is harder to define precisely, but it is important in order to distinguish this type of religious association from the one to be described next. This first type of religious association deals directly with what in Chapter 4 I called core religious beliefs (that is, beliefs and practices that address ultimate questions) in distinction from dealing with applications or consequences of those core beliefs. For example, it is in the context of churches that — in the Christian tradition — religious doctrines are developed and propounded and affirming religious rituals and ceremonies such as the mass and baptism are conducted.

A second type of religious structure consists of religious associations whose primary purpose is to provide a structure for the living-out and application in society of a religion's core beliefs. The clearest examples are that of religiously based service agencies such as schools, adoption agencies, hospitals, homeless shelters, and disaster relief agencies, but they also include religiously based policy advocacy groups. Again, all these are religious associations: They are formal organizations rooted in explicit, self-consciously held religious beliefs. However, they are distinguished from such associations as churches and synagogues in that they specialize in the application or living out of core religious beliefs. It is especially important to take note of them because in the present U.S. context, they are put under pressures to deny their religious roots and to act in some important ways like similar or parallel, but secularly based, associations. However, the fact that they specialize in the application of religious beliefs out in the broader society does not make them any less religious in nature than structures dealing more directly with a group's core religious beliefs. Although some of them have become largely secularized and thus cannot be considered religious associations, many are still deeply and profoundly religious in nature and, under pluralism, have as much right to a quasi-sovereignty as do religious associations dealing directly with a religion's core beliefs.

A third type of religious structure consists of faith communities bound together by organic, affective ties, even in the absence of a formal organization. Faith communities are not formal organizations; rather, they are communities rooted in ties of faith, shared traditions, and feelings of self-identity. They are tremendously important and usually provide much of the impetus on which the more concrete religious associations run, due to the deeply felt emotions and sense of mutual self-identity that they engender.

Rights Possessed by Religious Associations and Faith Communities

The basic right possessed by religious associations and faith communities — and by their individual members — is full freedom of belief and action. Here one is at the heart of what it means for a religious association or faith community to possess a quasi-sovereignty in the sphere of religion. Persons and religious structures simply must be free to develop, practice, and act on the basis of their religious beliefs. They possess as a right, and not at the sufferance of the state, the freedom to engage in all four of the roles or activities outlined in Chapter 4: to develop and teach their core beliefs, shape their members' behavior and attitudes, provide a wide range of services, and participate in the policy-making process. These roles help define the nature and meaning of religion in U.S. life. To the extent that religious associations and faith communities are blocked or discouraged from fulfilling any or all of these roles, freedom of religion is violated. They define the appropriate sphere of religion's activity within which structural pluralism insists that religion possesses a quasi-sovereignty. The rights possessed by religious structures emerge out of the need to protect religion's ability freely to fulfill these four roles or functions. Rights, and the freedom they imply, are always limited, not absolute, and we will explore some of the limitations later. At this point, however, the emphasis is on the freedom to believe and to act on the basis of those beliefs.

A broader view of religious freedom is being advanced here than may immediately be apparent. If freedom of religious belief and action is to be real — if religious structures and their members are to possess a true autonomy in their religious sphere of activity, churches and other religious associations that develop and teach core religious beliefs, a wide variety of religiously based and motivated associations whose function is to live out a religion's core beliefs in society, and informal faith communities must all be free to engage in the four roles listed in the previous paragraph. They are not to be directly blocked or prohibited from engaging in them, nor is any religious association or faith community, or their members, to be discouraged from or disadvantaged in engaging in them, as compared to other religious or secular structures and their members. No government, no business corporation, no school or university, no labor union, nor any other societal force may either directly forbid a religious belief or practice or impose indirect burdens on a religious belief or practice. Obviously, government is not to imprison the members of some new religious sect, nor is a law school to refuse admittance to Jews, a business concern to refuse to hire black Muslims, or a university to refuse to hire a Mormon. However, true freedom of belief and action extends beyond this. Government and the rest of society must not pressure and indirectly discourage or disadvantage religious beliefs and religiously rooted practices. For government to provide fire protection to a building owned by a secular literary club, but not to a church — simply because it is a church — would be a form of pressuring and limiting the free exercise of religion. Similarly, for government to give aid to a secular hospital but not to a Catholic hospital — simply because it is Catholic — is to discourage and disadvantage religion, or for a private insurance company to charge a Jewish youth camp — simply because it is Jewish — more for fire and liability insurance than it does a similarly situated Christian youth camp would clearly be to pressure and limit the freedom of religion. The key here is neutrality: the right of religious structures to autonomy is violated if their freedom in their sphere is blocked by the actions of other spheres' structures, or if such actions place a burden or withhold a benefit as compared to similar religious structures of other religious traditions or compared to similar structures that are secularly based. More specifically, powerful structures in the political sphere are not to use their power to advantage or disadvantage (1) certain particular structures in the religious sphere, (2) structures in the religious sphere as a whole, or (3) structures in the religious sphere as compared to structures of a similar or parallel nature outside the religious sphere. This is true neutrality; this is respecting the autonomy of the spheres. It is crucial to keep in mind that this right is not absolute, however. The religious sphere possesses a quasi-autonomy, not an absolute autonomy.

Responsibilities Possessed by Religious Associations and Faith Communities

Religious structures possess not only rights but also responsibilities or obligations. Just as other spheres must respect religious structures' rights to a quasi-sovereignty in their realm, so also religious structures must respect the other spheres and the autonomy they possess in their realms. This gives rise to obligations or responsibilities. More specifically, religious structures have obligations toward other religious structures, the state, and society more broadly.

Toward other religious structures and individuals of no religious faith, religious structures and their members owe a sense of respect or civility and an honoring of their rights and freedoms. A sense of respect, civility, and self-restraint needs to characterize the relationships of Christians with Jews, Episcopalians with Fundamentalists, Unitarians with charismatics, Shirley McLain's New Age devotees with Muslims, and all of them with committed secularists. This does not mean that differences have to be submerged or that proselytizing cannot take place. Structural pluralism is not rooted in relativism, that is, in the belief that religious differences ultimately do not matter since all contain the truth for their adherents. Instead, it is rooted in the belief that religious differences matter, and because they matter, religious associations, faith communities, and their members must be free to speak, argue, and act. However, one can be firm and forthright in one's sincere beliefs without being hateful and intimidating. The obligation being highlighted here means that the opposite side of structures' and persons' religious freedom is their obligation to avoid pressure tactics, threats, intimidation, and hateful, untruthful, or slanderous attacks. It is as a religious association and individuals in a faith community eschew such tactics that the quasi-sovereignty of other religious associations and faith communities will be safeguarded. If all religious associations and their members are to experience freedom of religion, each must respect the rights (the autonomy or quasi-sovereignty) of all the others. This includes the respect and civility being stressed here.

Religious structures and their members also have certain responsibilities toward government. Their responsibility essentially comes down to respecting the state's exercise of its responsibilities in its appropriate sphere. This entails three things: First, it means accepting and building up the authority and legitimacy of government and obeying its lawful decisions. Many political theorists have stressed the fact that effective government is rooted in the attitudes and traditions of the public, which accord it legitimacy and support it with obedience to its decisions.[7] Religion can be very important in achieving this state of affairs. In fact, it is hard to think of a single polity that has successfully achieved the voluntary, willing acceptance of governmental authority without the strong support of religion. Religion by its very nature touches on matters of the heart: on matters of feelings, attitudes, and faith. When one speaks of authority, legitimacy, and support for government and its policies, one is discussing the exact area in which religion reigns supreme. Second, religion has a responsibility to support or develop what has been termed civic virtue. As seen in Chapter 4, Alexis de Tocqueville (in the nineteenth century) and A. James Reichley (today), among others, have noted that religion in the process of simply being religion builds attitudes and virtues that are essential to the continuance of a healthy, effective, free society.[8] Virtues such as discipline, truthfulness, self-restraint, and respect for self and others are all key examples. These are essential to a peaceful, effective society in which people live and work together in relative harmony and peace. Religious structures have a duty to promote and inculcate them.

These first two points ought not to be interpreted to mean that religious structures may not critique government and its policies. Religious structures and their leaders, with their values and perspectives, may appropriately evaluate government and its policies. They may react negatively to and call for changes in certain public policies, and should even withdraw their generalized support from government when it moves beyond its proper sphere of responsibilities, as totalitarian governments do. Dietrich Bonhoeffer, who, as a Lutheran pastor in Nazi Germany, withdrew his support for the Nazi regime and actively worked for its overthrow (actions that cost him his life) stands in a noble tradition of religiously motivated persons who opposed and worked to change the state based on their understanding of God's will.

A third implication of the religious sphere's obligation to respect the state's exercise of its responsibilities is its duty not to try to take over or exercise the authority that rightly belongs to the state. The government's appropriate sphere of activity (in keeping with the definition developed in Chapter 4) is the continuing, ongoing exercise of authority over all persons in a defined geographic area. In doing so, government should (as will be shortly stressed) play a coordinative, empowering, protecting role in relationship to all the other societal spheres. Religious associations must not seek to take over that role. Structural pluralism would thus agree with the Supreme Court in objecting to what has been termed "vesting entanglement," which "doctrine prohibits the state from vesting government powers in religious bodies."[9] It would agree with the conclusion — if not necessarily all the reasoning — of the Supreme Court in *Larken v. Grendal's Den, Inc.* (1982), which held a Massachusetts statute unconstitutional that had delegated to churches the authority to veto the issuance of liquor licenses within 500 feet of a church. The Court concluded that the law was an improper "delegation of legislative zoning power to a nongovernmental entity."[10] Normative, structural pluralism says that religious structures have a responsibility not to aspire to exercise governing authority of this nature. If they do so, they will leave their proper sphere and invade that of the state, and in the process, inappropriately limit the sovereignty of the state in its proper sphere.

Admittedly, in the age of the comprehensive, intrusive administrative state, which has taken over many functions that in an earlier age were exercised by religious and other voluntary associations (such as education, care of the ill and elderly, and family counseling), in practice it is often difficult to delineate the boundary between the religious and political spheres. The key is the exercising of a decision-making authority for society, broadly conceived, which is the exclusive province of the state, not a supposed actual division of labor in terms of concrete tasks, which in today's world often does not exist.

Finally, religious structures also have responsibilities toward society as a whole. These essentially fall under the duty (as with the last point made about the religious sphere's responsibilities toward the state) not to interfere improperly in society's various autonomous spheres, such as economics, science, and art. Churches and other religious associations are not business enterprises, scientific research institutes, nor academies of the performing arts, and they need to respect the quasi-sovereignty of these other spheres. Religious associations and faith communities can — and indeed should — establish and teach certain norms that ought to guide endeavors in these other spheres, such as a commitment to truth, fairness, civility, and beauty. However, even if such norms are violated, it is not the duty of the religious structures in and by themselves to set things right by taking over these other sphere's functions. If they did, religion would be totalitarian, not limited.

The Political Realm as a Quasi-Sovereign Sphere

Government in the United States consists of over eighty thousand separate governing entities: one national government, fifty state governments, and thousands of local governments, including cities, counties, school districts, and a bewildering variety of special districts.[11] The political realm — within which one finds these eighty thousand separate governments — is a separate sphere of activity that possesses a quasi-sovereignty. This sphere is delineated by the nature of the state and the role it plays in society. Chapter 4 defined government as the formal, purposeful organization that exercises authority over all persons in a defined geographic area on a continuing basis. This authority of government must be exercised in pursuit of justice, the common good, the public interest, or some other such norm. However that norm is defined, pluralism insists it must be rooted in protecting, coordinating, and empowering the other societal spheres. All must be given their due. In pursuit of this objective (as Chapter 4 pointed out), the modern state seeks to provide for national security and public safety, to manage the economy, and to provide an array of needed services. This is the political sphere. As is the case with religious structures, the state has certain rights that safeguard its autonomy in its sphere, and it has certain responsibilities or duties toward religion and the other societal spheres. An understanding of these rights and responsibilities helps clarify the relationship between religious structures and government.

Rights Possessed by Government

The basic right of government is to possess the freedom it needs to exercise an autonomy or sovereignty in its sphere without intervention and interference by other social structures. This means that government has a right to exercise a decision-making authority backed by sanctions. However, it does not mean that government possesses a full sovereignty that permits it to set society's goals and then limit or empower the other structures of society in their pursuit. Doing so would uphold the absolute, and not the quasi-sovereignty of government. Pluralism sees the state playing a limited role in society on the basis that its authority is limited by the right to autonomy that the other spheres possess in their realms. Thus, the state's authority is to be exercised so as to coordinate, protect, encourage, and empower the other structures in society, thereby enabling them to play their assigned roles. Those associations and communities that would overreach and expand their role and power beyond that of their appropriate sphere must be restrained and limited, while those that are too weak or hesitant to exercise their roles in their areas need to be encouraged and supported and the gray areas between spheres need to be defined and regulated. Government, in short, possesses the right freely to make authoritative policy decisions aimed at coordinating, protecting, encouraging, and empowering society's various spheres of endeavor so as to promote justice, the public interest, the common good, or some other such normative goal.

In relationship to religion, this means that pluralism sees the state as having the right to assure that religious structures do not transgress on other spheres of activity. There have been times in Western history, for example, when the church has overstepped its bounds, trying either to get the state to enforce for it or itself to enforce suppression of Jews or other non-Christian groups, certain specific economic relationships, or certain limitations on scientific investigations. Then the government has the right to resist the church and insist that it is overstepping its sphere. An important distinction is needed at this point, however. In pursuit of the policy-influencing role mentioned earlier, religious associations are free to try to change public policies in keeping with their beliefs. The key limiting factor in their doing so is that they should only advocate public policies that are compatible with the nature and role of the state. They should only ask the state to make authoritative public policies that they are convinced will promote the public interest or the common good, or in some way will be to the benefit of society as a whole. In other words, they should be seeking only to influence policies that the state pursues in its role of coordinating, empowering, and enhancing the various societal spheres. They have no right to try to influence the state to do that which it has no business doing. The medieval church erred in its attempts to use the state to persecute Jews because it was asking the state to act contrary to its role of protecting and enhancing the various faith communities and instead to violate the rights of the Jewish faith community. However, churches do not err — to take a very specific, contemporary issue — to work either for or against requiring businesses to grant their workers leaves at the time of the birth or illness of children. This is a point at which the economic and family spheres interact and the rights and duties of families and business concerns need to be sorted out. The state has a proper role to play in doing so, and therefore, churches and other religious associations can appropriately seek to influence the public policy that the state adopts.

A corollary of the basic right of the state to assure that religious structures are respecting the autonomy of the other spheres is its entitlement to support from religious associations and communities. This support includes a sense of legitimacy which authenticates the state's authority, the material and financial wherewithal needed by government, and persons willing to play governmental roles as civil servants, elected officeholders, citizen activists, and military and law enforcement personnel. Through exhortations, teachings, and example, religious associations (such as religiously based colleges and universities, churches and synagogues, and religious publishing houses) can play a vital role in assuring that the rights of government are respected and met. This entitlement of the state to the support and help of the religious sphere is the mirror image of the responsibilities of the religious sphere (discussed earlier). As already stressed, religious associations and faith communities have an important responsibility to help assure that the needs of the state are met as long as it is fulfilling its proper role in its sphere.

The Responsibilities of Government

Government also has certain key responsibilities or obligations toward the various societal spheres, including the religious structures in society. The key one is to assure that it does not transgress on the sovereignty of the other spheres in their proper fields of endeavor. The state is not to limit scientific investigation and discovery, try to dictate artistic standards, or run the economy. As just seen, it has the right, under pluralist thought, to encourage, empower, and coordinate such societal spheres as these, but it has an obligation not to try to take them over and itself engage in science, art, or economics. The Catholic pluralist Yves Simon has written of the need "to keep the state confined within the functions that belong to it irreducibly and to hold in check its always threatening tendency to trespass, to encroach, to invade, and to destroy."[12]

In regard to religion, government has the responsibility to assure that religious structures have full freedom within their sphere of activity; that is, that other religious structures, other spheres' structures, and government itself are not transgressing on the religious structures' exercise of their proper autonomy. The goal is that of positive neutrality. Government is to be neutral toward religious structures, thereby recognizing their right to a quasi-autonomy. However, when necessary, it takes positive steps to achieve this. It does not take a hands-off approach to religion if the result of its doing so is to disadvantage or handicap religious structures in the playing of their role in their sphere. Sometimes, a hands-off, strict separation approach will achieve this goal; at other times, it will not. It is the achievement of the goal that is controlling, and not the rigid, unbending application of the separation approach.

Structural pluralism, in summary, recognizes the nature and importance of the rights and obligations that both religius structures and the state possess in the spheres or realms of endeavor in which each possesses a semi-sovereignty. Both religious structures and the state must exercise their rights and meet their obligations to other spheres faithfully. It is out of this mind-set and out of the recognition of the sovereignty of the religious and political spheres guaranteed by the reciprocal recognition of rights and obligations that the principle of positive neutrality emerges.

POSITIVE NEUTRALITY

The principle of positive neutrality has two interlocking sides or facets to it. The first is rooted in the rights possessed by the religious sphere and seeks to assure that religious associations and communities, and their individual members, are not constricted or disadvantaged in the living-out of their religious beliefs. The second facet seeks to assure that religious structures, in the exercise of their beliefs and rights, do not transgress on the rights and prerogatives of the other spheres and that one religious structure does not transgress on those of another or of nonbelievers. The first facet, therefore, says that religious associations, faith communities, and their individual members must be free to (1) believe what their consciences and traditions dictate and act on the basis of those beliefs; (2) seek to influence by persuasion the political process and public policies, in keeping with their religious beliefs; and (3) receive recognition and material aid from the state in support of activities with public, this-world benefits to the broader society, provided the state does not discriminate among religious groups and provided the state gives recognition or material aid to secularly based groups with similar or parallel programs. The second facet of positive neutrality states that religious associations, faith communities, and their individual members have an obligation to assure, and the government has the right to insist, that (1) religious associations and communities in the exercise of their rights do not interfere with the freedoms of other religious structures or endanger the health, safety, order, and freedom of society; and (2) that in the case of material aid to religiously based groups, they do not misuse or misspend the aid given in support of programs with public benefits. That is the heart of the principle, but it needs explication.

The first right of religious structures on which positive neutrality insists is the freedom of belief and the freedom to act on the basis of those beliefs. This right safeguards religion's autonomy in relation to two of its key, defining roles: developing core beliefs and shaping adherents' behavior and attitudes. Positive neutrality recognizes that if religion is to enjoy its rightful quasi-autonomy, both religiously based beliefs and religiously based actions must be protected. It rejects the belief-action distinction that the Supreme Court has at times asserted. If this right is to have meaning, society and the public policies of government, at times, will have to accommodate themselves to the practices of religious groups. This is familiar ground. Current public policy already seeks to accommodate those whose religious belief forbids participation in war, for example. Moreover, the Supreme Court has required state education systems to allow the Amish, based on their religious scruples, to withdraw their children from school after the eighth grade.[13] This aspect of the positive neutrality principle applauds such policies and would make additional accommodations and allowances to religious groups in order to allow them the fullest possible freedom of practice as well as belief.

This first right that is protected by positive neutrality is partially balanced by the first obligation of the religious sphere: In the pursuit of freedom of religious belief and action, the health, safety, order, and freedom of the rest of society — including that of other religious structures — are not to be violated. Pluralism is not anarchy: The quasi-sovereignty of religious associations does not mean that they should be allowed to engage in, for example, human sacrifice. There will be some hard cases here, requiring a careful balancing of the rights of deeply religious persons to practice and live out their religious beliefs freely and their obligation not to endanger or restrict the freedom of others or to disrupt the social order. The principle is clear, but reasonable persons will sometimes disagree on its proper application in concrete cases. Sensitivity to competing values and a genuine respect both for religion and for societal needs are crucial here. Chapter 6 considers how I see the somewhat abstract standard presented here applying to ongoing, concrete issues and controversies.

These two aspects of the positive neutrality principle are a departure (but not a radical one) from current legal doctrine and culturally dominant attitudes. They certainly run counter to the sharp belief-action distinction that the Supreme Court made in *Reynolds v. United States* (1879). However, they are in keeping with the compelling state interest test discussed in Chapter 2, which seeks to weigh the right of religious groups to practice their beliefs freely against the need of society for order, safety, and other compelling societal interests. However, as also seen in Chapter 2, the Supreme Court has often taken very weak positions in protecting unpopular or nonmainstream religious practices, and in some recent decisions, the Court majority has virtually done away with the compelling state interest test. As discussed more fully in the next chapter, positive neutrality has grave concerns about this recent trend. Nevertheless, positive neutrality is close to the position taken by the Court in some other cases. Its application would clearly require a shift in emphasis by the Supreme Court and the rest of the political system toward a greater willingness to tolerate and accommodate a wide range of religious practices, yet it is only a shift in emphasis that is called for, not a wholly new standard.

The second right of religious groups that positive neutrality seeks to protect is the right to freely influence the political process and the formation of public policies. The quasi-sovereignty of religious associations and faith communities in their key role of influencing public policies is thereby protected. Under this right, the United States Conference of Catholic Bishops would have every right to try to influence U.S. military or foreign policy; a Jewish group, to influence U.S. policy toward Israel; a legislator, to introduce legislation based on her evangelical Protestant beliefs; and a president to argue for a foreign policy initiative based on his religiously rooted values. All could do so openly, explicitly, and on the basis of particularistic religious beliefs. They would not have to do so implicitly, in veiled language, or on the basis of religion-in-general. This aspect of positive neutrality requires a shift in the culturally dominant opinion that now often questions the propriety of religious groups, religious leaders, and deeply religious public officials using their religiously rooted values and perspectives to guide and shape their reactions to questions of public policy — or at least to do so openly and explicitly. This aspect of positive neutrality would require the Supreme Court to drop the "secular purpose" prong of the three-part *Lemon* test of constitutionality (critiqued in Chapter 2), since religious motivations of legislators would no longer be held suspect.

The third right of religion on which positive neutrality centers marks the sharpest departure from current legal doctrine and culturally dominant opinion, and no doubt is the most controversial. It is rooted in the fact that if the state is to be truly neutral toward similar or parallel secularly based and religiously based groups and perspectives, it will sometimes have to take positive steps of accommodation, recognition, and material aid toward both, rather than singling out the secularly based groups and perspectives for accommodation, recognition, or aid. Because of the comprehensive administrative state, a radically different situation exists today than existed a hundred or even sixty years ago. For centuries, much of whatever aid was available to the ill, orphaned, poor, or others buffeted by life's tragedies came from religiously based associations and networks. Whatever formal education oppor-tunities there were also were largely provided by religiously based structures. However, in the age of the administrative state and a religiously pluralistic society, this has changed radically because both government and private, secularly based associations also provide an incredibly wide range of services. It is out of this situation that the problem noted in Chapter 2 emerges in stark, persistent dimensions: If neutrality is defined purely in terms of no state recognition or support for religion, it, in fact, is not neutral but rather is promoting a secular cultural ethos.

Several implications flow from this conclusion. When government runs certain educational and other service programs, it must recognize, or make allowance for, the religious beliefs of the persons being served. Thus, religious beliefs should be recognized and accommodated, as long as the full range of religious beliefs present in the community and similar or parallel secular beliefs are also recognized and accommodated. Thus, positive neutrality says that if prayer is an important part of the day for many children attending a state-run educational program, some allowance for prayer should be made, as long as no single religious tradition is favored and allow-ance is made for those who do not believe in prayer. Otherwise the implicit message will be that although the many subjects and activities engaged in during the course of the day are important prayer is not.

Similarly, if government takes positive steps to recognize or honor secularly based groups, in order to be truly neutral it must take positive steps to give the same sort of recognition or honor to similarly situated religiously based groups, for example, ceremonial recog-nitions such as governmental proclamations honoring an associa-tion or club or the displaying of symbols or providing space for information booths on public property. Positive neutrality simply says that if this sort of recognition is given to secular groups such as the Boy Scouts, Rotary Club, or an environmental protection advocacy group, neutrality demands that such recognition be given to reli-giously based groups as well. They should not be systematically excluded from public recognition thereby sending the not-so-subtle message that the secularly based groups are an important, con-tributing part of the community while the wide variety of religiously based groups are not.

In the same vein, when government gives material aid to secularly based homeless shelters, child-care agencies, schools, and a host of other such agencies that provide valuable public benefits to society, similar agencies that are religiously based and also provide shelter to the homeless, care for children, and education should be eligible to receive state-sponsored material aid in support of their programs with public benefits for society. Genuine neutrality demands no less. This aid should not, of course, go to a church to support, say, its construction of a new house of worship or to buy new hymn books. It is to be limited to programs with direct, this-world benefits to society. However, religiously based groups should receive this aid even if religious values and activities are integrated into the programs receiving assistance. I purposely have referred to programs with "public benefits to society," not to "secular programs." A Christian drug treatment program that includes prayers and Bible study as a component could still receive aid. The key is the direct, this-world benefit that society receives from the program. Religious groups should not have to secularize their programs in order to make them eligible for aid, nor should they have to pretend that the secular and religious aspects of a single program can be sorted out, with only the secular aspect receiving aid, as Chapter 2 demonstrated is now often required. To put such requirements on religiously based groups and programs would force them to become (or to pretend they have become) something they are not. This would be a violation of their sovereignty in their role as providers of services, which, in turn, means that their full freedom of religious belief and practice would be violated.

The key limits that positive neutrality demands is that material aid has to be given to a wide variety of religious and secular groups without discrimination among them, and religious groups receiving aid would have to be held financially accountable in order to assure that the funds given are, in fact, going for the purposes intended. This latter limit is an obligation religious associations have, and the state has a right to enforce it.

Positive neutrality thereby solves the dilemma of having to choose between, on the one hand, a neutrality by government defined in negative terms (no government recognition, accommodation, or support for religion in any form), which ends up favoring secularism over religion, and, on the other hand, an aiding of religion that ends up favoring one religion over another or religion over secularism. Positive neutrality escapes this dilemma by opening the political process to all. Its neutrality is not based on a separation that welcomes secularism but excludes religion from public affairs, nor does it accommodate itself to civil religion or religion-in-general, which then is made into an official, semiestablished faith. Instead, it allows those of all religious faiths, and of none, free access to the public forum. This public forum thereby comes to resemble society as it is in all its religious diversity. Government is neutral in that it favors no religion over any other nor religion nor secularism over each other. It is evenhanded, but it is an evenhandedness achieved only by the state taking certain positive steps. A full, genuine religious freedom for all believers and nonbelievers is the final result. In the terms of pluralism, the quasi-sovereignty of the religious sphere is recognized and safeguarded. Freedom of conscience is thereby protected and religion is free to participate fully in the social, public life of the nation, yet no special recognition or material aid (special in the sense that one has to be religious in nature to receive it) is accorded religion as a whole or any religious group.

In addition, positive neutrality protects the integrity of religion from the deadening effects that government establishment and support has historically proven to have. Religion seems to thrive best in a situation of independence and competition, not in a situation of governmental subsidization and standardization. The fact that under positive neutrality, the widest possible variety of religious associations and communities are assured freedom of belief and action, and are recognized, honored, and allowed equal access to social, public forums should, if anything, heighten competition among religious groups and thereby increase their flexibility and popular appeal, rather than resulting in a staid comfortableness.

Some may object that the neutrality of positive neutrality is not neutral at all, but rather is supportive or positive toward religion. There is both truth and error in this observation. Pluralism says that for the state to be positive and supportive of secularly based groups and programs and to fail to give any support or recognition to religiously based groups and programs, even when they are engaged in the same or similar activities of benefit to society, is to discriminate against religion. Government is no longer neutral. Similarly, to allow all points of view into public debate except those with a religious base is to discriminate against religion. (This was a basic contention of Chapter 2.) The only viable answer that pluralism sees to this unfairness is not, of course, for government to fail to give any recognition or material aid to secularly based groups or to question the legitimacy of secularly based points of view in public debate, but for it rather to welcome, recognize, and support religiously and secularly based groups alike. This is neutrality, but it is a neutrality rooted in a favorableness toward, or a favoring of, religion and secularism alike. This is one sense in which positive neutrality is supportive of religion. It recognizes, honors, and supports religion and encourages its participation in the public life of the nation. It is still neutral, however, for it offers the same type of support to all religions and to religion and secularism alike. This is the only way in which a true neutrality can be maintained, because only in this way can the state avoid singling out any one religious tradition over another, or either religion or secularism over the other.

Positive Neutrality and Other Church-State Theories

The more exact contours of the positive neutrality principle and the new perspectives it brings to church-state relations can be seen by comparing it with three other church-state theories: the accommodationist, the strict separationist, and strict neutrality. This section compares and contrasts positive neutrality with each of these three perspectives and suggests why it offers an approach that is more fully in keeping with the ideal of full, genuine freedom of religion.

The Accommodationist Position

Accommodationists (also often called nonpreferentialists) believe that the state should be allowed, as legal scholar Carl Esbeck has put it, "to aid or favor religion in general over those professing no religious belief. They argue that, although the first amendment prevents the establishment of a national church, the founding fathers never contemplated prohibiting government aid to religion on a nondiscriminatory basis."[14] Accommodationists believe that strong, vibrant religious faith is a positive help to the state in fostering civic virtue. Thus, it is in the state's own self-interest to encourage and accommodate religion in a nonpreferential manner. Religion is to be encouraged over nonbelief. As historian John F. Wilson pointed out, accommodationists "believe that the First Amendment excludes only the direct establishment of, or preferential treatment for, a particular religion. Indeed, government should facilitate the practice of religion by both individuals and collectivities as essential to the common good."[15] If the state fails to be supportive of religion and instead pursues policies of strict separation, it ends up, in practice, supporting an antireligious secularism that was never intended by the authors of the Constitution.

Based on underlying beliefs such as these, accommodationists end up supporting two types of government accommodation to religion. One is a support for broad, religion-in-general. Thus, they have, for example, supported the New York Board of Regents' prayer for use in public schools ("Almighty God, we acknowledge our dependence upon Thee, and we beg Thy blessings upon us, our parents, our teachers and our Country"), prayers at the start of legislative sessions, the display of religious symbols on public property, and Bible reading and the posting of the Ten Commandments in public schools. The second type of accommodation to religion that nonpreferentialists often support is governmental aid to a variety of religiously based service organizations such as schools, colleges, and child-care agencies. Such support usually rests in a religious-secular dualism, which argues that religiously based organizations provide clearly distinguishable secular and sacred services and that the secular ones may be supported by government.[16] Even when these agencies or programs are run by distinctly religious groups, state aid can go to them as long as the aid only funds their secular, and not their sacred, programs.

The accommodationist approach to church-state issues is the chief alternative to the strict separation approach to be examined next. When the Supreme Court has approved deviations from strict separation standards, it has usually done so on accommodationist-like grounds.

Positive neutrality agrees with the accommodationists' emphasis on the important role that religion plays in society. The two approaches share a friendliness or supportive attitude toward religion in society. Both reject the strict separation interpretation of the First Amendment and see the wall of separation metaphor as an extralegal dictum that does not reflect the intent of the authors of the Bill of Rights. Both see the strict separation position as leading not to neutrality, but to the implicit support of an antireligious secularism.

Here, however, the points of agreement run out and basic differences begin to emerge. In fact, positive neutrality rejects both the underlying contentions of accommodationists. In regard to nonpreferential support for and recognition of religion-in-general, positive neutrality sees this as an improper support for a nondescript civil religion or a bland lowest-common-denominator faith, which is far removed from the deep, rich beliefs of religion-in-particular: Roman Catholicism, Native American religion, Protestant Fundamentalism, Orthodox Judaism, and the hundreds of other specific, concrete manifestations of religious faith. Moreover, this sort of nonpreferential support of religion-in-general discriminates against those of no faith. Such nonpreferential support for religion-in-general is usually not much more than an attempt to hang onto some pale remnants of the nineteenth-century de facto establishment of Protestantism.

Structuralist pluralists also reject the sacred-secular dualism that is present in much of accommodationist thought. Within Christianity down through the centuries, the entire point of establishing schools, hospitals, orphanages, and other such programs of charity and service has been to live out the commands of Jesus and to give concrete expression to the beliefs of one's faith. To call these programs and service activities secular, and presumably indistinguishable from those offered by groups that have no religious orientation at all, is to demean religion and its power to transform persons in all aspects of their lives. The same point could be made in regard to a Nation of Islam drug treatment program or to other religions and their service programs. Positive neutrality and structural pluralism see attempts to gain state aid for religiously based organizations on the basis of supposedly secular activities as themselves a denial of religious freedom. To receive aid under such conditions would encourage, if not require, the organization or agency to deny its religious roots and substitute a secular faith. For example, a 1988 bill designed to provide financial assistance to child-care centers provided that church and other religiously based centers could receive aid as long as none of the funds would go to "sectarian" purposes. Moreover, "all religious symbols and artifacts" would have to be "covered or have been removed" from rooms in which child care was given.[17] A religiously based center could only receive assistance if it had been stripped of all aspects of its religious tradition, including something as minor as a cross or picture of Jesus on the wall. This is where the accommodationist sacred-secular dualism leads.

Accommodationalism is thereby the very antithesis of pluralism. It does not recognize or seek to give full freedom to the plurality of religions in the United States, but rather seeks to accommodate religion and the state by denying religious pluralism and advocating either a lowest-common-denominator type of religion or a religion that has been stripped of much that makes it distinctively religious. In either case, the state can accommodate itself to religion because religion has been turned into an old, tired, defanged tiger. In pluralist terms, religion is being limited and constricted in its sphere, where it should possess a quasi-sovereignty.

In contrast, positive neutrality argues that religion, in all its particularity and colorful diversity, should be allowed into the public life of the nation. Neutrality is not to be gained by trying to shape prayers, religious exercises, and other recognitions of religion in public life to meet a nonexistent societal consensus. The days of a Protestant consensus are long over, and there is no point in trying to recapture them or create some new, broader, and less meaningful consensus. Positive neutrality seeks neutrality by welcoming the adherents of all religious faiths, and of none, into the public life of the nation. In addition, positive neutrality rejects the sacred-secular dualism as a fiction. To pretend that the sacred and the secular aspects of a parochial school kindergarten class, a family and marriage counseling center, or a host of other educational and service programs can be disentangled is clearly untenable. It may be a convenient fiction, making it easier for a few governmental aid programs to slip by Congress and the Supreme Court, but it is not rooted in reality, and in the long run it merely forces religious programs to give up more and more of their religious overtones in order to qualify for governmental aid. Positive neutrality says that the direct, this-world benefits to society should make religiously based programs — along with their secular counterparts — eligible for public aid.

The Strict Separationist Position

Strict separationists support the erection of a high, impregnable wall of separation between the realm of religion and the realm of the state. To the strict separationist, this means that there is to be no encouragement, support, or aid of any kind by the government to religion: either religion-in-general or specific religious groups. The extremes to which strict separationists will go to strain out the smallest gnats of state support for religion is seen in many separationists' opposition to equal access programs in public schools, which merely allow student-initiated and student-led religious clubs and groups to meet on school property during times when the school is not in session.[18] The strict separationists fear that somehow this might be interpreted (that is, misinterpreted) as giving official endorsement or support to religion.

By the same token, under strict separation, religion is not to influence the state. As Esbeck described strict separation: "In the public sphere, civic issues and affairs of state are to be debated and resolved in a wholly secularized medium, since religious views are effectually leached of any serious public consequence."[19] A little later he went on to explain: "Strict separationists believe that little harm will occur if religious speech is not given unimpeded access to the public marketplace, and that some good may result."[20]

Even when strict separationists recognize that the wall they would erect between church and state in practice cannot be totally impregnable, they continue to hold the absolute separation of religion and state as an ideal. The prominent strict separationist lawyer Leo Pfeffer boldly wrote:

> Those defending the strict separationist interpretation of the First Amendment's Establishment Clause recognize that the absolute separation of church and state is not possible, but what does that prove? Does the reality that no person is immortal mean that the medical and pharmaceutical profession should be abolished? Realistic separationists recognize that the absolute separation of church and state cannot be achieved, else what's a secularist heaven for? Nevertheless, that is the direction they would have constitutional law relating to the Religion Clause take, fully aware that perfection will never be reached.[21]

There are three key beliefs or assumptions underlying the strict separationist position. The first is the assumption that the strict separation of church and state equates to the state being neutral toward religion. Some strict separationists are themselves deeply religious persons who see their support of strict separation as a means to protect freedom of religion. If the state and religion are kept separate, obviously, the state will not be able to favor one religion over another or religion over secularism; the state will be neutral, and neutrality implies full religious freedom. Closely related to this belief is a sacred-secular dualism. The political forum is viewed as being secular, and religion has nothing to contribute, since religion is a purely private affair dealing with personal salvation, family, and home. "Education, law, economics or military defense are declared to be secular and are to be publicly debated in such terms."[22] Third, strict separationists think only in terms of individual rights and individual freedom, and do not see religious associations or faith communities as having any rights. The only rights that a collectivity has are those of its individual members. This makes it easier to privatize religion and seal it off from the public realm.

Positive neutrality and structural pluralism agree with strict separationism in their desire for a state that is neutral toward religion and that thereby assures its full, genuine freedom. However, they profoundly disagree that strict separation leads to either neutrality or genuine religious freedom since they strongly disagree with all three assumptions that strict separationists make. Positive neutrality says that if a wall of separation is created between church and state, discrimination against religion, not neutrality, results. As has been developed throughout this book, strict separation means that religion alone — and not the host of competing secular faiths and beliefs — is excluded from influencing public policies, from government run programs, and from receiving support and encouragement from public policies. Structural pluralism also says that the secular-sacred dualism of the strict separationists is a false dichotomy. Religion (as seen in Chapter 1) speaks deeply and persistently to issues of war and peace, social justice, human rights, poverty, and a host of other politically relevant topics. To privatize religion is to force it onto the margins of society and human existence. Strict separation is a friend only of a truncated, limited, privatized religion; it discriminates against all other forms.

Finally, pluralism sees a variety of social structures as having ontological status and, as such, possessing rights that all governments should recognize. Many persons find meaning and direction within the confines of religious associations and faith communities, and if their religious faith is to be protected, the structures within which they find faith must be protected. Full and complete freedom of religion must include the freedom to do one's duty before God as dictated by conscience and confirmed by the faith community and religious association of which one is a member. In short, a basic theme of this book is that strict separationism — which is held in high regard in the United States — is doing immense harm to religious freedom.

Strict Neutrality

In the 1960s, legal scholar Philip Kurland propounded what he called the principle of strict neutrality with these words:

> The thesis proposed here as the proper construction of the religion clauses of the first amendment is that the freedom and separation clauses should be read as a single precept that government cannot utilize religion as a standard for action or inaction because these clauses prohibit classification in terms of religion either to confer a benefit or to impose a burden.[23]

Political scientist Paul Weber more recently referred to this concept as "equal separation" and slightly redefined it: *"Equal separation* rejects all political or economic privilege, coercion, or disability based on religious affiliation, belief, or practice, or lack thereof, but guarantees to religiously motivated or affiliated individuals and organizations the *same* rights and privileges extended to other similarly situated individuals and organizations."[24]

Strict neutrality or equal separation recognizes that if the two religion clauses are read separately, an inevitable conflict between the two develops. If the free exercise provision is emphasized, religion is given a benefit or advantage that strict neutrality finds troubling; if the no-establishment provision is emphasized, religion is saddled with a penalty or disadvantage that strict neutrality finds equally troubling. It concludes that the way to avoid these twin dangers is to treat religion neutrally, with neutrality defined in terms of treating religiously motivated beliefs and practices and religiously rooted associations in the same manner as nonreligiously motivated beliefs and practices and nonreligiously rooted associations. Weber put it this way:

> Classification in terms of religion may tend to discriminate either by favoring religious interests at the expense of other similarly situated interests or by burdening religious interests in such a way as to have a "chilling effect" on religious liberty. The most equitable solution to this dilemma is to treat religious groups and interests like similar [nonreligious] groups and interests.[25]

Strict neutrality or equal separation thereby argues that it escapes the problem of religion being disadvantaged by public policies that prevent governmental recognition or aid going to religious persons and groups when it is going to similarly or parallel persons or groups that are not religiously based. Neutrality is attained by achieving a complete evenhandedness between the religious and nonreligious, and that evenhandedness is attained by treating religion and secularism in the same manner. Thus, religious arguments and motivations could be used in support of public policies, since secular arguments and motivations may, of course, be used. Financial aid could go to religious organizations providing societal services as long as comparable aid was going to similar, secularly based organizations. Correspondingly, religious groups could be honored and recognized by the state as long as similar secular groups were also being honored and recognized. The religious or nonreligious character of an organization would be irrelevant, for religion as a classification would virtually be wiped out. Laws and policies that were discriminatory against religion would also thereby be wiped out.

The principle of strict neutrality has some strong similarities to positive neutrality. Both are committed, as their names imply, to neutrality of government toward religion, that is, to a situation in which the state gives neither advantages nor disadvantages to one religion over another or to either religion or secularism over each other. Also, both recognize that present public policies often disadvantage or handicap religion as compared to secularism, and both recognize the conflict that arises when the two religion clauses are interpreted separately.

Nevertheless, there are also some basic differences between the two principles, especially in terms of the underlying reasoning or concepts. Strict neutrality seems to be rooted in the concept of neutrality as a value in and by itself; while positive neutrality sees neutrality not as a value in itself, but as a means by which to assure that religious structures can realize the autonomy or freedom that is theirs in their proper sphere of endeavor. This basic perspective of pluralism helps to condition and define the neutrality of positive neutrality, while strict neutrality does not have similar concepts conditioning the way in which, in practice, it interprets neutrality.

The implication of this underlying difference between strict neutrality and positive neutrality can best be seen by thinking in terms of three important areas and the implications of strict neutrality for religious freedom in each. First, in regard to religious beliefs and expression, strict neutrality would grant religious beliefs and expression the same protections accorded nonreligious beliefs and expression, while positive neutrality would grant religious beliefs and expression the explicit protection of the free exercise provision of the First Amendment. The practical difference here, however, is small, since belief and expression (religious belief and expression included) are already fully protected by other First Amendment provisions. Here, the free exercise protections are largely duplicative of other First Amendment protections and thus, not much is lost by strict neutrality.

Things change, however, when one focuses on the right to freely put one's religious beliefs into practice. If, in Kurland's words, which were quoted earlier, "government cannot utilize religion as a standard . . . to confer a benefit," what happens to public policies that, for example, allow adherents of Native American religions to use peyote or a religious pacifist to escape military conscription? As Chapter 2 demonstrated, the free exercise protections of the First Amendment have already been interpreted very narrowly by the Supreme Court. By not offering religiously inspired practices any special protections that are rooted in their religious nature, strict neutrality would seem to support — or even go beyond — the Supreme Court's position. Weber has sought to escape this problem by suggesting that under strict neutrality, the free exercise rights of religion would not be reduced to the level of those of secularism, but rather, the rights of secularism would be raised to those of religion. He has written that the free exercise clause "is of central importance in setting the standard of freedom. The free exercise clause provides protection for religious groups and activities, but that protection must then be extended to other similar [secular] groups and individuals."[26] If other supporters of strict neutrality would accept this position, most of the practical problems noted here would be resolved, but until Weber's position is accepted more widely, the danger that strict neutrality poses for free exercise protections remains. In contrast, positive neutrality's concept of religion as a key societal sphere within which religious associations, faith communities, and their members possess a fundamental autonomy firmly roots the free exercise protections of religion in the nature of the quasi-autonomous sphere of religion. Religion *as religion* is safeguarded.

Finally, there is the area of state aid to religious groups or agencies offering services or programs with benefits to society as a whole. Strict neutrality says that these groups or agencies would be eligible for such aid as long as similar or parallel ("similarly situated," in Weber's terms) secular organizations were also receiving aid. Since strict neutrality reaches this conclusion on the basis of wiping out all legal distinctions between religious and nonreligious organizations, however, religious organizations "would have to keep the same records, maintain the same standards, and follow the same regulations as other participants."[27] This may appear innocuous, but it could be interpreted to mean that to be eligible to receive state assistance, an Orthodox Jewish school would have to hire a Christian teacher, a Fundamentalist Protestant teenage counseling service could not present premarital sex as being against God's law, and a Catholic social service agency would have to hire practicing homosexuals in violation of Catholic moral teaching.[28] As I have written elsewhere, "It is only a slight exaggeration to say the [strict] neutrality principle says to Orthodox Jewish, fundamentalist, and Catholic organizations that they, along with parallel secularly based organizations, may receive governmental aid as long as they cease to be Jewish, fundamentalist, or Catholic!"[29] Such a position continues to disadvantage religion, since it would often put a religious organization in the dilemma of having to choose between being disadvantaged by foregoing aid similar secular organizations are receiving or being disadvantaged by giving up key elements of its religious distinctiveness. Weber has argued that under strict neutrality, religious associations could still maintain certain policies in keeping with their religious nature, but the entire thrust of strict neutrality is to place religious associations on a par with nonreligious associations.[30] The pressures against maintaining a religious distinctiveness are clear. Pluralism's vision of religion as a quasi-autonomous sphere within which religious associations and faith communities have certain inherent rights and obligations is a powerful corrective. Neutrality must constantly be interpreted and defined in light of that perspective.

Strict neutrality is a major advance toward a greater degree of governmental neutrality in regard to religion and nonreligion, but it falls short of assuring full freedom of religion in a fully free society. Positive neutrality, with its pluralist thinking, is in a stronger position to maintain the distinctive nature and contributions of religious structures. If neutrality is to be truly neutral, it at times must support positive steps of state accommodation, recognition, or aid to religious structures. Religion must be recognized and respected for what it is.

Positive Neutrality and the Constitution

Does the principle of positive neutrality that was developed in this chapter mesh with the First Amendment and its guarantees of freedom of religion? Since positive neutrality is rooted in structural, normative pluralism, which has not played a major role in U.S. political thought, one might suppose that positive neutrality would be at sharp variance with the First Amendment, in particular, and the U.S. experience, more generally. This final section of the chapter makes the case that positive neutrality is fully compatible with the First Amendment and, although at variance with most of the Supreme Court's current interpretations of the First Amendment, is in keeping with goals often expressed by the Court and even in keeping with some more specific principles that it has articulated. Following positive neutrality would set the U.S. political system in some fundamentally new directions in church-state relations, yet it is compatible with much in U.S. thinking and experience.

Positive Neutrality and the First Amendment

Positive neutrality reads the religion language of the First Amendment as containing a single injunction, not as two different clauses doing two different things. It agrees with political scientist William Carroll when he wrote:

> The religion clauses are all designed to protect the broadest possible liberty of conscience, to allow each man to believe as his conscience directs, to profess his beliefs, and to live as he believes he ought to live, consistent with the liberty of others and with the common good. Therefore, both the free exercise and the establishment clauses of the First Amendment must be regarded as directed toward the end of liberty of conscience. . . . The establishment clause and the free exercise clause, each with a role to play, must be regarded as complementary rather than in conflict.[31]

The free exercise of religion — full freedom of belief and practice — is the basic goal of the First Amendment, and the no-establishment language is one means of reaching that goal. However no-establishment is interpreted, it is not an end in itself, whereas full and complete religious freedom is. Richard John Neuhaus saw this clearly:

> The no-establishment part of the religion clause is entirely and without remainder in the service of free exercise. Free exercise is the end; no-establishment is the necessary means to that end. No-establishment simply makes no sense on its own. . . . The purpose of the non-establishment of religion is to establish religious freedom. It follows that any interpretation of no-establishment that hinders free exercise is a misinterpretation of non-establishment.[32]

Positive neutrality, therefore, does not define religious freedom in terms of separate, distinct free exercise and no-establishment guarantees. To do so is to confuse means with ends. Instead, positive neutrality defines religious freedom in terms of a governmental neutrality toward religion in which no religion is favored over any other and neither religion nor secularism is favored over each other. Positive neutrality believes that no-establishment — when interpreted as some variation of religion-government separation — sometimes helps lead to genuine government neutrality toward religion, but other times does not. No-establishment in and by itself should not be controlling. Instead, it is the neutrality of government — rooted in religious structures' right to a quasi-autonomy in their sphere, which assures that they will neither be advantaged nor disadvantaged by the actions of other spheres — that should be controlling.

Is such an interpretation compatible with the plain words of the First Amendment and the intentions of its authors? Both the logic of the words and historical circumstances surrounding the First Amendment's adoption suggest that it is. Logically (as Neuhaus argued), the goal of the First Amendment is to assure full religious freedom: the ability freely and fully to express and live out one's religious beliefs and convictions. What defense is there for no-establishment in cases when it is not contributing — and is perhaps even detracting from — complete freedom of religious belief and practice? I know of none. Logically, one is driven to the conclusion that the no-establishment provision can best be read, not as a value in and by itself, but as a means by which to attain some other value, namely, the value of full religious freedom. Its interpretation needs to be qualified by the goal of attaining that value.

Historically, much debate has surrounded the question of the exact intentions of the First Congress in its writing of the First Amendment religion language (as discussed in Chapter 2). Two basic observations concerning original intent relevant to the discussion here can, however, be made. The first is that the basic concern or goal of the authors of the First Amendment was protecting the fundamental right to freedom of religious belief and practice. Full freedom of religion was their goal. Arlin Adams and Charles Emmerich, with the help of Justice Arthur Goldberg, clearly made this point:

> We begin with what may seem a rather obvious proposition — that the Founders intended the establishment and free exercise clauses to be complementary co-guarantees of a single end. As Justice Goldberg observed in *Abington School District v. Schempp*, the "single end" of the clauses is "to promote and assure the fullest possible scope of religious liberty and tolerance for all and to nurture the conditions which secure the best hope of attainment of that end." . . . The separation concept . . . is really a servant of an even greater goal; it is a means, along with concepts such as accommodation and neutrality, to achieve the ideal of religious liberty in a free society.[33]

This commitment to the full freedom of religious belief and practice as the fundamental goal of the First Amendment authors is captured in identically worded resolutions adopted by the ratifying conventions of Virginia and North Carolina, which urged the following language be included by amendment in the new Constitution:

> That religion, or the duty which we owe to our Creator, and the manner of discharging it, can be directed only by reason and conviction, not by force and violence; *and therefore* all men have an equal, natural and unalienable right to the free exercise of religion, according to the dictates of conscience, and that no particular religious sect of society ought to be favored or established by law in preference to others.[34]

Both the idea of the freedom of religious belief and practice and of government not favoring or establishing a particular religion are contained here, but both are clearly subservient to the goal of "religion [being] directed only by reason and conviction, not by force and violence." That was the goal; the free exercise and the no favoring or establishing by law were means. There is no evidence that the members of the First Congress disagreed with the goal articulated in the Virginia and North Carolina resolutions. Where the disagreement came was over how to word the language to achieve this goal.

A second observation is that, as argued in Chapter 2, there is compelling evidence indicating that it was never the intent of the First Congress to erect a wall of separation between religious associations and government, with government prohibited from supporting or accommodating itself to religion generally without favoring any particular religion over another. They did not see a wall of separation as essential to full religious freedom. Thus, when positive neutrality argues that at times, a true neutrality requires government to take some positive steps to accommodate, recognize, or support religion along with doing so for secularism, it is not going against the intent of the First Congress. It may be going against the wall of separation metaphor, but the evidence indicates that this is not the same as going against the intent of the First Amendment authors.

The conclusion that these two observations suggests is that the authors of the First Amendment were motivated by a desire to promote and protect the full freedom of religious conscience and did not believe that a no-establishment position that was absolute in the sense of outlawing nondiscriminatory aid to religion generally was essential to full religious freedom. Thus, when I suggest that under positive neutrality, full freedom of religious belief and practice is what is crucial and that no-establishment in the sense of strict separation of religion and government must be evaluated on the basis of whether it contributes to or distracts from that freedom, I am not running counter to the basic intent of the authors of the First Amendment.

*Positive Neutrality and Supreme
Court Church-State Principles*

In seeking to compare the principle of positive neutrality with the
key principles currently used by the Supreme Court in interpreting
the First Amendment religion language, one's task is complicated by
the confusing mishmash of principles, practices, and contradictions
marking Supreme Court church-state decisions. However, some
additional light may be thrown on the principle of positive neutrality
that I am advancing here by comparing it with two principles or, if
not exactly principles, two lines of reasoning frequently invoked by
the Court in church-state cases.

Neutrality. It is helpful to recall (as discussed in Chapter 2) that
the Supreme Court has frequently held up governmental neutrality
toward religion as a fundamental goal or aim of the Court. Here
there is common ground between my position of positive neutrality
and the reasoning often invoked by the Court. Nowhere is this more
true than in Justice Tom Clark's 1963 majority opinion in *Abington
School District v. Schempp*, which found Bible reading in public
schools to be unconstitutional. In this opinion, Clark used the word
"neutral" or "neutrality" some nine times.[35] At one point he clearly
declared: "In the relationship between man and religion, the State is
firmly committed to a position of neutrality."[36] This is a basic point to
which the Court has frequently returned. Chapter 2 noted that this
position was articulated most clearly by Justice Abe Fortas in a
unanimous opinion:

> Government in our democracy, state and national, must be
> neutral in matters of religious theory, doctrine, and practice.
> It may not be hostile to any religion or to the advocacy of no-
> religion; and it may not aid, foster, or promote one religion or
> religious theory against another or even against the militant
> opposite. The First Amendment mandates governmental
> neutrality between religion and religion, and between religion
> and nonreligion.[37]

In short, the Supreme Court has often — whether explicitly or
implicitly — held up the concept of neutrality as a fundamental goal
that its interpretations of the First Amendment's religion provisions
seek to attain. I would argue that the Court has an overly limited
understanding of neutrality and certainly is off the track when it
assumes that neutrality is attained by the strict separation of church
and state, yet there is some common ground between positive
neutrality and current Supreme Court reasoning. Both at least begin
by holding out neutrality between the state and religion as a goal or
ideal. Where they differ is on the nature of that neutrality and how it
is to be attained.

Equal Access. A second line of reasoning that has periodically shown itself in Supreme Court decisions is that no-establishment limits are not breached even when government grants certain benefits to religion, as long as those benefits are given indiscriminately to a wide variety of religious groups and to religious and nonreligious groups alike. This is the line of reasoning that comes closest to being supportive of structural pluralism's concept of positive neutrality.

In the ground-breaking *Everson* case, Justice Black, writing for the Court, declared that government "cannot exclude individual Catholics, Lutherans, Mohammedans, Baptists, Jews, Methodists, Non-believers, Presbyterians, or the members of any other faith, because of their faith, or lack of it, from receiving the benefits of public welfare legislation."[38] He then went on to conclude: "Measured by these standards, we cannot say that the First Amendment prohibits New Jersey from spending tax-raised funds to pay the bus fares of parochial school pupils as a part of a general program under which it pays the fares of pupils attending public and other schools."[39] Because the assistance being given by government was generally available to believers and nonbelievers and to believers of all faiths, the particular aid program under challenge was constitutional, even though it admittedly helped "to get [children] to church schools."[40] Religion was benefitting from the governmental aid, yet it was permissible under the First Amendment: "That Amendment requires the state to be a neutral in its relations with groups of religious believers and non-believers; it does not require the state to be their adversary. State power is no more to be used so as to handicap religions, than it is to favor them."[41] If this line of reasoning had been fully developed and consistently followed, it could have led to what I have termed positive neutrality. All religions, plus religion and nonreligion alike, were granted equal access to government assistance; not to have done so would have violated the norm of neutrality and made government to be the adversary of religion and to handicap it.

Also instructive is the reasoning that appeared in the Supreme Court's handling of the issue of whether student-initiated religious clubs or groups could use publicly owned school facilities for their meetings. On the university level, the Court concluded: "Having created a forum generally open to student groups, the University seeks to enforce a content-based exclusion of religious speech. Its exclusionary policy violates the fundamental principle that a state regulation of speech should be content-neutral."[42] The Court decided this case on free speech and association grounds rather than free exercise grounds, but it held that the First Amendment's no-establishment provision was not violated since the university had created a forum "available to a broad class of nonreligious as well as religious speakers."[43] The Court felt that "an open forum," such as this,

> In a public university does not confer any imprimatur of state approval on religious sects or practices. As the Court of Appeals quite aptly stated, such a policy "would no more commit the University . . . to religious goals" than it is "now committed to the goals of the Students for a Democratic Society, the Young Socialist Alliance," or any other group eligible to use its facilities.[44]

The Supreme Court thereby took a stand for neutrality based not on excluding religion from the public realm, but on welcoming religion as well as other forms of human belief and expression into the public realm on equal terms. Structural pluralism and positive neutrality ask for no more.

In a similar case dealing with secondary public schools rather than a public university, the Supreme Court allowed a religious club to be officially recognized by the school and to use school facilities for its meetings. Again, the Court justified its decision on the basis of a plurality of religious and secular clubs of a noncurriculum nature being recognized and allowed on campus.

> The broad spectrum of officially recognized student clubs at Westside, and the fact that Westside students are free to initiate and organize additional student clubs . . . counteract any possible message of official endorsement of or preference for religion or a particular religious belief. . . . Under the Act, a school with a limited open forum may not lawfully deny access to a Jewish students' club, a Young Democrats club, or a philosophy club devoted to the study of Nietzsche. To the extent that a religious club is merely one of many different student-initiated voluntary clubs, students should perceive no message of government endorsement of religion.[45]

Governmental neutrality toward religion was not violated because a policy of equal treatment of religious and nonreligious associations does not confer any special favors or endorsement on religion, whether religion generally or any particular religious faith. Positive neutrality says that this is the basic way to allow religion its full free exercise rights without violating no-establishment concerns. Religion is free to act; yet it is not being singled out for special endorsement, favors, or treatment.

I would, however, add that the standards that the Supreme Court has generally utilized in its church-state decisions are not at all what positive neutrality and structural pluralism believe they should be.

The "equal access" line of reasoning just discussed remains more in embryo than in adult form. It has not been fully developed or consistently followed. All that can be claimed is that the concept of positive neutrality and some of its approaches to church-state issues are not totally foreign to the U.S. experience and Supreme Court decisions. Their emphasis on neutrality is already embraced by the Supreme Court, plus their emphasis on allowing a plurality of religious and nonreligious expressions into the political sphere has some significant precedents.

The Supreme Court needs to set out on a new path in a new direction, but it could do so by singling out and developing several precedents and lines of reasoning that are already available. This new path has already been tested and probed by a few decisions. What is now needed is for the Court to move further down that new path, always — as is necessary in the real world — ready to adapt and modify its position as it proceeds down and explores that path. It is by doing so that the promise of full, genuine freedom of religious belief and practice can be realized in a religiously pluralistic society and in an age marked by the comprehensive administrative state.

NOTES

1.   I use the term *secular philosophy* to refer to a system of interrelated beliefs and values, such as Marxism or humanism, which in no way rely on the supernatural. By a *secular mind-set* I am referring to what James Hunter (as noted in Chapter 2) called a *secular cultural ethos*. It is a diffuse moral ethos that excludes the supernatural and that, often unconsciously, conditions a person's way of thinking and reacting to the world of events and people. I will often also use the terms *secularism, secularists,* or *nonbelievers* to refer to secular philosophies and mind-sets and to their adherents. In making these distinctions I am, of course, following the definition of religion established in Chapter 4 and the definitions of secularism and humanism established in Chapter 2.

2.   The Second Vatican Council, "The Political Community," in James W. Skillen and Rockne M. McCarthy, eds., *Political Order and the Plural Structure of Society* (Atlanta, GA: Scholars Press, 1991), p. 203.

3.   Abraham Kuyper, *Calvinism: Six Stone Foundation Lectures* (Grand Rapids, MI: Eerdmans, 1943), p. 107.

4.   Leicester C. Webb, "Corporate Personality and Political Pluralism," in Leicester C. Webb, ed., *Legal Personality and Political Pluralism* (Melbourne, Australia: Melbourne University Press, 1958), p. 56.

5.   Jacques Maritain, *Man and the State* (Chicago: University of Chicago Press, 1951), p. 161.

6.   Ibid., pp. 151–152. Maritain's emphasis.

7.   See, for example, David Easton, *A Systems Analysis of Political Life* (New York: John Wiley, 1965), pp. 153–170, 278–288.

8.   This same point has also been made by Charles Taylor in "Religion in a Free Society," in James D. Hunter and Os Guinness, eds., *Articles of Faith, Articles of Peace* (Washington, DC: Brookings, 1990), pp. 93–113; and Glenn Tinder, "Can We Be Good without God?" *Atlantic Monthly*, December 1989, pp. 69–85.

9.   Laurence H. Tribe, *American Constitutional Law*, 2d ed. (Mineola, NY: Foundation Press, 1988), p. 1228.

10.   Louis Fisher, *American Constitutional Law* (New York: McGraw-Hill, 1990), p. 708.

11.   See David C. Nice, *Federalism: The Politics of Intergovernmental Relations* (New York: St. Martin's, 1987), p. 2.

12.   Yves R. Simon, *Philosophy of Democratic Government* (Chicago: University of Chicago Press, 1951), p. 134.

13.   *Wisconsin v. Yoder*, 406 U.S. 205 (1972).

14.   Carl H. Esbeck, "Five Views of Church-State Relations in Contemporary American Thought," *Brigham Young University Law Review* 371 (1986): p. 396.

15.   John F. Wilson, "Religion, Government, and Power in the New American Nation," in Mark A. Noll, ed., *Religion and American Politics* (New York: Oxford University Press, 1990), p. 80.

16.   Esbeck wrote, "The [nonpreferentialists] argue the dualism that religious organizations perform easily discernible sacral and secular activities, and the latter may be state-supported." Carl H. Esbeck, "A Typology of Church-State Relations in Current American Thought," (an unpublished paper presented at the Calvin College conference on "The Role of Religion in American Public Life," October 5–6, 1990, Grand Rapids, MI), p. 19.

17.   See *Congressional Quarterly Weekly* 46 (February 27, 1988): p. 515.

18.   See, for example, the comments made by Marc Stern of the American Jewish Congress on *Westside Community Schools v. Mergens*, 58 U.S.L.W. 4720 (1990), in which the Supreme Court upheld the equal access law of Congress. "Equal Access or Open Season?" *Church and State*, July/August 1990, pp. 152–153.

19.   Esbeck, "Five Views of Church-State Relations," p. 381.

20.   Ibid., p. 382.

21.   Leo Pfeffer, *Religion, State and the Burger Court* (Buffalo, NY: Prometheus Books, 1984), p. xi.

22.   Esbeck, "Five Views of Church-State Relations," p. 381.

23.   Philip B. Kurland, *Religion and the Law: Of Church and State and the Supreme Court* (Chicago: Aldine, 1962), p. 18. Also see the description of strict neutrality in Tribe, *American Constitutional Law*, pp. 1188–1189.

24.   Paul J. Weber, "Neutrality and First Amendment Interpretation," in Paul J. Weber, ed., *Equal Separation: Understanding the Religion Clauses of the First Amendment* (Westport, CT: Greenwood, 1990), p. 5. Weber's emphasis.

25.   Ibid., p. 11.

26.   Weber, "Response to Dean M. Kelley," in Weber, ed., *Equal Separation*, p. 40.

27.   Weber, "Neutrality and First Amendment Interpretation," p. 10.

28.   These are not totally hypothetical. See the exchange of views among Kelley, Weber, and myself. Weber, ed., *Equal Separation*, pp. 43–44, 82–83, 90–93.

29.   Stephen V. Monsma, "The Neutrality Principle and a Pluralist Concept of Accommodation," in Weber, ed., *Equal Separation*, p. 83.

30.   See Weber, "Response to Stephen V. Monsma," in Weber, ed., *Equal Separation*, pp. 91–93.

31.   William A. Carroll, "The Constitution, the Supreme Court, and Religion," *The American Political Science Review* 61 (1967): p. 663.

32.   Richard John Neuhaus, "A New Order of Religious Freedom," *First Things* 20 (February 1992): p. 15.

33.   Arlin M. Adams and Charles J. Emmerich, *A Nation Dedicated to Religious Liberty* (Philadelphia: University of Pennsylvania Press, 1990), p. 37. The Goldberg quotation is from his concurring opinion in *Abington School District v. Schempp*, 374 U.S. 305 (1963).

34. Quoted in Michael J. Malbin, *Religion and Politics: The Intentions of the Authors of the First Amendment* (Washington, DC: American Enterprise Institute, 1978), p. 4. Emphasis added.

35. See Carroll, "The Constitution," p. 660.

36. *Abington School District v. Schempp*, 374 U.S. at 226 (1963).

37. *Epperson v. Arkansas*, 393 U.S. at 103–104 (1968).

38. *Everson v. Board of Education*, 330 U.S. at 16 (1947).

39. Ibid., p. 17.

40. Ibid.

41. Ibid., p. 18.

42. *Widmar v. Vincent*, 454 U.S. at 277 (1981).

43. Ibid., p. 274.

44. Ibid.

45. *Westside Community Schools v. Mergens*, 58 U.S.L.W. at 4727 (1990).

6

Positive Neutrality in the
Political Arena

The principle of positive neutrality is not intended to serve as a mere theoretical construct that is only useful in arcane academic discussions and abstract legal speculations. Instead, positive neutrality is intended to be a working principle, bringing clarity to the confusions and direction to the meanderings that now mark the U.S. church-state scene. Thus, it is important to understand how positive neutrality, if consistently applied and followed, would deeply affect relations among religious structures and governments at all levels.

Positive neutrality allows church-state cooperation in areas and in ways now not considered constitutional and disallows other forms of cooperation now allowed. However, the potential effects of positive neutrality go beyond this. It has powerful public policy implications, since current church-state practices and restrictions have such implications. Compared to most other modern democratic polities of Western Europe, as well as those of Canada, Australia, and New Zealand, the United States has more serious social problems in such areas as education, drug abuse, homelessness, teen-age pregnancies, and urban decay. One cannot draw a direct cause-and-effect relation between the constricted role that U.S. church-state practices allow religious associations in U.S. public life and social pathologies such as these, yet a case can be made that the two are related. Changes in church-state relations that empower religious associations to play a more fulsome role in society have a potential to unleash powerful new forces for dealing with persistent social ills. At the very least, they would greatly expand the public policy options available to decision makers who are wrestling with seemingly intractable social problems.

All this is the subject matter of this chapter. In it I take the principle of positive neutrality developed in Chapter 5 and demonstrate how in practice it would work itself out in the real world of court cases and public policy debates. I do so in two stages: First, I explore how positive neutrality would affect Supreme Court decisions in five key, prominent areas of church-state relations, and second, I discuss the effects it would have on the public policy options available to decision makers.

POSITIVE NEUTRALITY AND SUPREME COURT DECISIONS

This section considers five areas of church-state relations, in each of which the Supreme Court has had to deal with a number of controversial cases that have divided both the Court itself and the U.S. public. In each of these areas this section looks at certain decisions that the Court has reached and the reasoning it has used in support of them. Then it contrasts these decisions and the reasoning underlying them with the decisions that positive neutrality would have reached and the reasoning it would use in their support. Doing so should give greater clarity to the nature and nuances of positive neutrality, plus shed new light on the practical implications of positive neutrality for church-state relations.

The Recognition of Religion

One set of cases raises the question of the permissible limits of governmental recognition and honoring of religion. I have in mind here such practices as opening legislative sessions with prayers, displaying religious symbols such as a menorah or cross on public property, official proclamations acknowledging or honoring a religious group, and the mottoes "In God We Trust" on coins and "under God" in the Pledge of Allegiance. What these practices have in common is an acknowledging or an honoring of God or the role of religion in the public life of the nation. These cases have raised particular difficulties for the Supreme Court because they undoubtedly are technically contrary to the wall of separation theory that the Court has embraced; however, due to their popularity with the vast majority of the public and their long-standing place in U.S. public life, it is hard for the Court to rule against them. Most, but not all, such practices have been approved by the Court on the basis of the long traditions in their support and the Court's perception that they have been largely secularized.

It is helpful to look at two decisions of the Court in greater detail. One deals with the use of a paid legislative chaplain in the Nebraska legislature to open its daily session with prayer and the other with the use of a Christmas crèche or nativity scene as part of a Christmas display in Pawtucket, Rhode Island.

The Nebraska state legislature had hired the Reverend Robert E. Palmer, a Presbyterian minister, to open its daily legislative sessions with prayer, and paid him a salary of $319.75 a month to do so. When the case was heard by the Supreme Court in 1983 the Reverend Palmer had been opening legislative sessions with prayer continuously for eighteen years. Ernest Chambers, one of the Nebraska legislators, challenged this practice as being an unconstitutional establishment of religion. In a 6–3 vote, the Supreme Court approved the Nebraska legislature's practice, holding it to be in keeping with the First Amendment's religion language. It did so even though it is hard to disagree with the reasoning of Justice William Brennan, who, in dissent, argued that the Nebraska practice violated all three prongs of the *Lemon* test. Officially sanctioned prayers by a paid chaplain of one faith on the surface would certainly appear to have a religious purpose, to have an effect that is primarily religious, and, only slightly less clearly, to lead to the entanglement of the state with religion. Nevertheless, the majority of the Supreme Court held that there was no violation of the establishment clause. It did so, first, by simply ignoring the *Lemon* test; then it argued original intent. The First Congress, at almost the same time when it adopted the First Amendment, also voted to hire a chaplain to lead the Congress in opening prayers — almost the exact same practice as that of the Nebraska legislature, which had been challenged. Obviously, the Court reasoned, the authors of the First Amendment did not see legislative prayers by paid chaplains as a violation of the First Amendment, which they had just written and adopted.

An even more fundamental argument of the majority was that legislative prayer was legitimized by the fact that, in the words of Chief Justice Warren Burger's opinion, it "is deeply embedded in the history and traditions of this country," is a "part of the fabric of our society," and represents "simply a tolerable acknowledgement of beliefs widely held among the people of this country."[1] The tenor of the Chief Justice's opinion is that (apart from the original intent argument) legislative prayers of this nature are a traditional, innocuous practice without any real meaning or significance in terms of specific religious tenets. It was seen more as a nice, innocent tradition than as a serious religious act of worship. Prayer at the opening of legislative sessions — even when offered by a paid cleric from a particular religious tradition — thereby managed to escape the Supreme Court's wall of separation doctrine.

Positive neutrality, reflecting the pluralism that underlies it, would approach this case with three important perspectives. The first is that religion and prayer are an important, and even awesome, aspect of human existence, and should not be trivialized as mere innocuous traditions. It agrees fully with Justice Brennan when in his dissent he wrote:

Reverend Palmer and other members of the clergy who offer invocations at legislative sessions are not museum pieces, put on display once a day for the edification of the legislature. Rather, they are engaged by the legislature to lead it — as a body — in an act of religious worship. If upholding the practice requires denial of this fact, I suspect that many supporters of legislative prayer would feel that they had been handed a pyrrhic victory.[2]

Second, positive neutrality has serious problems with Nebraska's practice of having the same Presbyterian minister as the chaplain for eighteen years, representative of a religious body constituting only 4 percent of the U.S. population.[3] In such a situation the Reverend Palmer presumably could (1) offer distinctively Presbyterian prayers since this is his religious belief, (2) offer broadly Protestant or perhaps even broadly Christian prayers, recognizing that most of the legislators and public are not Presbyterians, or (3) offer lowest-common-denominator, religion-in-general prayers reflecting no particular religious tradition, since many Nebraskans and some legislators are not Christian. However, pluralism says that in following any one of these three options, the Reverend Palmer would not be reflecting the actual religious beliefs and preferences of some of the legislators and of large segments of the public. Even a religion-in-general prayer would favor religion over secular philosophies and mind-sets. In fact, it probably would not reflect the beliefs of anyone, since almost all persons' religious beliefs contain elements specific to them or their tradition. A generic prayer, for example, could not be trinitarian, for it would offend Unitarians, Jews, and probably others. However, to cast a supposedly generic prayer in unitarian terms would align it with a position that a majority of Christians down through the centuries have rejected as a heresy. The dilemma faced by the Reverend Palmer is that whatever option he adopts leaves out many, if not most, persons. Thus, on the basis of the deeply religious meaning of prayer and the inability of one clergyperson to reflect the religious pluralism of society, positive neutrality would find the Nebraska practice violative of religious neutrality and therefore unconstitutional.

However, a third perspective remains. Positive neutrality has as much a problem with Justice Brennan's dissenting opinion as it does with Chief Justice Burger's majority opinion, for Brennan would order all prayers out of all legislative bodies. If this position would be followed the government would be no more neutral than it is with a Presbyterian minister offering all the prayers. Under Brennan's approach of no prayers, the only persons whose beliefs would be accurately recognized and honored are those of no religious beliefs, about 9 percent of the population.[4] It would discriminate in favor of the secular, humanist cultural ethos identified by James Hunter (as discussed in Chapter 2). Under the Brennan approach, secularism is favored over religion; under Nebraska's and Burger's approach, Presbyterianism, Christianity, or religion-in-general is favored over all other religions and secularism.

Positive neutrality would resolve this dilemma by allowing daily legislative prayers but having them reflect the religious pluralism of U.S. society. The state would maintain its neutrality by inviting a rotating schedule of representatives of a wide variety of religious associations and faith communities, each of whom would be encouraged to offer a prayer within his or her religious tradition. One day a Fundamentalist Protestant would open the session with prayer; the next, a Unitarian; the next, a Catholic priest; the next, a Mormon; the next, a mainline Protestant; the next, a Jewish rabbi; and so on. Confirmed secularists should also be asked to take their turn by opening the daily session with a moment of quiet reflection on the importance of the tasks lying ahead that day or in some other appropriate manner. Thereby, religion would be given its due. It would be recognized in the halls of government as it is in the hearts of a majority of the public. However, by making allowance for the religious pluralism of the nation, no religious association or faith community will be favored over any other, nor will either religion or secularism be favored. Thus, neutrality is maintained.

There are, of course, some practical limitations to the number and type of religious associations and faith communities that have a right to be represented. Two are especially worth noting. First, only religious structures with a measurable representation in the population need to be included. Even small religious movements amounting to 1 or 2 percent of the population ought occasionally to be included, but self-proclaimed religious leaders whose following falls below even 1 or 2 percent of the population would have no right to demand recognition. Second, under the same rationale that leads to the compelling state interest test in free exercise cases (to be discussed more fully shortly), those religious movements that teach hatred or reject the legitimacy of the social order, or whose beliefs and practices are otherwise inimical to public health, safety, and social order, would not need to be included. Here is a clear instance in which the concepts of structural pluralism that underlie positive neutrality are needed to interpret and apply it. Structural pluralism emphasizes the quasi-sovereignty of religious associations and faith communities in their sphere, but also emphasizes other societal spheres, such as the political sphere, as well as governments' responsibility to coordinate and empower all of the various spheres in order to assure that they do not exceed their proper role. This includes the religious sphere. Religious structures and their leaders who teach hatred and incivility have violated their basic responsibility toward other religious structures and the nation's common life together. The state can appropriately act to restrict them — and surely does not need to honor or recognize them. Religious associations and faith communities have a rightful sovereignty in their sphere, but it is always a qualified or quasi-sovereignty.

A second case that raised the issue of what is and is not appropriate in regard to government recognizing or honoring religion dealt with a Christmas holiday display of Pawtucket, Rhode Island, which contained a crèche or nativity scene. For forty years Pawtucket had owned, and each Christmas season displayed in a privately owned park in the downtown area, a holiday display consisting of Santa Claus, reindeer and sleigh, candy canes, colored lights, and so forth — plus a crèche. It was this city-owned and city-displayed crèche on which the Supreme Court in 1984 was called to rule. In a very close, 5–4, decision the Court held the display of the crèche to be constitutional. To do so — given the Supreme Court's neutrality by way of separation doctrine — the Court majority had somehow to find the crèche to be of no great religious significance. As seen in Chapter 2, it did so by noting that the nativity scene "depicts the historical origins of this traditional event long recognized as a national Holiday." It declared the crèche to have a secular purpose, namely "to celebrate the Holiday and to depict the origins of that Holiday. These are legitimate secular purposes." As a result, "whatever benefit to one faith or religion or to all religions, is indirect, remote, and incidental."[5]

Justice Brennan again wrote for the four dissenting justices. He argued that the crèche had a clear and significant religious meaning, and therefore the city including it in an otherwise secular display violated the establishment language of the First Amendment. Only the secular elements — such as the Santa Claus, reindeer, and candy canes — could remain.

Positive neutrality begins its analysis of this case by agreeing with Justice Brennan that the nativity scene possesses a Christian religious significance — one, in fact, of deep and profound meaning to the sincere Christian. It does not argue with what the justice wrote:

> The essence of the crèche's symbolic purpose and effect is to prompt the observer to experience a sense of simple awe and wonder appropriate to the contemplation of one of the central elements of Christian dogma — that God sent His Son into the world to be a Messiah. Contrary to the Court's suggestion, the crèche is far from a mere representation of a "particular historic religious event." It is, instead, best understood as a mystical re-creation of an event that lies at the heart of Christian faith. To suggest, as the Court does, that such a symbol is

merely "traditional" and therefore no different from Santa's house or reindeer is not only offensive to those for whom the crèche has profound significance, but insulting to those who insist for religious or personal reasons that the story of Christ is in no sense a part of "history" nor an unavoidable element of our national "heritage."6

Positive neutrality argues that a case such as this — as with the Nebraska legislative prayer case decided the previous year — reveals the gaping hole that the Supreme Court has dug for itself and all U.S. society by its current interpretation of the First Amendment. Its high wall of separation doctrine and the assumptions underlying it clearly should ban governmentally sponsored religious displays. However, the Court's own common sense and respect for the opinions of the people of the United States leads it to recoil from fully following its own enunciated doctrine. In order to find legislative prayers and Christmas displays constitutional under the terms of its strict separation standard, the Court has had to do violence to religion, turning it into just another secularized tradition.

Positive neutrality, however, also recoils from the solution that the dissenting justices advance, namely, of government having to ignore the special holidays of religious traditions or — in a self-contradiction — recognize religion by way of secularized displays. This is not being neutral. Many Christian groups — especially those who take the biblically described, miraculous events surrounding Christ's birth literally — often look askance at the commercialization of the U.S. celebration of those events. They support efforts to "Keep Christ in Christmas," as it is often put. Sermons are preached from pulpits warning of the danger of having Santa Claus, present, and "Jingle Bells" crowd out what is seen as the true, deeply religious meaning of Christmas. Others in the Christian tradition see no particular danger of Christmas being subverted and readily join in the emphasis on gift giving, office Christmas parties, and general feelings of good cheer. What Justice Brennan and the other dissenting justices would do by removing all religious aspects from a municipal Christmas display is to weigh in on the side of those without special concerns to maintain the religious dimension of Christmas. The government through its official acts would be lending its support, influence, and encouragement to those who have turned Christmas into a largely secular holiday. Those Christians for whom Christmas is a deeply religious occasion would be sent the message that their views are not the ones to be favored or acknowledged by government. This is not neutrality.

However, neither would neutrality be achieved by simply removing all displays commemorating religious traditions or holidays. If a variety of secularly based organizations, such as the Rotary Club and

Boy Scouts, are recognized and honored for their community contributions by occasional public displays but religious organizations are never recognized or honored for theirs, nonreligion is clearly being favored over religion. Again, a secular cultural ethos is being advanced by the state.

The current standards of the Supreme Court cannot escape the horns of a dilemma. If the crèche is included, Christianity — and especially those Christians for whom the crèche is deeply meaningful — is favored; if it is excluded, those who would tend to secularize Christmas are favored. Moreover, if the display is totally removed while secular organizations are recognized, a culture of secularism will be favored over a culture that is respectful of religious values. A truly neutral state appears to be an impossibility.

Positive neutrality, however, says that there is a way to escape this dilemma. As with legislative prayer, it would maintain government's neutrality by recognizing and acknowledging religious groups and secular groups alike. It would allow the crèche in the Christmas display, but would also allow the display of a menorah at Hanukkah, recognize the Islamic feast of Ramadan if there is a significant Muslim presence in the community, and honor the contributions of a secular group such as the American Civil Liberties Union. Justice Brennan hinted at the possibility of such an approach when he wrote in his dissent:

> The effect on minority religious groups, as well as on those who may reject all religion, is to convey the message that their views are not similarly worthy of public recognition nor entitled to public support. . . . Pawtucket itself owns the crèche and *instead of extending similar attention to a broad spectrum of religious and secular groups*, it has singled out Christianity for special treatment.[7]

This statement suggests that if Pawtucket had only given due recognition to a wide variety of religious and secular groups, Brennan and his dissenting colleagues would have been willing to approve the crèche. Positive neutrality asks for no more than this.

In both these cases, and in other similar issues of official acknowledgment, honor, or recognition of religious groups and their important contributions to the nation's history and to its communities today, the proper approach — if government is to be truly neutral — is for government to recognize and celebrate the religious diversity of the nation, not by trying to keep all religions at arm's length but by embracing them all. Here is where true neutrality requires certain positive steps be taken. To acknowledge only secular groups and movements and their contributions is to send the message that only they are important in the life of the nation. To acknowledge the existence and achievements of only one religious group or of only religion-in-general would be equally discriminatory. Positive neutrality says that all religions, and religion and nonreligion alike, should be part of the public life of the nation. That includes being recognized and acknowledged by the government.

These two cases by themselves do not have profound, earth-shaking implications for the future of U.S. society, yet they clearly reveal underlying attitudes and assumptions that have enormous consequences for all U.S. society and politics. Chapter 3 speaks of a fault line underlying U.S. church-state relations ever since the eighteenth century. That fault line consists of the position of the eighteenth-century Enlightenment, which saw particularistic religion as a purely private affair and, therefore, as having no place in the public realm, and the position of the Great Awakening, which favored disestablishment but assumed that Christianity would continue to be a presence in the public realm. This fault line was covered over during the nineteenth and early twentieth centuries by an overwhelming Protestant consensus, but with the collapse of that consensus and the greater religious pluralism of today, it has made itself felt. In the Nebraska legislative chaplain and Pawtucket crèche cases the dissenting justices are heirs of the Enlightenment, which define religion as a personal, private affair with no place in the public realm; the majority justices are heirs of the Great Awakening, which just assumed that religion would continue to play a role in the public realm but never developed a thought-out, theoretical defense of it doing so. The eviscerating of religion, in an attempt to preserve a public role for it, clearly reveals that the heirs of the Great Awakening still have not developed a theoretical defense of their position. The concepts and theories of normative, structural pluralism are — as illustrated here — one attempt to articulate a rationale for safeguarding a place in the public life of the nation for religion.

Free Exercise Cases

In a number of cases the Supreme Court has dealt with the issue of whether and to what degree society and its legal codes must — or may — accommodate themselves to religiously motivated practices. Freedom of religion is an ideal that all support, but does it allow persons to engage in practices that otherwise would be forbidden or to refrain from practices in which they otherwise would be required to engage? As seen in Chapter 2, the Supreme Court has struggled to define what, in practical terms, the free exercise language of the Constitution means. Most observers agree that the Court has drawn an uncertain, wavering line in delineating the forbidden, the permissible, and the required.

Much of the uncertainty arises from two basic principles that the Supreme Court has articulated but not consistently followed. One separates religious belief from religious practice and declares that while the former is constitutionally protected, the latter is not. Positive neutrality, in contrast, insists that religiously motivated practices as well as religiously rooted beliefs must be afforded Constitutional protection if religious freedom is not to become a hollow shell. As developed earlier in Chapter 2, actions emanate out of and reflect beliefs. To attempt to separate them and protect only belief is to do violence to religion and thereby, also, to religious freedom. Structural pluralism, which underlies and shapes positive neutrality, sees governmental actions that disadvantage, constrict, or flatly prohibit religious practices — with the important qualification highlighted in the following paragraphs — as violating the autonomy that, by right, the religious sphere possesses. No government has a right to dictate or inhibit religious practices any more than it has a right to dictate or inhibit religious beliefs. Happily, the Supreme Court has not always held to the belief-practice dichotomy but has sometimes been willing to step in to protect the freedom of religious action as well as religious belief.[8]

A second standard that the Supreme Court has at times followed in interpreting the free exercise language of the First Amendment is the compelling state interest principle (also discussed in Chapter 2). This standard states that the government may only disadvantage or constrict the free exercise of religion if it has a compelling interest in doing so. If the health or safety of the public or the social order is threatened by a religious group's free exercise of its beliefs, the Court has held that such free exercise of its religion may be curtailed. For example, persons can be forced to receive smallpox vaccinations and Orthodox Jews cannot escape mandatory Sunday closing laws.[9]

Structural pluralism and positive neutrality are in full agreement with the compelling state interest standard. There is an important point to be made here. Pluralism, with its strong emphasis on religious diversity and the need to protect the right of a wide spectrum of religious groups, ought not to be seen as anarchistic. "Anything goes" is not its watchword. Structural pluralism sees the state as having a significant coordinative role to play among the various societal spheres, with the overall goal of promoting the common interests or welfare of society. Thus, pluralism has no problem in recognizing the state as having a proper role in limiting or disadvantaging a religious group's practices, if there are compelling societal interests in its doing so. Thus the description in Chapter 5 of positive neutrality emphasized the state's right to protect the health, safety, and order of society from threats that certain religious practices would pose.

This principle is clearly relevant when a religious group's practices pose a direct threat to society's health or safety. Most of the difficult cases, however, are of one of two types. One deals with a situation in which a religious group is disadvantaged or inconvenienced by a regulation or practice of the comprehensive administrative state. The health or safety of the public is not at stake in the sense that people are likely to die if an exception is made for the religious group, yet, cumulatively, the workings of the government and its administrative apparatus would be significantly handicapped if all sorts of exceptions were allowed. Here, pluralism and positive neutrality would tilt in the direction of favoring the exceptions for religious reasons, but would also give due weight to the inconveniences and disruptions that the rest of society would endure. As is often the case with law, a careful balancing process is called for.

A second type of difficult case is posed by a religious practice that goes against very strongly held societal values. A hypothetical example is that of a religious cult that engages in the ritualistic torture and sacrifice of animals. The health and safety of the public are not threatened, nor are the normal administrative processes disrupted, yet I would argue that under pluralism and positive neutrality, such practices could be stopped. The social order is seriously threatened when the underlying values that unite the people of the United States as a nation are openly flaunted. This is dangerous ground since this reasoning could be used to suppress almost any unpopular, nonmainstream religion. However, this does not change the fact that weight must be given to the need for societal unity. "*E Pluribus Unum*," as the great seal of the nation declares. If there is to be "*unum*" as well as "*pluribus*," the social fabric of the nation must be protected. Lebanon, Northern Ireland, and Yugoslavia all stand as testimonies of what happens when social order breaks down. Pluralism leans over backward to give all religions full freedom of belief and practice, but there are limits. I would argue that the Supreme Court could have better upheld laws against the nineteenth-century Mormon practice of polygamy on this basis than on a false, constitutionally unjustified belief-practice distinction.

These points can be made clearer by recalling *Employment Division v. Smith* (1990), as discussed in Chapter 2. This is the case that originated in Oregon and concerned two Native Americans who were fired from their jobs at a private drug rehabilitation agency because they had ingested peyote as part of the official rituals of their Native American religion. They were denied unemployment compensation because the Oregon authorities held that they had lost their jobs for work-related "misconduct." By a 6–3 majority, the Supreme Court upheld Oregon's action. Justice Antonin Scalia, in the majority opinion, essentially rejected using the compelling state interest test and upheld Oregon's actions on the basis that "an individual's religious beliefs [do not] excuse him from compliance with an otherwise valid law prohibiting conduct the State is free to regulate."[10] He took a very constricted view of the compelling state interest standard when he went on to hold that it was "inapplicable" to challenges to a state's criminal laws, stating that "we cannot afford the luxury of deeming *presumptively invalid*, as applied to the religious objector, every regulation of conduct that does not protect an interest of the highest order. The rule respondents favor would open the prospect of constitutionally required religious exemptions from civil obligations of almost every conceivable kind."[11]

Justice Sandra Day O'Connor concurred in the result of the decision that the Court reached but objected to its reasoning. She defended the compelling state interest test and argued that the Court should "apply this test in each case to determine whether the burden on the specific plaintiffs before us is constitutionally significant and whether the particular criminal interest asserted by the State before us is compelling."[12] In her judgment, Oregon had demonstrated a compelling state interest in banning the possession of peyote and therefore she agreed with the outcome of the Court's decision.

Justice Harry Blackmun wrote for the three dissenting justices. He began by restating the compelling state interest standard:

> This Court over the years painstakingly has developed a consistent and exacting standard to test the constitutionality of a state statute that burdens the free exercise of religion. Such a statute may stand only if the law in general, and the State's refusal to allow a religious exemption in particular, are justified by a compelling interest that cannot be served by less restrictive means.[13]

The dissent then went on to conclude that "Oregon's interest in enforcing its drug laws against religious use of peyote is not sufficiently compelling to outweigh respondents' right to the free exercise of their religion."[14]

Positive neutrality argues that the Court's majority opinion, by severely restricting the compelling state interest standard, is destructive of religious freedom in a major way. The maintaining of that standard as applicable in cases of this nature is more important than the outcome reached in any particular instance. Positive neutrality thus is comfortable with both O'Connor's concurring opinion and Blackmun's dissenting opinion, although it leans in the direction of making as many allowances as reasonably possible for religious practices that the majority of society might reject. Whether one favors in this particular case the conclusion reached by O'Connor or that of the dissenting justices is less important than upholding the compelling state interest standard, as both these opinions did. What positive neutrality objects to is leaving the country's accommodation to religious practices up to the political process, as did the Court's majority opinion, and then calling doing so an "unavoidable consequence of democratic government."[15] The Bill of Rights stands as a testimony that in a free society, some rights are beyond the reach of legislative majorities. The majority was wrong when it interpreted the compelling state interest test to mean that there would need to be "religious exemptions from civic obligations of almost every conceivable kind." Pluralism and its concept of quasi-sovereign spheres offers a basis on which to insist that religious associations and faith communities may be restricted when the health, safety, and order of society clearly demand it.

One final point needs to be considered. I have repeatedly defined positive neutrality in terms of being neutral not only among religions but also between religion and secularism. This raises a potential problem: Does not government's granting exemptions to otherwise valid laws and regulations on the basis of religious beliefs favor religion over secular philosophies and mind-sets? A sincere adherent of Native American religion would be able to use peyote as a part of a religious ceremony, while a nonreligious recreational user of peyote would face fines and even imprisonment.

The answer to this problem is found in giving equal consideration to religious beliefs and practices and to certain deeply held beliefs and practices based on those beliefs even when they technically are of a nonreligious nature. If a person holds to certain beliefs of an ethical or moral nature that seek to answer life's ultimate questions, and if those beliefs are deeply and sincerely held — as evidenced by their being held over a period of time, by a life lived consistently with them, and by association with others of like mind — they serve as a functional equivalent of religion, even though they may not be rooted in the supernatural (and therefore technically do not qualify as religion under my definition). In an increasingly diverse United States, pluralism's respect for those of no faith as well as those of deep religious faith is crucial. However, this position guards against potential abuses by distinguishing, in the realm of nonreligion, between mere preferences, convenience, self-interest, and lightly held opinions, on the one hand, and deeply held and sincerely believed convictions of conscience, on the other. Even if the latter are not rooted in what I have defined as religion because of an absence of a sense of the supernatural, they nevertheless, in a pluralistic society, should have the same protections as religiously rooted beliefs and practices.[16] The standards these secular beliefs would have to meet are sufficiently high that relatively few would qualify under them. However, for those few individuals, it is important that they not be excluded. To do so would be to favor religion over secularism.

Religion in the Public Schools

Some of the Supreme Court's most difficult decisions have dealt with the question of whether and in what form religion may be brought into the public schools. This issue has been extremely controversial, and Supreme Court decisions ruling against certain religious exercises in the public schools have aroused intense opposition from large segments of the public. Congressional majorities and Presidents Ronald Reagan and George Bush have paid at least lip service to proposals that organized prayer — contrary to what the Supreme Court has ruled — should be allowed in the public schools.

Intense feelings over Supreme Court decisions regarding religion in the public schools have probably been aroused, first, by the central role of the public schools in the lives of students and their families. With compulsory attendance laws, a majority of the prime daytime hours of children's lives from age five to sixteen are under the control of the public school. There certainly is time for the family and for churches and other religious associations to have a crucial influence on the lives of children, but many feel that they are in a competitive disadvantage with the schools, with their monopolization of children's daytime hours; elaborate instructional materials; professional, highly trained personnel; and high status. The degree of controversy in this area is also increased by the fact that well into the twentieth century, elements of the informal, de facto nineteenth-century Protestant establishment of religion remained in the public schools. Until after World War II, Bible reading, prayers, Christmas and Easter celebrations, and other Christian religious exercises were commonplace in many public schools. A series of Supreme Court decisions have had the effect of rooting out long-established practices. It is not surprising that opposition and controversy have accompanied these efforts.

In dealing with cases in this area, the Supreme Court has generally taken a strong position against allowing religious observations and exercises into the public schools. It has held released-time programs for religious instruction on school property. Offering state-composed, nonsectarian prayers, Bible reading, reading of the Lord's Prayer, posting the Ten Commandments in classrooms, a minute of silence for meditation and prayer, teaching scientific evidences in support of creation along with those for evolution, and praying at graduation ceremonies are all in violation of the establishment provision of the First Amendment.[17] On the other hand, it has ruled that released-time programs for religious instruction held off school property, objective teaching about religion, a minute of silence for meditation, and the official recognition of voluntary, student-initiated, and student-led religious clubs are all permissible under the First Amendment.[18] As these listings reveal, what the Court has disallowed is greater than what it has allowed. The basis for these decisions has generally been the Court's insistence that the state may not engage in or support any activity that could reasonably be interpreted as advancing or endorsing religion over nonreligion. The public schools, thereby (in the Court's view) are held to a position of neutrality in relation to religion and nonreligion. It is helpful to look briefly at several specific decisions of the Court.

Abington School District v. Schempp (1963) ruled against a Pennsylvania requirement that the Bible be read, without any comment, at the beginning of each school day. The majority opinion in this 7–1 decision held that the Bible reading was a religious exercise intended to inculcate religious values:

> It might well be said that one's education is not complete without a study of comparative religion or the history of religion and its relationship to the advancement of civilization. It certainly may be said that the Bible is worthy of study for its literary and historic qualities. Nothing we have said here indicates that such a study of the Bible or of religion, when presented objectively as part of a secular program of education, may not be effected consistently with the First Amendment. But the exercises here do not fall into those categories. They are religious exercises, required by the States in violation of the command of the First Amendment that the Government maintain strict neutrality, neither aiding nor opposing religion.[19]

The Court drew a plain distinction here and has, for the most part, consistently followed it. Religion may be objectively taught and analyzed; it may not be favored. Thus, all activities that could be interpreted as advancing or tending to advance religion are unconstitutional.

The stringent degree to which the Court has held to this distinction can be seen in *Wallace v. Jaffree* (1985), which held that although an Alabama law providing for a minute of silence in the public schools for "meditation" was constitutional, an amendatory law that provided that the minute of silence was "for meditation *or voluntary prayer* " (emphasis added) was unconstitutional. As the Court said, "The addition of 'or voluntary prayer' indicates that the State intended to characterize prayer as a favored practice. Such an endorsement is not consistent with the established principle that the Government must pursue a course of complete neutrality toward religion."[20]

The dissenting opinion by Justice William Rehnquist largely consisted of a compelling argument against the assertion that the original intent of the authors of the First Amendment was to ban all government actions which favored religion over nonreligion. Thus, the dissent concluded, "Nothing in the Enlightenment Clause of the First Amendment, properly understood, prohibits any such generalized 'endorsement' of prayer."[21]

Also instructive is *Stone v. Graham* (1980), in which the Supreme Court ruled that a Kentucky statute requiring the Ten Commandments be posted in all school classrooms to be unconstitutional. The Kentucky legislature had attempted to escape constitutional condemnation by asserting a claimed secular character for the Ten Commandments. The statute had required the following notice to be printed at the bottom of each copy of the Ten Commandments placed in classrooms: "The secular application of the Ten Commandments is clearly seen in its adoption as the fundamental legal code of Western Civilization and the Common Law of the United States."[22] The Court majority did not accept this secular disclaimer, but insisted: "The pre-eminent purpose for posting the Ten Commandments on schoolroom walls is plainly religious in nature. The Ten Commandments are undeniably a sacred text in the Jewish and Christian faiths, and no legislative recitation of a supposed secular purpose can blind us to that fact."[23] The Court went on to conclude: "If the posted copies of the Ten Commandments are to have any effect at all, it will be to induce the schoolchildren to read, meditate upon, perhaps to venerate and obey, the Commandments. However desirable this might be as a matter of private devotion, it is not a permissible state objective under the Establishment Clause."[24] In a dissenting opinion Justice Rehnquist gave greater credence to Kentucky's secular claim: "It is . . . undeniable, however, as the elected representatives of Kentucky determined, that the Ten Commandments have had a significant impact on the development of secular legal codes of the Western World."[25]

In contrast, the Court held in *Westside Community Schools v. Mergens* (1990), as seen in the previous chapter, that student-led and student-initiated religious clubs did not violate the First Amendment. In an 8–1 decision, the Supreme Court held that the norm of neutrality was not violated by a high school officially recognizing a religious club because the existing conditions were such that no endorsement of the club or religion was implied by the actions of the school. "To the extent that a religious club is merely one of many different student-initiated voluntary clubs, students should perceive no message of government endorsement of religion."[26]

Positive neutrality reacts to these decisions, first, by arguing that trying to gain constitutional approval by clothing religion in secular garb is inappropriate and self-defeating. Clearly, the Ten Commandments are a sacred text. If there is value in posting them in classrooms, that value is largely due to their religious character. The same is true of daily Bible readings. This "secularity" approach to allowing religion into the public schools is at heart dishonest, and in any case is destructive of religion. At the most, only a few scattered, anemic remnants of once powerful religious beliefs and principles would be able to gain constitutional approval on the basis of this defense.

Positive neutrality begins what it considers a much more theoretically sound approach to religion in the public schools with a basic point made in Chapter 2: the inaccuracy of the underlying assumption that a true neutrality between religion and secularism is gained by the removal from the public schools of all practices or references that are favorable to specific religions or to religion generally. The absence of religion in the life of the school in any sort of a favorable context — even one as minor as a moment of silence designated for prayer or meditation — is to send the implicit message that religion as a living, controlling force is unnecessary and irrelevant to most of life. Alone among the opinions of Supreme Court justices to raise this issue in clear terms is the dissent of Justice Potter Stewart in *Abington School District v. Schempp*. As noted in Chapter 3, he wrote:

> If religious exercises are held to be an impermissible activity in schools, religion is placed at an artificial and state-created disadvantage. Viewed in this light, permission of such exer- cises for those who want them is necessary if the schools are truly to be neutral in the matter of religion. And a refusal to permit religious exercises thus is seen, not as the realization of state neutrality, but rather as the establishment of a religion of secularism.[27]

Stewart then went on to argue that a genuine neutrality requires "the extension of evenhanded treatment to all who believe, doubt, or disbelieve."[28] He concluded with an eloquent expression of the ideal of governmental neutrality toward religion and irreligion: "What our Constitution indispensably protects is the freedom of each of us, be he Jew or Agnostic, Christian or Atheist, Buddhist or Freethinker, to believe ofr disbelieve, to worship or not worship, to pray or keep silent, according to his own conscience, uncoerced and unrestrained by government."[29] To all this, positive neutrality wholeheartedly agrees.

However, all this does not mean that the path to recognizing and accommodating religious pluralism in the public schools is easy or clear. Positive neutrality opposes favoring either religion or secularism, yet if today's almost total ban on the favorable treatment of religion favors secularism over religion, the old practice of reflecting and advancing the majoritarian religious beliefs of society favored religion over secularism, and even favored a particular religious tradition over all others. That was not neutrality either.

Justice Stewart's answer in his *Abington School District v. Schempp* dissent was to allow Bible reading in the public schools but to excuse or otherwise seek to avoid coercing those for whom such a religious exercise would violate their religious beliefs or their lack of a religious faith. However, one can immediately sense problems. Clearly, those for whom Bible reading complements their religious beliefs would be in a favored position over those such as Muslims or nonbelievers, for whom this would not be the case. The absence of the theoretical underpinnings that structural pluralism gives to positive neutrality, and which Justice Stewart did not have, both weakened the persuasiveness of the position that he urged and blinded even him to the lack of a genuine neutrality that his own conclusion entailed.

The response that positive neutrality makes to most church-state issues — guided by the concepts of pluralism, which inform it — is to allow the full and free play of all religious groups and of both religion and secularism. Thus, positive neutrality's approach to the posting of the Ten Commandments in the public schools would be to allow their posting, as long as comparable, key writings of other religious or secular traditions represented in the classroom and community are also periodically displayed. The basic principle is not to try to achieve a neutrality by driving all religion out of the classroom — which results in a false neutrality that, in fact, favors a secular cultural ethos, but by welcoming and recognizing all religions and secular philosophies and mind-sets alike.

However, it is harder to apply this principle in other aspects of religion and public K-12 education. In a legislature it makes sense to have daily sessions opened with prayers from a wide spectrum of religious traditions, but how can that same principle be applied in a community's public schools? One theoretical response would be to have all the children take turns each morning in reading from their religions' sacred writings and offering a prayer in keeping with their traditions. However, when thinking of a kindergarten or even a high school class, one can quickly recognize practical problems in implementing such a solution. One is dealing with immature persons who themselves are just beginning to relate to and sort out their reactions to their families' religious traditions. Moreover, such an approach does not touch on the problem of how to deal with religious values and beliefs in such sensitive areas of the curriculum as sex education and human origins.

The response that is most fully in keeping with structural pluralism is to encourage differing religious traditions to establish their own schools, as some, in fact, have done. The interests of every religious tradition in bringing up its young is so strong, and the improbability of a single public school being able to deal adequately with the increasingly diverse religious beliefs of U.S. society, suggest that different schools, each committed to the religious beliefs and traditions of the parents who send their children there, is the most thoroughgoing way in which to reflect the religious diversity of U.S. society. Those who wish their children to receive an education that is, for example, in keeping with the evangelical Protestant tradition, could better establish their own schools than try to make the public schools into evangelical Protestant schools.

However, this approach has its limitations. It is very expensive to create new, privately owned schools, plus it takes organizational skills and time. This is an option that at best is available only to the better-educated, wealthier portion of the population. It thereby contains its own form of religious discrimination: Professional families and others with money, time, and organizational skills can have their children educated in keeping with their religious beliefs; others cannot. The government can take some steps to ease this discrimination (as discussed later in the chapter), but it is unlikely ever to be eliminated totally. Plus, certain numbers are necessary for a successful, religiously based school. Religious traditions that are in a very small minority have no real alternative but the general public school. They, too, have no real choice.

Recognizing these limitations that adhere in nonpublic alternatives to public schools, I would suggest three additional approaches in keeping with positive neutrality that would help to assure greater pluralism in the public schools than is now the case. All three are aimed at developing appropriate means to recognize and accommodate a diversity of religious beliefs to which students and their families hold, while also recognizing and accommodating the beliefs of those of no religious faith. One approach consists of moments of meditation and prayer at the beginning of the school day, and perhaps at lunch time and the end of the day as well. Here, school children are totally free to speak (or not to speak) to the Deity in any way they please as long as they are not disruptive of others' prayer or meditation. Those who are nonreligious can meditate or reflect on the upcoming day, or, for that matter, plan their after-school television viewing.

The Supreme Court's rejection of such an option in *Wallace v. Jaffree* (1985) went squarely against the religious neutrality that the Court itself has often professed. It did so on the basis that the Alabama law implicitly (and perhaps explicitly) endorsed religion by specifically mentioning prayer along with meditation as a purpose of the minute of silence. In one sense, the Court was right. Of course, the Alabama statute endorsed prayer, but that is beside the point. As Chapter 5 argued, the norm of neutrality is not violated as long as all religions, as well as religion and secular points of view, are equally endorsed or supported. Under positive neutrality, the relevant question is whether the statute favored any one form of prayer and whether it favored prayer over nonprayer. Neutrality means even-handedness among religions and between religion and nonreligion. By mandating a one-minute period of silence "for meditation or voluntary prayer," Alabama law was neutral. The religious individuals could pray in whatever form they wished; the irreligious could meditate on anything to which their beliefs or values would lead. Religion and secularism were equally endorsed, yet to single out the endorsement of religion — or, more specifically, religious traditions that accept the possibility and need for human communication with the Deity — as unconstitutional, and not to hold the endorsement of meditation unconstitutional, is to favor secularism and religions not believing in prayer over religions believing in prayer. In contrast, structural pluralism and positive neutrality hold that one appropriate — that is, neutral — way in which to introduce religion into the public schools is to allow times of silence for personal, individual, voluntary prayer; otherwise, due deference to the religious traditions represented in the classroom is bound to be lost.

Positive neutrality says that this is a better way to defend the Alabama law than Justice Rehnquist's dissent, which argued that indeed, the law favored or endorsed religion over nonreligion, but that this was not a violation of the intentions of the authors of the First Amendment. Factually, Rehnquist's position on original intent is on solid ground, but in a society becoming increasingly pluralistic, a more equitable, defensible argument is that of neutrality assured by a government that affirms religious and secular beliefs alike.

A second way in which religion can be accommodated within the existing public schools is through the equal access approach approved by the Supreme Court in *Westside Community Schools v. Mergens* (1990) and released-time programs such as the one that was rejected in *McCollum v. Board of Education* (1948). Positive neutrality says that students surely should be free to meet for religious purposes if they meet voluntarily during noninstructional times, as long as all religious traditions and similar or parallel secularly based student groups are equally free to organize and meet. They should be free to meet on school property, to invite outside speakers in, and to advertise their meetings — just as all other student groups are free to do. The key here is a neutrality or evenhandedness by the school officials. Positive neutrality says that both the majority and the dissenting justices were wrong when they decided the *Mergens* case on whether in their judgment religion was being endorsed by the school. Endorsement or nonendorsement of religion is not the issue; equal treatment of all religious points of view and religion and nonreligion is.

Similarly, a plurality of religious points of view can be recognized and given their due without any one being favored or coerced by way of released-time programs. Here, various religious groups are invited to come into the public schools and teach the students who are adherents of their faith each week during an hour or so that has been set aside for such purposes. All religious faiths are invited to teach students of their faiths. Adherents of ethical or value-oriented associations that are not technically religious organizations could also have their representatives come in to teach their students, while those of no faith would have an extra study period.

The Supreme Court, from the point of view of structural pluralism, got it wrong back in 1948 when it judged a released-time program in Champaign, Illinois, on the basis of whether religion was being helped. Of course religion was being helped, but no more so than secularism, and no one religion any more than any other religion. It was religiously neutral. However, the Court simply asserted that the "wall between Church and State . . . must be kept high and impregnable" and then went on to note that the state's tax-supported public school buildings [were being] used for the dissemination of religious doctrines."[30] As far as the Court was concerned, that sealed the fate of Champaign's released-time program. The support or endorsement of religion was enough to find the practice unconstitutional. The question that pluralism considers to be the key one — namely, whether all religions, as well as secular perspectives, were being treated equally — was never brought up, not even in the dissent written by Justice Stanley Reed. He made his dissent on the very weak basis that the "Court cannot be too cautious in upsetting practices embedded in our society by many years of experience" and that the "accepted habits of the people" should not be interfered with.[31] He gave the argument away when he stated: "If abuses occur, such as the use of the instruction hour for sectarian purposes, I have no doubt . . . that Illinois will promptly correct them."[32] Pluralism wants the instruction hour to be used for sectarian purposes: that is, to teach specific tenets and values of specific religious associations and faith communities. The constitutionality of the program should have been affirmed on the basis of a neutrality based on the equal treatment of all religions and secularism, not on the basis of long practice, which may have more to do with a dying nineteenth-century Protestant establishment than religious freedom nor on the supposed nonsectarian nature of the religious instruction.

A third and final way in which positive neutrality suggests dealing with the issue of religion in the public schools is to make certain that religion is given its full due in an objective sense and that secular philosophies and points of view are also given their due, but no more than their proper due. Public schools today often do not even give religion the recognition and consideration it can be given without running afoul of the Supreme Court's church-state doctrines. This fact came out in a 1987 District Court case in the United States

District for the Southern District of Alabama (*Smith v. Board of School Commissioners of Mobile County*, No. 82-0544-BH, 1987). Although the District Court's decision — which found that certain public school textbooks used in the Alabama schools promoted the religion of secular humanism in violation of the establishment clause of the First Amendment — was attacked by many commentators and was overturned by the Federal Court of Appeals, yet it brought to light some startling facts.[33] For example, it noted the findings of Timothy Smith of Johns Hopkins University's History Department, which documented a systematic tendency to slight the role that religion has played in U.S. history:

> The pattern in these books is the omission of religious aspects to significant American events. The religious significance of much of the history of the Puritans is ignored. The Great Awakenings are generally not mentioned. Colonial missionaries are either not mentioned or represented as oppressors of native Americans. The religious influence on the abolitionist, women's suffrage, temperance, modern civil rights and peace movements is ignored or diminished to insignificance. The role of religion in the lives of immigrants and minorities, especially southern blacks, is rarely mentioned. After the Civil War, religion is given almost no play.[34]

Positive neutrality — with its emphasis on genuine governmental neutrality among religions and between religion and secular perspectives — says that to drive the role religion has played in U.S. and world history out of textbooks and public school classrooms and to fail to acknowledge what various religious traditions have said in regard to issues such as sexual ethics, personal values, and economic relationships is to do violence to neutrality. The goal should be the fair, unbiased, equal representation of religion's views and perspectives — as fair, unbiased, and equal as those given views and perspectives of secular origin. Positions and evidence on various sides of controversial issues should be presented honestly and accurately.

When Louisiana enacted legislation requiring that so-called creation science be taught along with evolutionary explanations of human origins, it was acting within the spirit of this third approach.[35] Whether this particular Louisiana law was the proper way in which to go about assuring that religion and secularism were treated evenhandedly is not the crucial issue (I personally have serious doubts); however, the underlying goal of "equal time" is. Assuring that a variety of religious and secular points of view are aired and treated fairly and respectfully is a key way in which to assure that the public schools practice a genuine neutrality toward religion and do not end up supporting a secular cultural ethos due to religion being left out of the curriculum.

In taking this position, as in other areas of religion in the public schools, positive neutrality stands in contrast to both sides in the current debate. It opposes those who argue that any explicit or implicit endorsement of or support for religion by the public schools is unconstitutional, but it also opposes those who would allow religion into the schools on the bases of an alleged secular character or the long-standing, traditional nature of some religious practices. In reading the many Supreme Court decisions in this area, I have been struck by the neat, tightly reasoned opinions of those opposing religion in the public schools and the often weak, uncertain opinions of justices supporting religion there in one form or another. The consequences of the historical patterns discussed in Chapter 3 continue to reverberate today. The justices who are wall of separation proponents can draw on the Enlightenment theories of church-state separation; however, the justices seeking a public role for religion have no similar theoretical base on which they can build. Neither the Great Awakening, the pietistic dissenters of the eighteenth century, nor the culturally dominant Protestants of the nineteenth century developed one. Structural pluralism seeks to offer at least the beginnings of a theoretically more defensible basis for judging when and in what forms religion should be allowed into the public schools and for defending those judgments.

State Aid to Nonpublic Schools

The large number of nonpublic schools and the large number of citizens who support them — combined with the often difficult financial straits in which they find themselves — have resulted in frequent attempts by government in one way or another to offer them material support or financial assistance. Given the religious nature of the vast majority of these nonpublic schools, the Supreme Court has time and again been called to rule on the constitutionality of such state aid.

The Supreme Court has made it very difficult for programs of governmental aid to nonpublic schools to pass constitutional muster. It has held that the states may not subsidize the salaries of nonpublic school teachers of secular subjects; subsidize the repair and maintenance of nonpublic school facilities; reimburse nonpublic school parents for tuition expenses they have incurred; pay for specialized counseling and testing services or most instructional materials and equipment such as maps, films, and projectors; nor pay for salaries of public school teachers offering classes in nonpublic school facilities.[36] On the other hand, the Supreme Court has allowed states to subsidize the transportation of children to nonpublic schools, pay for some limited assistance for standardized testing and diagnostic services, and permit tax deductions for school expenses incurred by nonpublic school parents.[37]

In reaching these decisions, the Supreme Court has repeatedly depended on the three-part *Lemon* test of a secular purpose, a primarily secular effect, and no excessive entanglement as the standard that the challenged program must meet. In determining if this test has been successfully passed, the Court has asked such questions as whether the aid goes to children and their parents or to the schools themselves, whether the aid is indirect and incidental or direct and significant, and whether the challenged program has the effect of advancing religion (either in general or in terms of specific religious teachings or traditions). Light can be shed on these issues by looking more closely at two decisions of the Court, one of which disallowed an aid program and one of which allowed a program of financial aid.

In *Grand Rapids School District v. Ball* (1985), the Supreme Court was called to pass judgment on two programs established by the public schools in Grand Rapids, Michigan. One placed full-time public school teachers in nonpublic schools to teach allegedly secular courses that supplemented the core curriculum, such as remedial and enrichment classes in various subjects, which otherwise the nonpublic schools would have been unable to provide. A second program offered enrichment classes after normal school hours in nonpublic schools, taught by part-time public school teachers (many of whom taught full-time for the nonpublic school during the regular class day).

The Supreme Court held in a 5–4 vote that both these programs were in violation of the First Amendment. The crux of the majority opinion, written by Justice Brennan, was: "The programs challenged here . . . have a similar — and forbidden — effect of advancing religion." This advantage given religion was "direct and substantial," not "indirect and incidental."[38] Justice Brennan argued (as seen in Chapter 2 also) that even though the teachers were teaching secular, not religious, subjects, and even though there was no direct evidence that they brought religious precepts into the classroom, the programs were unconstitutional. In reaching this conclusion, he quoted favorably a commentator who had written: "In short, the parochial school's operation serves to fulfill both secular and religious functions concurrently, and the two cannot be completely separated."[39] From this, Brennan concluded that the "pervasively sectarian" atmosphere of the nonpublic schools indicated their teachers may inadvertently inculcate "particular tenets or beliefs," that an impermissible "symbolic link between government and religion" was created, and that religion was directly promoted by providing a subsidy to the religious institution.[40]

Writing the dissent, Chief Justice Rehnquist argued that the subjects being taught were purely secular subjects and that there was no "instance of attempted religious inculcation existing in the records of the school aid cases decided today."[41] It is also helpful to note that Justice O'Connor, who dissented in part in the *Grand Rapids* case and also dissented in a companion case that was decided along with the *Grand Rapids* case, openly embraced the no advancement of religion test. She wrote in her dissent in the companion case that "direct state aid to parochial schools that has the purpose or effect of furthering the religious mission of the schools is unconstitutional. I agree with that principle."[42] She judged that because the subjects being taught were secular subjects and there was no evidence or reason to presume that teachers were bringing religious views into those secular subjects, the program should be held constitutional.

In *Mueller v. Allen* (1983), the Supreme Court, in another close 5–4 vote, upheld the constitutionality of a Minnesota statute that allowed parents to deduct up to $700 on their state income taxes for expenses they had incurred in educating their children. Parents sending their children to nonpublic schools could deduct money spent on tuition, books, and other such expenses, while parents sending their children to public schools could deduct money spent on school supplies, books, or any other school expense not covered by the state. The majority opinion, written by Chief Justice Rehnquist, applied the three-prong *Lemon* test and found that the Minnesota statute passed all three facets of the test. It had the secular purpose of aiding in the education of the state's children. It also had a primarily secular effect, as indicated by the fact that "the deduction is available for educational expenses incurred by all parents, including those whose children attend public schools and those whose children attend non-sectarian private schools or sectarian private schools."[43] Chief Justice Rehnquist summed up his case for a secular effect in this way: "The historic purposes of the clause simply do not encompass the sort of *attenuated* financial benefit, ultimately controlled by the private choices of individual parents, that eventually flows to parochial schools from the neutrally available tax benefit at issue in this case."[44] Finally, the majority opinion held that there clearly was no excessive entanglement of religion and government, especially since the aid was funneled through parents, and there was no need for state supervision of any significance.

Justice Thurgood Marshall wrote for the four dissenting justices and argued that the Minnesota statute "has a direct and immediate effect of advancing religion." He went on to conclude:

For the first time, the Court has upheld financial support for religious schools without any reason at all to assume that the support will be restricted to the secular functions of those schools and will not be used to support religious instruction. This result is flatly at odds with the fundamental principle that a State may provide no financial support whatsoever to promote religion.[45]

Positive neutrality and the tenets of structural pluralism underlying it argue that the appropriate issue in both of these cases is not whether religion is being advanced. Of course, the aid programs were advancing religion in some sort of manner. When justices who oppose state aid to nonpublic schools argue that "a State may provide no financial support whatsoever to promote religion" and that even a "symbolic link between government and religion" may not be allowed, governmental neutrality toward religion is not being promoted. Rather, what is being promoted is the government's favoring of secular perspectives over religious ones. Justice Brennan in the *Grand Rapids* case failed to see that if the aid program advanced religion by creating a symbolic link between religion and the state, the state, by eschewing all such aid, creates a symbolic link between government and nonreligion, thereby promoting a secular, humanistic cultural ethos over one that is neutral toward religion. Justice Marshall objected to any "financial support whatsoever to promote religion," but what about financial support to promote a nonreligious, secular outlook? That, of course, in his view was permissible. As noted in Chapter 2, however, A. James Reichley put the issue particularly clearly: "Banishment of religion does not represent neutrality between religion and secularism; conduct of public institutions without any acknowledgment of religion *is* secularism."[46] Thus, the norm of neutrality is being violated by the position of Justices Brennan and Marshall.

Positive neutrality, however, also has deep problems with the reasoning being advanced in the two cases examined here by those favoring state aid to nonpublic schools. It says they ought not to argue — as they did in the *Grand Rapids* case — that religion was not being advanced, since the secular and religious facets of education in a religiously based school had been effectively sorted out, and only the secular facet was granted state financial assistance. Nor should they argue — as was done in the *Minnesota* case — that religion is really not being advanced since it is being helped only minimally and indirectly. To make either of these arguments — in the view of pluralism and positive neutrality — is to give the argument away to those who would block all such aid.

In regard to the secular-sacred distinction, pluralism says that Justice Brennan was absolutely right when he noted in the *Grand Rapids* case that the secular and religious aspects of religious schools are intertwined and inseparable. Pluralism, which welcomes religion as a strong, robust force into the public realm, would expect religiously based schools to be "pervasively sectarian," to use the Court's term. The whole point of a religious association in establishing schools is to have its children learn and study in an atmosphere that respects and seeks to cultivate knowledge and attitudes in keeping with its beliefs. Even a purportedly secular science course in a Catholic school might very well discuss and critique the Church's clash with Galileo differently than would a secular school. Similarly, a black Nation of Islam school might very well cover different topics in a secular history course than would the typical public school. The point is even more clearly seen in courses on family life and social relations, philosophy, home economics, and literature. The Supreme Court's opinion in another case dealing with aid to religiously based schools at one point said: "We simply recognize that a dedicated religious person, teaching in a school affiliated with his or her faith and operated to inculcate its tenets, will inevitably experience great difficulty in remaining religiously neutral."[47] Pluralism's response is to exclaim, "I would hope so!" For those who favor state aid to nonpublic schools to do so by claiming that such schools teach many subjects in a totally secular manner and that government may therefore support them without supporting religion is self-defeating. The more this approach would succeed, the more the point of having religiously based schools would shrink, since its successes would mean that religiously oriented schools would have to increasingly limit their religious nature.

A similar point is even easier to make in regard to another argument used by some supporters of the constitutionality of state aid to nonpublic schools: that such aid may be supporting religion, but it is doing so only indirectly and minimally. In the Rehnquist majority opinion in the Minnesota tax deduction case, he argued for the constitutionality of the program, in part (as quoted earlier) on the attenuated nature of the financial benefit that the religiously based schools were receiving. Among the terms used to define *attenuate* in *Webster's New Collegiate Dictionary* are "to lessen the amount, force or value of; to weaken; to reduce the vitality of." Under this approach, state aid that is weak, minor, or of no vital significance can be approved; any that gives real help fails. The problem this causes for a pluralism that wants religiously based and secularly based points of view and schools to be treated in a neutral, evenhanded fashion is all too clear.

Positive neutrality says that a better, more defensible test for the constitutionality of a program of state aid to nonpublic schools than both sides were using in these two cases is a test of whether any particular religion, or either religion or nonreligion, is being favored, and whether the state aid is supporting programs with direct, this-world benefits for society generally. Religion admittedly is being advanced by most if not all, nonpublic school aid programs that have come before the Supreme Court. However, taking governmental aid in the field of education as a whole, education within a religious context is hardly being favored over education within a secular, nonreligious context. The state is providing massive assistance and support to secularized, nonreligious education through governmentally owned and operated public schools. State aid programs for religiously rooted schools that have come before the Court do not begin to compare in scope or size with state programs in support of secular, nonreligiously oriented education. Nor have any of these programs of state aid singled out any one religious tradition for the aid they provide: Catholics, Protestants, Jews, Muslims, and others are all eligible. Pluralism argues that government is not violating the norm of neutrality when it seeks to even the balances by providing at least some financial support to those whose consciences compel them to assure that their children receive an education in keeping with their religious beliefs. Here is a clear instance of a genuine neutrality on the part of government that requires it to take certain positive steps.

As Chapter 5 argued, positive neutrality does not support state aid going to support programs whose primary benefits are religious in nature, but rather only supports ones that have a direct, this-world benefit for society as a whole. Given society's great need for an educated population, the education that religiously based schools give their students clearly has a nonreligious, this-world benefit for society. It is important to be clear, however, that it is the benefits that the broad public gains from an educational program that are controlling, and not the existence of allegedly purely secular courses of study. Educational programs in which religious perspectives and precepts are mixed in with secular facets are eligible for funding, as long as the programs have nonreligious, this-world benefits for society generally.

This position of positive neutrality does not mean that government should aid any and all nonpublic schools without examining their nature and demanding accountability. Chapter 5 made it clear that in cases where the pursuit of a positive neutrality leads government to give material aid to a religiously based association, it has a right to demand, and the religious association has an obligation to meet, reasonable standards to assure that the aid is, in fact, contributing to attaining benefits for society as a whole. Thus, religiously based schools under positive neutrality could, for example, be required to hire certified teachers, offer certain basic courses, meet a certain number of days each year, not teach blatantly false material, and refrain from teaching racial or class hatred. If conditions such as these are not met, the public benefits of a school's program for society are, at the very least, drawn into question. Moreover, in the case of a school teaching class or racial hatred, it would not be fulfilling all religious structures' obligation to act with a sense of respect and civility toward other religious traditions and society more broadly. Government could — and should — deny such a school material aid. The quasi-sovereignty — and not the absolute sovereignty — of religious associations put forward by pluralism helps assure that the freedom and rights possessed by religious associations are limited or qualified by the larger societal context within which they exist. They are accountable.

State Aid to Other Religiously Based Organizations

Nonpublic, K-12 schools are only one type of religiously based and motivated organization that federal or state governments have sometimes sought to aid financially. Colleges and universities, hospitals, nursing homes, old age retirement facilities, homeless shelters, drug treatment centers, spouse abuse shelters, child-care centers, and adoption and foster care agencies are among the host of religiously rooted organizations that have received state aid. This raises the same question of permissible and impermissible state aid raised by aid to K-12 nonpublic schools.

In surprising contrast to the Supreme Court's decisions in regard to aid to nonpublic, K-12 schools, it has approved aid in several forms to religiously based colleges and universities, hospitals, and agencies dealing with teenage sexuality and unmarried pregnant teenagers.[48] The Court approved some of these programs by very narrow majorities, but I have not been able to uncover a single Supreme Court case in which a program of material or financial aid to religious organizations other than K-12 schools has been found unconstitutional. In surveying this issue, one is also struck by the very few cases of this nature that have even been litigated before the Court, again in sharp contrast to the numerous cases concerning aid to nonpublic schools. Every indication is that this has been the case, not because the Court has frequently refused *certiorari* but rather because few cases have been litigated in the lower federal and state courts and appealed to the Supreme Court. This indicates that U.S. society as a whole does not have the same concern for governmental aid to a host of religiously based programs as it does for aid to K-12 education. Organized groups such as the American Civil Liberties Union and Americans United for Separation of Church and State, which have raised challenges even to minor forms of state aid to nonpublic schools, seem to share this lack of concern. One thing, however, is beyond dispute: The lack of litigation is not due to a lack of governmental financial aid to a host of religiously based programs and agencies. The large number of religiously based colleges and universities — almost all of which receive various forms of direct and indirect governmental aid — is well known.[49] Less well known is the fact that the Roman Catholic New York Archdiocese, for example, provides foster care for thousands of children and is paid $50 to $60 million dollars a year in federal, state, and local funds for doing so.[50] In Michigan, of the over 9,000 children in foster care, 75 percent are receiving that care from private agencies, half of which are religiously based. The state of Michigan pays out approximately $28 million a year to the private agencies.[51]

On the few occasions when the Supreme Court has been called on to judge the constitutionality of such programs, it has generally approved them by distinguishing their religious from their secular aspects and arguing that the state is only funding the secular aspects. An especially clear expression of this principle is found in a dissenting opinion by Justice William Douglas:

> Churches perform some functions that a State would constitutionally be empowered to perform. I refer to nonsectarian social welfare operations such as the care of orphaned children and the destitute and people who are sick. A tax exemption to agencies performing those functions would therefore be as constitutionally proper as the grant of direct subsidies to them.[52]

Douglas's contention is that direct subsidies even to churches would be constitutional as long as those subsidies went to support "nonsectarian social welfare operations."

Due to the paucity of cases dealing with this issue coming before the Supreme Court, there are not many examples of the application of this principle enunciated by Justice Douglas. However, there are two that are especially helpful. One is a 1899 case that dealt with a challenge to the provision of federal funds to a hospital in the District of Columbia that was affiliated with a Roman Catholic order, the Sisters of Charity. A unanimous Court held that there was no violation of the establishment clause. The Court acknowledged the religious character of the hospital, but in the same breath declared the irrelevancy of this fact: "The fact that its members . . . are members of a monastic order or sisterhood of the Roman Catholic Church, and the further fact that the hospital is conducted under the auspices of said church, are wholly immaterial."[53] The Court's holding that the religious character of the hospital was immaterial in part rested upon the fact that the hospital had been separately incorporated by an act of Congress. Thus, the Court ruled: "It is simply the case of a secular corporation being managed by people who hold to the doctrines of the Roman Catholic church."[54] Moreover, the secular character of the corporation was assured by the secular nature of its operations:

The charter itself does not limit the exercise of its corporate powers to the members of any particular religious denomination, but on the contrary those powers are to be exercised in favor of any one seeking the ministrations of that kind of an institution. . . . There is nothing sectarian in the corporation, and "the specific and limited object of its creation" is the opening and keeping a hospital in the city of Washington for the care of such sick and invalid persons as may place themselves under the treatment and care of the corporation.[55]

The Supreme Court never really inquired into whether in fact the hospital was carrying out its tasks in a wholly secular fashion. I would be surprised if there were no crucifixes in patients' rooms, no priest who would stop by to visit the patients, and no deeply devout sisters who would speak of the "Great Physician" as they ministered to the ill. In fact, I cannot help but hope that they did not deprive suffering and dying patients whatever solace they could offer from their religious faith. However, closing its eyes to such possibilities, the Court built a shaky foundation for state aid to a host of religiously related social welfare programs. In 1988, these weaknesses came to light.

The 1988 case of *Bowen v. Kendrick* dealt with the Adolescent Family Life Act (AFLA), which makes federal grants available for services provided by public and private agencies relating to adolescent sexuality and pregnancy. It seeks to fund programs aimed at reducing premarital teenage sexual relations and pregnancies and at assisting unwed adolescents who are pregnant. Among the private agencies funded under the terms of the act were several with religious roots and connections. In fact, in the act, Congress specifically directed that aid should be given to programs that seek to increase the involvement of family members and religious and charitable organizations.

A majority of five on the Court held that on its face, the act did not violate the establishment clause of the First Amendment, although it left open to further legal proceedings whether the act as applied may have violated it. The heart of the majority opinion, written by Chief Justice Rehnquist, consisted of two key arguments that sought to demonstrate the act passed the second prong of the *Lemon* test, namely, that it had a primarily secular effect. One argument that Chief Justice Rehnquist advanced was that the aid given did not violate the norm of neutrality because it flowed to religious and nonreligious agencies alike.

Although the AFLA does require potential grantees to describe how they will involve religious organizations in the provision of services under the Act, it also requires grantees to describe the involvement of "charitable organizations, voluntary associations, and other groups in the private sector." In our view, this reflects the statute's successful maintenance of "a course of neutrality among religions, and between religion and nonreligion."[56]

A second argument advanced by the chief justice in the majority opinion hinges on his assertion that the religious organizations who were receiving aid were not "pervasively sectarian." Thus, as the Court had similarly argued in cases dealing with state aid to religiously based colleges and universities, there was little chance that, as agencies use the federal funds to carry out secular tasks, religion would inadvertently creep in and be advanced. Chief Justice Rehnquist concluded:

> But nothing in our prior cases warrants the presumption adopted by the District Court that religiously affiliated AFLA grantees are not capable of carrying out their functions under the AFLA in a lawful, secular manner. Only in the context of aid to "pervasively sectarian" institutions have we invalidated an aid program on the grounds that there was a "substantial" risk that aid to these religious institutions would, knowingly or unknowingly, result in religious indoctrination.[57]

On this basis the majority opinion concluded it is highly relevant whether aid under the act "is flowing to grantees that can be considered 'pervasively sectarian' religious institutions."[58] Moreover, it said "it would be relevant to determine, for example, whether the Secretary [of Health and Human Services] has permitted AFLA grantees to use materials that have an explicitly religious content or are designed to inculcate the views of a particular religious faith."[59]

In the dissenting opinion Justice Blackmun argued that tax dollars had been used "to support religious training."[60] Later, he went on to quote favorably the District Court, which had held that religious doctrines were bound to creep into the teachings of religious organizations' counselors:

> To presume that AFLA counselors from religious organizations can put their beliefs aside when counseling an adolescent on matters that are part of religious doctrine is simply unrealistic. . . . Even if it were possible, government would tread impermissibly on religious liberty merely by suggesting that religious organizations instruct on doctrinal matters without any conscious or unconscious reference to that doctrine. Moreover, the statutory scheme is fraught with the possibility that religious beliefs might infuse instruction and

never be detected by the impressionable and unlearned adolescent to whom the instruction is directed.[61]

This, the dissent argued, is contrary to the First Amendment: "It should be undeniable by now that religious dogma may not be employed by government even to accomplish laudable secular purposes."[62]

Positive neutrality argues that the dissenting opinion had its facts right, but its conclusion wrong. Clearly, Justice Blackmun and the District Court were right when they argued that religious counselors working with teenagers would not be able simply to set aside their deeply held religious beliefs. Positive neutrality would underscore and reemphasize this point, which was made by the dissenting opinion. For the state to try to force them to do so on pain of losing state funding would violate the rightful autonomy of the religious realm. However, the conclusion of the dissenting opinion that aid could not go to religiously based agencies is as discriminatory as conditioning the receipt of aid on their having to set aside their religious values and beliefs. Justice Blackmun assumed that neutrality would be gained by the government not using tax dollars "to support religious teaching." However, positive neutrality would counter that to use tax dollars to support secular perspectives supportive of certain "laudable secular purposes" and to deny them to religiously rooted ones is not neutrality, but discrimination against religion.

Positive neutrality, therefore, argues that the first point in the Rehnquist majority opinion cited earlier is the key one: namely, that the aid was going to a wide spectrum of agencies and organizations, religious and nonreligious alike. It did not benefit either religious groups or nonreligious groups over the other. Nor were the religious groups' eligibility to receive aid linked to their being of any one denomination or religious tradition. This is true neutrality.

However, positive neutrality has major problems with the second argument used by the majority opinion, namely, that since the religious groups receiving aid were not "pervasively sectarian," they could separate out their religious and secular facets and act as secular agencies in running the programs at issue here. Thus religion would not be advanced. At this point the premise of the Rehnquist majority opinion and the premise of the Blackmun dissenting opinion is the same: governmental aid can be given a religiously based counseling program only if it acts in a thoroughly secular, nonreligious manner. This premise also lay at the heart of the Court's approval of federal funds going to the hospital of the Sisters of Charity eighty-nine years earlier.

A basic tenet of structural pluralism, however, is that religious associations should be free to participate fully in the public realm, and to participate as religious associations. To say that religious groups may participate in a state aid program of this nature but may not advance the teachings of their religious tradition in support of teenage, premarital chastity, or other such sexual issues is to force religion to deny its heart and soul. The very reason why religious groups should be active in dealing with the enormous social problem of teenage pregnancies is because they have something uniquely powerful to offer, especially to those within their own tradition. A program associated with a Nation of Islam mosque can speak to its young adherents with a power and effectiveness that no secular agency could ever muster. However, for this to be true it must be free to speak the language of religion. True, religion will, in the process, be advanced — and advanced with tax dollars. However, pluralism does not shy away from this as long as all religious traditions and secular traditions as well are treated evenhandedly, are offered the same governmental resources. Thus a family and its teenagers can freely choose whether to go to a Catholic, Baptist, Pentecostal, Islamic, or secular agency for counseling and help. The religious pluralism of U.S. society is affirmed and recognized.

Within a pluralist perspective to say religious agencies may participate in programs as long as they cease to be religious and behave like their secular counterparts is to infringe their freedom of religion. Their right to a quasi-autonomy is violated. For the government to give to two counseling agencies — one religiously based and the other secularly based — financial aid to help them in their programs, and then say that the secularly based agency is free to speak, teach, and act on the basis of its secular values and beliefs while the religiously based agency must put aside its religious values and beliefs and act just as the secular agency is to discriminate against the religious agency. To force it to do so infringes on the freedom of religion of the agency and its supporters and workers.

As soon as the Supreme Court majority tries to make its case on the basis of the secularity of the religious groups' programs and their lack of a thoroughgoing religious nature, it has given the argument away to those who oppose all governmental aid to religious social service agencies. It is impossible not to agree with the dissenters when they favorably quoted Patrick Sheeran, an official in the Office of Adolescent Pregnancy Programs: "Broadly speaking, I find it hard to find any kind of educational or value type of program that doesn't have some kind of basic religious or ethical foundation, and while a sex education class may be completely separate from a religious class, it might relate back to it in terms of principles that are embedded philosophically or theologically or religiously in another discipline."[63] If this is true — and pluralism would argue wholeheartedly that it is — it is impossible to argue with a straight face that sex education can be taught by a deeply religious agency without advancing religion or religious doctrine. Indeed, one would not want it to do so.

Neutrality — and thereby conformity with the First Amendment — must be defended and advanced on the basis of an evenhandedness among all religious groups and between religion and secularism, not on the basis of a supposed secularity that religious groups can put on and off as easily as a hat. Positive neutrality says that as long as the Court defines the issue as being simply whether religion is being advanced in some manner, the ability of public policy goals to be achieved through cooperative programs between the government and religious associations is bleak. Therefore, positive neutrality says that governmental aid may go to religiously based associations running a wide variety of programs, as long as these programs have a direct, this-world benefit for society and as long as there are sufficient checks to assure that the aid is indeed going to support those programs.

Running through the decisions of the Supreme Court in all five issue areas considered in this section are some common threads. Almost all Supreme Court justices are agreed that under the First Amendment no governmental actions may advance or endorse religion. This is crucial. Once this is conceded, a trap snaps shut on those who wish religion to be a full participant in the social, public life of the nation. Once it is granted that religion may not be endorsed or advanced by government — even if all religions are endorsed or advanced equally and even if religion is not advanced or endorsed any more than secularism — then there are only two ways in which religion can be let into the public realm. One is if religion is seen as only a nice tradition or a common practice that has lost any real, specifically religious meaning. The other is if sacred and secular aspects of what in fact are integrated religious beliefs and practices are distinguished, and only the allegedly secular aspects are allowed into the public realm. In either case, religion as religion is kept isolated and limited to the private, personal aspects of individuals' lives. It is not allowed or empowered to play a social or public role as almost all religions down through the centuries have sought to do. The rightful autonomy of the religious sphere is violated, for the power of the state is being used to favor secular philosophies and mind-sets over religious ones.

This is the modern outcome of the conditions under which the terms of church-state relations were initially defined in the eighteenth century (as described in Chapter 3). They have led to a present-day dilemma. If religion seeks openly and honestly to remain a particularistic force, acting on the basis of its deeply felt beliefs, it is kept out of the public life of the nation. Its irrelevancy to social life is assured. If, on the other hand, religion is allowed into the social life of the nation only on the basis of a sacred-secular distinction, it is required to eviscerate itself by denying that which makes it unique and to put on the garb of a harmless tradition or of a secularized force. Religion is forced to choose between irrelevancy by exclusion or irrelevancy by denying its essence. One needs the assumptions, perspectives, and concepts of structural pluralism and positive neutrality in order to escape this choice.

THE PUBLIC POLICY CONSEQUENCES OF POSITIVE NEUTRALITY

Positive neutrality has highly significant public policy consequences. It is a living, dynamic concept which, if followed and implemented, would unleash fresh breezes to move through the institutions and practices of U.S. public policy. Old relationships would be redefined, new relationships would emerge, and extensive possibilities for change would exist. Clearly, one cannot predict with confidence the exact contours of the public policy changes to which a general adherence to positive neutrality would lead. Much would depend on the exact form and timing of the move toward positive neutrality and on the ever-shifting forces impinging on the public policy making process. However, it is helpful to contemplate briefly the sort of public policy potentialities that positive neutrality carries with it. That is what this section of the chapter does. It first considers a basic fear engendered by the vision of deeply religious associations and persons playing a fuller, freer role in the public policy forum, and it next considers two potentially positive consequences of their doing so.

Positive Neutrality: Social and Political Divisiveness

Structural pluralism and positive neutrality hold forth the vision of full and complete religious freedom for those of all religious faiths and of none, a freedom that encompasses the right by religious associations and religiously motivated persons to influence public policies and to take part in public policy debates *as religious associations and persons*, to have their practices as well as beliefs protected, to have their beliefs recognized and accommodated by governmental programs in the same way as secular beliefs are, to be recognized and honored by government in the same way similarly situated secular groups or movements are, and to receive material or financial aid in support of their programs with this-world benefits to society, just as similarly situated secular associations do.

Freedom of religion of this sort — which would liberate religiously motivated persons and organizations to participate in the political realm as fully as their secular counterparts — arouses sincere fears in many persons. They fear the consequences for the common life of the U.S. people of bringing large numbers of deeply religious citizens and public officials into the public policy process who would participate as deeply religious persons. They fear allowing large numbers of such persons into the system's policy debates would make it more difficult to forge a public policy consensus. As noted in Chapter 2, there is a prevalent attitude in U.S. society that believes religious divisions are likely to be especially bitter and difficult to resolve by a process of negotiation and compromise. Those taking this position point to the bitter Catholic-Protestant division in Northern Ireland or other historical or contemporary religious divisions that are particularly sharp. In addition, they argue that religious divisions are based on traditional cleavages that touch deeply-felt truths believed to have been revealed by God and thus are not susceptible to the consensus building process of negotiation, trade-offs, and compromise. Therefore, they reason, allowing religion into the policy arena is to introduce a new and potentially explosive element that has been foreign to the U.S. experience. The present-day abortion debate — with its commitments to fundamental values, its bitterness, and, at times, its civil disobedience and even occasional violence — is pointed out as a testimony to the dangers religion can pose when it enters public policy debates.

Neither historical experience nor logic indicates that religion poses particularly acute dangers to political unity and consensus building. Logically, most religious traditions (as I pointed out in Chapter 2) distinguish between certain basic, revealed, perhaps even nonnegotiable truths, and the application of those truths in the uncertain, complex world of public policies. The application is normally seen as being open to discussion, negotiation, and compromise. There are very few religious traditions that believe God has revealed to them the proper level of taxation, how many aircraft carriers are needed for national defense, or the appropriate minimum wage. There is little prospect — outside of a handful of small fringe groups — that religious groups would introduce a new element of rigidity into the U.S. system. Even those few, fringe religious groups are unlikely to be any more rigid than some existing groups the system is able to handle, such as the National Organization of Women (NOW) on abortion rights or Aids Coalition to Unleash Power (ACT-UP) on gay rights.

Historically — as also pointed out in Chapter 2 — religion has not been a particularly divisive force in U.S. history. Those who fear the potential divisiveness of religion can, of course, answer that the lack of religious divisiveness in the U.S. experience is due to particularistic religion having been largely kept out of the policy arena. In response to this, the present-day experience of Western Europe is instructive, where governments often endorse and aid religion — sometimes even to a greater degree than the principle of positive neutrality would allow. Religiously oriented schools and other religious agencies receive state aid, religious ceremonies are integrated into political ceremonies, various forms of religious establishment exist, and Christian political parties freely compete alongside secularly based, and even strongly anticlerical, parties. All this is the case without political debate degenerating into particularly bitter or divisive strife. One scholar has argued that the interjection of religion into the politics of a divided nation such as Belgium in the form of Christian political parties has in fact served as a basis for greater national unity: "The Belgium case is particularly interesting, for both the Walloon PSC and the Flemish CVP . . . have regarded their commitment to Christian values as a means by which the two Belgian communities can, as it were, rise above their particularism by committing themselves to the higher values of European Christendom."[64] In both Germany and the Netherlands Christian Democratic parties, composed of Catholics and Protestants, have worked to pull together the predominantly Catholic and the predominantly Protestant regions. In addition, the Christian Democratic parties have been key in establishing common ground among the nations of the European Community, helping to move Western Europe more quickly toward economic and political union. Clay Clemens has observed:

> Indeed, the founding fathers of Christian Democracy — Adenauer, De Gasperi, Schuman — doubled as the architects of European reconciliation, cooperation and, eventually, integration. Collaboration between European Christian Democrats, within and outside of the evolving European Community, has remained a feature of international politics ever since. Four decades later Christian Democrats still espouse and, in general, pursue the ideal of interstate cooperation and eventual European union.[65]

The Italian Christian Democratic party is typical of Western European Christian Democratic parties in its being marked, not by ideological rigidity and uncompromising stances, but rather, by "pragmatism and adaptability."[66]

In short, the historical experience of the United States and Western Europe and the nature of religion in the United States indicate that allowing religion to play a freer, more fulsome role in the public life of the nation would not pose a clear, imminent danger of increasing the rigidity or divisiveness present in the U.S. polity.

Positive Neutrality: Nonelite Access

One positive result of allowing religious associations and their spokespersons freer, fuller access to the public policy-making forum is to increase nonelite access to the political system. Many political scientists over the years have noted that a perennial problem of political systems professing democratic norms is a tendency toward elite domination.[67] Analysts differ on the extent to which this is a problem in present-day United States, but almost all agree that elite domination is a danger to the actual realization of democratic norms. Thus, forces that serve as counterweights to socially and politically dominate elites are to be welcomed.

Political scientist Allen Hertzke, in an excellent study of religiously based interest groups, noted that some observers have asserted that the proliferation of interest groups has worked to make the system more elitist by giving even more representation and influence to those individuals who were already well represented and influential in the political arena. However, he then went on to state:

> This assertion appears *not* to be wholly accurate . . . when religious political advocacy is included in the analysis. Religion in America . . . is characterized by an activism and pluralism that enhance its importance in American cultural life, particularly in the experience of non-elites. The national religious lobbies — in their growing diversity — now roughly mirror this pluralism. When these religious groups mobilize constituencies and articulate their competing religious values, they are playing a unique representational role in the "pressure system," however imperfectly or incompletely. My thesis is that in light of their mobilization efforts and their pluralism, the national religious lobbies, collectively, enhance the representativeness of the modern American polity.[68]

Hertzke pointed out that churches and other religiously based groups have three characteristics that suggest why they possess this potential to act as a strong counterweight to the elitist tendencies posed by the structure of interest groups and — many would add — by other features of the U.S. political system. First, Hertzke suggested that "of all the potential reasons for violating economic self-interest, . . . the religious motivation is one of the most compelling. The religious message, at least in its Christian form, is a supranational, paradoxical call for transcendence over one's narrow selfish interest. Christians are called on, as Jesus says, to 'lose their lives' to gain the Kingdom."[69] If one assumes that the entire interest group structure is motivated purely by economic self-interest, then there is little room to expect either the poor and weak or the broader common interests of society to receive much notice. However, the altruism and the sense of social responsibility taught by Christianity and other religions can serve as a counterweight to the politics of economic self-interest. That this altruism is not pure theory is revealed by a recent Independent

Sector/Gallup poll showing that weekly church attenders (37.3 percent of the population) gave an average of $1,386 a year to charities and volunteered an average of 3.4 hours a week of their time, while nonattenders contributed an average of only $293 a year to charities and volunteered an average of only 1.8 hours per week.[70]

Second, Hertzke argued that religiously based groups often see themselves as explicitly speaking for the disenfranchised, for those on the margins of society who otherwise would have no voice. He reported that many religious groups are marked by a "conscious attempt to articulate the needs and concerns of the poor, both at home and abroad."[71] He concluded that "the diverse representational roles of religious lobbyists enable them, in some cases, to articulate broad but otherwise underrepresented values in the American polity."[72]

Third, Hertzke pointed out that religious groups tend to be composed of lower-middle-class and lower-class persons to a greater degree than are other politically mobilized groups. Political advocacy groups typically are composed of upper-income, better-educated persons, but that is not true of most religious associations. Church membership and church attendance generally do not differ between upper-income, highly educated persons and lower-income, less-well-educated persons.[73] Polling data also indicate that increased education actually correlates with decreased religious activities and beliefs "in a number of key areas."[74] Therefore, as religious associations become politically mobilized, a significant broadening of political participation is achieved. Paul Weber has noted that "identifiable religious societies are important for interest group theory partially because they are by far the largest non-elite group in the nation."[75]

If broader participation in the policy-making system is considered a key mark of democratic, egalitarian politics, religious associations — by playing a key role in increasing and broadening public participation — are one important means of achieving a more democratic, egalitarian polity. Religion is already helping to achieve this sort of a polity, in spite of the present-day attitudinal and legal imitations noted in Chapter 2 and elsewhere. Pluralism and positive neutrality say that religiously motivated groups and public officials should be welcomed as full partners in the public life of the nation and, more specifically, in the public policy-making system. If this point of view would prevail, religion, now freed to play a more significant role in the body politic, would be empowered to serve as an even greater counterweight to the elitist tendencies of the U.S. system than what it is now. There is a powerful force for stronger, more effective nonelite representation waiting to be freed from its present-day limitations.

Positive Neutrality: Religion as a Mediating Structure

Mediating Structures

In an excellent little book, sociologist Peter Berger and theologian John Richard Neuhaus have argued that there are important "institutions standing between the individual in his private life and the large institutions of public life," which they term *mediating structures*.[76] Their study focuses on four key mediating structures: neighborhood, family, church, and voluntary associations, such as labor unions and clubs. Berger and Neuhaus persuasively argued that the public policy options typically considered in the United States are unduly constricted by a failure to take into consideration and make use of the mediating structures of society. Policymakers tend to see the individual and the state, but little in between. Thus, it is assumed that if individuals run into such troubles as unemployment, poverty, or drug dependency, or if there are certain goals that individuals cannot achieve on their own, the only alternative is the modern administrative state. Either individuals are left to struggle on their own, or governmental bureaucracies and programs are created to deal with the demonstrated needs.

Berger and Neuhaus, in contrast, focused on the importance and the potential public policy role of mediating structures. They put forward three basic propositions: "Mediating structures are essential for a vital democratic society. . . . Public policy should protect and foster mediating structures, and Wherever possible, public policy should utilize mediating structures for the realization of social purposes."[77] These propositions, they argue, offer a third way besides the enormous governmental bureaucracies that U.S. liberals tend to advocate and the inaction in the face of severe social problems U.S. conservatives tend to support. By taking mediating structures into account, by making certain that they and their roles in society are safeguarded, and by making use of them where practical, a whole new world of public policy options are opened up.

Some societal needs, Berger and Neuhaus argued, can be met simply by government helping to assure that mediating structures can operate fully and freely. Many of the worst abuses of industrial workers of the early twentieth century were corrected not by direct governmental intervention, but by government simply protecting the rights of workers to organize into labor unions. Similarly, some big city neighborhoods have stemmed the slide of urban decay by organizing neighborhood associations that have directly tackled circumstances fueling the decay. Thus, Berger and Neuhaus's second proposition says that sometimes public policy goals can be attained simply by government safeguarding the freedom and ability of mediating structures themselves to deal with certain needs.

At other times, when direct action by mediating structures is insufficient or impractical, governmental involvement is called for. Even then, however, as Berger and Neuhaus argued in their third proposition, the more government can make use of and work through mediating structures, the better. If, for example, there is a need for more overnight shelters for the homeless in a particular area of a city, this third proposition suggests that instead of the city buying property, erecting shelters, and hiring civil servants to staff and operate the shelters, it could better approach groups that already are active in the target area and encourage and enable them to develop or expand their capacity to provide overnight shelters for the homeless.

By recognizing the importance of associations and communities in the life of a society, and in seeking public policies that will not thwart or weaken them but rather will empower and utilize them, Berger and Neuhaus's three propositions are fully in keeping with pluralism's view of society. Whether one fully agrees with them, the public policy possibilities of mediating structures should certainly be discussed, weighed, and considered. They and their role in society need to be on the public policy agenda of the nation in a way they now are not.

Among the four mediating structures Berger and Neuhaus discussed, churches — or, more neutrally, religious associations — are especially crucial. As they noted, "Religious institutions form by far the largest network of voluntary associations in American society."[78] The fact that a majority of people in the United States belong to a church or other religious association, and the fact that this membership plays a more central role in many of their lives than other memberships, suggest that if mediating structures as a whole have an important role to play along the lines that Berger and Neuhaus suggested, religious associations surely do. Religious associations have long traditions of being active in education and care for the ill, orphans, poor, and drug-dependent. Rescue missions on skid rows, orphanages, retirement homes, and schools are all part of the U.S. religious tradition. In most of these areas, churches and their auxiliaries, as well as other religious associations, were active long before the state.

Limitations on Religiously Based Mediating Structures

There are two ways in which religious associations as mediating structures are limited or handicapped by prevailing church-state attitudes and practices. One consists of subtle and sometimes overt pressures that work to discourage them from playing an active role in society as religious associations, that is, speaking and working out of a particular religious tradition. The subtle pressures usually arise from societal expectations that a religious association should downplay its religious commitments in a variety of ways, such as by not necessarily hiring its employees only from out of its own faith community. In 1988, for example, there was a minor flap when the First Presbyterian Church of Sherman Oaks, California, announced in the future it would only hire persons "who profess faith in Jesus Christ" to work in its preschool nursery program. The pastor of the church explained that the church simply wanted its nursery school to be a Christian one — not too unreasonable an expectation for a Christian church. However, many parents and teachers were reported to be "angered and shocked," the director of the preschool resigned, and many parents withdrew their children from the school and laid plans to start a new one.[79] The point is that as soon as a religious association moves into the community and begins to offer certain services, there are societal expectations that it should not do so as a religious association but rather as any other secular association. It should lay its distinctive religious character aside.

The pressures to lay aside one's religious nature become overt when legal action is taken. For example, New York City had long followed the practice of placing children with foster care agencies of the same faith as that of the children being placed (that is, Jewish children with Jewish agencies, Catholic children with Catholic agencies, and Protestant children with Protestant agencies). In 1988 this practice was challenged in court by the American Civil Liberties Union. In an out-of-court settlement, the city agreed to place children on a first-come, first-serve basis without regard to religion, and the religiously based child-care agencies were required not to "impose their religious beliefs on children in their care."[80] Their freedom to act as religious child-care agencies, serving the children of their faith in keeping with the tenets of their faith, was compromised. They would have to secularize.

Both the more subtle and the overt pressures work as powerful disincentives for churches, their auxiliaries, and other religious associations against becoming involved in public service activities. Structural pluralism teaches that religious associations possess a rightful quasi-autonomy in their appropriate sphere of endeavor. This means that they should be free to act as religious associations, yet under current circumstances, they know that they risk condemnation and even legal action if they do so in certain areas of activity.

A second way in which current church-state practices negatively affect religious associations acting as mediating structures is through a certain hesitation or outright inability of government to work through or make use of religious associations in achieving its secular public policy goals. It is hard for public policymakers to follow the third proposition put forward by Berger and Neuhaus. The clearest example here is that of K-12 schools, where most forms of state aid to religiously based schools have been found unconstitutional by the Supreme Court. Although there are some programs of state aid funneled through religious associations that have not been challenged in court, they continue to operate under the cloud of possible constitutional challenge. Even when such aid is available, subtle and overt pressures against religious associations operating as religious associations are often present: Witness the religiously based child-care agencies of New York City just mentioned and the Supreme Court's reactions to the Adolescent Family Life Act discussed in the prior section.

These pressures create enormous problems both for religious associations seeking to live out their faith by providing social benefits or programs and for society as a whole, which is in need of the religiously based programs' help in meeting severe social needs. If religiously oriented agencies provide services in the context of their distinctive religious beliefs, they are subjected to public approbation and can expect little or no encouragement or financial support from the broader society. They may do a very good job at serving a limited clientele, but from the point of view of societywide needs, they are unlikely — even collectively — to have a major impact. If, on the other hand, they provide services in a context of watered-down religious beliefs, they may receive public funds and encouragement, but at the cost of losing much of the rationale for their being active in the first place. This results in their giving up the major advantages — to be discussed shortly — that religious associations can bring to the struggle against social ills. They end up looking and acting much like any secular agency — to their loss and that of society. Religious associations, therefore, are forced to choose between running very limited programs with minimal financial resources, or they must water-down and secularize the religious aspects of their programs, leading them to become more and more like any other secular agency. In either case, religion as a powerful, active force is handicapped and crippled, and society loses most of the contributions that the largest, most vital networks of voluntary associations could provide.

Positive Neutrality's Response

Positive neutrality emphasizes the importance of giving religious associations full freedom of belief and action, including their actions in pursuit of living out their beliefs in the social and political worlds. As they do so, a true neutrality insists on religious associations' right to maintain their religious distinctiveness. Pluralism accepts and affirms the resulting diversity and does not try to impose a secular uniformity. If a mosque of the Nation of Islam establishes a preschool nursery program, positive neutrality says that there should be no overt or subtle pressures on it to hire white Christian teachers. Similarly, a Hasidic synagogue and a Presbyterian church should be able to run nursery schools that are in keeping with their distinctive traditions. Pluralism does not fear diversity of this nature.

The situation becomes more controversial when the issue of state financial aid enters in. However, pluralism says that as long as the aid goes to a wide variety of religious and nonreligious programs without discrimination, and as long as it supports programs of direct, this-world benefit to society, it is constitutional, and, under most circumstances, advisable. The concept of mediating structures and the three propositions put forward by Berger and Neuhaus help explain why pluralism suggests that advantages to society adhere in the government working through, empowering, and aiding religious associations' programs with secular benefits to society, rather than establishing its own programs. It is not that pluralism would argue government should work through religious associations exclusively, but only that it should work through them along with working through secular agencies and, often, through governmentally owned and operated programs as well.

There are three especially important advantages to government working through private, religiously based associations. The first is that the government can make use of and build on the sense of dedication, empathy, and closeness to the people being served that tends to mark the workers in religiously based programs. Religious associations — because of their religious nature — are able to tap into a reservoir of volunteers and dedicated workers that governmental and secular agencies cannot. The key incentive for persons to give money and time to a religiously based agency or to give up other, perhaps more promising, careers to come and work full-time for it, is the religious dimension. In the Christian tradition, volunteers, financial contributors, and paid staff all see themselves as following Jesus' example of the Good Samaritan and acting in keeping with his teaching that whatever you do "for one of the least of these brothers of mine, you [do] for me."[81] It is religious motives and a sense of mission that lead many deeply religious persons to give time and expend efforts above and beyond what they otherwise would do. Although most do not reach the heights of self-sacrifice and dedication to others of a Mother Theresa, she stands as a symbol of the self-sacrificing, religiously motivated worker. As long as religious associations are able to maintain their distinctive religious character, this factor can serve as a powerful force.

A second advantage of government working through religiously based agencies in addressing a range of societal needs is that religious associations have a basis on which to build a bond or sense of trust and to motivate persons with whom they are working that governmental and other secularly based agencies lack. Religion, of course, can have a powerful effect on how persons view the world, themselves, and their relationships to others. It is not that religion is a magic wand that changes persons quickly and effortlessly, but it can be an effective basis on which agencies can encourage individuals to reach outside themselves for inspiration, guidance, and a sense of moral standards. Especially when a religiously based program is working with adherents of the same religious tradition, there immediately is a basis for trust that is important in achieving agency goals. A Catholic agency has a basis on which to appeal to a Catholic teenager for premarital chastity that a secular agency would never have. An African Methodist Episcopal Church's drug awareness program has a basis to appeal to a young African-American to refrain from drug use that white, middle-class civil servants running a governmental agency could never have. A little reflection reveals a host of basic, powerful incentives and bonds on which religious agencies can build their programs that secular and governmental agencies do not have.

A third advantage of public policies building upon religiously based programs already in existence is the flexibility thereby given public policy. When government creates a service agency, staffing it and buying a physical facility and equipment, it is hard to eliminate that program if it proves ineffective or budgetary constraints so advise. It is easier to cancel or reduce contracts or other commitments to private agencies. There is also evidence that a certain competitive element among governmental and private agencies, all seeking to provide the same service, improves the effectiveness and efficiency of the services produced. John Donahue of the Kennedy School of Government at Harvard concluded, "It isn't that the private sector or the public sector is better; it's the competition between the two of them that works."[82] Sometimes the competition can be provided by for-profit companies, but often it can best be provided by nonprofit, and especially religiously rooted, organizations. The pervasiveness of religious service agencies offers the potential for competition between them and public sector agencies, which, from the public policy point of view, could result in both savings and increases in the quality of services provided. Especially in services to the disadvantaged of society, it traditionally has been religious associations that have stood as the only alternative to governmentally provided services. Public policies that allow private and public agencies to compete in providing education to inner-city youths, helping drug addicts, counseling teenagers at risk of pregnancy, sheltering the homeless, and offering programs to a host of other needy persons may well be an advantage to both the taxpayer and the needy.

In all this I have tried to pick my words carefully. I would not claim in sweeping terms that following the principles of positive neutrality — and the resulting shift in attitudes toward religiously based mediating structures and governmental cooperation with them — would be a panacea for all, or even most, social ills.

However, doing so would give public policymakers new possibilities and fresh alternatives for dealing with persistent, seemingly intractable social ills. That is no small achievement. Exploring two problem areas — drug abuse and education — can help give a better understanding of how the basic principles of structural pluralism would open up new possibilities and alternatives for dealing with severe social problems and how current church-state interpretations are limiting the policy options available to policymakers.

Case Study No. 1: Drug Treatment

One of the most persistent, debilitating problems facing the United States today is a continuing epidemic of illicit drug use. It is estimated there are 10 million cocaine users and .5 million heroin users in the United States.[83] Attempts at enforcement of antidrug laws cost about $10 billion a year.[84] Some 30,000 to 50,000 babies are born each year with long-term brain damage due to their mothers using cocaine, usually "crack," while pregnant, and the vast majority of heterosexual persons with acquired immune deficiency syndrome (AIDS) have contracted the disease through illegal intravenous drug use.[85] It is estimated that one-half to two-thirds of all street crime is drug-related, while warfare over drug territories among rival youth gangs in cities such as Washington, D.C., and Los Angeles result in hundreds of deaths each year.[86] As a result, whole areas of cities have a siege mentality, with people living in fear and economic development or recovery proving virtually impossible. Thousands of lives are being wasted, and millions of persons are suffering negative consequences.

Thus, President Bush declared a war on drugs. However, attempts at interdicting drugs coming into the United States have failed to make significant dents in the availability of drugs on the streets. Most treatment programs have failure rates of over 90 percent.[87]

Against this picture of gloom and failure, the one glimmer of hope comes from a number of religiously based treatment and rehabilitation programs. For example:

> The interdenominational Teen Challenge ministry, founded in 1969, staffs 114 highly successful recovery centers throughout the country — seven are in Southern California — where young people can get off drugs and out of gangs. A survey found that 86% of those who completed the program were drug-free five years later, said Phil Cookes, director of the Teen Challenge office in Los Angeles.[88]

Similarly, a Methodist-sponsored drug treatment center in Los Angeles reported 65 to 70 percent success levels one year after treatment.[89]

The type of resources that churches can bring to the fight against drugs that no government agency can is revealed in a program that Glide Memorial United Methodist Church in San Francisco recently undertook:

In January, 800 members and supporters marched into the Valencia Gardens housing project in the drug-infested Tenderloin district, proclaiming "unconditional love" and announcing that "recovery time" had arrived for addicts and their families. Rather than simply forcing drug dealers away — a "drug-busting" technique that Glide's effervescent pastor, Cecil Williams, doesn't favor — "We told the pushers, and the users, 'You stay here,'" he said. "'The total community needs recovery. We're coming in with unconditional love. We're your family.'"

"Most dope addicts feel lost, ashamed, rejected and empty," Williams continued. "They've lost all their friends and family and relationships. So what I did was fix them a new family."[90]

As a result of this effort, Captain Michael Hebel of the San Francisco police department reported a significant decrease in crime in the targeted Valencia Gardens housing project and a renewed sense of pride in the area.[91] William J. Bennett, former head of the National Drug Control Policy Office, stated: "I believe with Harvard psychologist Robert Coles that drugs are fundamentally a spiritual problem for many people. Drug use is a misguided attempt to find meaning in life."[92] If Bennett is correct, it is clear why a religious component to drug treatment efforts appears to be important.

However, religiously based drug treatment efforts are limited in nature. The United Methodist Church recently commissioned one of its African-American bishops, the Reverend Felton May, to spend a year developing anti-drug efforts in Methodist churches. A newspaper story reported that at the end of the year, the Reverend May observed that churches were in a much better position to reach people on the streets than were government programs. He pointed out that his own denomination alone — the United Methodist Church — has more churches than the Postal Service has post offices.[93] The newspaper reporter, however, went on to comment: "But chances of funding such a grand plan seem unlikely, given the fact that the United Methodists are having difficulty funding and staffing just the 14-church project in Southeast Washington through the summer."[94]

How much potential churches, synagogues, mosques, and their auxiliary agencies have in fighting the war on drugs by loving and rehabilitating drug users is hard to say with any degree of confidence. The available evidence (such as I just cited) is largely anecdotal, and not systematic. However, there are enough success stories to indicate that religiously based drug treatment programs constitute one of the few promising answers available. Nonetheless, the religious associations themselves are hard-pressed to muster the financial resources that they need to carry out the needed massive programs. If government would attempt to use religious associations as a major answer to fighting illicit drug abuse, one can imagine enormous church-state problems emerging under present Supreme Court standards and societal attitudes. Under *Bowen v. Kendrick*, Christian drug treatment centers presumably could not unequivocally condemn drug use as an offense before God and attempts to integrate help and support for the addict with spiritual assurances of God's love and his presence would risk legal action. As a result, the most promising path for dealing with drug addiction and its accompanying social horrors remains unexplored.

Positive neutrality says that if public policymakers believe there is enough promise in the use of religiously based drug treatment centers to embark on a large-scale government program of encouraging, recognizing and aiding those centers, the First Amendment should be no bar. The only conditions that would need to be met are that (1) the support must go to a wide variety of religiously based drug treatment centers and not only to Christian ones or disproportionately to those of one or a few Christian denominations; (2) support must also go to nonreligious, secular drug treatment programs; and (3) there be financial accounting measures to assure that the funds are going to treating drug addicts and not other programs of the sponsoring religious associations. There would be no requirement that the drug programs be segregated out from the religious teachings and programs of the religiously based agencies. The controlling factor would be that the government would, with its tax dollars, be purchasing a valuable this-world benefit for all of society — in this case that of a society more free of illicit drug use, with all its attendant social ills — without favoring any religious group or either religion or secularism. My point in all of this is that the area of drug abuse is just one example of how present church-state doctrines are constricting the policymakers in their attempt to wrestle with a severe social problem. Fresh air is needed. Positive neutrality would open up a new, promising avenue that current Supreme Court doctrine and societal attitudes have closed off.

Case Study No. 2: K-12 Education

U.S. education at the beginning of the 1990s presented a troubling picture. The president of the highly respected Brookings Institution reflected a widespread concern when he wrote in the foreword to a recently published book:

By most accounts, the American education system is not working well. Children appear to be learning less in school today than they did a generation ago. Some 25 percent of the nation's high school students drop out before graduating, and in large cities — whose poor and minority children desperately need quality education — the figure can climb to 50 percent. On math and science achievement tests, American teenagers trail students from other nations — a pattern with alarming implications for America's ability to compete in the world economy.[95]

This present-day concern over the state of U.S. education was graphically captured by the National Commission on Excellence in Education: "If an unfriendly foreign power had attempted to impose on America the mediocre educational performance that exists today, we might have viewed it as an act of war. As it stands we have allowed this to happen to ourselves."[96]

In an exceedingly complex area, one can question whether U.S. education is doing as bad a job as its critics claim, but two facts are undeniable: The people of the United States are dissatisfied and troubled by the state of education in their country, and today's U.S. students do less well on standardized tests than an earlier generation of U.S. students did and students in most other modern, industrialized countries do today.

Given these two facts, the political system is struggling to respond. President Bush indicated that he wanted to be known in history as the "education president." Moreover, the 1980s saw what two observers have called the "greatest and most concentrated surge of educational reform in the nation's history."[97]

However, one obvious, and in some ways compelling, response to the concerns over the health of U.S. education — while beginning to receive some attention, for the most part remains unexplored by public policymakers. Again, current church-state doctrine is constricting policymakers, and the closing off of a promising avenue for dealing with that is a critical national problem. This avenue is encouraging and helping to finance the education that is currently being provided by the thousands of private, religiously based schools.

Two factors suggest that keeping this option largely unavailable to public policymakers is an unfortunate constriction. The first of these factors consists of mounting evidence indicating that private, religiously based schools — and the Catholic schools in particular — are doing a better job of educating students than are the public schools. James Coleman and his associates, after an exhaustive study, concluded that "achievement in both the sophomore and senior years is somewhat higher in Catholic schools and in other private schools than it is in public schools."[98] The differences, while not dramatic, were clear and consistent. Some might argue that these successes on the part of religiously based schools was due to their starting out with more homogeneous, better motivated, superior students. However, a significant and surprising finding of the Coleman study was that Catholic schools had more racially and ethnically diverse student bodies than did the public schools.[99] Even more significant, the Catholic schools did a better job of achieving educational equality for children coming from families of dissimilar backgrounds than did the public schools:

> That is, the performance of children from parents with differing educational levels is more similar in Catholic schools than in public schools (as well as being, in general, higher). . . . Thus we have the paradoxical result that the Catholic schools come closer to the American ideal of the "common school," educating all alike than do the public schools. Furthermore, . . . a similar result holds for race and ethnicity. The achievement of blacks is closer to that of whites, and the achievement of Hispanics is closer to that of non-Hispanics in Catholic schools than in public schools.[100]

A follow-up study led Coleman and his associates to state flatly: "The achievement growth benefits of Catholic school attendance are especially strong for students who are in one way or another disadvantaged: lower socioeconomic status, black, or Hispanic."[101] The authors concluded: "This [public school] stratification has in effect produced a 'public' school system which not only no longer integrates the various segments of the population of students, but appears no more egalitarian than private education, and considerably less egalitarian in outcome than the major portion of the private sector in America — the Catholic schools."[102]

What one can claim from these data is that religiously based schools — and especially the Catholic schools — offer very clear potential advantages in raising education achievement levels and in equalizing educational opportunities for children from disadvantaged backgrounds. Surely they deserve close attention by the makers of public educational policies.

A second key advantage that private, religiously based schools offer policymakers is the possibility for competition and parental choice. The public school system comes close to being a monopoly. To have true educational choice now, families need sufficient private financial resources, first to pay their educational taxes, and then to pay for their own children's education in addition. Families without such resources have no choice but to send their children to the local public schools, and usually to a particular school that is dictated by where they live. Public school administrative structures and teachers have a guaranteed source of students and thereby guaranteed employment, no matter how good or bad a job they do.

A number of scholars and analysts have advocated variations of voucher systems, in which the parents of every school-age child would receive an educational voucher representing that child's share of educational money. The parents could send this child to any school in the state that was certified as meeting basic standards of health, safety, and accreditation, whether public or private, whether religiously or secularly based. This would maximize parental choice, thereby maximizing competition.[103] Schools doing a poor job of educating students would go out of business; good ones would prosper. The large number of Catholic and other religiously based schools help assure that such a plan would result in genuine choice and competition.

The problem, however, is that the present constricted, rigid concept of church-state separation casts any such plan into the grey area of constitutionality. One only has to recall *Mueller v. Allen* (1983), the Minnesota case in which a much more modest plan of tax deductions for educational expenses barely passed Supreme Court scrutiny. I personally favor voucher plans or other forms of aid to religiously based schools, but that is not my point here. I am only arguing that policymakers, while struggling with problems of declining test scores and public dissatisfaction with the public schools, should have a full range of policy options to weigh, consider, and debate. Writing off a whole set of promising policy options is unwise.

Positive neutrality would clearly hold voucher plans to be fully in keeping with the First Amendment. The key is assurances that religious schools from the entire spectrum of religious traditions as well as secularly based schools would be equally eligible to receive student vouchers. Government would thereby not be advancing any religion over any other, nor either religion or secularism over each other. With such options opened up to political debate and consideration, fresh breezes would blow through the corridors of educational policy-making.

This second section of the chapter dealing with the public policy effects of following positive neutrality has necessarily been somewhat speculative. There is no firm proof that the pervasive social ills that U.S. society is facing at the close of the twentieth century have been caused to any appreciable degree by the absence of public policy options that other modern, industrialized democracies have been able to utilize and that have not been available to the United States due to the constricted interpretation given church-state relations. However, circumstantial evidence and logic point in this exact direction. No one can deny that current church-state interpretations have constricted the use that policymakers can make of religiously based organizations and programs; that these options are available in most of the Western European democracies; nor that these countries have fewer social ills of the sort that plague the United States. Moreover, there are logical reasons to believe that religiously based mediating structures could play a vital role in dealing with these social ills. However, currently, these approaches cannot even be explored and tested. One cannot help but speculate on the costs U.S. society is paying by its rigid adherence to a doctrine that constricts the public policy role of the most powerful, vital force in U.S. society.

With these observations I come to the end of my considerations of church-state relations in the United States. It has been a long journey. The issues are complex and the problems deeply rooted in long-standing assumptions and patterns of thought and action. To trace out the failures of the past, to go back to basics, and to develop new foundations so that church and state can live in a freedom that is respectful of each other is not easy. This book should be seen more as a beginning than as an end; more as a foundation than a completed building. However, I am convinced that if the concepts and perspectives that make up that foundation gain wide currency in the U.S. body politic, a persistently troublesome feature of U.S. politics — and one that is unduly restricting U.S. public policy with unknown negative results for society — will be resolved in a manner that is respectful of both the religious and the nonreligious among us.

NOTES

1. *Marsh v. Chambers*, 463 U.S. at 786 and 792 (1983).
2. Ibid., p. 811.
3. George Gallup, Jr., and Jim Castelli, *The People's Religion: American Faith in the 90's* (New York: Collier Macmillan, 1989), p. 27.
4. Ibid.
5. *Lynch v. Donnelly*, 465 U.S. at 680, 681, and 683 (1984).
6. Ibid., pp. 711–712.
7. Ibid., pp. 701–702. Emphasis added.
8. See *Wisconsin v. Yoder*, 406 U.S. at 205 (1972); *Sherbert v. Verner*, 374 U.S. at 398 (1963); and the cases cited in note 14 of Chapter 2.
9. See *Jackson v. Massachusetts*, 197 U.S. at 11 (1905); and *Braunfeld v. Brown*, 366 U.S. at 599 (1961).
10. *Employment Division v. Smith*, 58 U.S.L.W. at 4435 (1990).
11. Ibid., p. 4438. Emphasis in original.
12. Ibid., pp. 4440–4441.
13. Ibid., p. 4443.
14. Ibid., p. 4446.
15. Ibid., p. 4438.
16. For a case involving statutory interpretation in which the Supreme Court essentially took this position, see *Welsh v. United States*, 398 U.S. at 333 (1970).
17. See *McCollum v. Board of Education*, 333 U.S. at 203 (1948); *Engel v. Vitale*, 370 U.S. at 421 (1962); *Abington School District v. Schempp*, 374 U.S. at 203

(1963); *Stone v. Graham*, 449 U.S. at 39 (1980); *Wallace v. Jaffree*, 105 S.Ct. at 2479 (1985); *Edwards v. Aguillard*, 107 S.Ct. at 2573 (1987); and *Lee v. Weisman*, 60 U.S.L.W. at 4723 (1992).

18.   See *Zorach v. Clauson*, 343 U.S. at 306 (1952); *Wallace v. Jaffree*, 472 U.S. at 38 (1985); and *Westside Community Schools v. Mergens*, 58 U.S.L.W. at 4720 (1990).

19.   *Abington School District v. Schempp*, 374 U.S. at 225 (1963).

20.   *Wallace v. Jaffree*, 472 U.S. at 60 (1985).

21.   Ibid., pp. 113–114.

22.   See *Stone v. Graham*, 449 U.S. at 41 (1980).

23.   Ibid.

24.   Ibid., p. 42.

25.   Ibid., p. 45.

26.   *Westside Community Schools v. Mergens*, 58 U.S.L.W. at 4727 (1990).

27.   *Abington School District v. Schempp*, 374 U.S. at 313 (1963).

28.   Ibid., p. 317.

29.   Ibid., pp. 319–320.

30.   *McCollum v. Board of Education*, 333 U.S. at 212 (1948).

31.   Ibid., p. 256.

32.   Ibid.

33.   For a discussion of this case, which was sympathetic to the District Court's ruling see James Davison Hunter, "Religious Freedom and the Challenge of Modern Pluralism," in James Davison Hunter and Os Guinness, eds., *Articles of Faith, Articles of Peace* (Washington, DC: Brookings, 1990), pp. 54–73.

34.   *Douglas T. Smith v. Board of School Commissioners of Mobile County* (no. 82-0544-BH, 1987), reprinted in Center for Judicial Studies, *American Education on Trial: Is Secular Humanism a Religion?* (Cumberland, VA: Center for Judicial Studies, 1987), p. 50.

35.   See the case in which the Supreme Court rejected this approach, *Edwards v. Aguillard*, 107 S.Ct. at 2573 (1987).

36.   See *Lemon v. Kurtzman*, 403 U.S. at 602 (1971); *Committee for Public Education v. Nyquist*, 413 U.S. at 825 (1973); *Wolman v. Walter*, 433 U.S. at 229 (1977); *Grand Rapids School District v. Ball*, 473 U.S. at 373 (1985); and *Aguilar v. Felton*, 473 U.S. at 402 (1985).

37.   See *Everson v. Board of Education*, 330 U.S. at 1 (1947); *Board of Education v. Allen*, 392 U.S. at 236 (1968); *Meek v. Pittenger*, 421 U.S. at 349 (1975); *Wolman v. Walter*, 433 U.S. at 229 (1977); and *Mueller v. Allen*, 463 U.S. at 388 (1983).

38.   *Grand Rapids School District v. Ball*, 473 U.S. at 394–395 (1985).

39.   Ibid., p. 391.

40.   Ibid., pp. 385, 390, 392.

41.   Ibid., p. 401.

42.   *Aguilar v. Felton*, 473 U.S. at 422 (1985).

43.   *Mueller v. Allen*, 463 U.S. at 396 (1983).

44.   Ibid., p. 400. Emphasis added.

45.   Ibid., pp. 404, 416.

46.   A. James Reichley, *Religion in American Public Life* (Washington, DC: Brookings, 1985), p. 165. Reichley's emphasis.

47.   *Lemon v. Kurtzman*, 403 U.S. at 618 (1971).

48.   See *Tilton v. Richardson*, 403 U.S. at 672 (1971); *Hunt v. McNair*, 413 U.S. at 734 (1973); *Roemer v. Board of Public Works*, 426 U.S. at 736 (1976); *Witters v. Washington Department of Services for the Blind*, 474 U.S. at 481 (1986); *Bradford v. Roberts*, 175 U.S. at 291 (1899); and *Bowen v. Kendrick*, 487 U.S. at 589 (1988). In the last case, the Supreme Court held that, on its face, the challenged statute was

constitutional, but reserved judgment on whether, as actually put into practice, it could pass constitutional muster.

49. For a good summary of the amounts and types of funding that private, religiously based colleges and universities receive, see Paul J. Weber and Dennis A. Gilbert, *Private Churches and Public Money: Church-Government Fiscal Relations* (Westport, CT: Greenwood, 1981), pp. 99–103, 193–233.

50. See Suzanne Daley, "Archdiocese to Continue Foster-Care Services," *New York Times*, September 3, 1988, pp. 25, 29.

51. Memo to the author from Harold Gazan, Director of Children and Family Services, Michigan Department of Social Services (September 16, 1991).

52. *Walz v. Tax Commission*, 397 U.S. at 708 (1970).

53. *Bradfield v. Roberts*, 175 U.S. at 289 (1899).

54. Ibid., pp. 289–299.

55. Ibid., pp. 299–300. No source is given in the Court's opinion for the quoted phrase, but from the context it appears to be from the act of Congress which incorporated the hospital.

56. *Bowen v. Kendrick*, 487 U.S. at 607 (1988). The first quotation is from the AFLA itself and the second is from *Grand Rapids School District v. Ball*, 473 U.S. at 382 (1985).

57. Bowen v. Kendrick, 487 U.S. at 612 (1988).

58. Ibid., p. 621.

59. Ibid.

60. Ibid., p. 626.

61. Ibid., 636.

62. Ibid., pp. 639–640.

63. Ibid., p. 640 n.9.

64. R. E. M. Irving, *The Christian Democratic Parties of Western Europe* (London: George Allen & Unwin, 1979), pp. 35–36.

65. Clay Clemens, *Christian Democracy: The Different Dimensions of a Modern Movement* (Brussels: Parliamentary Group of the European People's Party, 1989), p. 23.

66. Irving, *The Christian Democratic Parties*, p. 108. On this point, also see Joseph LaPalombara, *Democracy Italian Style* (New haven, CT: Yale University Press, 1987), pp. 121–122.

67. See, for example, E. E. Schattschneider, *The SemiSovereign People* (New York: Holt, Rinehart and Winston, 1960); Thomas R. Dye, *Who's Running America?* 5th ed. (Englewood Cliffs, NJ: Prentice-Hall, 1990); and Daniel Hellinger and Dennis R. Judd, *The Democratic Facade* (Pacific Grove, CA: Brooks/Cole, 1991).

68. Allen D. Hertzke, *Representing God in Washington: The Role of Religious Lobbies in the American Polity* (Knoxville: University of Tennessee Press, 1988), p. 16. Hertzke's emphasis.

69. Ibid., p. 10.

70. "Religious Faith: Firm Foundation for Charity," *Christianity Today*, November 19, 1990, p. 63.

71. Hertzke, *Representing God*, p. 116.

72. Ibid.

73. See Gallup and Castelli, *The People's Religion*, pp. 29–35.

74. Ibid., p. 86.

75. Paul Weber, "The Power and Performance of Religious Interest Groups" (paper presented at the meeting of the Society for the Scientific Study of Religion, October 1982). Quoted in Hertzke, *Representing God*, p. 220.

76. Peter L. Berger and Richard John Neuhaus, *To Empower People: The Role*

of *Mediating Structures in Public Policy* (Washington, DC: American Enterprise Institute, 1977), p. 2. Berger and Neuhaus's emphasis removed.

77.   Ibid., p. 6. Berger and Neuhaus's emphasis removed.

78.   Ibid., p. 26.

79.   See Steve Padilla, "'Christian-Only' Furor Sparks New School Plan," *Los Angeles Times*, June 5, 1988, p. II-2.

80.   See Daley, "Archdiocese to Continue Foster-Care Services," p. 25.

81.   Matthew 25:40.

82.   Quoted in Louis Uchitelle, "Public Services Found Better if Private Agencies Compete," *New York Times*, April 26, 1988, p. A1.

83.   Thomas R. Dye, *Understanding Public Policy*, 6th ed. (Englewood Cliffs, NJ: Prentice-Hall, 1987), p. 95.

84.   Ethan A. Nadelmann, "Should Drugs Be Legalized? Yes," in George McKenna and Stanley Feingold, eds., *Taking Sides*, 7th ed. (Guilford, CT: Dushkin, 1991), p. 245.

85.   James Q. Wilson, "Should Drugs be Legalized? No," in McKenna and Feingold, eds., *Taking Sides*, p. 257; and Nadelmann, "Should Drugs Be Legalized? Yes," p. 248.

86.   Clarke E. Cochran, Lawrence C. Mayer , T. R. Carr, and N. Joseph Cayer, *American Public Policy: An Introduction*, 3d ed. (New York: St. Martin's, 1990), pp. 188–189.

87.   Ibid., p. 189.

88.   Russell Chandler, "Churches Take Up Drug Fight," *Los Angeles Times*, July 6, 1990, pp. A1, A19.

89.   Ibid., p. A19.

90.   Ibid.

91.   See ibid.

92.   Quoted in Kim A. Lawton, "Churches Enlist in the War on Drugs," *Christianity Today*, February 11, 1991, p. 46.

93.   See Chandler, "Churches Take Up Drug Fight," p. A19.

94.   Ibid.

95.   Bruce K. Maclaury, "Foreword," in John E. Chubb and Terry M. Moe, *Politics, Markets, and America's Schools* (Washington, DC: Brookings, 1990), p. ix.

96.   Quoted in Cochran, Mayer, Carr, and Cayer, *American Public Policy*, p. 336.

97.   Denis P. Doyle and Terry W. Hartle, *Excellence in Education: The States Take Charge* (Washington, DC: American Enterprise Institute, 1985), p. 1. Quoted in Chubb and Moe, *Politics, Markets, and America's Schools*, p. 1.

98.   James S. Coleman, Thomas Hoffer, and Sally Kilgore, *High School Achievement: Public, Catholic, and Private Schools Compared* (New York: Basic Books, 1982), p. 176. Similar findings are reported in another Coleman study: see James S. Coleman and Thomas Hoffer, *Public and Private High Schools* (New York: Basic Books, 1987).

99.   Coleman, Hoffer, and Kilgore, *High School Achievement*, pp. 28–64.

100.   Ibid., p. 144.

101.   Coleman and Hoffer, *Public and Private High Schools*, p. 213. Also see Jean Merl, "Inner-City Students Find Success at Catholic Schools," *Los Angeles Times*, March 31, 1992, pp. A12, A18–A19.

102.   Coleman, Hoffer, and Kilgore, *High School Achievement*, p. 196.

103.   See, for example, Chubb and Moe, *Politics, Markets, and America's Schools*, pp. 185–229; and John E. Coons and Stephen D. Sugarman, *Education by Choice: The Case for Family Control* (Berkeley: University of California Press, 1978).

Selected Bibliography

BOOKS

Adams, Arlin M., and Emmerich, Charles J. *A Nation Dedicated to Religious Liberty*. Philadelphia: University of Pennsylvania Press, 1990.

Alley, Robert S., ed. *James Madison on Religious Liberty*. Buffalo, NY: Prometheus, 1985.

Bellah, Robert N., and Greenspahn, Frederick E., eds. *Uncivil Religion: Interreligious Hostility in America*. New York: Crossroad, 1987.

Benson, Peter L., and Williams, Dorothy L. *Religion on Capitol Hill: Myths and Realities*. New York: Harper & Row, 1982.

Berger, Peter L., and Neuhaus, Richard John. *To Empower People: The Role of Mediating Structures in Public Policy*. Washington, DC: American Enterprise Institute, 1977.

Berns, Walter. *The First Amendment and the Future of American Democracy*. New York: Basic Books, 1970.

Beth, Loren. *The American Theory of Church and State*. Gainesville, FL: University of Florida Press, 1958.

Bradley, Gerald V. *Church-State Relationships in America*. New York: Greenwood, 1987.

Buckley, Thomas E. *Church and State in Revolutionary Virginia, 1776–1787*. Charlottesville: University Press of Virginia, 1977.

Caplow, Theodore, Bahr, Howard M., Chadwick, Bruce A., Hill, Reuben, and Williamson, Margaret Holmes. *Middletown Families: Fifty Years of Change and Continuity*. Minneapolis: University of Minnesota Press, 1982.

Cochran, Clarke E. *Religion in Public and Private Life*. New York: Routledge, 1990.

Coleman, James S., Hoffer, Thomas, and Kilgore, Sally. *High School Achievement: Public, Catholic, and Private Schools Compared*. New York: Basic Books, 1982.

Cord, Robert L. *Separation of Church and State*. New York: Lambeth, 1982.

Chubb, John E., and Moe, Terry M. *Politics, Markets, and America's Schools*. Washington, DC: Brookings, 1990.

Figgis, John N. *Churches in the Modern State*, 2d ed. New York: Russell and Russell, 1914.

Fowler, Robert Booth. *The Dance with Community*. Lawrence: University of Kansas Press, 1991.

___. *Religion and Politics in America*. Metuchen, NJ: American Theological Library Association, 1985.

Gallup, George, Jr., and Castelli, Jim. *The People's Religion: American Faith in the 90's*. New York: Macmillan, 1989.

Goldwin, Robert A., and Kaufman, Art, eds. *How Does the Constitution Protect Religious Freedom?* Washington, DC: American Enterprise Institute, 1987.

Greenawalt, Kent. *Religious Conviction and Political Choice*. New York: Oxford University Press, 1988.

Griffith, Carol Friedley, ed. *Christianity and Politics: Catholic and Protestant Perspectives*. Washington, DC: Ethics and Public Policy Center, 1981.

Handy, Robert T. *A Christian America: Protestant Hopes and Historical Realities*. New York: Oxford University Press, 1984.

Hatch, Nathan O. *The Democratization of American Christianity*. New Haven, CT: Yale University Press, 1989.

Heimert, Alan. *Religion and the American Mind from the Great Awakening to the Revolution*. Cambridge, MA: Harvard University Press, 1966.

Hertzke, Allen. *Representing God in Washington: The Role of Religious Lobbies in the American Polity*. Knoxville: Tennessee University Press, 1988.

Howe, Mark DeWolfe. *The Garden and the Wilderness: Religion and Government in American Constitutional History*. Chicago: University of Chicago Press, 1965.

Hunter, James Davison. *Culture Wars: The Struggle to Define America*. New York: Basic Books, 1991.

Hunter, James Davison, and Guinness, Os, eds. *Articles of Faith, Articles of Peace*. Washington, DC: Brookings, 1990.

Hutcheson, Richard G., Jr. *God in the White House*. New York: Macmillan, 1988.

Irving, R. E. M. *The Christian Democratic Parties of Western Europe*. London: George Allen & Unwin, 1979.

Koyzis, David T. *Towards a Christian Democratic Pluralism: A Comparative Study of Neothomist and Neocalvinist Political Theories*. Ann Arbor, MI: University Microfilms International, 1986.

Kurland, Philip B. *Religion and the Law: Of Church and State and the Supreme Court*. Chicago: Aldine, 1962.

Kuyper, Abraham. *Calvinism: Six Stone Foundation Lectures*. Grand Rapids, MI: Eerdmans, 1943.

___. *The Problem of Poverty*, ed. James Skillen. Grand Rapids, MI: Baker, 1991.

Levy, Leonard W. *The Establishment Clause: Religion and the First Amendment*. New York: Macmillan, 1986.

McCarthy, Rockne M., Skillen, James W., and Harper, William A. *Disestablishment a Second Time*. Washington, DC: Christian University Press, 1982.

McLoughlin, William G. *Isaac Backus and the American Pietistic Tradition*. Boston: Little, Brown, 1967.

Magid, Henry Meyer. *English Political Pluralism*. New York: Columbia University Press, 1941.

Malbin, Michael J. *Religion and Politics: The Intentions of the Authors of the First Amendment*. Washington, DC: American Enterprise Institute, 1978.

Maritain, Jacques. *Man and the State*. Chicago: University of Chicago Press, 1951.

___. *The Person and the Common Good*, trans. John J. Fitzgerald. Notre Dame, IN: University of Notre Dame Press, 1966.

May, Henry A. *The Enlightenment in America*. New York: Oxford University Press, 1976.

Mead, Sidney E. *The Lively Experiment*. New York: Harper & Row, 1963.

___. *The Nation with the Soul of a Church*. New York: Harper & Row, 1975.

___. *The Old Religion in the Brave New World*. Berkeley: University of California Press, 1977.

Neuhaus, Richard John. *The Naked Public Square*. Grand Rapids, MI: Eerdmans, 1984.

___, ed. *Unsecular America*. Grand Rapids, MI: Eerdmans, 1986.

Noll, Mark A., ed. *Religion and American Politics*. New York: Oxford University Press, 1990.

Peterson, Merrill D., and Vaughan, Robert C., eds. *The Virginia Statute for Religious Freedom*. Cambridge: Cambridge University Press, 1988.

Pfeffer, Leo. *Church, State and Freedom*. Boston: Beacon Press, 1953; rev. ed., 1967.

___. *God, Caesar, and the Constitution*. Boston: Beacon, 1975.

___. *Religion, State and the Burger Court*. Buffalo, NY: Prometheus Books, 1984.

Podell, Janet, ed. *Religion in American Life*. New York: H. W. Wilson, 1987.

Reichley, A. James. *Religion in American Public Life*. Washington, DC: Brookings, 1985.

Sanders, Thomas G. *Protestant Concepts of Church and State*. New York: Holt, Rinehart and Winston, 1964.

Skillen, James W., and McCarthy, Rockne M., eds. *Political Order and the Plural Structure of Society*. Atlanta, GA: Scholars Press, 1991.

Swanson, Wayne R. *The Christ Child Goes to Court*. Philadelphia: Temple University Press, 1990.

Tinder, Glenn. *The Political Meaning of Christianity*. Baton Rouge: Louisiana State University Press, 1989.

Wald, Kenneth D. *Religion and Politics in the United States*, 2d ed. Washington, DC: Congressional Quarterly, 1992.

Walzer, Michael. *Spheres of Justice*. New York: Basic Books, 1983.

Webb, Leicester C., ed. *Legal Personality and Political Pluralism*. Melbourne, Australia: Melbourne University Press, 1958.

Weber, Paul J., ed. *Equal Separation: Understanding the Religion Clauses of the First Amendment*. Westport, CT: Greenwood, 1990.

Weber, Paul J., and Gilbert, Dennis A. *Private Churches and Public Money: Church-Government Fiscal Relations*. Westport, CT: Greenwood, 1981.

LAW REVIEW AND SCHOLARLY JOURNALS

Ahlstrom, Sydney E. "The Scottish Philosophy and American Theology." *Church History* 24 (September 1955): pp. 257–272.

Baer, Richard A., Jr. "The Supreme Court's Discriminatory use of the Term 'Sectarian.'" *The Journal of Law and Politics* 6 (1990): pp. 449–468.

Bellah, Robert N. "Civil Religion in America." *Daedalus* 96 (Winter 1967): pp. 1–21.

Bradley, Gerard V. "Church Autonomy in the Constitutional Order: The End of Church and State." *Louisiana Law Review* 49 (1989): pp. 1057–1087.

Caplow, Theodore. "Religion in Middletown." *The Public Interest*, no. 68 (Summer 1982): pp. 78–87.

Carroll, William A. "The Constitution, the Supreme Court, and Religion." *American Political Science Review* 61 (1967): pp. 657–674.

Chopper, Jesse H. "Defining 'Religion' in the First Amendment." *University of Illinois Law Review* 1982 (1982): pp. 579–613.

Cochran, Clarke E. "The Thin Theory of Community: The Communitarians and Their Critics." *Political Studies* 37 (1989): pp. 422–435.

Durham, W. Cole, Jr., Gaffney, Edward Mcglynn, Laycock, Douglas, and McConnell, Michael W. "For the Religious Freedom Restoration Act." *First Things*, no. 21 (March 1992): pp. 42–44.

Esbeck, Carl H. "Five Views of Church-State Relations in Contemporary American Thought." *Brigham Young University Law Review* 371 (1986): pp. 371–404.

Jellema, Dirk. "Abraham Kuyper's Attack on Liberalism." *Review of Politics* 19 (1957): pp. 472–485.

Johnson, Phillip E. "Concepts and Compromise in First Amendment Religious Doctrine." *California Law Review* 72 (1984): pp. 817–846.

Laycock, Douglas. "A Survey of Religious Liberty in the United States." *Ohio State Law Journal* 47 (1986): pp. 409–451.

Little, David. "Thomas Jefferson's Religious Views and Their Influence on the Supreme Court's Interpretation of the First Amendment." *Catholic University Law Review* 26 (1976): pp. 57–72.

McConnell, Michael W. "Neutrality under the Religion Clauses." *Northwestern University Law Review* 81 (1986): pp. 146–167.

____. "The Origins and Historical Understanding of Free Exercise of Religion." *Harvard Law Review* 103 (1990): pp. 1409–1517.

McLoughlin, William G. "Isaac Backus and the Separation of Church and State in America." *American Historical Review* 73 (June 1968): pp. 1392–1413.

Mueller, Franz H. "The Principle of Subsidiarity in the Christian Tradition." *The American Catholic Sociological Review* 4 (October 1943): pp. 144–157.

Neuhaus, Richard John. "The Naked Public Square: A Metaphor Reconsidered." *First Things*, no. 23 (May 1992): pp. 78–81.

____. "A New Order of Religious Freedom." *First Things*, no. 20 (February 1992): pp. 13–17.

Pepper, Stephen L. "The Conundrum of the Free Exercise Clause — Some Reflections on Recent Cases." *Northern Kentucky Law Review* 9 (1982): pp. 265–303.

Tinder, Glenn. "Can We Be Good without God?" *The Atlantic Monthly*, December 1989, pp. 69–85.

Tushnet, Mark. "The Constitution of Religion." *Connecticut Law Review* 18 (1985–86): pp. 701–738.

Utz, Arthur. "The Principle of Subsidiarity and Contemporary Natural Law." *Natural Law Forum* 3 (1958): pp. 170–183.

Van Der Slik, Jack R. "Respecting an Establishment of Religion in America." *Christian Scholar's Review* 13 (1984): pp. 217–235.

Witte, John, Jr. "The Theology and Politics of the First Amendment Religion Clauses: A Bicentennial Essay." *Emory Law Journal* 40 (1991): pp. 489–507.

Weber, Paul J. "Excessive Entanglement: A Wavering First Amendment Standard." *Review of Politics* 46 (1984): pp. 483–501.

____. "James Madison and Religious Equality: The Perfect Separation." *Review of Politics* 44 (1982): pp. 163–186.

West, John G., Jr. "The Changing Battle over Religion in the Public Schools." *Wake Forest Law Review* 26 (1991): pp. 361–401.

Index

ABOUT THE AUTHOR

STEPHEN V. MONSMA, Professor of Political Science, Pepperdine University, is the author or editor of several studies dealing with religion and politics, including *Responsible Technology: A Christian Perspective* (1986), *Pursuing Justice in a Sinful World* (1984), and *American Politics* (1976).